Recapturing
the
Constitution

RECAPTURING THE CONSTITUTION

Race, Religion, and Abortion Reconsidered

Stephen B. Presser

REGNERY PUBLISHING, INC.
Washington, D. C.

Library of Congress Cataloging-in-Publication Data

Presser, Stephen B., 1946–
Recapturing the Constitution / Stephen B. Presser.
p. cm.
Includes bibliographical references and index.
ISBN 0-89526-492-7 (alk. paper)
1. United States—Constitutional law—Moral and ethical aspects.
2. United States—Constitutional law—Interpretation and construction.
3. United States—Constitutional history.   4. Law and politics.   I. Title.
KF4552.P74   1994
342.73′029—dc20
[347.30229]   94-19331
                                                                                    CIP

Published in the United States by
Regnery Publishing, Inc.
An Eagle Publishing Company
422 First St., SE, Suite 300
Washington, DC 20003

Distributed to the trade by
National Book Network
4720-A Boston Way
Lanham, MD 20706

Printed on acid-free paper.

Manufactured in the United States of America.

10 9 8 7 6 5 4 3 2 1

Books are available in quantity for promotional or premium use. Write to
Director of Special Sales, Regnery Publishing, Inc., 422 First Street, SE,
Suite 300, Washington, DC 20003, for information on discounts and terms
or call (202) 546-5005.

To Sidney and Estelle Presser

CONTENTS

Contents

Contents

Chapter Five:
LAW, POLITICS, AND RECAPTURING THE CONSTITUTION   252

PREFACE

By the end of 1993 it had become clear, even to President Clinton, that the United States was facing a moral crisis. The country was, in the words of *U.S. News & World Report*'s Michael Barone, "slouching toward dystopia." Charles Murray's electrifying October 29 op-ed piece in the *Wall Street Journal*, "The Coming White Underclass," described the dangers now facing America. Murray argued that the overall number of illegitimate births in America had begun to approach the percentage that, twenty-eight years ago, led to the formation of a black underclass. Today the figure among whites is 22 percent. In 1965 the black figure was 26 percent, now it is 68 percent. There seems to be general consensus that the collapse of the two-parent black family among the black underclass is the most important factor contributing to the epidemic of crime, drugs, poverty, welfare, and homelessness that now ravages our inner cities. Murray's op-ed piece suggested that our whole society may be headed in that direction. The spate of random killings and other acts of violence at the end of 1993 seemed to bear him out.

Murray's solution is to end welfare, which he argues rewards single mothers who have children. Other social theorists, most prominently the president of the United States, but significantly also black leaders such as Jesse Jackson, following the lead of George Bush's vice president, Dan Quayle, have called for a moral renewal. They now appear to recognize that sexual license and the irresponsible production of children out of wedlock are pernicious and wrong, and that it might be possible for a renewal of rectitude to improve our national condition.

At the same time as these ever-increasing calls for moral responsibility are made, however, the nation's chattering classes continue to strive to ensure that our society remains committed to secular humanism. In a notable break from this consensus, earlier this year, the governor of Mississippi made *his* call for a moral renewal, describing the United States as a "Christian nation." He immediately found himself roundly condemned and forced to apologize. The 1993 holiday season brought with it our now traditional disputes over whether menorahs, Christmas trees, or crèches can or should be displayed in schools or on public property.

Strangely, the relationship between the recent transformation of the United States into an aggressively secular society and our country's moral collapse goes all but unrecognized in the media. Similarly barred from widespread national discussion is the possibility of some linkage between the current state of federal constitutional law and the secularization and concomitant moral distress of the country. The relationship between morality and religion, and their connection to constitutional law are the principal subjects of this book. The main thesis is that the framers got it right, and we, departing from their understanding, have got it wrong. The moment is ripe to return to this original understanding of the framers, and to bring the best of their experience back into our lives.

The arguments presented here are made to persuade concerned members of the public that it is time to act to prevent further deterioration of our constitutional tradition. This book calls for the renewal and the exercise of virtue on the part of the American people. It is not a treatise on constitutional law for legal scholars; it is an introduction and commentary on the issues for troubled laymen. For too long constitutional law has been exclusively the province of specialists. Just as war is too important to be left in the hands of the generals, the Constitution is too important to remain exclusively in the hands of the judges and the professoriate. Still, there may be something of value here for legally trained readers as well. They will find here a perspective somewhat different from that encountered in law schools today. There, history is slighted in favor of the politically correct or the unreflectively practical. Here history will provide both the framework for analysis and the moral worth of the arguments. The lengthy notes that follow the text are crafted to encourage further reading by those new to the topics, and to provide scholarly substantiation for the cognescenti.

If our current social crisis is to be solved, as Myron Magnet argues in his persuasive *The Dream and the Nightmare: The Sixties' Legacy to the Underclass* (1993), economic solutions, such as abolishing welfare, will not be enough. There must be a moral and cultural renewal, because social actions are ultimately shaped more by the culture than by the economy. The most pressing cultural need in America, then, is to regain an understanding of our basic cultural statement, the United States Constitution. We have become a more diverse nation since the late eighteenth century, and we wisely acknowledge a broader base for the exercise of popular sovereignty and political rights than did the framers, but this does not mean that we can or should lose sight of some of the eternal truths of moral and political life known to those who drafted the Constitution.

Given the obscurity in which the document has been recently veiled by the judges and law professors, such an effort at recapture is not easy. As a law professor, I am aware that a simple presentation often eludes me. There is a risk, when encountering abstruse constitutional doctrine, that lay readers may come too close to utter bafflement and consequent despair. In order to alleviate the problem, the Introduction and each chapter are followed by a "Summary of the Argument," which simplifies and unifies the presentation. Risk-averse readers may wish to read the summaries first, and then tackle the text.

If there is anything of value in the book (and, sharing the standard law professor's arrogance and immodesty, I confess that there is an abundance of importance here) much of the credit belongs to Alfred Regnery, my publisher, and Terry Eastland and

Trish Bozell, my editors. Alfred signed on to the project when it was little more than a series of hunches, and harnessed and shaped my enthusiasm into this book. That Alfred invited me to participate in the celebrated tradition of his and his father's publishing house is something for which I will be ever grateful. Terry tried to ferret out the inconsistencies and incoherencies in the argument, suggested several important avenues to pursue, and generally sought to make the work comprehensible to real people. Trish furthered this effort by gently and elegantly sharpening and polishing my prolix professional prose.

Early stages of research for this book were underwritten by the Washington Legal Foundation (WLF), a public interest law firm committed to the preservation of the free market. I am particularly grateful to Daniel Popeo, WLF's chairman and general counsel, who made that commitment possible and who has continued to offer encouragement and enthusiasm over the years.

My wife and best friend, ArLynn Leiber Presser, convinced me of the importance of religion and morality in constitutional discourse. She was aided in that enterprise by Mark Simpson, Robert Ferrigan, Mike McNulty, and Richard Eastman. Mark Melickian, my research assistant, flailed at me from the other side of the political spectrum, but still ferreted out the sources unflinchingly and brilliantly. Robert Bennett, Northwestern Law School's dean, and Martin Redish, its director of research, were generous in support. Pat Franklin, my secretary, assembled the manuscript with her usual aplomb. David, Elisabeth, Joseph, and Eastman kindly indulged their dad.

STEPHEN B. PRESSER
Chicago, Illinois
December 1993

Recapturing the Constitution

Beyond Jefferson and Self-Actualization, and Back to the Original Understanding

For a generation longer than did the Children of Israel we Americans have been wandering in a wilderness. Our wilderness is one of theory, of the spirit rather than of the material world, and most of us are only vaguely aware of our plight. Our bewilderment is real enough, however, and our guides who have themselves lost their way have been sitting on the United States Supreme Court. Too many of the Justices appear to have forgotten that their appointed task is to determine the law, and instead have been inappropriately engaged in the business of legislating policy, and the wrong policy at that. This ought to be obvious, but the obvious must often be embarrassed in the academy and in the courts.

In American colleges and law schools, and often in judicial opinions, information now comes wrapped in gorgeous cloaks of theoretical refinement and subtlety. Law Professor Gene R. Nichol, writing recently in the *Michigan Law Review*, bemoaned what he called the inward turn of many "sophisticated commen-

3

tators" on constitutional law. These academic legal scholars have concerned themselves not with the application of legal principles, nor with the operation of law and its institutions. Instead, they have produced a body of constitutional thought that "cast itself adrift, whether out of desperation, disgust, or despair, and engaged itself in spinning gossamer webs of republicanism, deconstruction, dialogism, feminism, or what have you."[1]

This glorious intellectual raiment in American legal scholarship often conceals the arbitrary ideological choices that lie at the heart of current academic and legal thought. Most current constitutional theory, so complex as to be virtually impenetrable,[2] is, at bottom, a rather shameless attempt to legitimate what ought properly to be regarded as the blatantly unconstitutional decisions of the Supreme Court of the past sixty years, and particularly those made during the time of the Warren and Burger Courts. Both conservatives and liberals—but primarily liberals in the past half century—have displayed what Judge Robert Bork quite properly regards as the "heresy . . . that the ratifiers' original understanding of what the Constitution means is no longer of controlling, or perhaps of any, importance."[3] Bork has argued that the Warren and Burger Courts are examples of a federal judiciary engaged in a form of "civil disobedience . . . arguably more dangerous, because more insidious and hence more damaging to democratic institutions, than the civil disobedience of the streets."[4] With this "heresy" and this judicial "civil disobedience" dominant, there are no longer firm guideposts in American constitutional law.

In recent years the Supreme Court, formerly given to relatively plain statement, has disguised its result-oriented jurisprudence in a variety of obscure doctrinal formulae. Former Solicitor General Charles Fried has lamented the manner in which most Supreme Court opinions are written, which he likens to "the modern bureaucratic style—a style typical of the law clerk-drafted effluvia of most of our courts and even of the Supreme Court, with its two-part, three-pronged tests ineffectively lightened (as with lumpy roux mixed into an already heavy sauce) by heavy-handed sarcasms and ponderous moralisms[.]"[5] Sadly, it is time to acknowledge that even the much vaunted Reagan revolution, which was to result in a much more conservative Supreme Court, and one devoted to interpreting rather than making law, has failed, and failed spectacularly.[6] President Reagan's appointments of Justice Sandra Day O'Connor and Anthony Kennedy, and the selection of David Souter by another Republican president, George Bush, have actually served to perpetuate the errors of their predecessors.[7] It is time for some plain speaking. Our Supreme Court has lost its way, and it is time for the people to recapture the Constitution and the country.

The errors on the part of the Court, the theoretical failings in the academy, and misunderstandings on the part of the press all have contributed to the persistence of judicial usurpation. The judicial errors, the theoretical failings, and the media misunderstandings can be explained by an ideological commitment, particularly in the academy and the press, to an odd and strangely debased version of democracy. Examination of the current state of constitutional law and our constitutional history makes clear that our nation is *not* a democracy, but *is* a republic. The framers of the Constitution understood this, and they tried to erect a structure of republican government that implemented the American principle of popular sovereignty. In American government, however, there was supposed to be a big difference between democracy and popular sovereignty, as we will seek to understand here.

That we are a republic, that we have popular sovereignty but *not* democracy is obscured by the modern and bizarre American democratic ideology that goes by the name of "liberalism" and which dominates most of our political discourse. This modern and bizarre view of the American polity is usually identified with the thought of Thomas Jefferson. As the political scientist Robert Dawidoff explains, self-confessedly a bit maladroitly:

> I conflate Jeffersonian and liberalism, knowing something of the historical awkwardness of that fit. Candidly, I mean the knee-jerk, bend-over-backwards embarrassing kind of liberalism, the kind that approaches politics and culture with a conscious air of difference in the hopes of bonding across difference . . . The name-

5

giving titan of any [such] version of American democracy [is] Thomas Jefferson.[8]

Among the elements of supposedly Jeffersonian thought now most commonly stressed are that humankind is infinitely perfectible, that societal problems can and should be solved by the application of human reason, that all men and women are inherently equal, that elitism is anathema, that there ought to be a maximum of freedom for individuals to live in the manner that they deem best for themselves, and that the government has no business interfering with any moral or religious choices any individual might make. Whether or not this *was* the thought of Jefferson is doubtful, as we shall see. In any event, another simple and blunt truth is that whatever his views, Thomas Jefferson was not the only Founding Father, nor was he the most important one. While Jefferson may have been the principal drafter of the Declaration of Independence, he had no hand in writing the United States Constitution,[9] and although Jefferson appears at least once to have acknowledged a need for judicial review of legislation,[10] he was no great friend of the judiciary.[11] Still, it seems that for some years now the American media, at least, if not also the universities and law schools, have been dominated by those who believe that the primary Founding Father (or "Founding Person," or "Founder") of the American republic was Thomas Jefferson.[12]

Jefferson has often emerged as the favorite Founder because among the members of the founding generation it is indeed Jefferson who appears to have come closest to believing in the concept of democracy. Jefferson is further idealized because he supposedly conceived of an American nation where there is a "wall of separation" between church and state, where, as indicated earlier, reason prevails, where all men are equal, and where the people actually rule.

There is some basis in fact for this Jefferson. Jefferson's ideas did appear to become increasingly democratic as the eighteenth century turned into the nineteenth. And he did define the form of government that was closest to a republic as that which had the maximum amount of popular participation. As he wrote to his friend Col. John Taylor:

> Were I to assign to this term ["Republic"] a precise and definite idea, I would say, purely and simply, it means a government by its citizens in mass, acting directly and personally, according to rules established by the majority; and that every other government is more or less republican, in proportion as it has in its composition more or less of this ingredient of the direct action of the citizens. . . . The further the departure from direct and constant control by the citizens, the less has the government of the ingredient of republicanism . . ."[13]

Finally, Jefferson's thought powerfully endorsed religious freedom. Jefferson condemned the folly of the government seeking to impose uniformity in religion, arguing instead that "difference of opinion is advantageous in religion," because it fosters "reason and persuasion." Those two, reason and persuasion, Jefferson believed, were the "only practicable instruments" to advance religion.[14]

Nevertheless, while we are about the business of speaking plain and perhaps unpopular truths, it should be early acknowledged that Jefferson, at least when he was a young man, appeared to understand that there was some difference between a democracy and a republic. Even Jefferson must have understood that the United States was to be constituted not as a *democracy*, but as a *republic*. The implications of this republican form of government will be developed in Chapter One, but for now it is enough to note that a republic, because it is governed by representatives, and not through the direct actions of the people, inevitably creates a sort of hierarchy in society.

The Jefferson who, in 1781 and 1782, wrote the *Notes on Virginia*, a masterpiece of early American practical philosophy, appears to have understood the inevitability of orders within society. The needs of the individual were not the centerpiece of the young Jefferson's philosophy. That young Jefferson was clearly opposed to the notion that ambition was a virtue. He believed that there were higher values than promoting maximum social mobility for individuals.[15]

Thus, in his *Notes*, Jefferson described his model of an essentially aristocratic system of education. He designed it to have "twenty of the best geniuses . . . raked from the rubbish annually, and be instructed, at the public expense." It was also crafted to furnish "to the wealthier part of the people convenient schools, at which their children may be educated, at their own expense."[16] This scheme was praised by Jefferson in that it provided "an education adapted to the years, to the capacity, and the condition of every one, and directed to their freedom and happiness."

Jefferson, in the *Notes*, appeared at pains to point out that he thought students should be educated in the Virginia schools with the "first elements of morality." This, to him, included the lesson that their "own greatest happiness . . . does not depend on the condition of life [the social status] in which chance has placed them, but is always the result of a good conscience, good health, occupation, and freedom in all just pursuits."[17] Recent scholarship on Jefferson has indicated that he was probably much more committed to religion, or at least its moral teachings, as an important positive force in society than are the secular humanists (even those on the Supreme Court) who embrace him today.[18] Indeed, even his comments about differing religious views leading to "reason and persuasion"[19] suggest that Jefferson saw merit in encouraging religion.

Much of what follows is written in the hope that we can return to the understanding of society reflected in the *Notes* of the young Jefferson. As he did, we will try here to understand how best to promote morality in society, and we will seek to understand the nature of social responsibilities under the original American conception of popular sovereignty. Eventually we will seek to apply this understanding to solve constitutional conundrums in three currently problematic areas: race, religion, and abortion. Before we can reach that point, however, we need to spend some time studying Jefferson's contemporaries, in order to arrive at the original understanding of the Constitution.

Whatever Jefferson believed, if one seeks the meaning of the federal Constitution as it was understood by those who conceived it—and it is difficult to believe that any other approach to the document can result in following the concept of the rule of law[20]—we would do better not to look exclusively to Jefferson for guidance. Instead, we should look to the group that dominated the Philadelphia Convention, which actually gave us the document that still forms the basis for our government and dominated national politics until 1800.

These actual Founders, usually called "Federalists," included men such as James Wilson, Oliver Ellsworth, Alexander Hamilton, and, at least for a time, James Madison.[21] They understood that to preserve the American republic it was necessary to erect barriers against the unreflective actions of individuals, even when the individuals in question constituted a majority of the society. The Founders, then, had profound reservations about pure democracy. They saw a need, in other words, to protect the people from themselves. This is the thrust of Madison's famous comment in *Federalist* 51:

> It may be a reflection on human nature that such devices [checks and balances in the structure of government] should be necessary to control the abuses of government. But what is government itself but the greatest of all reflections on human nature? If men were angels, no government would be necessary. If angels were to govern men, neither external nor internal controls on government would be necessary. In framing a government which is to be administered by men over men, the great difficulty lies in this: you must first enable the government to control the governed; and in the next place oblige it to control itself. A dependence on the people is, no doubt, the primary control on the government; but experience has taught mankind the necessity of auxiliary precautions.[22]

The Federalist framers of the Constitution were *not* monarchists or proponents of an hereditary aristocracy, Antifederalist propaganda to the contrary notwithstanding.[23] They understood that the only legitimate basis of American government was the consent of the people, and they were thus committed to popular sovereignty. But though they embraced popular sovereignty, they were still committed to avoiding the foibles of direct democracy. Indeed, the Founders' core insight was that popular sovereignty itself could succeed only if the rule of law was maintained, and if the form of government included checks and balances against popular tempests and popular disturbances. These checks and balances, as every American schoolchild used to be taught, were secured by the Constitution, which separated and balanced the three branches of our government, and limited the power of the federal government so that popular sovereignty could flourish at the level of the states as well. Thus the passion of the people that might manifest itself in acts of the federal government would be restrained by the tripartite structure of the federal government, by the limitations on the powers delegated to the federal government, and by strong and vigorous state governments, which would be expected to respond to most of the problems of their citizenry. Some of the most notable aspects of this Federalist thought, and, in particular its belief that law could not be separated from morality and religion, will be explained in Chapter Two.

Unfortunately, most recent constitutional history has been a tale of the lessening of the authority of state governments, and of the failure of federal officials in all three branches to follow either the rule of law or the constitutional scheme of checks and balances. Since the New Deal, as a leading constitutional text asserts, there has been

inaugurated an American version of bureaucratic centralization. Intended to provide social and economic security against the perilous forces of modern industrial organization, the New Deal established federal authority in areas previously the preserve of the states. It created a regulatory welfare state that altered the federal system and possibly transformed the spirit of American constitutionalism by inducing groups and individuals to turn to the federal government to guarantee their basic needs.[24]

The notion of checks and balances against the passions of democracy has been nearly lost to us in the late twentieth century, when, in the pursuit of popular policy goals, particularly at the federal level, we have—erroneously—come to see no difference between democracy and popular sovereignty, or more precisely between a republic (which we are) and a democracy (which we are not). Chapter Three is devoted to an exploration of where and how our constitutional theory went wrong.

Perhaps we have fallen into a dangerous late Jeffersonian error of believing that if a little democracy is good much more of it is much better. Thus the federal government increasingly appears to set its agenda based on what it thinks a majority of the people want. Even judicial appointments are now made recognizing that they may be withdrawn or fail depending on the popular consensus that crystallizes around a candidate. This is not the first time in our history that this error has dominated our politics. We made the same mistake in the period leading up to our Civil War, and we succumbed to its siren call as well during the presidency of Franklin D. Roosevelt during the New Deal.

This book, touching on these and other developments, attempts to explore how we might regain the original understanding of the operation of our Constitution, and how we might go back and relearn lessons we forgot in 1800, in 1860, and in 1937. We cannot, of course, go back to exactly the understanding of society of the late eighteenth century. There has been some social movement since that time, and we will attempt only to capture the best and the still relevant aspects of the framers' thought, for the light that it casts on our current constitutional conundrums. Chapters Four and Five suggest what might happen in several areas of current constitutional controversy if these original insights were restored. This book is thus what Jeffrey Hart has called "An Act of Recovery,"[25] and is the same sort of exercise Allan Bloom was attempting in his *Closing of the American Mind* (1987)[26]; it is an attempt to recapture an understanding of the life of American law that has recently eluded us.[27]

We are in a period where in several fields we see emerging an understanding that not all change is progress, that perhaps the clock can be turned back (and, indeed, as C.S. Lewis told us, the clock should be turned back when it is set ahead too far in error, and when it fails to give the correct time).[28]

Let the reader be warned: This is a politically incorrect tract for our time. I start with a set of profoundly obvious assumptions about the federal Constitution in particular and about law in general that have fallen sadly out of favor in the academy at least, but without which, I believe, the American concept of the rule of law makes no sense. As the political philosopher Hadley Arkes recently wrote, "For the Founders, for Lincoln, the case for natural rights claimed its force and its coherence only with the recognition that it was grounded in certain necessary, moral truths. But in our own time nothing is more likely to stir discomfort among liberals, in dining rooms or courts, than the willingness to speak seriously about moral 'truths' that are 'absolute' and 'eternal.' "[29]

The world of the Constitution's framers was a world in which law was believed to be more than simply the dictates of the temporal wielders of power. In the late eighteenth century, at the time of our nation's founding, the English common law was the basis of the liberties of Englishmen and of Americans. Americans considered themselves to be at least the heirs of, and perhaps the perfection of Englishmen, and the English common law was still thought to be the foundation for state and federal law. This was a time too when morality and religion were believed to be inescapable concomitants of anything that could survive as the rule of law. It was thus a time when the law and the Constitution were thought to reflect the divinely inspired natural order. At that time, no supposed Jeffersonian wall of separation existed between religion and the state; rather it was believed that there could be no popular government or rule by law without morality and that there could be no morality without religion.

Perhaps the best known contemporary statement of this set of beliefs on the part of the Founders was George Washington's "Farewell Address," the first president's "one outstanding piece of writing," comparable in importance to Jefferson's Declaration of Independence, Hamilton's financial plan, or Madison's journal of the proceedings of the Constitutional Convention.[30] Said the outgoing president, in pertinent part:

> Of all the dispositions and habits which lead to political prosperity, religion and morality are indispensable supports. In vain would that man claim the tribute of patriotism, who should labour to subvert these great pillars of human happiness, these firmest props of the duties of men and citizens. The mere politician, equally with the pious man, ought to respect and to cherish them.—A volume could not trace all their connexions with private and public felicity. Let it simply be asked, where is the security for property, for reputation, for life, if the sense of religious obligation *desert* the oaths which are the instruments of investigation in courts of justice? And let us with caution indulge the supposition that morality can be maintained without religion. Whatever may be conceded to the influence of refined education on minds of peculiar structure, reason and experience both forbid us to expect, that national morality can prevail in exclusion of religious principle.
>
> It is substantially true, that virtue or morality is a necessary spring of popular government. The rule, indeed, extends with more or less force to every species of free government. Who that is a sincere friend to it can look with indifference upon attempts to shake the foundation of the fabrick?[31]

These sentiments of Washington's as they were expressed by other Federalists, particularly the first Supreme Court Justices, will be developed in Chapter Two.

The Constitution was framed in an era when it was generally believed that one's duties to the community and to the diety took precedence over individual desires. Thus, the world of the Federalist Founders (and even that of the early Jefferson) was not a world where the primary goal was, to slip into contemporary psycho-babble, individual "self-actualization." We have lately come to conflate democracy itself with "self-actualization," and the notions that result are other aspects of the debased form of Jeffersonian thought that have led us into grave constitutional error.

"Self-actualization," or "self-fulfillment," which seems to mean the same thing, appears to be a pervasive theme in interpreting the Constitution these days, particularly with regard to explicating the First Amendment's guarantees of religious freedom, free speech, and a free press. A search for "self-actualization" in the Lexis/Nexis Lawrev/Allrev data base (the most prominent law journals going back about ten years) yields eighty-eight entries (as of July 21, 1993). "Self-actualization" occurs in a staggering 458 articles in the Nexis/Omni database (general purpose newspapers and journals going back about ten years). The Supreme Court has used the term "self-fulfillment" in eight opinions, generally to make the point that "to permit the continued building of our politics and culture, and to assure self-fulfillment for each individual, our people are guaranteed the right to express any thought, free from government censorship."[32]

In the 1970s and the 1980s, First Amendment theory was "dominated by theories about self-actualization." Those theories are still of profound importance, although there has been an increasing interest in a less individualist, more communitarian conception of the First Amendment.[33] Still, at the present, the "self-actualization" legal theorists[34] occupy prominent places in the academy and on the Court. Their coupling of individual self-actualization and democracy is probably still the dominant theme in American constitutional culture.

The most curious legal exercise involving "self-actualization" was a recent United States District Court opinion which found that "secular humanism" (and "self-actualization" as an important component part) was a religion, and prohibited a state from advancing it. Said the United States District Court for the Northern District of Alabama:

> This highly relativistic and individualistic approach constitutes the promotion of a fundamental faith claim [that] assumes that self-actualization is the goal of every human being, that man has no supernatural attributes or component, that there are only tempo-

ral and physical consequences for man's actions, and that these results, alone, determine the morality of an action.[35]

In the course of a prior opinion in the case, noting the Supreme Court's earlier decision that no state could promote prayer in its public schools, the Alabama federal court observed:

> It was pointed out in the testimony that the curriculum in the public schools of Mobile County is rife with efforts at teaching or encouraging secular humanism—all without opposition from any other ethic—to such an extent that it becomes a brainwashing effort. If this court is compelled to purge "God is great, God is good, we thank him for our daily food" from the classroom then this Court must also purge from the classroom those things that serve to teach that salvation is through one's self rather than through a deity.[36]

The words of the Alabama federal court are quite useful for putting "self-actualization" in its psychological and social context. "Self-actualization" is thus seen to be a component part of "secular humanism," of a supposedly democratic political and cultural philosophy that puts the individual at the center of the universe and has no place for a divinely ordained hierarchy of authority. The Alabama federal district court appears to have understood this. On rather dubious grounds, however, the Alabama federal district court's holding that the religion of "secular humanism" was unconstitutionally advanced by the conduct of Alabama school officials was reversed on appeal.[37]

Undeniably, however, the Alabama federal court was on to something. Perhaps it sensed the dangers of "self-actualization" had gone too far. In the context of modern "self-help" groups, indeed, the modern concept of "self-actualization" appears to have gone completely bonkers.[38] When the term "self-actualization" was originally coined by the psychologist Abraham Maslow, it might have had a more benign purpose. As the term is now used, it seems to be a means of promoting the

15

notion that *all* individuals ought to regard themselves as the damaged victims of pernicious societal practices. Such individuals, so the argument goes, can repair their wounded psyches only through twelve-step programs and group or individual therapy. The view that we are all damaged victims, of course, supports a huge self-help industry, which thrives on convincing everyone that every complaint they might have is the result of some injury *others* have inflicted. Originally Maslow might have been railing against these

> "[l]ow grumbles, high grumbles, and meta-grumbles," this "pessimistic tendency we have to focus on our deficits, deficiencies, and problems. Why not, he asked, radically 'shake free of this cultural relativism, which stresses passivity, plasticity, and shapelessness?' Why not, instead, realize our potential by concentrating on autonomy and growth? Why not think about the 'maturation of inner forces?' "[39]

But whatever the value of Maslow's conception of "self-actualization," it was not a concept of great importance to the framers. In the framers' thought, the purpose of the presumably God-given talents distributed equally among the rich and poor was not to enrich or actualize individuals, but to contribute to the betterment of all.[40] In the late eighteenth century there grew an increasing awareness of the importance of economic development as the key to American independence and greatness. It was not a belief that the primary purpose of commerce and economic development was to gratify individual desires. Instead, economic progress was considered as only a tool of moral and spiritual growth for the American people, and a means of promoting virtue and civic pride.

The liberty of individuals in America *was* of primary importance to the framers, of course, but that liberty was regarded as a means not of furthering selfish desire, but of perfecting one's self morally and spiritually.[41] Because of the frank acknowledgement and understanding of the importance of religion and morality in American public life, individuals could derive meaning in their lives from participating in the common construction of an American culture of republican altruism.

In spite of their glorious vision, and the inherent wisdom in their theories, the Federalist framers were outwitted by the shrewder politics of the Jeffersonians in the presidential election of 1800. With Jefferson's election, and with the turn toward demagoguery that his victory represented and encouraged, the debased notions of democracy described earlier entered American political life. More often than not, as these debased notions have matured, they have obscured the ideas of the Federalist framers. In a sense, then, the Federalists failed to continue to convince a majority of their fellow Americans to pursue their particular ideals. By 1800, the Federalists' original understanding of the Constitution had begun to erode as the competing Jeffersonian conception flourished.

From time to time in the next two centuries the beliefs of the Constitution's framers were powerful enough to enjoy an occasional renaissance on the Supreme Court. This happened, for example, with the work of Supreme Court Justice Joseph Story in the first third of the nineteenth century.[42] It happened with the jurisprudence of Rufus Peckham and others in the late nineteenth and early twentieth century, and it happened with the opinions of the "Four Horsemen" in the early years of the New Deal. We will have more to say about Justice Story in due course,[43] but a word or two about Peckham and the "Four Horsemen" might help clarify the argument here.

Rufus Peckham, who served on the Supreme Court from 1895–1919, was one of the most prominent Supreme Court critics of state regulation of employment contracts. He was a zealous upholder of the Sherman Antitrust Act, but his opinions generally had a nostalgic cast to them, as was true of his opinion in *United States v. Trans-Missouri Freight Association* (1897).[44] In *Trans-Missouri* Justice Peckham wrote movingly of his conception of American "real prosperity," which involved maintaining an economy in which individual entrepreneurs were not crushed by monolithic economic giants. The "real prosperity" of the community, for Peckham and his late nineteenth-century colleagues, was to be guaranteed also by attention to "liberty of contract." Peckham explicated this conception in his opinions in *Allgeyer v. Louisiana* (1897)[45] and *Lochner v. New York* (1905).[46] Peckham looked back to the original Federalist fondness for the protection of private property as a means of promoting individual liberty in service to the community and preserving the existing hierarchical social and economic order.

The term, "Four Horsemen," meant to evoke the legendary Four Horsemen of the Apocalypse, has been used by constitutional historians to refer to Justices Pierce Butler, Willis Van Devanter, George Sutherland, and James McReynolds. The term is one of opprobrium, used by members of the legal academy sympathetic to the goals of Franklin Roosevelt's New Deal. These men, we are told, were "four justices of the Supreme Court who consistently opposed New Deal economic and social legislation." Like Peckham, they sought to promote traditional Federalist beliefs. "The Four Horsemen" sensed that there was something not only very new but very wrong about the New Deal. They believed that the measures of the New Deal were unconstitutional because they usurped traditional areas of state authority and eroded the traditional liberty of contract.[47]

Yale Law School's Bruce Ackerman describes the period from 1865 to 1935, the period of Peckham and the "Four Horsemen," as an important "middle period" of constitutional jurisprudence. It was a period in which the Court was essentially restrained, noninterventionist, procontract, and pro-private property. During this "middle period," according to Ackerman, the Supreme Court went about the noble business of attempting to synthesize the jurisprudence of the Founders with the constitutional mandate of the Reconstruction amendments. Ackerman feels that the results of the "middle period," for example, Peckham's opinion in *Lochner v. New York* (1905), holding that New York could not regulate wages and hours for bakers,[48] have been too often maligned by those who have not understood the subtlety of the jurisprudence involved. Such opinions, he believes, have been repeatedly simply dismissed by most modern liberal proponents of the activist state.

Ackerman builds a convincing case that the Supreme Court's efforts during this period should not be regarded merely as an era of morally bad law, as liberals have tended to do. This condemnation of the Four Horsemen and Peckham, of course, is promulgated by those who regard the New Deal's redistributionist thrust as the only morally justified course. Ackerman is correct in believing that the Court's decisions during the "middle period" were a reasonable understanding of proper constitutional interpretation and the rule of law.[49] Since Ackerman is a man of the Left (his thought will be explored in the concluding chapter), the argument of this book will have a more conservative cast than Ackerman's, but (as will be explained more fully in Chapter Five) we conservatives have much to learn from the theorists of the Left. In particular, there is something that those seeking to recapture the original understanding can learn even from the proponents of Critical Legal Studies, a group generally more radical than Ackerman and a supposed scourge of the legal academy.[50]

In any event, as Ackerman's work suggests, the body of belief of the original Federalists never flickered completely out, but has smoldered all along in the writings of assorted judicial, political, and legal scholars.[51] It is time, once again, to fan these embers of thought, to light torches to pave the way for another renewal of Federalist constitutional theory and practice.

In the chapters that follow, then, we will seek to recover what is an obvious constitutional philosophy, that, *pace* Oscar Wilde, virtually dares not speak its name, at least in the American legal academy today. This is the simple notion that the Constitution's text is the only valid guide to constitutional interpretation, and, further, that there is only one valid meaning to the text,[52] the meaning ascribed to it by the founding generation. In our time, as indicated earlier, almost every constitutional law professor has his or her pet theories about constitutional interpretation. In our time as well, the misuse of the notion of a "living Constitution,"[53] usually in the service of "self-actualization" or other debased Jeffersonian goals, has been endorsed by virtually all legal academics and most Supreme Court Justices. This has led many conservative theorists virtually to throw up their hands in despair.

19

The words of law professor Richard S. Myers, making some of the points that will be developed in the next chapter, are typical of this feeling:

> The long conservative battle to reshape the Supreme Court—the battle to promote the principle of judicial restraint—may have ended in June 1992 when the Court decided *Planned Parenthood v. Casey*. In *Casey*, the Court reaffirmed *Roe v. Wade*, the modern exemplar of judicial activism. Although the joint opinion in *Casey* spent a great deal of time discussing *stare decisis*, the jurisprudential core of its opinion is its acceptance of philosophical liberalism. I do not think it was simply a rhetorical flourish when the opinion announced that "[a]t the heart of liberty is the right to define one's own concept of existence, of meaning, of the universe, and of the mystery of human life."[54]

With "self-actualization," and the equally daffy notion that constitutional liberty consists of "the right to define one's own concept of existence, of meaning, of the universe, and of the mystery of human life" we are in a bad way. One of the most pernicious signs of the degeneracy of current constitutional jurisprudence is the scorn heaped upon the traditional Federalist "single-meaning" hypothesis, when, that is, any conservative dares to advance it. When Edmund Meese and Robert Bork tried to expound its virtues during the presidency of Ronald Reagan, the one was ridiculed and the other was denied a seat on the Supreme Court.[55]

Stephen Carter, a Yale law professor, confesses that "my constitutional law scholarship . . . has consistently adhered to a vision of the original understanding as the basis for constitutional adjudication, a claim that is practically anathema among serious legal theorists, most of whom come from the Left."[56] Carter, who is black, tries to suggest that originalism transcends the labels conservative or liberal and he takes special pains to argue that he is not simply a conservative. He is leery of the label because "to be black and also a conservative . . . 'is perhaps not considered as bizarre as being a transvestite, but it is certainly considered more

20

strange than being a vegetarian or a birdwatcher.' "[57] Notre Dame law professor Gerard V. Bradley has pungently observed that although originalism has some very able defenders,[58] "most of its detractors do not take it seriously. They consider it impossible (John Ely), intellectually naive (Mark Tushnet), a cynical apology for a conservative political agenda (William Brennan), or all of the above. And worse."[59]

As Meese, Bork, Carter, and Bradley know, however, this philosophy of constitutional interpretation, usually called "original intention," "originalism,"—or, more properly, "original understanding"[60]—though despised in most of the academy, has the virtue of being the original constitutional philosophy, the philosophy of the framers of the Constitution. It is more than a little curious that originalism is hooted at in the academy, and yet virtually every Justice on the Supreme Court, at one time or another, has tried to justify his or her position through recourse to originalist arguments. At some level even the Justices appear to appreciate Robert Bork's sentiments that once one departs from originalist arguments one is leaving the realm of the rule of law and entering the realm of unbridled discretion.[61] Modern theorists may seek to escape from constitutional originalism, but it cannot be done if our constitutional rule of law is to endure.

Why then did Meese and Bork encounter such rough going? One of the reasons they were not able to win public acceptance of their theories may have been that neither was in a position to put forth the valid historical pedigree of original understanding, and neither sought to present the essentially moral and religious basis on which this constitutional philosophy ultimately rests.[62] Both of those tasks will be attempted here, but the trickier will be to recapture the religious and moral basis for the Constitution; and it is in that regard, incidentally (and ironically), that Critical Legal Studies thought is useful.[63]

We have many fine volumes on the framers' era, and even a few that have accurately portrayed much of the conservative nature of their thought.[64] Most of these, however, have suggested that the framers' world was hopelessly different from ours. In the late twentieth century, concepts such as self-actualization, multiculturalism, political correctness, feminism, and diversity are dominant. Their expositors are dismissive of the supposed unfeeling elitism, patriarchy, racism, and sexism of the Founders.[65] According to conventional wisdom in the legal academy, there is little to be learned from the understanding of the framers of the late eighteenth century.[66] The conventional wisdom is wrong.

By emphasizing the natural law and religious dimensions of the framers' thought and showing its relevance to our time, we can not only recapture some of the glory that was rightfully theirs, but also move towards solving some of the dilemmas of current constitutional practice. This will not be an attempt to return completely to the framers' world, however. Many of them held beliefs about race and gender, for example, that flowed from inexperience, fear, and prejudice. Their world was fatefully compromised on slavery, and it denied fundamental rights of person, property, and the franchise to women as well. The attempt to implement racial and gender equality before the law is one of the great and laudable struggles of the modern era, and should not be abandoned. The Reconstruction Amendments—Thirteen, Fourteen, and Fifteen—as Ackerman has reminded us, must be made a part of our working constitutional jurisprudence.

All this notwithstanding, it is appropriate to try to return to some aspects of the judicial land of Canaan, as the framers knew it. We can leave in the past the errors of the framers' time, but we should try to regain their best political, moral, and constitutional principles and apply them to our own day. But before we can explore the framers' understanding further, it might be helpful to describe in more detail our current set of constitutional conundrums.

Summary of the Argument

Our current constitutional law doctrines are bewilderingly complex, and are usually attempts to justify the blatantly unconstitutional actions taken by the United States Supreme Court in the course of the last sixty years. The Supreme Court has lost its way, and it is time for the people to recapture the Constitution. Our way was lost when the Court, the media, and the academy adopted a bizarre, debased version of democracy attributed to Thomas Jefferson. Jefferson did favor a maximum of popular participation in government, and also a maximum of religious freedom. But, at least as a young philosopher, Jefferson also believed in the inculcation of morality in the young, in a natural aristocracy, and in an hierarchically structured society. In order to grasp the original understanding of the federal Constitution, we must look not only at the thought of Jefferson, but also at that of the Federalist founders, men such as Wilson, Ellsworth, Hamilton, and Madison. Such an examination demonstrates the framers' fidelity to popular sovereignty, but also to their simultaneous desire to restrain the passions of the people and to move beyond the selfish desires of individuals. In our current mania for self-actualization, we have ignored the lessons of the framers, we have neglected checks and balances, strong state governments, and the rule of law itself. This book is an attempt to recapture the original understanding, it is an "Act of Recovery." The framers did not believe in "secular humanism," or individual self-actualization as the primary goals of society. They believed in natural law, and in the furthering of individual liberty to promote morality, religion, and the creation of a natural aristocracy. The framers believed in economic progress and social mobility, but they placed the interests of the community above those of the individual. Their beliefs were somewhat eclipsed by a trend toward more democracy by 1800, but their core insights never vanished from American law. Federalist constitutional theory showed up again in the work of Joseph Story, Rufus Peckham, and the Four Horsemen. It is time once again to fan the embers of Federalist constitutional thought, and to return to "original understanding" as the dominant philosophy of interpretation. Robert Bork and Edwin Meese were not permitted to do so, and neither is Stephen Carter. But we might if we emphasize the moral and religious roots of original understanding. The next chapter goes further into detail in describing our current constitutional conundrums.

Chapter One

CLARENCE THOMAS, THE CONSTITUTION, RELIGION, PROPERTY, AND THE RULE OF LAW

A. Introduction

The angular patrician president stood before the microphone on a windswept July day in front of his aristocratically shabby summer home in Maine. Off to the side, looking a bit abashed, stood a muscular mustachioed black man of medium build. He was somewhat dwarfed by the chief executive, but this was the man the president proposed for the vacancy on the highest court in the land. His nominee, George Bush assured the assembled press corps, was "the best qualified man for the job," and race "played no part in his selection."

The president's credibility had been strained by his abandonment of his "read-my-lips: no new taxes" campaign pledge, but what he had to say about Clarence Thomas, a black man nominated to the position vacated by the nation's first black Supreme Court Justice, Thurgood Marshall, appears instantly to have been regarded by most as a blatantly hypocritical falsehood. Clarence

Thomas graduated somewhere in the middle of his class at Yale Law School. At the time he was nominated, he was a judge on the United States Court of Appeals for the District of Columbia Circuit (widely regarded as second in importance only to the Supreme Court itself). Even so, Thomas had not yet issued any judicial opinions of great significance. He was not generally thought of in the legal academy as a serious scholar. Were it not for his race, and the fact that he had been a loyal Republican bureaucrat in the Reagan and Bush administrations, virtually all commentators noted, he would never have been seriously proposed for such a position.

I cannot profess to know whether George Bush actually meant what he said about Clarence Thomas. Perhaps Bush's critics were right, and he *was* engaged in a cynical political act to seek some support for his party in the black community by keeping an African-American seat on the Court.[67] Nevertheless, whether the President believed it or not, Clarence Thomas *was* one of, if not the most, qualified persons to sit as an Associate Justice of the United States Supreme Court—but not because of his rise from rural poverty to national fame or because of his race. Indeed, it will be argued here that it is wrong to make judicial appointments to favor particular political constituencies,[68] and that the attitude out of which this practice springs is dangerously weakening the fabric of our civil order.

But there was something unmistakeably right about Clarence Thomas, something that was clear to those who had been following his speeches and behavior over the last few years before he ascended the bench. And this was that he was one of the few potential jurists who had publicly gone on record in favor of what is the only correct American judicial philosophy for our time or for any time, the philosophy labeled "original understanding" in the preceding introduction. Moreover, Thomas, nearly alone among public figures of our era, appeared to remain true to the original eighteenth-century conservative jurisprudence itself. Thus, his views emphasized that ours is a government of laws, not men, and he manifested at the same time a set of beliefs including (1) that there ought to be a relatively modest role for the judiciary, (2) that the judges should demonstrate fidelity to the original understanding of the framers of the Constitution, and (3) that judges should show an awareness of the continuing importance of morality and religion in constitutional interpretation.[69]

Thomas's appointment made good sense because it represented an effort to return to jurisprudential traditions honored throughout most of our history, but abandoned in recent years. The effort in which Bush was engaged, to remake the Court, is one that Presidents Nixon and Reagan had undertaken before him, but without much success. From the time that Dwight Eisenhower was astonished and appalled by the radioactive constitutional liberalism of Earl Warren, Republican presidents have tried to nominate Justices who would eschew the Warren Court's habit of abandoning virtually all traces of our original jurisprudence to make way for new constitutional law. Thus Richard Nixon "had said he would not pick as a Justice a 'super-legislator with a free hand to impose social and political viewpoints on the American people.' "[70] During his campaign for the presidency in 1980, Ronald Reagan "said he wanted judges who 'would interpret the laws, not make them.' "[71] The Republican party platform for 1980 "included a pledge that Reagan would select judges (at every level) 'who share our commitment to judicial restraint.' "[72] Strangely, this effort has continually failed to achieve its ends, at least insofar as nominations to the Supreme Court are concerned.[73] Though the Thomas nomination was a step in the right direction, even his nominator, George Bush, through his appointment of David Souter, seemed to frustrate his professed laudable goals.

Indeed, what led to this book were two decisions in the first term that Clarence Thomas served on the Court, *Planned Parenthood v. Casey*[74] and *Lee v. Weisman*.[75] In those decisions, Republican appointees, though not the new Justice Thomas, participated in the judicial majorities which outrageously flaunted the essential attributes of the American notion of the rule of law.

B. Two Terrible Decisions

In *Planned Parenthood v. Casey*, in an odd opinion purportedly written by three Republican nominees, Justices Sandra Day O'Connor, Anthony Kennedy, and David Souter (no one of whom apparently had the courage to claim the opinion as his or her own), a plurality of the Court both did and did not overrule the Court's most controversial recent decision, *Roe v. Wade*. *Roe* was the case that found in the Constitution an unfettered right for a woman to have an abortion during the first trimester of her pregnancy.[76] In *Casey*, *Roe v. Wade*'s approach to abortion as a matter to be handled by reference to the particular trimester in which the pregnancy was sought to be terminated and *Roe*'s particular constitutional standard of "strict scrutiny" to be applied to restrictions on abortions, were both abandoned. At the same time, however, the three-person *Casey* plurality claimed *not* to be overruling *Roe*. It threw out as unconstitutional one of Pennsylvania's restrictions on abortion, a husband-notification provision, as imposing an "undue burden" on a woman's purported "right to choose" to terminate her pregnancy—a right supposedly established by *Roe v. Wade*. While the three Justices clearly implied that the constitutional foundation on which *Roe v. Wade* had been erected was faulty, they claimed that to overrule the case would be to cave in to "political pressure" and would somehow diminish respect for the integrity and independence of the judiciary.

The back-breaking exercise in judicial gymnastics of the three-person plurality in *Planned Parenthood v. Casey* is probably the single worst opinion yet written by Supreme Court Justices. Perhaps it did take three of them to get it this spectacularly, hideously, and horribly wrong. The problem with the case is that it fails to recognize that the integrity of and the respect due the judiciary depend only on the judiciary's fidelity to the Constitution itself, and not on some latter-day political scientist's view of the role of the late twentieth-century judge. The fact that the *Casey* plurality opinion makes only the "slightest of nods in the

28

direction of traditional legal analysis," and that it is more concerned with the "preservation and enhancement of judicial authority" than with the interpretation of the Constitution has led one commentator to label *Casey* "the most significant Supreme Court decision in decades."[77]

The other outrageous case from the October 1991 term when *Casey* was decided, *Lee v. Weisman*, held that a Rhode Island public middle school violated the First Amendment when it provided for a rabbi to open a graduation ceremony with a nonsectarian prayer. Justice Kennedy, a Reagan nominee who wrote for the five person majority in *Weisman*, held that the First Amendment's prohibition against the establishment of religion by Congress ought to be extended, through the Fourteenth Amendment (which prohibits states from taking away any person's life or liberty without due process), to cover an invocation at a middle school's graduation ceremony. Specifically, Justice Kennedy declared that the Constitution was violated when any student or invitee at a public school graduation was coerced, by school authorities, into having to listen to a prayer. Justice Souter wrote a concurring opinion, which will be analyzed in a later chapter.[78]

Even after *Weisman*, apparently it is still permissible under the Constitution to have "In God We Trust" on our coins, and to open congressional sessions with a prayer, but such convocations can now have no place in our public schools, at least where school authorities initiate them.[79] To be fair to Justice Kennedy, he was simply making a logical extension from earlier (though equally questionable) Supreme Court decisions forbidding prayer during actual public school classes.[80] Nevertheless, as the four dissenters (including Justice Thomas, who also dissented in *Casey*) in *Weisman* observed, the majority's opinion flew in the face of hundreds of years of American tradition. The majority in *Weisman* arrived at a result fraught with dubious psychology and freighted with dubious constitutional logic. *Weisman* represents the triumph in America, particularly in the American legal academy, of a secular humanist spirit[81] associated with leftist approaches to society from the time of the French Revolution[82] through that of the Bolsheviks[83] and on to today in the United States.

Thomas's two dissenting votes, in *Casey* and *Weisman* suggest that his jurisprudence was sound. Nevertheless the fact that Thomas's views, and those of his colleagues who dissented along with him,[84] remain in the minority on the Court suggests that Republican presidents have failed in the task they set for themselves. They have not yet managed to reverse the wrong-headed approach of the dominant constitutional theorists of this and the last generation.

Of course, Republican presidents are not entirely to blame for this outcome. Except for a brief period at the beginning of Ronald Reagan's term, Republican presidents nominated candidates who could survive hearings and votes in the Democratically-controlled Senate. The Senate's Democratic majority apparently had no interest in bringing constitutional jurisprudence back to the original understanding. Their lack of interest in this project is easily explained: The deviant constitutionalism of the past two generations, with its plethora of new constitutional rights to be enforced against state and federal governments (the so-called "unenumerated rights") has been widely perceived as benefiting many of the core constituencies of the Democratic party. Thus, judicial candidates of strong conservative jurisprudential views, candidates committed to a Court that interprets rather than makes constitutional law, like Robert Bork and Clarence Thomas, encountered rough going. Indeed, one commentator, Terry Eastland, has persuasively argued that following Bork's defeat, at least so long as Democrats control the Senate, "no Republican president will nominate a lawyer who does not pledge allegiance to judicial enforcement of at least some unenumerated rights."[85]

Even Democratic constituencies have been ill-served by their party's abandonment of the original understanding, however. Perhaps when this is better understood, public pressure may build for the Senate majority to reconsider its hostility to conservative jurisprudence—which, by the way, ought not be the monopoly of either party. As we will soon see, one of the most important exponents of a conservative jurisprudence, Felix Frankfurter, was a Franklin Roosevelt nominee.

C. Recapturing the Constitution

The appointments made to the Court during the remainder of the nineties—by either Republican or Democratic presidents—may be the last chance to correct nearly six decades of accumulated constitutional error. This legacy of misinterpretation does not serve the professed interests of either of our major political parties, even though the current chaos in constitutional law and American life might improperly serve the interests of some politicians and some special interest groups who support them. Still, what is said here should be of interest to persons of all political persuasions. This essay is offered for the use of all the citizenry in recapturing the Constitution itself by insisting on an appropriate judicial philosophy in nominees to the Court. Such an insistence is probably best expressed in voting for particular candidates to the United States Senate, or in furnishing them with constituents' views. That public clamor can affect the judicial nomination process is clear from the unconscionable episode that nearly cost Clarence Thomas his position on the Court,[86] and from the travesty that did cost Robert Bork his.[87] In Thomas's case the favorable impression he made during his travails with Anita Hill, when he shed his assumed attitude of amiable deference and attacked his critics, apparently caused majority public sentiment to shift in his favor. This convinced most senators to vote for his confirmation. In Bork's case a series of unscrupulous distortions and blatant falsehoods insufficiently rebutted by Bork's backers, particularly President Reagan, or even by Bork himself roused the public and caused the Senate to reject him.[88] "Borking," seeking to tar the reputation of a nominee through outrageous lies, should not be allowed to happen again to the nominees of either a Democratic or a Republican president.

A primary purpose of this book, then, is to bring popular understanding of the process of constitutional adjudication to a higher level. Should this occur, the public, by influencing its elected officials at the time of Senate confirmation hearings of judicial nominees, can help future Republican or Democratic Thomases and prevent disasters that might befall bipartisan Borks. If Americans are to succeed in recapturing the Constitution through future nominations to the Supreme Court, sooner or later it may be necessary to end the current vagaries and the circus-like atmosphere of the nominating and confirmation processes for Supreme Court Justices.

For example, the Twentieth Century Fund's wise suggestion that judicial nominees not personally appear before Senate committees ought to be adopted.[89] There is no reason why senators and their staffers should grill and fry nominees in person. There ought to be sufficient evidence from nominees' public writings, previous opinions, or personal standing in their professional communities for the Senate to fulfill its advise and consent functions. It is instructive, for example, that Felix Frankfurter, the second Supreme Court nominee in history to testify before the Senate Judiciary Committee—who subsequently encountered a politically motivated, hostile roasting at the hands of a senator—began his testimony by stating:

I, of course, do not wish to testify in support of my own nomination. I should think it improper for a nominee, no less than for a member of the Court, to express his personal views on controversial political issues affecting the Court. My attitude and outlook on relevant matters have been fully expressed over a period of years and are easily accessible.[90]

It is time to stop nomination hearings from degenerating into interest-group politics and posturing, and to return them to their original purpose of evaluating jurisprudential qualifications. Terry Eastland has recently summarized what went wrong with the Thomas nomination proceedings once liberal interest groups realized that they were headed for hard times if Thomas were confirmed:

The very fact that Thomas was opposed [with charges levied by Anita Hill of sexual harassment] by means of a news leak [probably from a liberal senator or one of his staffers allied with liberal interest groups to whom Thomas was anathema], especially one that apparently did not have the blessing of Anita Hill herself, suggests a corruption of a constitutional process by a corrupted liberalism. Not content to abide by formal procedures—once a hallmark of liberalism—by which it was apparent that Thomas would be confirmed, liberals decided to publicize Hill's charge in hopes that it would undermine the nomination [and convince Thomas and his backers to withdraw his name]. Senate Judiciary Chairman Joseph Biden was right to wonder during the second set of hearings [on the Anita Hill charges] how "we could call ourselves civil libertarians any more" when leaks of this fashion occur.[91]

This "corrupt liberalism" ought to be countered by full and frank discussion of nominees' qualifications by those who nominate them, and by exposing distortions, falsehoods, and improper procedures for what they are. This task will probably be best performed by future chief executives, however.[92]

Nevertheless, there is much that the public can do. One possible project is to build some safeguards into the Constitution itself; these would ensure that at least after nominees make it onto the Court their behavior is appropriately circumscribed. In our concluding chapter, three constitutional amendments that could profitably be pursued in the course of recapturing the original understanding of the Constitution are proferred. But before reaching that point, it is necessary to spell out just what proper constitutional jurisprudence might be.

D. A Republic and a Government of Laws

We might profitably start with the core notion of our constitutional jurisprudence: that ours is a government of laws, not men (or, if you like, of laws, not *persons*). What can this mean? Laws appear to us late twentieth-century moderns as the acts of men and women, particularly those in the legislatures. We understand that even the Constitution was promulgated by human beings whose existence has been carefully documented. How can we say that we are governed not by the flesh and blood men and women who made the laws, but by some abstract bloodless disembodied rule?

One useful answer in the constitutional context, of course, is to remember that the framers are all dead. Thus when we are governed by their work—the law of the Constitution—it is not the men, but their work—the law—that governs us. Still, there is more than that to the concept of a government of laws not men. One still useful description of the working of the concept was offered by an otherwise obscure federal judge, Richard J. Hopkins, in 1941, in the course of a criminal trial:

> Our American system represents the collective wisdom, the collective industry, the collective common sense of people who for centuries had been seeking freedom, freedom from the tyranny of government actuated or controlled by the personal whims and prejudices of kings and dictators. The result is a government founded on principles of reason and justice, a government of laws and not of men.[93]

As this little quote suggests, one way of understanding the notion of a government of laws and not of men is to remember, as Judge Hopkins did, that there are certain things in existence prior to the Constitution itself that circumscribe, and to a certain extent dictate what it is that the framers did when they drafted the Constitution.[94] These "things in existence," which Hopkins appears to mean by the "principles of reason and justice" that the 1787 document sought to implement, are prior to the acts of men. They form the essential stuff out of which our legal system is really built. The philosopher Hadley Arkes calls them "principles of 'natural justice' that existed before the formation of any government."[95]

This "essential stuff," then, is the set of basic concepts at the core of our constitutional order, and includes, among other things, the notion that we have a republic, not a democracy, that there are certain ends that any constitution must serve, and that the ends partake, ultimately, as much of morality and religion as they do of positive law. As Arkes noted, "For the founders these principles of right and wrong helped to explain, in the first place, just why they were morally enjoined to found a constitutional government rather than a despotism."[96]

This preexisting body of constitution-shaping precepts, what Hopkins meant by "principles of reason and justice," is also what Clarence Thomas meant in his prenomination speeches by "natural law." Thomas's views, remarkably like those of Hadley Arkes, are most cogently spelled out in Thomas's Heritage Lecture, "Why Black Americans Should Look to Conservative Policies." This talk was a major political statement about the attractiveness of conservative ideas and ideas about natural law in the modern age.[97] Among other things, Thomas there noted the connection "between natural law standards and constitutional government." He also observed the connection between "ethics and politics" as remarked upon by Abraham Lincoln. Finally he commented on the "moral horizons" of Lincoln and others, which suggested that "Equality of rights, not of possessions or entitlements, offer[s] the opportunity to be free, and self-governing." In that lecture Thomas also indicated that although ideas about natural law go back at least to St. Thomas Aquinas, until recently they were "an integral part of the American political tradition," and invoked even by Martin Luther King, Jr.

Perhaps as a gesture to his hosts at the Heritage Foundation, Thomas also suggested in his lecture that "Heritage Foundation Trustee Lewis Lehrman's recent essay in *The American Spectator* on the Declaration of Independence and the meaning of the right to life [was] a splendid example of applying natural law." This last comment generated much of the opposition to him at the Senate hearings on his nomination for Supreme Court Justice, and it is a position with which I cannot fully agree.[98] Nevertheless, the essence of Thomas's approach to natural law was not the issue of the fetus's right to life, but rather as Thomas suggested, quoting John Quincy Adams, it was that

> "Our political way of life is by the laws of nature [and] of nature's God, and of course presupposes the existence of God, the moral ruler of the universe, and a rule of right and wrong, of just and unjust, binding upon man, preceding all institutions of human society and of government."

Thomas further stated in a peroration:

> Without such a notion of natural law, the entire American political tradition, from Washington to Lincoln, from Jefferson to Martin Luther King, would be unintelligible. According to our higher law tradition, men must acknowledge each other's freedom, and govern only by the consent of others. All our political institutions presuppose this truth. Natural law of this form is indispensable to decent politics. It is the barrier against the "abolition of man" that C.S. Lewis warned about in his short modern classic.[99]

As important as the foundation in "natural law" of our constitutional government is the form chosen for that government, the structure erected on the natural law foundation. Thus we ought to continue, in working out these "Constitution-shaping" precepts, by considering what it is to have a "republic," the form of our government which the Constitution guarantees to each state, and the form chosen for our federal government.[100] As suggested in the Introduction, believing that we are following the work of "framers" like Jefferson, we often speak of the Western "democracies," and most Americans today probably regard their country as a "democracy." But this popular understanding is wrong.

There is no clause in the Constitution guaranteeing us federal or state democracies. Instead, Article IV §4 of the United States Constitution provides that "The United States shall guarantee to every State in this Union a *Republican* Form of Government. . . ."[101] This "guarantee clause," as it is called, was inserted into the Constitution in order to protect the people of the

36

states from having their right to representative government, and their right to enjoy "order and law," usurped by factions or even by duly constituted state officials.[102] The purpose of the clause was to enable the might of the national government to be used to prevent representative state governments either from being violently supplanted by popular dictators or despots, or from having monarchies established in the individual states.[103] The clause was designed to prevent state mobocracy, monarchy, or an hereditary aristocracy. It was designed to promote popular sovereignty through representative government, but not democracy.

What, then, does this word "republic" mean? "Republic" comes from the Latin *res publica*, or "thing public," and refers to the commonwealth, the polity in which the citizenry, as a whole, shares. "Republican" can refer to anything that redounds to the common benefit, and, in fact, the concept did mean many things to the framers' generation.[104]

We know, for example, as already indicated, that for Thomas Jefferson, particularly as he grew older, the word "republic" came to mean something very close to "democracy," since he believed that the more democratic a government was the more republican it would be. Contrary to the conventional wisdom, however, Jefferson was not a representative thinker of his time on this issue. For most of the framers, a "republican" form of government meant simply one in which the people elected representatives who were expected to govern in the public interest. This meaning, of a "republic" as a representative form of government, appears to have been clearly understood until about a generation ago, when the United States began to be spoken of increasingly as a "democracy" rather than a republic.

In a pure democracy, however, the people govern themselves, and do not employ the intermediary of representatives. Democracy existed in its relatively pure form in classical Athens, but even there whole classes of the population were excluded from participating. While all adult Athenian males took part in the law-making process, women, children, resident foreigners, and slaves (who together made up a substantial majority of the population) played no part. It is simply wrong and misleading, then, to speak

37

of a country of almost 300 million souls as a democracy. We must act through our representatives, and hence we are a republic, not a democracy. There was much wisdom in John Adams's comment that "No democracy ever did exist or can exist."[105] We ignore that wisdom at our peril.

This all seems obvious enough, but there is a subtle point to be made about the implications of our being a republic rather than a democracy, and about our Constitution's assuming a republican form of government. It is that a republic (a government operated in the public interest) which acts through representatives must to a certain extent be a hierarchy, a society in which some have greater responsibilities and accompanying greater privileges to enable them to meet those responsibilities. Indeed, at the time of the framing of the Constitution, one of the thornier problems was how to create a special class with the requisite intelligence to govern and the wealth to assure independence to act in the public interest.

Throughout most of our history demagogues from Jefferson through Bill Clinton suggested that we are all equal, that no one should be significantly better off than anyone else, and that progress can be associated with the redistribution of wealth to render the citizenry substantially equal in wealth and power. It has never worked out that way, it never will, and it never could.[106] Some citizens will always be more industrious than others, some will always have greater abilities than others, and some will always be born with greater advantages than others.

As John Adams, perhaps the most sophisticated American political philosopher of the early republic, made clear, there were two senses in which all men were equal. First, as children of the God of nature, they were all subject to *"equal laws* of morality." Second, as members of a just society they were entitled to "a right to equal laws for their government" (what we now think of as "the equal protection of the laws," or equality under the law, or no person being above the law).[107]

As Professor Jeffrey Hart recently observed, referring to the ringing early phrases in the Declaration of Independence, "Men are equal in their right to govern themselves through a representative assembly and to enjoy, as individuals, those (but only those) rights that the assembly confers in its pursuit of the general good."[108] Still, according to John Adams, "a physical inequality, an intellectual inequality, of the most serious kind, is established unchangeably by the Author of nature; and society has a right to establish any other inequalities it may judge necessary for its good."[109]

This meant to Adams, and it ought to mean to any discerning student of politics, that there will be some "aristocracy" in any society. As Russell Kirk, a modern conservative philosopher, and a disciple of Adams, explains:

> Aristocracy is not simply a creation of society; it is in part natural, and in part artificial; but in no state can it be eradicated. Its existence may be denied by hypocrites; but it will survive, all the same, for in any society imaginable, some men will exercise political influence over their fellows—some will be followers, others leaders, and the leaders of political society are aristocrats, call them what we will.[110]

Indeed, the lesson of the events in Eastern Europe in the late eighties and early nineties, learned over seventy years of experience with the Marxist redistributionist ethic, is that utopian democratic theories for society, such as Marxism, eventually only replicate the hierarchy of bourgeois societies but in a more repressive and less economically efficient manner.

The Constitution's framers understood the inevitability of hierarchies. Like Adams, they embraced the principle that we all ought to be equal before the law; that is, that the same laws ought to apply to all, rich or poor, laborer, merchant, or landowner. They similarly embraced the principle that all men were equal in the sight of God, and owed obedience to his moral dictates, particularly the "Golden rule" of Christianity, "do as you would be done by." Thus, for Adams, "The precept . . . *do as you would be done by*, implies an equality which is the real equality of nature and Christianity."[111] Nevertheless, virtually all of the framers did *not* believe that in the matters of the world that counted—intelligence, wit, wisdom, piety, virtue, or industriousness—all Americans would be equal. As we have already seen, even Jefferson, the great Democrat, appeared to believe in a "natural aristocracy" of men of superior parts who ought to be educated at public expense in order the better to serve their fellows.[112]

E. The Purpose of Political Life in a Republic

Jefferson and Adams's notion of a "natural aristocracy" that ought to serve its fellow citizens illustrates an important aspect of the philosophy of our eighteenth-century "republican" constitutional and political framers. They believed that just as the classic meaning of the word "republic" indicated, the primary purpose of political life was to better the life of all. In contrast to the modern constitutional philosophy of self-actualization, as we saw in the Introduction, for the framers the individual was not the primary end of society. Rather it was the task of individuals, comfortable with their rightful place in the societal hierarchy, to contribute to the common good. Altruism, and as John Adams shows, a rather specific Christian strand of altruism, rather than a selfish individualism, was our earliest common civic philosophy.[113] In some academic quarters this altruistic philosophy of the framers is once again being called "republicanism."[114]

The republicanism of our framers did not mean that individuals were not to be rewarded according to the fruits of their individual efforts. It did not mean that individuals were to be denied the means to better the situation of themselves or of their families. Nor even did the framers' republicanism mean that all citizens were not to have some recognized individual rights. What the founding-era "republican" theory did mean was that one's primary societal duty was to others, or perhaps to God, but certainly not to one's self.

Here Russell Kirk's suggestion about the "liberalism" of Adams and Burke is apposite. It demonstrates the difference between the "liberalism" of self-actualization, and the framers' "liberalism":

Edmund Burke and John Adams were liberals in the sense that they believed in prescriptive liberties, though not in an abstract liberty. They were individualists in the sense that they believed in individuality—diversity of human character, variety of human action—although they abhorred the apotheosis of Individualism as the supreme moral principle. When the doctrinaire liberals [such as the French revolutionaries and their sympathizers in England and America] repudiated the idea of Providence, they retained only a moral concept shorn of religious sanctions and left to wither into mere selfishness.[115]

Early American republican theory taught that the task of framers of government was to build a structure that would encourage the development of altruistic virtue in the citizenry, and that would restrain inevitable tendencies toward selfishness and self-aggrandizement on the part of individuals. It was recognized that this task, in a republican government, necessitated the creation of a means to elevate the best individuals to positions of responsibility in the executive, legislative, and judicial branches. These individuals were to possess the requisite wisdom and independence to operate in the public interest, and were to be the "fittest characters" of the new nation. For example, the Pennsylvania Constitution of 1776, in many ways the most democratic of the new state constitutions, nevertheless expressly provided in Chapter II, Section 7, that "The house of representatives of the freemen of this commonwealth shall consist of persons most noted for wisdom and virtue, to be chosen by the freemen of every city and county of this commonwealth respectively . . ."[116]

As indicated earlier, also bound up with the notion of altruistic virtue and rule by an enlightened hierarchy as essential qualities of republican government was the idea that in a republic the rule of law prevailed. Indeed, for Jean Jacques Rousseau, "republic" actually meant a government in which the rule of law was followed:

Any state which is ruled by law I call a "republic," whatever the form of its constitution; for then, and then alone, does the public interest govern and then alone is the "public thing"—the *res publica*—a reality. . . .[117]

It can still be argued today that the real meaning of the Constitution's guarantee clause was to secure the rule of law itself.[118] The rule of law, or the theory that ours was a government of laws not men, was regarded as one of the essential checks on individual tendencies toward selfish error. The essential check of the rule of law was to operate along with the institutional safeguards of checks and balances among the three branches of government, and the delicate interplay of dual state and federal sovereignty.

In one sense, its usual popular sense, the rule of law means nothing more than an absence of arbitrary procedure. Those in government are not to impose their selfish will on the citizenry in accordance with nothing other than their individual crass desires. Instead, the government is to proceed according to prearranged and publicly accepted standards for the good of all. Indeed, the notion of *stare decisis,* of adherence to previous precedent, is often thought to embody the essence of the rule of law, the essence of following a preordained path. This aspect of freedom from arbitrary official acts as an essential part of the rule of law was clearly flagged by Judge Hopkins in the excerpt from his 1941 opinion quoted above.[119]

To the framers, however, the idea of the rule of law inherent in the concept of a government of laws not men meant much more than freedom from arbitrary power. And it is to this—the content of the rule of law beyond republicanism, hierarchy, altruism, and virtue—that we now turn.

F. The Vision of the Framers: Law and Religion

To reinhabit the world of the framers and once again to see their vision of the rule of law is not an easy task, because it requires looking beyond what the law has become today, and back to a time when it was something else. Today, too often, law is big business—urban firms employ hundreds of lawyers and thousands of support personnel; they have become legal factories—operated on a business basis to serve the interests of giant corporations. John Gresham's recent thriller, *The Firm*, describes some of the pressure to generate billable hours:

> Once you pass the bar your billing will be monitored weekly . . . It's all computerized and [the partners] can tell down to the dime how productive you are. You'll be expected to bill thirty to forty hours a week for the first six months. Then fifty for a couple of years. Before they'll consider you for partner, you've got to hit sixty hours a week consistently over a period of years. No active partner bills less than sixty a week—most of it at the maximum rate.
>
> . . . You'll start off working long, crazy hours, but you can't do it forever. So you start taking shortcuts. Believe me, Mitch, after you've been with us a year you'll know how to work ten hours and bill twice that much. It's sort of a sixth sense lawyers acquire.[120]

The truth, of course, is not quite that bad, but the bottom line has become all that matters for many in these firms, and for the first time in our national history young lawyers are judged as much for the hours they bill as they are for the quality and wisdom of the legal advice they offer. The amount of billable hours expected from young associates has doubled over the past fifteen years, and requirements of 2,000–2,500 billable hours a year are apparently commonplace.[121] Billable hours usually represent only a portion of the workday, with even the most efficient lawyers only being able to bill ten hours for every twelve worked. When billable hours reach these larger figures, it is probable that lawyers often are working up to ninety-hour weeks, and there is virtually no time for families or anything else.[122]

It was not always thus. There was a time, not so very long ago, when the profession of law, much like the ministry, was a "calling," a profession one undertook not to make millions, but to serve others. Indeed, there was a pervasive feeling that a lawyer's primary duty was not to the individual clients he or she served, but rather to the law itself and through the law to society.[123] This feeling has not vanished from the bar, but it is kept alive more in the provinces than in the metropolis, and the national media and national university law schools have all but forgotten it.

Curiously, this notion that the law can serve society and that it can mystically link us with something greater and better than ourselves is what still leads young men and women into law school, although they now see the noble goals of the law in rather crabbed and narrow terms. Ask first-year students why they have entered law school, and they will tell you that they want to practice "public interest law," today meaning rendering legal service on behalf of the nation's poor and downtrodden. Or they will tell you that they want to practice "international law," applying concepts of "public interest law" on a worldwide scale, seeking to reform the globe and lead to a utopian community of humankind. But these first-year idealists, in order to pay back massive student loans, usually end up working in a sort of "indentured servitude" at domestic corporation law for urban law firms, and their idealism is all but squeezed out of them.[124] In 1986 the average Harvard Law student left "with a diploma and more than $30,000 in debt."[125] By 1991 that figure was probably closer to $50,000.[126] In order to service debt of that magnitude young lawyers are forced to find jobs paying from $50,000 to $70,000 or more a year, and these are almost always with the large urban corporate law firms.[127]

One or two generations ago "public interest law" as we know it didn't exist, or rather all law was regarded as in the public rather than the private interest. All law—domestic or international— was commonly believed to partake of something greater than the will of the strongest or the richest. Our law, and particularly our law as expressed by the Constitution and the courts, was thought to embody the moral and spiritual aspirations of the nation itself.

The law and the Constitution were once generally believed to reflect American efforts to fashion a national code of conduct that would help our citizens not only to serve each other and our country, but God as well. This last notion was expressed by those who adopted the language in the last part of the Declaration of Independence, where the delegates invoked their "sacred honor."[128] As Garry Wills has observed, "sacred" referred to the source of all the framers' moral philosophy in the law of nature and nature's God; "honor" referred to the responsibilities of all men to abide by this law, to live virtuously, and to serve as virtuous exemplars to their fellows. Thus, in closing with the phrase "sacred honor," the delegates who signed the Declaration were indicating that Americans were undertaking to create a new nation pursuant to their obligations from a divinely inspired natural law. These men displayed, on behalf of the new nation, an understanding of what they perceived to be their duty—to serve as exemplars of virtue to the world.[129]

Because of the manner in which we have recently been led to believe (by the leaders of the bench and bar) that our philosophy of government is a thoroughly secular one, and (in profound error) that our framers meant to erect "a wall of separation" between church and state, this idea of the law as a moral and religious depository will seem strange, bizarre, and perhaps even shocking. It was not so to the framers. The political scientist Ellis Sandoz has recently demonstrated how the founding generation conceived of its new government as one that built upon and incorporated Christian tenets and morality. His work strongly suggests that the framers would have found it strange, incomprehensible, yea even perverse, that modern scholars and jurists should attempt to discover, or fashion, law out of purely secular materials.[130]

The attitude of the young Jefferson who drafted the Declaration *was* typical. As Clarence Thomas appears to have understood,[131] when, in the Declaration of Independence, Jefferson used the idea of "nature and nature's God" entitling each citizen to certain inalienable rights, he was underscoring the religious basis of American jurisprudence. Without this basis, as the young Jefferson knew, our law could not really be properly understood or admired. Remove this basis, as we have been repeatedly urged to do, most recently by the majority in *Lee v. Weisman,* and the whole structure of the rule of law begins to crumble. This seems to have been understood even by the more commercially minded in the early days of our Republic. Thus Alexander Hamilton, Russell Kirk reminds us, ought not be classed as a "Utilitarian,"

45

someone committed simply to the greatest production of wealth for society. Instead "[Hamilton] remained a Christian, in the formal eighteenth-century way, and wrote of the follies of the French Revolution, 'The politician who loves liberty, sees [the events in France] with regret as a gulf that may swallow up the liberty to which he is devoted. He knows that morality overthrown (and morality *must* fall with religion), the terrors of despotism can alone curb the impetuous passions of man, and confine him within the bounds of social duty.' "[132]

After all, if ours is a government of laws not men, and if the law does not come from men, from whence does it come? It will, alas, not do simply to stop with Judge Hopkins's notion of the rule of law as embodying "principles of reason and justice." We still need to ask where those "principles," where that "reason" and that idea of "justice" come from. The answer of the framers, it would appear, was that all of these, "reason," "justice," and "law," proceed ultimately from God. There is plenty of direct and indirect evidence of this belief on their part (some of which will be explored in the following chapter). The framers were certainly aware that the English common law, expressly adopted in each of the original thirteen states, was grounded in reason, and that the judges who interpreted it, as Oxford Professor William Blackstone explained, were engaged in an activity that partook of divine design.

In the first volume of his *Commentaries*, published eleven years before the American Revolution, Blackstone observed, "Man, considered as a creature, must necessarily be subject to the laws of his Creator." He went on to state:

This will of his Maker is called the law of nature. For as God, when he created matter, and endued it with a principle of mobility, established certain rules for the perpetual direction of that motion; so, when he created man, and endued him with free will to conduct himself in all parts of life, he laid down certain immutable laws of human nature, whereby that free will is in some degree regulated and restrained, and gave him also the faculty of reason to discover the purport of those laws.[133]

46

Moreover, Blackstone explains, another characteristic of the law of nature that governs man is that it is not only discoverable by the use of our God-given reasoning powers, and not only revealed to us in the Bible,[134] it is consistent with the principle of "our own self-love," because it is conducive to human happiness. Further, says Blackstone:

> This law of nature, being co-eval with mankind and dictated by God himself, is of course superior in obligation to any other. It is binding over all the globe, in all countries, and at all times: no human laws are of any validity, if contrary to this; and such of them as are valid derive all their force, and all their authority, mediately or immediately, from this original.[135]

Finally, Blackstone observed that in the common law process of decision-making, the English judges sought to *find*, not to *make* law, by following prior decisions. There was one and only one instance in which the common law judges would be expected to repudiate former decisions. This was where those prior decisions could be demonstrated to be in error because "manifestly absurd or unjust" (in which case they would not be "*bad law*" but rather "*not law.*")[136] The prior decisions could then be ignored. Normally however, precedent, that is prior decisions, ought to be followed. Blackstone explained that this was so because "though their reason be not obvious at first view, yet we owe such a deference to former times as not to suppose they acted wholly without consideration."[137] In this manner the English common law would develop, and occasionally change, all pursuant to the usually imperceptible workings of the hand of God.[138]

The English common law formed the basis of American private law for most of the nineteenth century, and Blackstone's *Commentaries* were the most commonly cited law books for the first few generations of our republic. Blackstone apparently received a warmer welcome in colonial America than in England, where his treatise was attacked with venom by Jeremy Bentham, among others. By the time Jefferson became president in 1801, Blackstone had become the acknowledged cornerstone of the developing American jurisprudence, thanks in no small part to Jefferson himself, who had included the *Commentaries* on a reading list he prepared for law students in 1790.[139] Blackstone, in essence, did what the king's armies had failed to do in the eighteenth century—instilled some of the aristocratic, Burkean principles of England into the hearts and minds of nineteenth-century Americans who, despite Jefferson's fears, generally became "good citizens of the republic."[140]

There is plenty of evidence that most of the early United States Supreme Court Justices believed that even the federal government had adopted the English common law and the law of nations,[141] and that these were, in the words of one of the great early Supreme Court Justices, James Wilson, "of obligation indispensable" and "of origin divine."[142] From Jefferson's Declaration of Independence to Lincoln's Gettysburg address,[143] our most basic political tenets have been borrowed from the English common law, and have included divine will as the bedrock of our constitutional ideals.[144]

But in our time this divine basis of American law has been obscured and nearly obliterated by the Supreme Court itself. The hierarchy, the deference, the inherent nobility and morality of much of the American constitutional system that flowed naturally from the nexus between religion and morality and the law has been lost to us. What has taken its place? If the rule of law in general and constitutional law in particular are no longer about religion and morality, what are they about?

Hadley Arkes remarks that we have recently witnessed ". . . the displacement of natural rights, in our public philosophy, with one variety or another of 'positivism' or 'moral relativism.' "[145] He proceeds to observe that virtually all current constitutional scholars have fallen into this positivist trap, including the Chief Justice of the Supreme Court himself.[146] Making a point that we will develop in Chapter Two, Arkes states:

> We should be aware then, that there is a radical separation between the jurisprudence of the Founders, and the jurisprudence offered by conservatives and liberals in our own day. The jurisprudence of

the Founders was built on the connection that was traditionally understood between morals and law. The Constitution they finally produced . . . could be understood and *justified*, only in moral terms, only by an appeal to those standards of natural right that existed *antecedent* to the Constitution. . . . [T]he Constitution produced by the Founders cannot be understood or defended if it is detached from those moral premises.[147]

A similar point is made by Harvard law professor Mary Ann Glendon:

Those views of law that have been so fashionable within the American legal profession since the late nineteenth century—that moral questions are out of bounds, and that the task of law is to adapt itself to behavior—impoverish discussion and diminish us. Such attitudes render insight and self-correction less likely to occur, and lend themselves to perpetuation of long cycles of decline. At worst they are counselors of nihilism and despair.[148]

Arkes, Glendon, and other social theorists such as Myron Magnet all acknowledge that we have cheated and damaged ourselves as a society by ignoring the moral dimension of our law and our constitutional tradition. They do not explicitly develop the linkage between the loss of morality and the loss of religion in the public sphere. But because we seek here the original understanding, and because the linkage of morality and religion was crucial to the framers, it is crucial to us. Given that we have lost our original divine bearings, then, what now guides our nation's jurisprudence?

G. *The Current Void: The Balancing Test Method*

The sad and dismal truth is that there is no current guide to American constitutional jurisprudence. While the Justices of the Supreme Court still claim to be following the Constitution, the words of our supreme law have lost their meaning. Instead, the swing Justices, at least—and in particular Justices O'Connor,

Souter, and Kennedy—appear to subscribe to what has been called a "balancing test" method of judging.[149] This "balancing test" method of jurisprudence has become "widespread, if not dominant over the last four decades."[150] Instead of applying clear rules that can be used to determine the outcome in future cases, the Court has approached the matters brought before it on an ad hoc basis, weighing the competing interests of the parties in a manner which traditionally was supposed to be done by legislatures. Thus, for example, in an early 1939 effort, the Court sought to "balance" the interests of the individual and the government, in order to hold that a municipality's interest in preventing litter was outweighed by an individual's wish to distribute handbills.[151] The Court has also sought to balance the interests of competing governmental entities, whether it be the interests of the state and federal governments,[152] or the interests of Congress and the president.[153] Probably the most widespread and questionable use of the balancing doctrine is when the Court has sought to "balance" the purported constitutionally secured rights of individuals—as, for example, it was implicitly doing in *Casey*, when it balanced a woman's purported right to terminate her pregnancy with her fetus's right to life.

Resort to balancing is a very new phenomenon. It is clearly "not nearly as old as the Constitution. As an explicit method of constitutional interpretation, it first appears in majority opinions in the late 1930's and early 1940's."[154] It is a jurisprudential approach that emerged when the Supreme Court abandoned the notion of the rule of law. One of the most astute critics of balancing, Professor T. Alexander Aleinikoff of the University of Michigan, has written:

> No Justice explained why such a methodology was a proper form of constitutional construction, nor did any purport to be doing anything novel or controversial. Yet balancing was a major break with the past, responding to the collapse of nineteenth-century conceptualism and formalism as well as to half a century of intellectual and social change.[155]

It was apparently formerly believed that constitutional law could proceed in a manner that recognized categories, and not simply matters of degree. For example, in the great case of *Mc-Culloch v. Maryland* (1817),[156] in which John Marshall encountered a state effort to tax the federal Bank of the United States, he did not seek to balance the state's interest in taxation with the federal government's need to regularize the nation's finances free from state interference. He simply declared that the state had no such power. As Aleinikoff has argued:

> To be sure, early Justices such as Marshall, Story, and Taney recognized great clashes of interests: federal versus state, public versus private, executive versus legislative, free versus slave. But they resolved these disputes in a categorical fashion. Supreme Court opinions generally recognized differences in kind, not degree: The power to tax was the power to destroy; states could exercise police power but could not regulate commerce; legislatures could impair contractual remedies but not obligations.[157]

Boldly making legal determinations by categories—what judges, of course, are supposed to be doing—is today little done on the Supreme Court. Often, if not exclusively, "balancing" involves the purported discovery of two contradictory principles or interests said to lie behind the constitutional provisions in question. Judges then "balance" the two principles or interests to see which should be dominant in the factual situation before them. For example, in the notorious *Casey* opinion, the three-judge plurality used a "balancing test"—called the "undue burden" standard—to determine when a purported Fourteenth Amendment right ought to entitle women to choose to have abortions. As it evaluated each provision of the Pennsylvania law in question, the plurality opinion sought to balance the state's purported right to regulate or discourage abortion (in the interests of protecting fetal life or the life of the mother) with the mother's purported right to choose to terminate her pregnancy. The source of both the protection of fetal life and the mother's supposed "right to choose" was the Fourteenth Amendment's "due process" clause which prohibits the impairment of "life, liberty, or property" without "due process."

"Due process," as understood by a majority of Supreme Court Justices, at least since Justice Harry Blackmun's majority opinion in *Roe v. Wade*, was supposed to guarantee a right to privacy similar to a right of property that included a woman's purported right to an early abortion. Presumably, "due process" also guarantees a fetal right to life, which the state is obliged to safeguard. Balancing the two guarantees, the *Casey* plurality concluded that some of the Pennsylvania restrictions—for example, the parental notification provisions for minors—could be sustained as not imposing an "undue burden" on a woman's "right to choose." But somehow the "husband notification" provision could not.

The Court sought to distinguish the two cases of parental and husband notification by citing social science data which seemed to suggest that unruly and abusive husbands might unjustly use the information that their wives had contemplated or executed abortions to torment them.[158] Thus the balance was tipped in favor of the woman's purported right to be free from an "undue burden." Never mind that nonabusive husbands might, in some cases, be able to persuade their wives to change their minds and bear children, and thus avoid a decision that both husband and wife might later regret. Never mind that the biological father of the child might also have a competing Fourteenth Amendment right to choose what to do with the fetus (the result, after all, of a physical contribution on his part) that ought to be accorded some weight.

The Court, in applying the "undue burden" standard, simply played the standard "balancing test" game—it invented two *and only two* policies and then arbitrarily chose between them. In doing so, of course, as always happens with the "balancing test," the Court made what can only be classified as a "legislative" judgment. Swallowing the dubious social science data with regard to husbands, the Court in *Casey* decided which policy it preferred and created a rule to implement it. This was one of the most naked instances of the Supreme Court making, not finding law. It showed starkly how the "balancing test" is nothing but an exercise in judicial law-making.

On the surface level, the "balancing test" approach seems to be a search for some sort of Aristotelian Golden Mean. But once one probes a bit, it is revealed for what it is—a license for judicial legislation and legerdemain. Too often—as in *Casey*—the policy or principle being "balanced" is simply an invention of the Court. In *Casey* the supposed "right to privacy" or "right to choose" had been manufactured by the majority of Justices who decided *Roe v. Wade*; they had simply declared by fiat that it be included in the due process clause.

The right to choose, or the right to privacy, of which it was a constituent part, had earlier been found to inhere in "penumbras, formed by emanations" from the First, Third, Fourth, Fifth, and Ninth Amendments. This was the doctrine advanced in *Griswold v. Connecticut* (1965),[159] where the Court found that a Connecticut law banning the sale of contraceptives violated a purported constitutional right of married couples to freedom from government coercion within a specified "zone of privacy."[160] The rather blatant constitutional creativity of the language and analysis in Justice Douglas's majority opinion in *Griswold* immediately led to criticism and controversy. For example, Justice Potter Stewart, in dissent (joined by Justice Hugo Black), put it commendably bluntly: "I can find no general right to privacy in the Bill of Rights, in any other part of the Constitution, or in any case ever before decided by this Court."[161] Some critics have suggested that Douglas's opinion sought to disguise its discretionary nature by cloaking itself in the objective language of specific provisions of the Bill of Rights.[162]

But whether one might be willing to concede a constitutionally protected zone of privacy to protect the use of contraceptive devices between consenting married adults aside, there is a deep chasm between such a right and the right of privacy as extended in *Roe*. Thus at least one noted constitutional scholar, William W. Van Alstyne of Duke University, has suggested that one might accept *Griswold* in principle yet still consider *Roe* to be an "aberration of judicial legislation."[163]

Perhaps it was something like this view that led Justice John M. Harlan, whose views we will extensively praise in Chapter Three, to render his puzzling opinion in *Griswold*, concurring in the result. In Harlan's *Griswold* opinion, referring to his earlier dissenting opinion in *Poe v. Ullman* (1961),[164] Harlan stated his belief that prohibiting the use of contraception by married adults violated "basic values 'implicit in the concept of ordered liberty.' "[165] Curiously, a bit later in his *Griswold* concurrence Harlan praised judicial self-restraint, remarking:

> It will be achieved in this area, as in other constitutional areas, only by continual insistence upon respect for the teachings of history, solid recognition of the basic values that underlie our society, and wise appreciation of the great roles that the doctrines of federalism and separation of powers have played in establishing and preserving American freedoms.[166]

What Harlan was up to in *Griswold* was hardly judicial self-restraint; it was the usual "balancing test" approach used to create new individual rights—a case of even Harlan being seduced by this approach, of Homer nodding.

Thus, in *Poe*, where Harlan set out his thoughts on the issue of prohibiting contraception by married couples at greater length, he declared that the due process clause's prohibitions in the Fifth and Fourteenth Amendments had to be understood in terms of a balancing test:

> Due process has not been reduced to any formula; its content cannot be determined by reference to any code. The best that can be said is that through the course of this Court's decisions it has represented the balance which our Nation, built upon postulates of respect for the liberty of the individual, has struck between that liberty and the demands of organized society. If the supplying of content to this traditional concept has of necessity been a rational process, it certainly has not been one where judges have felt free to roam where unguided speculation might take them. The balance of which I speak is the balance struck by this country, having regard to what history teaches are the traditions from which it

developed as well as the traditions from which it broke. That tradition is a living thing. A decision of this Court which radically departs from it could not long survive, while a decision which builds on what has survived is likely to be sound. No formula could serve as a substitute, in this area, for judgment and restraint.[167]

But in *Griswold* and in his *Poe* dissent Harlan's embrace of the idea of the due process clause as a "living thing" led him to substitute his own policy preferences for "judgment and restraint."

In *Poe* Harlan conceded that the state could properly seek to address the moral character of its citizens—the argument of the Connecticut legislature was that the availability of any contraceptive would encourage fornication and adultery.[168] But because the "due process" privacy rights of married couples were involved, Harlan insisted that "close scrutiny and stronger justification" than the mere rational basis to the state's decision were required.[169] Applying this "close" or (as it is usually called) "strict scrutiny" test, Harlan failed the Connecticut legislature, because he believed that the state had failed to demonstrate that criminalizing use of contraceptives would further Connecticut's moral policy of preventing adultery and fornication.[170]

The "balancing" performed in this kind of jurisprudence, when one element in the balance is so clearly the inappropriate product of constitutional alchemy, is like the Justices' thumbs being applied to the scales of Justice.[171] This is what Harlan was up to in *Griswold*, with his invocation of "close scrutiny" and "strong justification." A standard was conveniently adopted to implement the Justice's policy preference for his newly minted individual constitutional right.

Inveighing against this sort of jurisprudence was Justice Antonin Scalia's dissent in *Casey*, in which Clarence Thomas joined. There Scalia suggested that the Court simply did not belong in the abortion business. Scalia argued forcefully that there was no constitutional, legal, or customary basis on which to find that any constitutional provision bore on a state's power to legislate in the abortion area. This politically divisive area, for Scalia, was no place for a Court to be dictating policy.

The three-person plurality in *Casey* was not blind to the problem of the politics of abortion, but somehow seemed to believe that the politics of the issue could be avoided by claiming that the Court was not overruling *Roe*. Their opinion claimed that to overrule *Roe* would be to give in to "political pressure," and that such an exercise would have an adverse institutional effect on the Court, because it would suggest that the Court was simply a political organ. Such a political posture for the Court, the plurality feared, would betray what we have already observed to be the core principle of our constitutional system—the rule of law and the ideal of a government of laws, not men.[172] The stand of the three-person plurality on this point was effusively and embarrassingly praised by liberal commentators who started making noises about the extraordinary "growth" on the part of Bush nominee Souter and Reagan nominee Kennedy, both of whom had been expected to vote to overrule *Roe*.

Justice Kennedy, in particular, has been singled out as either an unwitting or almost-willing victim of what happened in *Casey* and *Weisman*, sometimes called the "Greenhouse Effect." A term coined to pinpoint obeisance to media views typified by liberal *New York Times* courtwatch reporter Linda Greenhouse, the "Effect" is seen when a jurist, seeking the approval of the predominantly liberal media and legal academy, moves to the left on constitutional issues. Conservative economist-journalist Thomas Sowell has flagged the two key factors comprising the "Greenhouse Effect." First is the hue and cry raised by Greenhouse and other journalists who fear a new direction in jurisprudence might emerge from a Court dominated by supposed conservatives. The second is the proclamations of impending danger from liberal constitutional scholars such as Harvard's Lawrence Tribe. These two factors, Sowell explained, have created an unwillingness on the part of "moderate" jurists such as Kennedy, Souter, and O'Connor, to overturn even clearly unconstitutional decisions such as *Roe*.[173] It has been regarded as significant that two of Tribe's proteges clerked for Kennedy and Souter in recent years, and some observers have attributed at least part of the Kennedy-Souter swing in the direction of the dominant liberal theology to their influence.[174] This is only speculation, but somehow the three-person plurality in *Casey* failed to understand the message of Scalia's dissent, and that of Chief Justice Rehnquist, that *Roe* itself had been playing politics, because the *Roe* majority had engaged in the essentially political practice of *making* not *finding* law. To continue this practice, and to proceed, in effect, to affirm *Roe*, as the plurality did in *Casey*, was to continue to engage in politics, not jurisprudence.[175] Had *Roe* been overruled, had its departure from sensible constitutional law been corrected, it would not have been an exercise in politics, it would not have been playing politics with the Court, it would simply have been a judicial act bringing the Court back in conformity with the rule of law.[176]

The 5–4 decision in *Casey*, upholding *Roe*'s rule that there was a constitutionally protected "right to choose," underscored the precarious political position in which the Justices found themselves. Their difficulty was exacerbated by *Roe* author Harry Blackmun's self-serving suggestion, made in his concurring and dissenting opinion in *Casey*, that he was eighty-three years old and that the appointment of his successor might well tip the balance against *Roe*.[177] Blackmun thus all but ensured that the next nominee for the Court would face the same kind of confirmation circus and shadow-boxing over his or her position on *Roe v. Wade* that had come to make a mockery of what should have been a sober examination of judicial temperament and philosophy.

The truly bizarre jurisprudence of the triumvirate's plurality opinion in *Casey* bore some resemblance to the notorious posture of some American forces in Vietnam who supposedly destroyed Vietnamese villages in order to "save them" from the Viet Cong. In order to preserve the "institutionalist" value of respect for the Court as above politics the three-person plurality was prepared to uphold a decision—*Roe*—that virtually all constitutional scholars conceded was barren of proper constitutional grounding. When *Roe* was promulgated, its critics made clear that to read the Fourteenth Amendment as including a woman's "right to choose" was to go far beyond anything the Fourteenth Amendment's framers could have intended, and to go far beyond anything that had been historically regarded as a fundamental right. This conclusion was inescapable, given the more than a century in which the states had regulated and in many cases prohibited abortion.

In the year that *Roe* was decided, even Harvard's Lawrence Tribe—who is now perhaps the most visible supporter among leading constitutional scholars of *Roe*'s embrace of a supposed constitutional "right to privacy"[178]—could find nothing of substance on which to base the majority's decision: "One of the most curious things about *Roe* is that, behind its own verbal smoke-screen, the substantive judgment on which it rests is nowhere to be found."[179] In Mary Ann Glendon's excellent comparative study of American and European family law, *Abortion and Divorce* in Western Law (1987), she observes:

> As time passes, not only does the *Roe* decision appear to be collapsing from within, but the opinions of leading constitutional law writers, many of them not opposed to abortion in principle, have been marshalled against it. Archibald Cox, Alexander Bickel, John Hart Ely, Harry Wellington, Richard Epstein, and Paul Freund have all been highly critical. Furthermore, at least two of *Roe*'s prominent defenders [Lawrence Tribe and Michael Perry], would, I believe, also be opposed to it if they consistently applied their own theories of constitutional hermeneutics to that case.[180]

In order to preserve what the three-person plurality in *Casey* thought was the rule of law, they were prepared to embrace a decision that represented a naked exercise of will and not a valid interpretation of the Constitution . This is where the "balancing test" frame of mind, and the supposedly value-neutral "institutionalist" perspective, had brought us.

How, then, do we get out of this "balancing test" mess? What was it that George Bush thought Clarence Thomas was going to do? What ought jurisprudence to look like in our republic? What really qualifies as a "republican" jurisprudence today?

H. *Turning Back the Clock in Order to Understand the Defects of Contemporary Constitutional Jurisprudence: Community and Property*

As should be clear by now, what is proposed here is a return to the basics of American jurisprudence. To recover these basics, we initially must consider the insights of the earliest federal judges during the crucial first years of our republic. At that time it was not at all clear that we would survive as a nation. France, Spain, and Great Britain were each, in their different ways, still seeking to divide and conquer us. From 1789 to 1800, the French Revolution threw Europe into turmoil, and the French revolutionary wars spilled over into the present and former European colonies. American constitutional law in these early precarious years became a device to preserve the republic against attack. In particular the judiciary had to deal with two armed insurrections in Pennsylvania which seemed to be fomented by those sympathetic to the French revolutionary cause.

By 1800, following the development of doctrines necessary to preserve the peace (explored in the next chapter), most of the Justices had declared their beliefs that there could be no law without morality and no morality without religion. These Federalist judges and theoreticians had concluded that no citizenry could be expected to exhibit the virtue necessary to preserve a republic unless it was understood that there were consequences in a world to come from failure to perform duties owed to the public in this one.

Political scientist Ellis Sandoz describes this understanding as an element of "civil theology," a grounding of the rights and obligations of citizens and governments within a framework of theological beliefs which, for Europeans and Americans, can trace their roots all the way back to Athens, in the works of Hesiod, Xenophanes, and Plato.[181] In America, of course, the civil theology or eschatology has a particularly Christian aspect.[182] It appears most prominently in late eighteenth-century homilies from American pulpits. Typical were the hortatory words of the election sermon given by Samuel Langdon, president of Harvard College, in the spring of 1775: "We must keep our eyes fixed on the supreme government of the Eternal King, as directing all events. . . . For the sins of a people God may suffer the best government to be corrupted or dissolved, and . . . nothing but a general reformation can give good grounding to hope that the public happiness will be restored."[183] In other words, not only might a breach of one's public duties on earth lead to one's suffering in the world beyond, but that breach might lead to a form of divine retribution in this world which would take the form of dissolving government and public order. The Founders' insistence on virtue in the people thus takes on both grave theological and practical political dimensions.

American "civil theology" made plain that a morality of social duty flowed from religious faith, and that this morality was essential in upholding the law. Not only must citizens bear their share of the financial burden of running the country, in terms of paying taxes and keeping contractual obligations, but each was responsible to see that the others similarly performed their duties. This responsibility was to be carried out by service on juries, and by following the instructions of enlightened judges.

These basic notions were not explicitly mentioned in the United States Constitution , but they certainly undergirded contemporary understanding of the document (as will be seen in the next chapter). Why not, however, make explicit what was implicit? Why not at least have part of the preamble of the Constitution remark on the necessary nexus between duty, morality, religion, and law? The most likely explanation, as the First Amendment made clear, is that religion as such was not regarded as something with which the federal government was primarily charged. The moral and religious edification of the citizen was left to the state and local governments, those closest to the people. The federal structure was imbued with American "civil theology," but there was enough variance in the strains of that theology for there to be resistance to imposing a detailed orthodoxy on the states. It was probably challenging enough to impose a new governmental structure on the formerly sovereign states. To dictate a new religious orthodoxy would have been perceived as too much. Moreover, the impossibility of any law existing without morality and any morality existing without religion would have been taken so much for granted in the founding era that it might have literally gone without saying. Just as there was no need formally and explicitly to declare that the Constitution was for air-breathers, there may have been no need to express the basic tenets of civil theology.

The late eighteenth-century constitutional world of the framers, revealed in their interpretation of the Constitution in the years immediately following its adoption, was a world in which individual rights existed but social duties were regarded as more important. The community took precedence over the individual, and, in fact, the individual, as a citizen, found meaning in life only from participation in the community. The world of the framers, then, was infused with a rather different philosophy from that which today dominates constitutional law. Now, as indicated in the Introduction, the individual is nearly everything. Now, the purpose of constitutional law often appears to be to protect the individual from the community—specifically from the imposition of community values, as happened, for example, in *Lee v. Weisman* and *Planned Parenthood v. Casey*.

The principal villain in American law in this regard was Oliver Wendell Holmes, Jr. (of whom more in due course). Mary Ann Glendon says that Holmes took the sophisticated liberalism of John Stuart Mill, sheared it of its moral seriousness and its notion of the hierarchy of goods, and replaced it with a rather vulgar notion "that respect for others meant that anyone's opinion was as good as anyone else's."[184] Hadley Arkes, who also advocates a return to the moral basics of constitutional law, similarly condemns Holmes by commenting on his "amorality," and his "characteristic thuggery."[185]

What the Holmesian individualistic positivist jurisprudence of today generally fails to understand, of course, is that no individual can supply him- or herself with values sufficient to live a meaningful life. These can only come from a community, even if that community is as small as a single family. For this reason the

American (and the English) common law tended to treat the family unit as a single legal entity—law suits were forbidden between members of a family, since it was assumed that their legal interests were actually identical. Children were legally subservient to parents, and had virtually no rights to assert against them. Even wives were submerged in the legal being of their husbands.[186] While this system undeniably led to particular individuals being ill-treated, and while I do not advocate a return to a time when women, children, minorities, and foreigners had no legal rights at all, it will still be argued here that there is something to be learned from an era when the community was more important than the individual.[187]

As we are now beginning better to understand after several generations of forgetting, much of the essence of the jurisprudence of community of our early republic turned on conceptions of property. It was property that guaranteed the independence necessary to exercise virtue in the republic. It was property that allowed citizens to act for the benefit of the community instead of their own selfish interests. The theory was that ownership of property conferred a stake in the community, and led one better to act in the interests of all.

In England, it had been traditional to limit the franchise to the possessors of property in order to ensure that the government act in the interests of the community. As in so many other things, Sir William Blackstone was the classic defender of the limited franchise in England:

> . . . The true reason of requiring any qualification, with regard to property, in voters, is to exclude such persons as are in so mean a situation that they are esteemed to have no will of their own. If these persons had votes, they would be tempted to dispose of them under some undue influence or other. This would give a great, an artful, or a wealthy man, a larger share in elections than is consistent with general liberty. If it were probable that every man would give his vote freely, and without influence of every kind, then, upon the true theory and genuine principles of liberty, every member of the community, however poor, should have a vote in

electing those delegates, to whose charge is committed the dis-
posal of his property, his liberty, and his life. But, since that can
hardly be expected in persons of indigent fortunes, of such as are
under the immediate dominion of others, all popular states have
been obliged to establish certain qualifications; whereby some,
who are suspected to have no will of their own, are excluded from
voting, in order to set other individuals, whose wills may be supposed independent, more thoroughly upon a level with each
other.[188]

In a similar manner to Blackstone, Justice Samuel Chase, of the
United States Supreme Court, made clear in his late eighteenth-
and early nineteenth-century jury charges that he feared abandoning property requirements for the franchise and moving toward universal suffrage. Such moves, he thought, would bring
into the political process men with no real attachment to, or
interest in, the community.[189] James Wilson, Chase's predecessor
on the Court, and one of the most influential framers of the
Constitution itself, as well as the 1789 Judiciary Act, also believed
that suffrage should be limited to property owners.[190]

As the excerpt from Blackstone indicates, however, this did not
mean that either Chase or Wilson was against popular government or the important American ideal of liberty. It merely meant
that true liberty—the state of society whereby there is freedom
from oppression and the property and person of both rich and
poor are protected—might better be secured through a limited
franchise. For this reason, in the early years of our republic, the
franchise was restricted to property holders, and, fairly quickly,
redistributive legislative measures began to be viewed as inconsistent both with the contracts clause of the Constitution and with
the due process clause of the Bill of Rights. It was this view,
prevailing into the nineteenth century, as reflected in the interpretation of the Constitution's "apportionment" clause, that finally led the Supreme Court to declare that a federal income tax
designed to further redistributive goals was unconstitutional.
Eventually, however, a constitutional amendment was passed
which allowed progressive taxation.[191]

I do not contend that we ought to repeal that constitutional amendment. Still, it deserves emphasis that in the early days of our republic, and for many years thereafter, it was recognized that there would inevitably be differences in wealth in America. The early constitutional faith of our framers was bottomed on the proposition that the possessors of great wealth could be persuaded to use it in the public interest without expropriating and redistributing it. This insight, incidentally, was not that different from what, under Ronald Reagan, came to be called "supply-side economics." That economic philosophy—lowering taxes and removing regulatory fetters that increased costs and operated like taxes—it will be remembered, brought us in the 1980s our greatest sustained period of postwar prosperity.[192]

Consideration of the historical pedigree of this idea, and its profound importance in the early years of the republic, ought to make us pause before reinstituting a more "progressive" system of taxation. Similarly, we ought to think hard before we adopt regulatory measures, such as the proposed Clinton Health Plan, which might increase significantly the costs of doing business for persons of modest means. Such large-scale tinkering with the national business environment, which could put many thinly capitalized but valuable small-scale businesses into bankruptcy, may ultimately result in discouraging the accumulation of capital and the exercise of the spirit of entrepreneurship on the part of family businesses.

Is it too much to suggest, then, that there is still much we can learn from the eighteenth century, that we might wish to return to some of the goals of the past? Ought we, perhaps, to recognize that the framers' world was, in many ways, a better one than ours?

Ours is a time when the vast majority of law teachers and constitutional scholars are philosophically rather far to the left—the right wing of the legal academy flapping down about where Edward Kennedy and Joseph Biden are, and the left wing settling somewhere in the neighborhood of Robespierre, Karl Marx, or Fidel Castro.

According to Mary Ann Glendon, professor at Harvard Law

special standards of constitutional review—especially when the interests of judicially favored minorities or formerly powerless groups are at stake. Nevertheless, there are still ambiguities, antinomies, and obscurities in the Constitution. Even paranoids have enemies, and even a devotee of the original understanding has to confess that some parts of the Constitution might legitimately admit of multiple meanings. These constitutional difficulties are what has made the present jurisprudential morass possible; and the obscurity of the meaning of many phrases or terms such as "freedom," "speech," "religion," "unreasonable," "search and seizure," "cruel and unusual," "equal protection," or "due process," have allowed too many "balancing test" jurists to see their own values reflected within the Constitution.

The position we will usually take is that the values of those who framed the document can even now illuminate those obscurities. Still, it is probably true that the Constitution and the Bill of Rights—as the products of one of our earliest political struggles—do indeed contain the kind of compromises between conflicting values that can be found in any modern political deal between ideological adversaries.[200] The nature of the compromise that took place is suggested by the fact that among the framers themselves there were identifiably distinct political ideologies. John Adams, James Madison, Alexander Hamilton, and Thomas Jefferson, for example, all considered themselves "Whigs" (men devoted to curtailing the arbitrary rule of the English sovereign) during the tumultuous time leading up to the Declaration of Independence. Nevertheless, the foundations of their divergent political beliefs about what ought to be done once independence was secured were built during this time, long before they split into the warring camps of the 1790s.[201]

Compromise was also a guiding force behind the drafting and ratification of the Judiciary Act of 1789, which created the federal judicial system.[202] It is also likely that the framers compromised not just among their varying political ideologies but with an eye toward just how visionary a document the eighteenth-century American public would accept. A minor figure at the Philadelphia gathering, Pierce Butler, on June 5, 1787, captured this feeling when he stated: "We must follow the example of Solon who gave the Athenians not the best Government he could devise; but the best they would receive."[203]

What all of this means, then, is that if we wish to be faithful to the values of the framers our primary focus ought to be on the way the compromises they reached were "originally understood" by those—particularly those instrumental in framing those compromises—who first interpreted the Constitution. Thus we favor the "original understanding" on which the interpreters, for the most part, seemed to agree rather than the "original intention" on which they may have differed. For this reason, in what follows, opinions of Supreme Court Justices such as James Wilson, who was of primary importance at the Philadelphia Convention, and Oliver Ellsworth, who was the principal draftsman of the first legislation setting up the federal courts, take on particular significance.

As amendments, which themselves spring from a political process, have been added to the Constitution, the problem of conflicting values has increased rather than decreased, since the values of those pushing for amendments are often different from those of the framers of the original document.[204] The clearest case of this, of course, is the Thirteenth Amendment, which abolished slavery, an institution carefully preserved (although not named) in the compromise that made the original Constitution possible. Particularly with the addition of the Reconstruction and Civil War amendments, Thirteen, Fourteen, and Fifteen, an original conflict or tension in the document between the preservation of the institution of private property and the need to recognize political and civil equality for all citizens became acute. It remains one of the most difficult constitutional dilemmas today.

How then, do we deal with this inescapable constitutional problem of competing values or principles, if not by what we believe to be the execrable "balancing test" approach? The scheme of constitutional interpretation offered here requires that in the case of competing constitutional principles one first look to see if the Constitution itself has clearly marked out for us the principle that is to prevail. Thus, Columbia law professor Herbert

Wechsler, in his oft-cited article declaring the need for judicial review according to "neutral principles," notes that a judge has a "duty of fidelity to the text of the Constitution, when its words may be decisive" on the proper interpretation of the issue at hand.[205]

If the words themselves are not decisive, pursuant to the mode of constitutional interpretation employed in the nineteenth century, one can look to the events surrounding the adoption of particular provisions, or to the particular problem that a given provision was designed to solve. One of the most pressing problems for those who drafted the Constitution was to create a climate of commercial certainty, to further American economic expansion, and to reassure America's foreign creditors. This need came about because of the wanton activity of state legislatures during the period after Independence but before the Constitution. Those state legislatures had created commercial chaos by suspending debts and annulling contracts. These events at the time of the adoption of the Constitution suggest that the community's interest in stability, hierarchy, and deference normally required that the constitutional protection of private property take precedence over individualized demands for political or civil rights that would involve the redistribution of existing resources.

University of Chicago Law Professor Richard Epstein argues, according to Herman Schwartz, that pursuant to the "original understanding" of the Fifth Amendment:

> Government may take property only for "public uses," which do not include redistribution of wealth or charity or any other purpose that does not benefit the parties equally. Thus, estate and gift taxes, urban renewal, rent control, land reform, and zoning are largely unconstitutional, as are most welfare laws. Because the property affected by the takings clause includes contract rights, any interference with such rights that does not benefit both parties equally is unconstitutional. Courts, therefore, should strike down much of modern labor relations law, including the National Labor Relations Act, which mandates collective bargaining, and

minimum wage and maximum hours legislation. As Professor Epstein proudly acknowledges, "It will be said that my position invalidates much of the twentieth century legislation, and so it does."[206]

Our argument will not go quite so far as Epstein's, because our primary concern is the Court's jurisprudence with regard to race, religion, and abortion. Still, we share his sense that much of current constitutional theory is fundamentally at odds with the original understanding of property rights.

The interests of the community, according to the original understanding, required a certain ascendance for property rights. We also argue that the interests of the community dictate a particular set of presumptions with regard to morality and religion. The historical materials explored in the next chapter strongly suggest that, for the framers, the interests of the community required that a sense of morality and the obligations of religion undergird the polity. Thus, where there is a conflict between an individual's claim to be free from any government establishment of religion and the community's efforts to preserve virtue in the citizenry through attention to a nonsectarian spirituality, the interests of the community ought to prevail.[207]

Nevertheless, where the historical record is intolerably obscure, or where the problem was unknown to the framers, a different methodology of constitutional jurisprudence from original understanding may be appropriate. This method involves resolving value conflicts on the basis of the established understanding of natural law, tradition, or custom, as was done in this country for almost three hundred years. While Americans of the late eighteenth century may have rejected British rule and much of English statutory law, they still embraced most of the English common law, which they believed to be solidly and laudably grounded in natural law. Indeed, for most American lawyers of the founding generation, common law, natural law, and custom were seen as virtually interchangeable. This perception lasted well into the nineteenth century.[208]

There are times, however, when the text, the surrounding events, custom or natural law still fail to clarify a course of interpretation. When this happens there really ought to be nothing that a court can do, and it should defer to the governmental entity charged with making public policy. The appropriate solution to political problems brought about by intractable constitutional value conflicts is usually to leave the matter to the legislature. As Gerard V. Bradley has argued, there is a "burgeoning load of scholarship showing that *the* fundamental natural right in the Revolutionary and early republican eras was the right of a community to be governed by laws of its own choosing."[209]

The exercise of Republican government through elected representatives, then, was "the paramount liberty."[210] "Liberty" was not viewed in terms of individual self-actualization; rather "liberty" was "identity between the people and its representatives."[211] In our time, of course, this notion of liberty has often been lost sight of as courts have freely frustrated the will of the people's representatives through implementing an improperly expanded conception of individual rights. Better, if one wants to be consistent with the original understanding, to leave areas of uncertainty and value conflict to the legislatures. This normally means leaving it to the *state* legislatures.

This idea of judicial deference, or judicial restraint, was most cogently argued in the recent past by Yale's Alexander Bickel, one of the twentieth-century's preeminent constitutional philosophers.[212] Bickel advocated strictly circumscribing the role of the Supreme Court. He believed that the Court should confine itself to declaring unconstitutional only those laws that were completely irrational or administratively arbitrary. In particular, Bickel doubted the capacity of the Court, through the promulgation of new doctrines, to promote and oversee social change, because

in dealing with problems of great magnitude and pervasive ramifications, problems with complex roots and unpredictably multiplying offshoots . . . the society is best allowed to develop its own strands out of its tradition; it moves forward most effectively

71

in empirical [legislative] fashion . . . as it retreats and advances, shifts and responds in accordance with experience, and with pressures brought to bear by the political process.[213]

Courts, Bickel maintained, were ill-equipped to undertake the empirical pragmatism necessary to make social policy:

The judicial process is too principle-prone and principle-bound— it has to be, there is no other justification or explanation for the [undemocratic] role it plays. It is also too remote from conditions and deals, case by case, with too narrow a slice of reality. It is not accessible to all the varied interests that are in play in any [social] decision of great consequence. It is, very properly, independent. It is passive. It has difficulty controlling the stages by which it approaches a problem. It rushes forward too fast, or it lags; its pace hardly ever seems just right. For all these reasons, it is, in a vast, complex, changeable society, a most unsuitable instrument for the formation of policy.[214]

Following Bickel, the most impermissible jurisprudential practice, we argue, is to do what was done in *Roe v. Wade, Planned Parenthood v. Casey,* or *Lee v. Weisman.* In those cases, and others like them (considered shortly), the United States Supreme Court substituted the values or beliefs of a majority of its Justices for the values inherent in the Constitution, or inherent in long-standing public practice.

Making matters worse, these acts of constitutional usurpation were performed by Justices informed not by belief in natural law, custom, or tradition, but by belief in the ephemeral principles of the descendants of those whom Burke scornfully regarded as "oeconomists, calculators, and sophisters"—modern economists, sociologists, and psychologists. It is time, as Clarence Thomas's speeches suggest he understands, for our people to take back the Constitution from the left-leaning secular social scientists. It is time we reclaim our legal traditions and a bit of ourselves.

Summary of the Argument

Clarence Thomas was one of the best nominations George Bush could have made to the Court, because of his belief in the original understanding of constitutional law. So far even the Republicans have failed to bring the Supreme Court back to this constitutional philosophy, as is made clear by two recent cases, *Planned Parenthood v. Casey* and *Lee v. Weisman. Casey* perpetuated errors regarding abortion, and *Weisman* errors regarding school prayer. It would serve the interests of both political parties to turn the Court back to the original understanding of the Constitution, and avoid future donnybrooks like those involving Thomas and Bork. One way to recapture the Constitution is by amendment, another is by understanding our jurisprudential tradition. The essentials of that tradition are (1) that ours is a government of laws, not men, (2) that there is a natural law moral basis for our constitutional structure, (3) that we are a republic not a democracy, and (4) that the idea of a republic implies hierarchy, and implies that substantive equality and redistribution are wrong; but (5) the idea of a republic also implies that we are equal in the sight of God and before the law. Our early republican traditions, absorbing these principles, emphasized altruism and Christian virtue. They clearly embraced the religious basis of law, an idea that appears, for example, in Blackstone, but that has been all but lost in our current secular culture. Now that we have lost our natural law and divine bearings, what guides constitutional law? Nothing really, except for hypocritical "balancing tests," such as the one used in *Casey*. So, how might we abandon the balancing test and substitute something different? This will be developed in subsequent chapters, but, as a preview, the framers understood the intersection of law and religion, and perhaps we could turn back the clock on this. The framers also understood the importance of ownership of property insofar as it guaranteed a stake in the community. The framers also knew that taxes enacted for the purpose of redistribution were unconstitutional, and that hierarchies were inevitable. In many ways the world of the framers was better than ours, and still has much to teach us. We should thus seek to recapture the Burkean framework of late eighteenth-century American jurisprudence. We'll do this by studying the world of the framers (Chapter Two), by observing the erroneous move away from their thought (Chapter Three), and by suggesting doctrines and a philosophy to bring us closer to the original understanding (Chapters Four and Five). Still, it must be admitted that there are problems caused by ambiguities in the Constitution, particularly with regard to individual rights, property, and freedom of religion. For the most part they can be resolved by reference to the "original understanding." Where that is not the case, natural law, custom, or the decisions of state legislatures ought to govern. What should not govern is the arbitrary will of Supreme Court Justices informed by economists, calculators, and sophisters.

Chapter Two

THE WORLD WE HAVE LOST:
THE INTERTWINING OF LAW AND
RELIGION IN THE EARLY REPUBLIC

We must recapture in our jurisprudence its original religious base and its reliance on natural law by looking primarily at a set of sources that were close to the ratification of the Constitution. Other works have noted the profound importance of religion, particularly Christianity, in forming the American republic.[215] And other commentators from time to time have noticed an early constitutional philosophy that understood the importance of religion and natural law, particularly in the work of Supreme Court Justice Joseph Story, who sat on the Court for many years beginning in 1811.[216]

Curiously, the richest source for the study of such a jurisprudence—one that helps us, for example, to understand whether the First Amendment was meant to exclude religious aspects from American institutions—has, for many years, been all but neglected by scholars. This source is the pronouncements by the Supreme Court Justices who decided cases during the first years of the republic, particularly when those Justices "rode circuit," and presided over grand jury inquests and jury trial proceedings in the lower federal courts of the individual states.

Most of the Supreme Court Justices' judicial business, in those days, in fact, consisted of circuit riding. This task was believed to be important both in order to keep the Justices in touch with the American people, and to instruct the people on the basics of American law and the new constitutional system.[217] Until recently, however, much of what these Justices had to say in their jury charges existed only in manuscript form in archives. While there were published reports of some of the cases the circuit-riding Justices decided, these have rarely beem consulted by lawyers or historians. Splendid published collections of the jury charges have recently appeared, however,[218] and the importance of what the Justices had to say about the nature of the early republic should soon be more widely appreciated. What is presented here ought to help in that effort, and ought to lead us closer to an appreciation of the importance of religion, natural law, and conservative political principles to the operation of the federal courts in the first decade of the new nation. Though we should not seek precisely to replicate all of the doctrines in use at the time of the framers, there is still much their jurisprudence has to offer us.

We will first examine the theoretical basis for the operation of the federal courts, set out in *The Federalist Papers*, and next review the jury charges of the Justices. We will then consider the disposition of several important cases that arose during those early years, including those involving the federal common law of crimes, seditious libel, and treason. And we will close with an extended examination of some of the trials and tribulations of Associate Justice Samuel Chase, and particularly the views he expressed regarding natural law and the importance of religion to the American legal system.

A. Federalist *78 and* Federalist *10*

For more than two hundred years the best guide to understanding the original intention of the Constitution's framers has been *The Federalist Papers.*[219] That collection, written by Alexander Hamilton, James Madison, and John Jay, was not intended as a treatise for the ages, but was rather a series of shrewd polemics designed to persuade the New York electorate to pressure its delegates to ratify the proposed Constitution.[220] The polemics failed somewhat in their intended purpose, because by the time New York got around to ratifying the Constitution enough other states had already approved the document to put it into operation. Nevertheless, the essays of these three men have long been recognized as the premier (some might say the *only*) original work of American political theory. To this day the *Federalist* appears to be, by consensus, the most reliable guide to the political philosophy of the framers of the Constitution. Even Thomas Jefferson, who was later quite out of sympathy with the *Federalist*'s perspective, said in 1788 that it was "the best commentary on the principles of government which ever was written." Historian Clinton Rossiter wrote in 1961 that the *Federalist* was "the most important work in political science that has ever been written, or is likely ever to be written, in the United States . . . the one product of the American mind that is rightly counted among the classics of political theory."[221] For our purposes, namely the recovery of the original understanding of the basic premises regarding interpretation of the Constitution by the courts, we can concentrate on two numbers of the *Federalist*, No. 78 by Hamilton, and No. 10 by Madison.

FEDERALIST 78

Federalist 78,[222] still read by law students, is Hamilton's famous description of the character of the judiciary and his justification for judicial review. Hamilton claims that the judiciary will be "the least dangerous branch," because it will possess neither the sword of the executive, nor the purse of Congress. It will neither exercise military might nor engage in taxation, Hamilton states;[223] it will only be able to exercise judgment. Hamilton recognized that the independent life-tenured judiciary created under the new federal Constitution would be, to a great extent, insulated from political pressures. Hamilton thus faced the task of justifying entrusting constitutional interpretation to this group of nonelected career federal bureaucrats. He responded by noting that the impeachment remedy would discourage misconduct, and further that life tenure and a guaranteed salary would attract some of the country's most respectable characters to the bench.

Even so, Hamilton needed to go further to justify judicial review, whereby the Court determined the validity of congressional legislation—that is, the power of the judges to declare an act of the Congress or of the state legislatures impermissible because it exceeds the limits of authorized power under the federal Constitution. Hamilton performed this difficult task by explaining that when judges practice judicial review, when they seek to determine whether laws are within constitutional limits, they are merely acting as the servants of the people themselves. It is *the people*, after all, who have approved (through the individual state constitutional conventions called to ratify the document) the United States Constitution. It is *the people* who, by the text of that Constitution, have made the Constitution itself "the supreme law of the land."[224] When a congressional act goes beyond the boundaries specified in the Constitution, the argument runs, Congress has disobeyed the will of the people. It then becomes the solemn duty of the judges—who swear an oath to uphold the Constitution—to reassert that popular will by declaring a congressional act unconstitutional.[225]

That it is for the courts to determine whether the legislature or the executive have exceeded popularly mandated constitutional bounds is plainly suggested by the Constitution's vesting "the judicial power" of the United States in one Supreme Court and in such lesser federal courts as Congress shall from time to time establish.[226] "The judicial power" is nothing more nor less than the power to judge whether the Constitution and the laws are being followed in a particular instance; to say, in a word, what the Constitution and the laws *mean*.

There has been a remarkable amount of ink spilled over whether the Supreme Court was intended to be the final arbiter of the constitutionality of acts of the legislative and executive branches of the federal government, and of the state governments.[227] Some caution was expressed with regard to the Court's power in this regard even by some of the earliest federal judges. The earliest Supreme Court Justices appear to have understood that the Supreme Court had the power, under the Constitution, to determine the legitimacy of laws passed by the state or federal legislatures, although they recognized that the power ought to be exercised sparingly, if at all.

It is noteworthy that one of the most cautious early Justices on the question of judicial review, James Iredell, conceded the validity of the practice even before the ratification of the Constitution. Thus, writing on August 17, 1787, Iredell considered the arguments against the judicial role in constitutional interpretation (in this case, a state constitution), and concluded that judicial review is a proper counterweight to the possible tyranny of the majority so long as judges do not abuse their power.[228] Later, as we will soon see, in *Calder v. Bull* (1798),[229] both Iredell and Justice Samuel Chase agreed that the power to void a legislative act should be exercised only in very proscribed circumstances. "I will not decide any law to be void, but in a very clear case," said Chase.[230] And Iredell said, "that as the authority to declare [a law] void is of a delicate and awful nature, the Court will never resort to that authority, but in a clear and urgent case."[231]

Nevertheless, other opinions by the earliest federal judges, coupled with what Hamilton had to say in 1788 in *Federalist 78*, make clear that the *Federalist* framers believed judicial review of constitutionality to be a vital part of the structure of government, and a task of the Supreme Court. For example, in a jury charge in 1798, Justice William Paterson told his jurors, "You have nothing whatever to do with the constitutionality or unconstitutionality of the sedition law. . . . until this law is declared null and void *by a tribunal competent for the purpose*, its validity cannot be disputed."[232] The tribunals competent for the purpose, of course, were the federal courts, and particularly the United States Supreme Court, where the judicial power was initially vested by Article III of the Constitution. Samuel Chase spoke to similar effect in rejecting the defense counsel's argument, in *U.S. v. Callender* (1800),[233] that the jury should be able to decide the validity of the sedition law under which Callender was being prosecuted. Said Chase, "[T]he judicial power of the United States is the only proper and competent authority to decide whether any statute made by Congress (or any of the state legislatures) is contrary to, or in violation of, the Constitution."[234]

Chief Justice John Marshall is customarily accorded credit for settling the issue in *Marbury v. Madison* in 1803. Properly understood, however, *Marbury* advanced nothing new, and John Marshall merely restated the arguments in the *Federalist* and those used by his predecessors on the Supreme Court, most notably Samuel Chase. According to Marshall's most famous biographer, Albert J. Beveridge, Marshall was in the audience during Chase's lengthy discourse on judicial review in *Callender*.[235] Beveridge observed that "Chase advanced most of the arguments used by Marshall in *Marbury v. Madison*."[236]

Some of Chase's further statements on the necessity for judicial review of the constitutionality of statutes, in words much like those which Marshall would use, but written three years *before* *Marbury*, are in his manuscript Jury Charge Book:

> . . . if Congress have, or should, from Inattending [?], or error in Judgement, or want of appreciation, pass laws in violation of the Constitution; or burthensome or oppressive to the people; a *peaceable, safe,* and *ample* remedy is provided by the *Federal* Constitution. *The people* therefore have established *the mode,* by which *such grievances* are to be redressed; and no *other* can be adopted *without a violation of the Constitution and the Laws.*
>
> If the *Federal* Legislature should at any time pass a Law *contrary to the Constitution of the United States, such Law* would be

80

void, because that Constitution is the *fundamental* Law of the United States, and *paramount any Act of the Federal Legislature; whose authority is derived from, and delegated by, that Constitution; & which imposes* certain restrictions *on the* Legislative authority that can only be preserved through the *medium* of the Courts of Justice. *The Judicial* power of the United States is *coexistent, co-extensive,* and *co-ordinate* with, and *altogether independent of* the *Legislature,* & *the Executive,* and the Judges of the Supreme and District courts are bound by their *Oath of Office,* to regulate their Decisions *agreeably to the Constitution.* The Judicial power, there-fore, are the only proper and *competent* authority to decide whether any Law made by Congress or any of the State Legisla-tures is contrary to or in Violation of the *Federal* Constitution.[237] [italics Chase's]

Chase continued, much like Paterson before him:

It is my opinion, that you [grand jurors] have *no right* to decide on the *Justice,* or the *validity* of the *Law;* and if you should exercise *the power,* that you would thereby usurp the authority entrusted by the *Federal* Constitution to the *Legislature* to judge of the *Justice* of its laws; and to the judiciary to determine their *constitu-tionality.*[238] [italics Chase's]

Indeed, if Marshall's opinion in *Marbury* is remarkable for anything, it is his use of power of judicial review in a timid manner to declare that his Court had no jurisdiction to give relief to a man whose official commission Marshall himself had failed to deliver some months before. Perhaps some of the doubt that has been cast on judicial review over the years has come from the wide-spread belief that John Marshall himself invented the doctrine, but this is far from the truth. Judicial review was being debated and argued profoundly even before the War for Independence.[239] The case for the judges throwing out unconstitutional statutes as agents of the people was, in any case, clearly established by Ham-ilton in the *Federalist* a decade and a half before *Marbury.*

Recently—for the last forty years—we have watched the Supreme Court throw out state and federal legislation on the grounds that it transgressed rights not expressly enumerated in the Constitution. And we have seen constitutional amendments interpreted in a manner that goes far beyond the intention of their framers or ratifiers. Thus we might be excused if we find Hamilton's argument—about the judges only implementing the popular will as specified in the Constitution—quaint, to say the least. Nevertheless, if the theory of popular sovereignty on which the Constitution itself is bottomed is to make any sense, Hamilton's justification for judicial review—that it merely enforces the will of the people—is the only valid one.

For Hamilton's theory of the judiciary as the expositor and enforcer of the popular will to make any sense, then, two important corollaries must follow. Not only must the judiciary only enforce the will of the people when it engages in constitutional interpretation, but (1) it must be able to discern the popular will as expressed in the document, and (2) there must be a clear original understanding—the popular will must have a single correct meaning. The search for the popular will, as expressed in the Constitution, is the only valid means of constitutional interpretation. If there are correct answers to constitutional questions—and if there are not, then the rule of law itself makes no sense—there can be only one meaning for the Constitution. Constitutional adjudication, then, is nothing more nor less than the search for the single correct expression of the popular will inherent in the document. There must be right answers to constitutional questions, and they are to be sought in the original understanding of the words and phrases ratified by the people in convention.

FEDERALIST 10

While Hamilton's implicit theory of objective constitutional interpretation and original understanding makes sense, other insights in the *Federalist* seem to run counter to *Federalist* 78's inherent notion of a single valid constitutional rule and a single

82

valid constitutional perspective. Thus Madison, in *Federalist* 10,[240] appears to celebrate not American uniformity of belief, but American diversity. Indeed, it is not uncommon to find in the literature of modern political historians, a celebration of Madison in particular and the *Federalist* in general as the forerunners of American liberalism.[241] Is *Federalist* 10 consistent with what we have said about the "single-meaning" hypothesis that ought to undergird popularly based judicial review?

In *Federalist* 10, Madison was answering critics of the new national republic. Those critics contended that the classic republican form of representative government worked well only in small geographic areas. In such small areas, it was thought, some uniformity of culture and a uniform set of ethical precepts could inform the government, cultivate virtue in the people, and lead to greater self-sacrifice and stability for the interests of all. The argument was borrowed by the Antifederalist critics of the Constitution from the celebrated French theoretician, the Baron de Montesquieu.[242] Madison famously turned the old argument about republics on its head. He argued that in a small geographic area self-interested factions would have an easier time taking over the government to serve their own rather than society's ends. In a larger republic, Madison reasoned, there would be many factions, with many interests, and the special interests of these particular factions would tend to cancel each other out. In a large republic, then, the true national interest could more easily emerge and remain dominant in the national government.[243]

There is something of a paradox here in that Madison appears to suggest that there will be competing visions of the good in American society. Indeed, Madison *does* sound something like a modern self-actualized value-neutral liberal. If America is expected to be rife with factions, can *Federalist* 78's implicit claim that there is a single meaning to constitutional provisions, and a single set of constitutional values still stand? The paradox may be more apparent than real, however, because Madison also appears to believe that there is a single, perceptible, sensible, noble, and valid national purpose that will emerge after the battle among competing factions. This is what Madison means by suggesting that the playing off of factions will arrive at "the public good," or "the true interest of [our] country."[244]

While Madison doesn't tell us in *Federalist* 10 precisely what the ultimate aim of constitutional government is to be, he is clear on what it will not be. Thus he says that his theory about controlling factions, by the large size of our republic, will result in less risk of the government's acceding to "a rage for paper money, for an abolition of debts, for an equal division of property, or for any other improper, or wicked project."[245] We might note in passing that Madison's condemning of the notion that there ought to be an equal division of property is consistent with the argument made here in Chapter One. Redistribution, to restate the argument, is an unacceptable governmental goal, and, indeed, a violation of natural law. To interpret the Constitution in a manner that creates new rights and implies redistribution of resources, then, has to be in error.

DIVINE PROVIDENCE AND THE CONSTITUTION

But how are we to be assured that what is essentially in the national interest will result from a battle of factions, and that the most powerful faction will not simply take control of the national government? Won't this happen if that faction is skillful enough either to persuade a majority of the public to go along with it, or to persuade the molders of public opinion, such as the press, to help it achieve its nefarious and self-centered ends?

The authors of the *Federalist* offered no definitive answer to this problem. Still, it seems fair to read their work as suggesting that it was Divine Providence itself that was to achieve the triumph of the public interest. Divine Providence, that is, was expected to guide the judges in making constitutional interpretations according to the sense of the people. Thus, in the first published commentary on the Constitution, in the New York *Daily Advertiser* on September 24, 1787, the anonymous author spoke of the advantages "by the blessing of Heaven" that Americans were likely to derive from the fruits of the Constitutional Convention.[246] Shortly thereafter, in November 1787, "A Citi-

84

zen of Philadelphia" [Peletiah Webster] suggested that Congress could be trusted to do the right thing under the federal Constitution because of "*the fear of God before their eyes,* for while they sit in the place of God, to give law, justice, and right to the States, they must be *monsters indeed* if they do not regard *his law,* and imitate *his character.*"[247] To similar effect, "Plough Jogger," writing in the *Newport Herald,* on April 17, 1788, stated that "He that has all power no doubt means that [magistrates under the new Constitution] should have power, not to do wrong but to administer justice in his fear, consistent with his law. . . ."[248]

Several individuals who urged that morality and religion ought to lead to ratification of the Constitution underscored the connection between the American Constitution and Divine Providence. Tench Coxe wrote in the *Pennsylvania Gazette,* on May 21, 1788, to the members of the Virginia ratifying convention, urging them, as "friends of religion and morality," to "seize this opportunity proffered you by the bounty of Heaven, and save your country from contempt and wretchedness" by ratifying the 1787 document. Benjamin Rush told the Pennsylvania ratification convention that the origin of the Constitution was "from heaven, asserting that he as much believed the hand of God was employed in this work, as that God had divided the Red Sea to give a passage to the children of Israel, or had fulminated the ten commandments from Mount Sinai!"[249]

Perhaps the most famous such encomium on the divine nature of American constitutional government was uttered by Benjamin Franklin, "the wisest of the Founding Fathers,"[250] using the pseudonym "K," in his extraordinary article in the *Federal Gazette* of Philadelphia, on April 8, 1788. Franklin there compared the Antifederalist critics of the Constitution to the Old Testament rejectors of divine beneficence:

> I beg I may not be understood to infer, that our General Convention was divinely inspired, when it form'd the new federal Constitution, merely because that Constitution has been unreasonably and vehemently opposed; yet I must own I have so much Faith in the general Government of the world by *Providence,* that I can

hardly conceive a Transaction of such momentous Importance to the Welfare of Millions now existing, and to exist in the Posterity of a great Nation, should be suffered to pass without being in some degree influenc'd, guided, and governed by that omnipotent, omnipresent, and beneficient Ruler, in whom all inferior Spirits live, and move, and have their being.[251]

Franklin and Rush's view of natural law and nature's God working to ensure a triumph of good government in the federal Constitution[252] is consistent with the position of those who believed, for example, in the divinely inspired nature of the common law. In the early years of our republic, as we will soon see, this common law itself was implemented in the federal courts. The notion of Divine Providence was at work as well in the minds of those who believed that natural law principles should be both embodied in and in control of the operation of the Constitution itself. As we will also explore, these theorists believed that these supraconstitutional principles prohibited particular legislative acts, such as *ex post facto* laws or uncompensated taking of one person's property to give to another.

B. The Earliest Federal Jurisprudence

It would appear, then, that belief in Divine Providence and in a religious foundation for American law was widespread during the founding and early national period of American history. If the authors of the *Federalist* and the early interpreters of a federal common law of crimes and of supraconstitutional principles that circumscribed any legislature were correct, then religion has been a part of our jurisprudence from the very beginning. A religious justification, in short, was offered to explain how the will of the people could be expressed and preserved, and, as we have seen, a religious justification was advanced to ensure that judicial review would be done in accordance with the popular and divine will expressed in the document. Early American jurisprudence, of the sort the *Federalist* and the other defenders of the Constitution described as necessary and inevitable, then, was a profoundly religious and, it will appear shortly, conservative enterprise.

The *Federalist's* argument for the influence of religion and natural law is implicit rather than explicit. But what was merely implied by Madison and Hamilton becomes express once we review more of the jury charges made by some of the first federal judges. As these judges rode the circuits, they explained the workings of the new constitutional order to the American people, demonstrating to them precisely what it was they had wrought. The principal task of the federal grand juries was to assist in determining whether there was evidence of crimes committed sufficient to begin prosecutions through indictments. Much of the evidence brought before them in the early years of the republic concerned suspected crimes involving violations of the law of nations. The law of nations was an ancient body of learning long predating the Constitution, but generally believed to be a part of *any* nation's jurisprudence.

It was necessary for the United States Supreme Court Justices who rode on circuit to lecture the grand juries on the basics regarding the constitutional order and the law of nations. For example, John Jay, one of the three authors of the *Federalist*, and the first Chief Justice of the United States, told a Virginia jury, in April of 1793:

> . . . nations and Individuals injure their essential interests in pro-
> portion as they deviate from order. By Order I mean that relational
> Regularity which results from Attention and Obedience to those
> Rules and principles of Conduct which Reason indicates and
> which Morality and Wisdom prescribe. [Jay further explained that
> order followed also from the Law of Nations, which was created by
> Him] from whose will proceed all moral Obligations, and which
> will is made known to us by Reason or by Revelation.[253]

Jay also referred to the necessary nexus between law and religion when he charged a Vermont grand jury in June 1792 regarding perjury: "Testimony is given under those solemn obligations

87

which an appeal to the God of Truth imposes; and if oaths should cease to be held sacred, our dearest and most valuable Rights would become insecure."[254]

When Associate Justice William Cushing addressed a jury in Rhode Island in 1794, he spoke to them of a nation's natural right to self-defense, and the concomitant requirement for citizens to cooperate in the national defense effort. Such cooperation on the part of citizens, he stressed, should be done "trusting to the justice of the Supreme Ruler, that innocence and virtue shall finally come off triumphant."[255] To similar effect was a charge by Justice Cushing to a Virginia jury in 1798, when he told them that he could see "a connection between the seditious publications [of the critics of the Adams administration] and the influence of the [atheistic revolutionary] French,"[256] and he warned against

> combinations of foreign influence and intrigue, of internal anarchy and discord, misrepresentation, calumny and falsehood, operating from POLITICAL, ambitious and selfish purposes—against all impious attempts to root out of men's minds every trace of Christian and natural religion, with all sense of a Deity and moral obligation—OF ALL which evil workings we have seen too many and lamentable specimens in America within a few years past.[257]

Cushing sought to explore the religious dimensions of good citizenship. He contrasted the impious—who would improperly operate in the political sphere acting pursuant to evil and selfish ambition—and more pious Americans—who, pursuant to the dictates of Christianity and "natural religion," would live lives of moral obligation and republican virtue. In a Burkean manner, Cushing sadly reviewed and deplored a whole series of revolutions and disorders throughout the world.[258] Hoping that these wouldn't be permitted to happen in the United States, Cushing railed against "atheism, military despotism, and the prostration of all principle, civil, moral, and religious."[259]

Chief Justice Oliver Ellsworth, who followed Jay, shared Cushing's sentiments against the radical principles of the French Revolution. Ellsworth warned a jury in New York in 1797: "So radically hostile to free government, are the impassioned and the impious."[260] In closing his charge to jurors in South Carolina in May of 1799, Ellsworth assured them that they needed no persuasion to perform their proper duties because "You *feel* that you have a *country*, and believe there is a *God*."[261] [italics his]

Similarly, when Associate Justice William Paterson, in 1795, was readying a Pennsylvania jury to hear charges of treason he explained to them that "We must be mindful of our duty, and be faithful to our country and its laws, to our oaths, our consciences, and our God."[262] When Paterson closed his grand jury charge to the Delaware jurors in June of 1795, he followed the common practice of doing so with a prayer: "May the God of heaven be our protector and guide, and enable us all to discharge our official, relative, and social duties with diligence and fidelity."[263]

In 1800, in the course of his charge to a New Hampshire jury, Judge Paterson said, "Religion and Morality were pleasingly inculcated and enforced, as being necessary to good government, good order, and good laws, for 'when the rightious are in authority, the people rejoice.' "[264] Finally, in another charge delivered by Justice Paterson, which is undated, he made clear that his grand jurors ought to "seek peace and be obedient to the laws; let us fear God, respect our government, and honor the constituted authorities of our country."[265] The practice of "fearing God," the sensitivity to what might happen in a world to come based on one's conduct in this one, was believed by Paterson to be linked with respect for the new government and its ministers.

Associate Justice Samuel Chase, perhaps the one individual who had the most to say about the necessary nexus between constitutional law and religious obligation,[266] told a Pennsylvania jury in 1800 that they were obliged to defer to the judges on questions of law because judges "are assigned and qualified to decide the Law, under the solemn obligations of religion . . ."[267] Like Paterson, Chase quoted Scripture when he told the Pennsylvania jurors that " 'Ye shall know them by their fruits: A good tree cannot bring forth evil fruit, neither can a corrupt tree bring forth good fruit."[268]

Chase indicated to some Pennsylvania jurors, who were trying a case of seditious libel against a critic of President Adams, the kind of good fruit he thought had been brought forth with the president. President Adams, he explained, was "the uniform friend of religion and piety, Morality and Virtue." He cautioned his jurors not to be lax in their duties, lest the nation be undermined by forces "subversive of the foundation of all religious, moral, and social obligations."[269]

According to Samuel Chase's manuscript Jury Charge Book, he exhorted his Baltimore Grand jurors in 1802 in the following language:

> Suffer me to entreat you, by the love of your Country, and a regard to its dearest rights, to exert your *utmost* endeavors to support your *national* Government; and to maintain sacred and inviolate the *Union* of the States, on which, under the care and protection of Divine Providence, your *Political safety, happiness, & prosperity* depend. As good *Citizens* you must know, that it is your indispensable duty to render a cheerful and ready obedience to the *Laws;* and as Sincere *Christians* you must consider it your duty to practice *religious, moral,* and *social* duties. Permit me, Gentlemen, to call to your remembrance *maxims,* sanctioned for their truth, by the wisdom and experience of ages, that there can be no "*political happiness* without *liberty;* that there can be no *liberty* without *morality;* and that there can be no *morality* without *Religion,*"— The distinction between *Liberty and Licentiousness;* between *virtue* and *vice,* and between *Religion* and *infidelity,* should be inviolable . . . in *all* Societies. You know . . . from the *highest* authority— "that *Righteousness* exalteth a Nation; and that *Sin* is a Reproach to *any people.*"[270]

Asking for the further indulgence of his jurors, Chase took the time to pass on to them the few "Principles, which I hold to be correct, and therefore necessary to be Known, and kept in memory by all my fellow Citizens":

> 1st That *our free Republican* Governments cannot be preserved without the *Republican* virtues of *probity,* and *industry, frugality,*

and *temperance*. 2d That without the restraint of Laws *Liberty* cannot exist in a State of Society. 3d That *good* Laws cannot be put in execution without *good morals*; and 4th That *Religion* and *piety; morality* and *virtue*, are the only pure foundations of *National* happiness.—Any Government, whatever may be its form, that does not give protection and Security to the *property* and the *Civil and religious liberties* of its Citizens is unworthy of obedience, *and* defense.—Any government that does not *distinguish* virtue; *discourage* vice; and *reward* merit, cannot deserve the respect and esteem of its Citizens.[271]

Chase thus recalls all of the religious themes we have observed so far in the work of the earliest federal judges. All of this adds up to the proposition that much was expected of American citizens, and that if their free republican government was to be preserved, they—and the government—would have to take care to exercise and promote virtue while discouraging irreligion and vice.

The need is no less today. The framers knew well that both the governors and the governed would have to understand that no one could enjoy true liberty unless it were under the rule of law, and unless the law was firmly undergirded by morality and religion. Chase's thought, and that of his Federalist judicial colleagues, might be fairly summed up by suggesting that they believed that *there could be no law*, constitutional or otherwise, *without morality and that there could be no morality without religion*.

Chase was also concerned that his jurors understand just what sort of liberties and rights they could expect to exercise. He seemed particularly worried that abstract revolutionary theories, such as those of the French, would be corrosive of real American liberty:

You know, Gentlemen, that our *National*, and *State* Institutions do *fully* secure to every member of Government *equal liberty*, and *equal rights.—Terms* grossly misunderstood; or wickedly misapplied!—An *Equality of liberty, and rights* can only mean, that every person, without respect to his *property*, or *Station*, should enjoy an *equal share* of *Civil Liberty:* an *equal protection* of

Law; and an *equal security* for his *person* and *property.*—Any other *idea* is, in my opinion, *visionary:* and destructive of all *Government,* and all *Laws.*[272]

One year later, in 1803, in the famous Baltimore grand jury charge that led directly to his impeachment by the Jeffersonians, Chase indicated his fears that what he believed to be the basic principles of good government were not being followed. Thoroughly upset by what he regarded as the demagogic behavior of the Jeffersonian majorities in the Maryland and federal legislatures, Chase bemoaned the fact that

> It is a very easy task to deceive & mislead the great Body of the people by propagating plausible but false doctrines; for the bulk of mankind are governed by their passions, and not by reason. *Falsehood* can be more readily disseminated than *truth,* and the *latter* is heard with reluctance, if repugnant to *popular* prejudice.[273]

This did not mean, Chase explained, that he was not "a decided & avowed advocate for a *Representative* or *Republican* form of Government." He was, but he clearly shared with John Adams the notions that even in a republican form of government there was a need for distinctions among the citizenry, and that abstract principles such as universal suffrage ought to be eschewed. Thus, he stated:

> It is my sincere wish that *freemen* should be governed by their *Representatives* fairly & freely elected, by *that class of Citizens,* described in our Bill of rights, "who have *property* in, a common interest with, and an attachment to the Community."[274]

In language that would later be used as evidence of Chase's "cloven hoof," and of his being a closet aristocrat or monarchist (a favorite Antifederalist tactic),[275] Chase gave his view of the current crisis in America, in language that has lost none of its relevance:

The purposes of Civil society are best answered in those Govern-ments, where the public *safety, happiness,* and *prosperity,* are best secured; whatever may be the Constitution or form of Govern-ment; but this History of mankind (in *Ancient* and *modern* times) informs us, "that a *monarchy* may be *free*; and that a *Republic* may be a *tyranny.*" —The true test of Liberty is in the *practical* enjoyment of protection to the *person,* and the *property* of the Citizen, from all injury.—Where the *Same* laws govern the *whole Society;* without any distinction, and there is no power to dispense with the execution of the Laws; *where* Justice is *impartially* and *speedily* administered, and the poorest man in the *Community* may obtain redress against the most wealthy and powerful, and riches afford no protection to violence; and where the person, and prop-erty of every man are Secure from insult or injury: in *that* Country *the people are free.*—This is our *present* situation. *Where* Law is *uncertain, Partial* or *arbitrary; where* Justice is *not impartially* administered to all; where property is insecure, and the person is liable to insult & violence, without redress, by *Law;* the people are *not free*; whatever may be their form of Government.—To *this situation* I greatly fear that we are fast approaching.[276]

Chase next explained just what actions at the national and local level had alarmed him, and what actions he thought threatened freedom:

... [O]ur State, and national Institutions were framed to Secure to every member of the Society *equal Liberty,* and *equal rights;* but the late alteration of the federal Judiciary [through the Federal Judiciary Act of 1802] by the abolition of the office of the sixteen Circuit Judges, and the *recent* change in our [Maryland] State Constitution, by the establishing *universal suffrage,* and the *fur-ther* alteration that is contemplated in our State Judiciary, (if adopted), will, in my Judgment, *take away all security for property,* and *personal Liberty.* The independence of the National Judiciary is already shaken to its foundation; and the virtue of the people alone can restore it. The independence of the Judges of this State will be *entirely* destroyed, if the Bill for the abolishing the two Supreme Courts, should be ratified by the next General assembly

93

[because it will make clear that the Judges are dependent for their continuation in office on the legislature, and thus the judicial power will unwisely be subordinated to the legislative].[277]

As Chase explained later in his Jury Charge Book:

If the independency of your State Judges, which your Bill of Rights wisely declared, "to be essential to the *impartial* Administration of Justice, and the great security to the rights & Liberties of the People," shall be taken away, by the Ratification of the *Bill* passed for that purpose, it will precipitate the Destruction of your *whole* State Constitution; and there will be nothing left in *it* worthy the Care, or support of freemen.[278]

Chase suggested what would happen if corrective measures were not soon taken:

The change of the State Constitution, by allowing *universal* suffrage, will in my opinion, *certainly & rapidly* destroy all protection to property, and all security to personal liberty; and our Republican Constitution will sink into a *mobocracy*, the worst of all possible Governments.[279]

In another part of the manuscript Jury Charge Book Chase amplified his views on the dangers of universal suffrage:

I can only lament, that the *main pillar* of our *State* Constitution has already been thrown down by the establishment of *Universal Suffrage*. By this shock *alone* the *whole* Building totters to its base; and will crumble into Ruins before *many* years elapse, *unless* it be restored to its *original* state.[280]

Indicating his firmly Burkean or perhaps even Hobbesian cast, Chase pinpointed the source of much of this mischief on the part of the Jeffersonian republicans and their backers. He targeted their leader specifically, and also appeared to criticize the works of John Locke, Jean-Jacques Rousseau, and Thomas Paine:

The Declaration [of Independence] respecting the Natural rights of man, which originated from the claim of the British Parliament to make Laws to bind America in *all Cases whatsoever;* the publications, since that period of visionary and theoretical Writers, asserting that men in a *State of Society* are entitled to exercise *rights* which they possessed in *a State of Nature;* and the *modern* Doctrines, by our late *reformers,* that all men in a State of *Society* are entitled to enjoy *equal Liberty,* and *equal rights,* have brought this mighty mischief upon us: And I fear that it will rapidly progress, until peace & order, freedom & property, shall be destroyed. . . . I have long since subscribed to the opinion that there could be no *rights of man* in a *State of Nature* previous to the Institution of Society; and that *liberty,* properly speaking, could not exist in a *State of Nature.* I do not believe, that any number of men ever existed together in a *State of Nature;* without Some head, leader, or chief, whose advice they followed, or whose precepts they obeyed.—I really consider a *State of Nature* as a creature of the *imagination* only, although a great many names give a sanction to a contrary opinion.[281]

Chase then reiterated his core belief that "The great object, for which men establish any form of Government, is to obtain Security to their *persons,* and *property* from violence," and rhetorically asked his jurors:

Will Justice be *impartially* administered by Judges dependent on the *Legislatures* for their *continuance in office,* and *also for their support?* Will *liberty,* or *property* be protected, or secured by Laws made by representatives chosen by electors who have no *property* in, a *common interest* with, *or attachment to the* Community?[282]

There was good reason for Chase to be concerned at the Jeffersonian legislative attack on the judiciary. The 1802 Judiciary Act was a blatant end-run around the federal Constitution's prohibition against removal of judges by any means save impeachment. The Jeffersonians claimed that they were not removing the judges, but were merely abolishing their positions. It amounted

95

to the same thing, of course, and, as Chase pointed out, was a fundamental betrayal (as was the Maryland tinkering with the state's supreme courts) of the independence of the judiciary from the legislature.[283] Thus, one of the dark blots on the career of John Marshall and his colleagues on the Supreme Court is that they were unwilling to join Chase in labeling the Jeffersonian 1802 Judiciary Act as unconstitutional.[284]

Chase's comments directed against universal suffrage underscore the point made in the Introduction that the earliest interpreters of the Constitution understood that an American republic was something other than a pure democracy, Jefferson and his adherents notwithstanding. It bears stressing that Chase's views on the need for the franchise to be exercised only by those with significant property and/or a similar attachment to the community were staples even in the most radical of the new states.[285] They were articulated not only by Chase, but by one of the most important architects of the federal Constitution itself, James Wilson. In his "Lectures on Law," prepared for the College of Philadelphia and delivered in 1790 and 1791, Wilson surveyed the state constitutions and noted that all states, including Pennsylvania, had some restrictions on the franchise—restrictions based on age, length of residency, family connections, property ownership, or some combination thereof. He concluded that the right to vote is properly extended only to one who could prove an attachment to the land and community either through the ownership of land, or the ability and willingness to own land, thereby possessing "a common interest with his fellow citizens."[286] These views of Wilson's are strikingly similar to those of the great conservative English legal commentator, Sir William Blackstone.[287]

For Samuel Chase, then, and for his brother Federalist judges, there were clear lessons from religion, history, and common sense that should inform the behavior of a virtuous citizenry and shape the conduct of trials and the content of legislation. Some consistently conservative and religious threads run through these jury charges, particularly those of Samuel Chase, as well as the federal cases we will soon consider: (1) belief in an objective legal standard dictating duties, and (2) a presumption that there are certain

96

natural divinely dictated guidelines involving the impartial protection of property and person that any legal system of a free people—whether of a monarchy, aristocracy, or democracy—must follow. Moreover, for these judges, as they began to formulate constitutional jurisprudence, the philosophy of *Federalist* 78—the notion of a single objective understanding of the federal Constitution that implemented the will of the people—took precedence over the philosophy of *Federalist* 10—the notion of accommodating to the conflicting views of factions.

C. Trials in the Early Federal Courts: Common Law Crimes, Seditious Libel, and Treason

The Federal Common Law of Crimes

One of the most important legal questions explored by the earliest federal judges was the so-called "federal common law of crimes."[288] This involved the determination of whether the United States courts could punish criminal acts that had never been proscribed in any federal statute. A review of this jurisprudence also demonstrates the conservative religious basis for interpretating the Constitution that we have so far observed in a variety of jury charges.

The Judiciary Act of 1789 gave the federal courts jurisdiction to punish "all crimes and offenses cognizable under the authority of the United States,"[289] but did not define or describe such "crimes and offenses." It was common in England for English courts to punish acts that, in the judges' opinions, were criminal, whether or not a particular statute had defined the crime and set forth a specific punishment for the act. If defendants were found guilty of such "common law crimes," they would simply be given a punishment that, in the judges' opinion, was appropriate to the particular case, usually by analogy to some similar crime for which punishment had been specified by custom or statute. The issue appears first to have gained public prominence in the United States in the 1790s. This was just a few years after ratification of the Constitution, and occurred in connection with the prosecution of persons who violated President Washington's proclamation of neutrality in the current European wars, prosecutions which had grown out of the French Revolution. In particular, Washington was concerned that Americans not become involved in the battle being waged between France and England.

One famous case involved Gideon Henfield, an American seaman struck by the similarity between the French struggle for liberty and that engaged in by the Americans a few years before. Henfield had sought to aid the French by commanding a French privateer. Henfield's actions actually occurred *before* Washington's neutrality proclamation, but Henfield was brought to trial, after Washington's pronouncement of neutrality, in the federal circuit court in Philadelphia. Henfield was prosecuted, not on the grounds that he had violated the president's proclamation of national neutrality, but rather on the basis of the legal reality that underlay the neutrality proclamation: Henfield had violated the treaty of friendship and amity between the United States and Great Britain.[290] No statute forbade Henfield's conduct, however, and the prosecution was styled one "at common law." It was a proceeding brought against a citizen who had violated international legal norms from the law of nations that were reflected in a treaty and, the prosecution argued, were binding whether or not spelled out in a criminal statute.

The norms invoked in Henfield's prosecution—these notions from the law of nations assimilated to the English and American common law—Associate Justice James Wilson had earlier explained, came from the "law of nature," and were "of obligation indispensible, and of origin divine."[291] Henfield's defense counsel argued, however, that no American could be punished unless a statute made his conduct clearly criminal. While the prosecutors and the judges appear to have disagreed with the defense, the jury did not, and proceeded to acquit Henfield.

The anti-administration press trumpeted Henfield's acquittal as a repudiation of the theory that people could be punished for conduct not made criminal by a statute. It is more likely that Henfield was simply viewed as an innocent patriot, interested in liberty, and espousing a popular cause. This is suggested by the fact that there *was* a successful prosecution, at common law, the next year against an individual who had sent threatening letters to a government official, even though his conduct had not been made criminal by statute.[292]

The issue of the common law of crimes did not become a hot political topic, however, until the famous case brought against Robert Worral in 1798.[293] Worrall was a contractor who sought to construct a federal lighthouse in North Carolina. In order to get the contract, Worrall offered a bribe to Tench Coxe, the federal commissioner of revenue, who was charged with building the lighthouse. While there were federal laws on the books prohibiting some crimes of bribery, none applied to the commissioner of revenue. Nevertheless, Worral was convicted of the crime of attempted bribery. The jurors who brought in a guilty verdict against Worrall were persuaded by the prosecution's contention that since what Worrall was accused of would have been a crime according to the English common law, and since that common law was of equal use in allowing the American government to defend itself against venality, Worrall deserved to be punished. Thus the jurors decided, and were eventually upheld by the judges in Worral's case, that a prosecution at common law—i.e., one undertaken without the benefit of statute, but with the guidance of previous precedents earlier decided by English judges—could be maintained in the American federal courts.[294]

Only one of the early federal judges doubted that the national government was constitutionally possessed of this natural law/common law power to punish crimes. And even he may have changed his mind eventually in favor of the jurisdiction.[295] Those jealous of the federal government who sought instead to preserve the maximum of power for the states, most notably Thomas Jefferson, were eventually vehemently to argue against the federal common law crimes jurisdiction. When the Jeffersonians later took control of the federal government, they eventually succeeded in getting a surprising declaration from the Supreme Court that there was no such jurisdiction.[296] This dubious holding, however, came more than twenty-five years after the Constitution's framing.

The lawyers closest to the events, and who participated in the framing of the Constitution and the Judiciary Act of 1789, most notably Oliver Ellsworth, the principal author of the Judiciary Act, and James Wilson, a major architect of the Constitution, appear to have believed in the validity and the need of the federal common law of crimes jurisdiction. They believed this jurisdiction to be bottomed in principles "of obligation indispensible," and "of origin divine." Indeed, there has yet to be a convincing refutation of the great Justice Joseph Story's statement that "excepting Judge Chase [who may have later changed his mind], every Judge that ever sat on the Supreme Court from the adoption of the Constitution until 1804 (as I have been very authoritatively informed) held a like opinion" on the legitimacy of the federal common law of crimes.[297]

This early federal common law of crimes, it should be stressed in passing, is quite different from the so-called "federal common law," which is advocated as a source of individual rights *against* officials of the state or federal governments. Such a "federal common law" was believed to exist, for example, by former Justice William Brennan, who maintained that federal judges could work out a veritable system of specially protected federal "property rights," through the due process clause, which could be implemented through the federal courts. Such rights, according to a view Brennan articulated in dissent, would, for example, permit injured plaintiffs to sue because of damages to reputation, in connection with a lawful termination from municipal employment,[298] or for economic or reputation injury caused by the public delivery of a federal subpoena.[299] Brennan's idea of a federal common law as a source of individual rights appears to have few bounds. He indicated that he "would recognize the existence of [individual] federal common-law rights of action 'wherever necessary or appropriate' for dealing with 'essentially federal matters.' "[300]

Fortunately, the Supreme Court has hesitated to embrace Brennan's view. It has dismissed Brennan's "remarkably innovative suggestion that [the Court] develop a federal common law of property rights."[301] Brennan's supposed federal common law of property rights served the modern individualistic goal of self-actualization. The late eighteenth-century federal common law of crimes was altogether different. Based solidly in tradition, it was a means of securing the people's government from its enemies. It protected the traditional republican right of the American people to be secure in their popular governments. It was not, as Justice Brennan's vision was, a means of undercutting those governments. It embraced the republican notion that duties (to refrain from attacking the government) were more important than individual rights (to secure damages against governments pursuant to self-actualization).

THE SEDITIOUS LIBEL CASES

Another area demonstrating the prevalence of conservative, religiously influenced views of the national will and purposes was the early federal criminal libel law. To criticize the government was clearly a crime of the English common law, even if the charges brought against the government were true. Eventually the English common law was changed by an English statute, in order to make truth a defense in a prosecution for seditious libel. In America, early Federal legislators wanted to make sure that the defense of truth to such a crime was available here as well, in order to avoid the kind of oppression that some English monarchs had perpetrated.[302] Similarly, Federalist expositors of seditious libel doctrine, like their enlightened English counterparts, wanted to make sure that even in seditious libel cases, the jury would fulfill its historic role as a barrier between individuals and possible government misconduct. It was thus necessary to reserve to the jury the final determination of the facts, and the application of the law to the facts.

As it was put in the statutes passed both in America and in England in the 1790s, the jury was to "have a right to determine the law and the fact, under the direction of the Court, as in other causes."[303] In America, the statute that clarified seditious libel doctrine was part of the frequently excoriated (by liberal historians) Alien and Sedition Acts of 1798. These acts have been termed part of a Federalist "reign of terror." The outcome of the acts, putting a few mendacious radicals in jail for some months at a time and fining them a few thousand dollars, does not seem quite the same as the murder of some twenty thousand in France during the real "reign of terror" in those days.

In any event, the 1798 American Act, and prosecutions under it, were thought to be necessary by the Federalist-controlled federal legislature. This was because of an exceptionally inflammatory and outrageously false series of publications by the partisans of Jefferson aimed at discrediting the Adams administration. At least two of these scribblers were subsidized by Jefferson himself.[304] At the time of the 1798 act, the Adams administration was embroiled in an undeclared war with France, having tilted in favor of England in its struggle against Napoleon. The partisans of Jefferson, many of them recent immigrants originally persecuted for their views in Scotland, Ireland, or England, favored a rapprochment with France. They began a campaign of circulating scurrilous allegations concerning Adams in particular and a host of other Federalist officials in general.[305]

Most of the accounts of the American 1798 sedition law trials have been written by Jeffersonian sympathizers and thus usually present them as a scandalous series of persecutions of noble quasi-public servants from the Fourth Estate.[306] It is likely that the truth is very different. This can be seen, for example, in the most famous of these trials, that of James Thomson Callender. The calumner in question was one of the paid hirelings of Jefferson. Callender's character is perhaps best demonstrated by the fact that his object of invective changed from Adams to Jefferson himself once the man from Monticello disappointed Callender's expectations of a position in the new administration. Callender was the source of the persistent rumor that Jefferson was the father of most of the mulattoes on his plantation. Callender was also once ejected from Congress for being covered with lice and filth and appears to have been habitually in trouble with local Virginia authorities for questionable personal habits.[307]

In 1800, Callender wrote a book-length attack on John Adams, *The Prospect Before Us*, which was read and approved in manuscript by Jefferson.[308] The clear implication of the book was that unless Adams, who was running for reelection, were defeated and someone else (Jefferson) elected in 1800, any chance of American democracy or prosperity would vanish. As Callender stated:

> The reign of Mr. Adams [from 1796 to 1800] has been one continued tempest of malignant passion. As president, he has never opened his lips, or lifted his pen without threatening and scolding; the grand object of his administration has been to exasperate the rage of contending parties, to calumniate and destroy every man who differs from his opinions. Mr. Adams has labored, and with melancholy success, to break up the bonds of social affection, and under the ruins of confidence and friendship, to extinguish the only gleam of happiness that glimmers through the dark and despicable farce of life.[309]

As one American historian of the period explained, in his book Callender

> compiled a catalogue of "presidential felonies": a standing army, a large navy, high taxes and a French war. Washington and Adams, he declared, raised "an effected yelp against the French Directory; as if any corruption could be more venal, more notorious, more execrated than their own." According to Callender, the only limit upon President Adams's career of profligacy and corruption was his stupidity: "this federal gem, this apostle of the parsons of Connecticut, is not only a repulsive pedant, a gross hypocrite, and an unprincipled oppressor, but . . . in private life, one of the most egregious fools upon the continent." Future historians, Callender predicted, "will enquire by what species of madness America submitted to accept, as her president, a person without abilities, and without virtues: a being alike incapable of attracting either tenderness, or esteem."[310]

All of this, to the Federalist prosecutors, seemed to go way beyond the bounds of fair criticism, and into the historically suspect territory of criminal and unfounded attacks against the people's government itself. Pursuant to the 1798 act, they brought charges of seditious libel against Callender in the federal circuit court in Virginia.[311] The hapless Callender was defended at his trial by three prominent young Virginia Jeffersonians. The three, had they really been interested in doing their job, would have sought to present a defense to the twenty distinct charges against their client (from twenty different alleged libels in Callender's book against Adams). Instead Callender's lawyers sought to use the trial as a forum to attack Adams's supposedly aristocratic and British-leaning proclivities. The Virginia defense lawyers also sought to get the Virginia jury to declare the 1798 federal act, under which Callender was being prosecuted, an unconstitutional usurpation. The lawyers, who clearly cared more for the political points they wanted to make then for their client,[312] were frustrated in their aims by Supreme Court Justice Samuel Chase, who was presiding.

Chase later suffered an impeachment proceeding at the hands of the Jeffersonians for his trouble, but he succeeded in excluding inflammatory political testimony from the only witness offered in the trial. Chase also refused to allow arguments to be made to the Virginia jury on the constitutionality of the federal seditious libel statute, since he correctly understood that constitutionality, as a matter of judicial review, was for the Court, not the jury.

Callender's lawyers, frustrated in their political aims, planned to embarrass Chase into a temper tantrum that could be used to discredit Adams and his Federalist supporters. They "deliberately baited the easily irascible Chase; anticipated his explosive response; and planned from the outset to walk out of the courtroom and leave Callender to his fate."[313] Their plan worked. They provoked Chase into making several disparaging comments on their abilities, into derisively putting their inappropriate arguments about seditious libel and the role of the jury down to their being "young gentlemen." Pursuant to their strategy, and perhaps even made to look foolish by Chase, the "young gentlemen" threw up their briefs, stalked out, and left their client to the mercy of the court and jury. The jury proceeded to bring in a guilty verdict. Callender went to jail, but was later pardoned by Jefferson, once he became president.

In all, approximately fifteen Adams administration critics were indicted under the 1798 act,[314] and only in cases where the prosecution believed that the falsity of what was published was apparent. The sedition act prosecutions were not, then, an attempt to silence a vigorous press, but only an attempt to prevent the people from being misled by a pernicious campaign of public mendacity.[315] This was in accordance with a longstanding belief, as expressed by the Federalist judges, that there were only two ways in which the American republic could be corrupted, and the virtue of the people diminished—by too much luxury, or by too much licentiousness in the press.[316]

To come to the relevance of seditious libel for our inquiry: what supported the doctrine of seditious libel, with its concomitant belief that it was wrong falsely to criticize the government, was the same set of conservative notions that we have been exploring in a variety of contexts. These principles might be applied in the seditious libel context roughly as follows.

(1) There was a single national popular will.

(2) The execution of that will required deference to the people's duly constituted leaders.

(3) Because of the Constitution's wise structural checks and balances and its divinely inspired natural law basis, the people's leaders could be relied upon to do what was in the national interest.

(4) If the people believed that the government was not doing its job they could replace officials when the time came for elections.

(5) But even then, given that the people were passionate and easily misled, it was important that truth be the standard for assessing official accomplishments.

Conversely, the collapse and the gradual abandonment of the doctrine of seditious libel in the nineteenth century may have indicated a popular decline of the notion that there was a single national will protected by a traditional deferential social order. As Jacksonian market democracy became the dominant ideology, and as the beliefs of the Federalists began to fade into secondary importance, deference and respect for authority were seriously weakened.

There is no need now to advocate a return to the seditious libel doctrine. It had a perfectly valid purpose when the government was still tottering on a shaky foundation, and when mendacity could threaten to topple it. When Pennsylvania itself could be wracked by two rebellions sparked by misinformation in a single decade the fragility of the government was evident. At the present, the federal and state governments are unlikely to be toppled by popular uprisings, and they do not need the doctrine of seditious libel to protect them. An argument could be mounted today that a seditous libel statute *would* be constitutional (as it was in 1798), pursuant to the original understanding, but given the absence of internal or external threats of a kind extant in the late eighteenth century, it would be imprudent legislation. (In America, seditious libel laws were the creatures of legislatures, and the 1798 act expired, by its own terms, in 1801.) In any event, pursuant to our usual approach to constitutional value choices, the determination of whether to impose a national doctrine of seditious libel rests with the legislature, in this case the federal legislature. The Constitution does not change its meaning with regard to seditious libel, but the legislature's choice of whether a constitutionally permitted doctrine is needed at any particular point may differ according to particular circumstances.

Still, even if we don't need a law of seditious libel now, our review of the old seditous libel doctrines and cases serves the purpose of suggesting the communitarian, deferential, conservative, and, ultimately, deeply religious nature of early American law. Some of *that*, it is argued here, has lost none of its necessity or appeal. After all, even if our government is not as precarious as it once was, much of the current social order seems as chaotic or anarchic as the worst nightmares of the Federalists. Even if we don't need seditious libel, we could use a renewal of the respect for authority and the deference to truth, morality, and established norms of conduct that undergirded the old doctrines. There are plenty of other legislative arenas in which such a renewal might take place (Chapters Four and Five).

THE TREASON CASES

Whatever the relevance of seditious libel to the present, it is clear that the Federalist judges who delivered the jury charges we have studied, and who presided in the seditious libel and the common law crimes trials, believed in good faith that popular government itself was put at risk by an irresponsible press. This was so because most people then had no means of discerning whether what was published was true or false. And false accusations against a government acting in the people's best interests could lead the people to rebel (as had happened in Shay's rebellion and other disturbances after the Declaration of Independence in 1776, and before the Constitution in 1789).

Worse, as indicated, two actual rebellions took place in the 1790s in Pennsylvania (the most populous, radical, and important state in the late eighteenth century—a sort of early analogue to modern California). Several of the federal judges we have already encountered believed that these two Pennsylvania rebellions were fomented by unscrupulous adventurers, encouraged by designing European powers, and abetted by misinformation from the press hostile to the administration. Some further feel for the religious and conservative nature of the jurisprudential and political concerns of the early federal judges can thus also be gained by reviewing their opinions and actions in the trials for treason of some of the alleged ringleaders of these two Pennsylvania disturbances.

The first of the two Pennsylvania rebellions was the Whiskey Rebellion, an uprising against the new federal excise tax on distilled spirits, which hit hardest in the rebellious counties of western Pennsylvania. Tax collection in those counties, and, indeed, all activities of the federal government, came to a halt for several months in 1794. Good order was restored only when the secretary of the treasury, the redoubtable Alexander Hamilton himself, athwart his charger, marched thousands of troops in to break the resistance.[317] He succeeded, and although at one point thousands of men were probably in arms against the federal government, they scattered after a vastly superior show of federal force.

Most historians have written off this armed resistance to the general government as an ineffective sideshow. But at the time, it appeared to bear too close a resemblance to the acts of anarchy, turmoil, and terror then transpiring in France not to be taken seriously. There were credible reports, read by the federal officials, that western Pennsylvania intended to secede from the Union and join with France or Spain in hostilities against the infant United States. It was believed that only by the strongest exercise of the federal military force could the existence of the nation be assured.[318]

Most of the ringleaders of the Whiskey Rebellion managed to escape, but a few were brought to trial and prosecuted for treason against the United States. Their trials and convictions established the precedent that armed resistance to a United States statute amounted to "levying war" and thus came within the constitutionally defined capital crime of treason.[319] Some English cases suggested that any time private citizens took up arms and tried to supplant the law enforcement authority it was treason, but it was not a foregone conclusion that this would come to be the law of America.

In England, as the defenders of the American rebels explained, treason was whatever a strong king declared it was against weak subjects, while weak kings could never punish strong barons for treason for any acts they cared to perpetrate. Further, particularly strong kings, such as Henry VIII, had found treason in virtually every criticism of royal authority. Henry had ordered prosecutions for acts as seemingly inconsequential as cursing the king and wishing for his death, or naming one's public house the "Sign of the Crown," and then informing one's son that he would someday be "heir to the Crown." These reported treason cases, and others like them, were examples of the English doctrine of "constructive treason," which the United States Constitution was often said to have eschewed.[320] The Constitution specified only two means of committing treason—waging war against the United States and giving aid or comfort to her enemies.[321] Nevertheless the federal judges who sat on the Whiskey rebels' trials accepted the prosecution's argument that the safety of the republic depended on a construction of the Constitution's treason clause which concluded that armed opposition to a statute constituted waging war against the United States.[322]

Whether armed opposition to a statute amounted to treason became an important issue with profound political implications in the trial of one of the principals in the 1799 Pennsylvania rebellion. This rebellion, the Northampton insurrection, is also known as the "Hot Water War," or the "Fries Rebellion," after the defendant in question, one John Fries. Fries and his fellows in some of the eastern counties of Pennsylvania were protesting a federal tax on houses, made necessary because of the high cost of quelling the Whiskey Rebellion, and because of anticipated expenditures in a possible war with France. The tax was calculated, according to the traditional method, by counting the numbers of windows in houses. The rebellion received its sobriquet of Hot Water War when some scalding liquid was poured from upper stories on hapless federal tax collectors counting windows on the ground.

This 1799 rebellion is dismissed by modern historians as being faintly Gilbert & Sullivanesque, and as having constituted no real threat to peace and good order. But as was true with the Whiskey Rebellion, federal tax collection was effectively stopped for some period in the affected areas in 1799. And at one time during the disturbance thousands of men were armed against the federal government, and there was a threat of real carnage.[323] As it turned out, the rebels did much marching and sabre rattling, and committed one clear act of unlawfulness—freeing some federal prisoners from the custody of a federal marshall, an act in which Fries participated.

When Fries was brought to trial for treason, his lawyers argued that even though there was a British common law precedent that "rescue" of a prisoner in custody amounted to treason, the jury should ignore it as being a manifestation of the odious "constructive treason doctrine." Fries's defense lawyers conceded that what Fries had done might have amounted to some crime—riot, perhaps; but since the protest could hardly have been regarded as a potent threat to the actual organs of government—Congress, the president, or the courts—it should not be construed as treason.

In a free republic such as America, the defense lawyers argued, a maximum of political expression was necessary, in order for the people to assert their will. Treason thus ought to be narrowly construed, lest public debate be unduly circumscribed.[324]

The argument of Fries's counsel on the law and politics of the case went on for some nine or ten days in the federal circuit court in Philadelphia before District Judge Richard Peters and Supreme Court Associate Justice Iredell. Peters and Iredell rejected the defense lawyers' arguments and concluded, following English authority, that the crime of treason was made out by an armed rescue of federal prisoners. Following the judges' instructions, a jury duly brought in a guilty verdict. But the verdict was set aside and a new trial awarded when it was found that one of the jurors had been prejudiced. He had been heard to comment, before trial, that the Northampton rebels "should be hung."

This news of possible juror prejudice did not much move the patrician District Court Judge Richard Peters, one of the two judges presiding over Fries's trial. Peters had been a firm champion of judicial prerogatives in the common law of crimes cases,[325] and he had even conducted a part of the Whiskey rebels trial in apparent violation of the clear mandates of the judiciary act of 1789. Section 29 of that statute required him to follow state procedures in selecting juries. Accordingly, Peters would have had to allow selection of jury from the very neighborhood that had recently been in open rebellion against the federal government. Believing that to have done so would deny the prosecution a fair trial, Peters simply ignored the act.[326]

In *Fries*, Peters, a champion of firm administration, was not troubled by the information that one juror might have declared his views about the necessity of punishing the participants in the second Pennsylvania rebellion. Peters believed that the juror in question had done no more than any other public-spirited citizen would have done in the same circumstances, namely, expressed disapproval of anyone who would rebel against the people's duly chosen government or its tax collectors.

Peters's partner on the bench, however, the circuit-riding Supreme Court Justice James Iredell, was not made of such stern stuff. Iredell is a perplexing and little-studied figure. He appears, among all the Federalist judges, to have been the least committed both to the practice of judicial review of statutes for unconstitutionality[327] and to the notion that there were supraconstitutional natural law principles that circumscribed the actions of legislatures.[328] He seems also to have been relatively wishy-washy about the need to convict Fries for treason. "I could not bear to look upon the poor man," Iredell wrote his wife after Fries had been convicted by the jury and before the purportedly biased juror was revealed. "I dread the task I have before me in pronouncing sentence on him," he lamented.[329] Accordingly, Iredell appears to have leaped at the chance to escape the dreaded task, and leave its possibility for other judges in a retrial.

The excuse of a biased juror was enough to make Justice Iredell persuade his colleague Judge Peters to put the case over for a new trial at the next term. Peters, who believed that the trial had been perfectly fair to Fries, was nevertheless willing to see a retrial in order to preserve the appearance as well as the substance of justice. Peters was, in spite of his patrician upbringing, a politically-adept former Speaker of both the Pennsylvania House and Senate. He undoubtedly sensed that the Jeffersonian opponents of the incumbent Federalist administration could make much of the charge that biased Federalist judges had railroaded Fries with a tainted jury.

If that was Peters's belief, then Peters was prescient. But even he would have probably underestimated the potential for Jeffersonian use of the case, even if a retrail was granted. When that retrial came that next year, the headstrong Samuel Chase, as he would later do in the *Callender* trial in Virginia, walked into several traps laid by defense lawyers, and unwittingly allowed himself to play the role of oppressor.[330] In doing so, and of primary interest to us, he strongly suggested the moral and religious basis for the rulings he felt obliged to make.

Associate Justice Chase, riding circuit instead of Iredell the following year, had heard about the long first Fries trial. Chase observed that because of the delay of that trial, a backlog of more than one hundred commercial cases remained to be heard. Chase, a stickler for courtroom efficiency, wanted to do all that he could to clear the Court's calendar and deliver justice in all the cases.[331]

Chase believed that the law of the Fries case—to wit, that armed rescue of federal prisoners constituted an act of war against the government, and thus treason—had been established both in the first trial of Fries and in the Whiskey rebels' trial some years before. Accordingly, Chase declared that he would not let defense counsel waste the time of court or jury arguing the law of the case, as had been done *ad nauseum* in the first Fries trial.

At the start of the second Fries trial, Chase delivered a written opinion to the two defense counsels to let them know that since the law of the case was clear, the jury would not be permitted to hear arguments that it was not. The jury was thus not to be distracted from their fact-finding task with citations of English abuses of the constructive treason doctrine. Nor were they to be misled with citations to statutes involving lesser crimes than treason. When Fries's defense counsel received this opinion they stormed out of court and refused to proceed further with the case. Chase's cooler colleague, Peters, who was sitting with Chase as he had sat with Iredell before, tried to persuade Chase to withdraw his written opinion. Knowing they risked falling into a political trap, Peters argued that it was imperative to allow defense counsel to mount the same lengthy argument, for appearance's sake, to give Fries's lawyers a chance to persuade the jury to disregard the previous legal definitions of treason. The district attorney, at whose home this conference took place, similarly sought to get Chase to back off.[332]

But by this time, Chase had become convinced that the issue was not what the jury could hear or not hear, but whether he should allow himself to be used to score political points by Fries's lawyers. He huffed and puffed, but was finally persuaded to withdraw his opinion. Nevertheless, at the court hearing in which he did so, and at which Fries's counsel, William Lewis and Alexander James Dallas, were present, he made clear that he "knew what it was about." Although he would allow counsel to make whatever arguments they chose, he fumed, they did so "at the hazard of their reputation." Chase apparently meant by this that everyone would know that in seeking to get the jury to ignore established law Lewis and Dallas were not behaving as men committed to the rule of law and proper procedures. But to no avail—the two publicly used Chase's comments as evidence of bias on his part, and as a further excuse to remain off the case.[333]

By this time Lewis and Dallas had determined that their client actually stood no chance of success at the trial, since the facts and the law were clearly against him. His only hope, they had concluded, was a presidential pardon. This was a real possibility, they reasoned, because similar pardons had been granted to the defendents in the Whiskey rebels trial. Lewis and Dallas further reasoned that the chances for such a pardon would be magnified if Fries proceeded without counsel, because it would look as if he were thus subject to greater oppression from the obviously overbearing Chase.

When Lewis and Dallas left the case, Peters and Chase offered to appoint other counsel for the defendant, Fries. Having been advised of the strategy that he would maximize his chances for a presidential pardon if he declined counsel, however, Fries did not accept the offer. Chase then declared, demonstrating for the first time under whose auspices he really thought he was operating, "[B]y the blessing of God, the Court will be your counsel, and will do you as much justice as those who were your counsel."[334] Chase sought fairly to see that any exculpative facts were brought out regarding Fries, but Chase also made certain that the facts which condemned Fries were brought to the attention of the jury. In the end, Fries was once again convicted.

It is noteworthy that Chase believed that his job as judge could comfortably allow him to represent the best interests of *both* the defendant Fries and the government. That was because Chase saw the criminal trial as simply an even-handed search for truth. He did not, as we moderns do, view a criminal trial as an adversarial battle in which partisans deploy every conceivable tactic or trick in defense of their clients, and in which the judge plays a relatively passive neutral role. The surprise here is that even the defendant Fries appears to have regarded his second trial—in which he had no counsel but the judge, Chase—as a fair one. There is a report that following his conviction, and following the presidential pardon successfully secured by his lawyers's tactics, Fries journeyed to Baltimore. Fries there met Chase face to face and thanked him "for his impartial, fair and equitable conduct" in Fries's second trial.[335]

This was a remarkable undertaking on Fries's part, to thank the man the opposition press had by then painted as such a partisan bully, and whom the Jeffersonians would soon seek to impeach for his role in the Fries and Callender trials. Why did Fries do it? Why thank the man who presided over his trial in which he was condemned to die? Fries's behavior is explained not only by the rulings Chase made in the course of the trial. Of more importance is what Chase did *following* Fries's conviction, at the hearing that Justice Iredell had dreaded, when Chase pronounced the death sentence on Fries.

We come now to the most important linkage between the earlier materials in this chapter on the Justices's jury charges and the criminal trials here reviewed. "I suppose you are a Christian," said Chase to Fries, "and as *such* I address you."[336] Chase then proceeded for some eloquent minutes to instruct Fries, according to orthodox Christian doctrines, how he might still save his immortal soul before the death sentence that Chase was to pronounce was carried out.

Chase explained to Fries that he had done what must have displeased the diety. First Fries had rebelled against the people's duly established government—clearly sinful conduct. Equally blameworthy, because of the high cost of troops necessary to quash Fries's rebellion, he in effect had imposed further taxes and burdens on his fellow citizens. This, for Chase, was wickedness itself. It amounted to the kind of sin that, if unatoned, would place Fries in great peril in the world to come. Still, Chase pointed out to his "guilty and unhappy fellow citizen"[337] that the government Fries had cruelly sought to damage was a beneficient one. It would grant Fries, before his execution, sufficient time with a minister of the Gospel to engage in the kind of spiritual aerobics that might result in penitence, which could trigger the sympathy of a merciful Christian God. For Chase, Fries's sentencing hearing was a time for religious instruction. The immortal soul of the defendant was as much a concern for the presiding Supreme Court Justice as it was for the minister of the Gospel the government was willing to supply.

Chase's concern for Fries's immortal soul is thus the most likely explanation for Fries's postpardon friendly visit to Chase. A repentant Fries, genuinely concerned that he had erred and wishing to make amends, may have been touched by the supposedly overbearing Federalist judge. Chase seldom administered "emollients,"[338] and his hair-trigger temper could embarrass him and his government in the courtroom. But of his firm commitment to an integration of benevolent Christian religion with jurisprudence there can be little doubt. This firm commitment is even more striking when we consider that unlike modern day analysts, Chase saw no conflict between the provision in the First Amendment that prohibited "an establishment of religion"[339] and his clearly Christian religious concern for and instruction of Fries.

D. Samuel Chase, Natural Law & Nature's God

CALDER V. BULL

One other aspect of Samuel Chase's understanding of the underpinnings of the constitutional system is of particular interest to us for the light it sheds on the integration of natural law with the Constitution. This is to be found in the key case for which Chase is generally known, *Calder v. Bull* (1798).[340] Many scholars have discussed the case, but it has rarely been placed in the context of the other late eighteenth-century jurisprudence that we have been considering.[341] Justice Chase, in *Calder v. Bull*, upheld a Connecticut statute that reversed a determination regarding the rights of private property made by a Connecticut court. The Connecticut legislature's act had been challenged as a violation of the United State Constitution's *ex post facto* clause. To quote

Chase, "The Constitution of the United States, article 1, section 9, prohibits the Legislature of the United States from passing any *ex post facto* law; and, in section 10, lays several restrictions on the authority of the Legislatures of the several states; and, among them, 'that no state shall pass any *ex post facto* law.' "[342] Chase eventually determined that the constitutional clause in question should be interpreted only to prohibit legislation that made crimes out of acts which, when committed, were perfectly legal. Thus, according to Chase, the clause had no application to the Connecticut legislation, which merely adjusted property rights, and had nothing to do with criminal law.

Nevertheless, in the course of reaching this conclusion, Chase added some dicta regarding the restraints on legislatures in general, restraints which were not expressly provided for in the United States Constitution. Because Chase's language is a good example of late eighteenth-century natural law thinking it is worth reproducing at some length:

> I cannot subscribe to the omnipotence of a State Legislature, or that it is absolute and without controul; although its authority should not be expressly restrained by the Constitution, or fundamental law, of the State. The people of the United States erected their Constitutions, or forms of government, to establish justice, to promote the general welfare, to secure the blessings of liberty, and to protect their persons and property from violence. The purposes for which men enter into society will determine the nature and terms of the social compact; and as they are the foundation of the legislative power, they will decide what are the proper objects of it: The nature, and ends of legislative power will limit the exercise of it. This fundamental principle flows from the very nature of our free Republican governments, that no man should be compelled to do what the laws do not require; nor to refrain from acts which the laws permit. *There are acts which the Federal, or State, Legislature cannot do, without exceeding their authority. There are certain vital principles in our free Republican governments, which will determine and over-rule an apparent and flagrant abuse of legislative power; as to authorize manifest injustice by positive law; or to take away that security for personal liberty, or private property, for the protection whereof the government was*

116

established. An ACT of the Legislature (for I cannot call it a law)
contrary to the great first principles of the social compact, cannot be
considered a rightful exercise of legislative authority. The obligation
of a law in governments established on express compact, and on
republican principles, must be determined by the nature of the
power, on which it is founded. A few instances will suffice to
explain what I mean. A law that punished a citizen for an innocent
action, or, in other words, for an act, which, when done, was in
violation of no existing law; a law that destroys or impairs the
lawful private contracts of citizens; a law that makes a man a Judge
in his own cause; or a law that takes property from A. and gives it
to B: *It is against all reason and justice, for a people to entrust a*
Legislature with SUCH powers; and therefore, it cannot be presumed
that they have done it. The genius, the nature, and the spirit, of our
State Governments, amount to a prohibition of such acts of legisla-
tion; and the general principles of law and reason forbid them. The
legislature may enjoin, permit, forbid, and punish; they may declare new crimes; and establish rules of conduct for all its citizens
in future cases; they may command what is right, and prohibit
what is wrong; but they cannot change innocence into guilt; or
punish innocence as crime; or violate the right of an antecedent
lawful private contract; or the right of private property. *To main-*
tain that our Federal, or State, Legislature possesses such powers, if
they had not been expressly restrained, would, in my opinion, be a
political heresy, altogether inadmissible in our free republican gov-
*ernments.*343 [italics mine]

Among the many interesting conclusions to be drawn from this
very rich language is that, for Chase, supraconstitutional restraints on legislatures spring from what he calls the "nature" of
"our free republican governments." I think the term "natural
law" is appropriate to describe these sort of legislative checks.
They ought to be regarded as fundamental laws that flow from
the "nature" of the compact originally made among the people
when "our free republican governments" were instituted.344 Today it is fashionable to label such restraints as "substantive due
process."345

It is important to understand that this view of "natural law" as
encompassing only what flows inevitably from the conception of

"free Republican governments" is not a license for arbitrary judicial law-making, nor is it the opening of a Pandora's box of limitless potential horribles.[346] While Chase may have used some loose language, linking his notion of supraconstitutional principles generally with "law and reason," this view of "natural law" is still limited to what is *essential* to "free republican governments." In order to invoke this natural law check to invalidate a legislative measure it must be demonstrated conclusively[347] (through recourse to historical example, learned treatises, and contemporary practice[348]) that such a measure is inconsistent with the original compact among the people. The measures that Chase described are such examples. The acts of unfairly transferring property from one person to another are abuses of which tyrannical English monarchs were often accused. The example of the prohibition against a person being a judge in his own cause comes from no less an authority than the greatest of the English common law judges, Sir Edward Coke.[349]

Chase's *Calder* opinion was criticized by Justice Iredell. Iredell actually concurred with Chase's holding that the Connecticut statute was not an *ex post facto* law. Still, he was moved to write his own opinion in the case, because he disagreed with Chase's dicta regarding the inherent limitations on the powers of legislatures. Said Iredell:

> If, then, a government, composed of Legislative, Executive and Judicial departments, were established, by a Constitution, which imposed no limits on the legislative power, the consequence would inevitably be, that whatever the legislative power chose to enact, would be lawfully enacted, and the judicial power could never interpose to pronounce it void. *It is true, that some speculative jurists have held, that a legislative act against natural justice must, in itself be void; but I cannot think that, under such a government, any Court of Justice would possess a power to declare it so.* Sir William Blackstone, having put the strong case of an act of Parliament which authorizes a man to try his own cause, explicitly adds, that even in that case, "there is no court that has power to defeat the intent of the Legislature, when couched in such evident and

express words, as leave no doubt whether it was the intent of the Legislature, or no." 1 Bl. Com. 91.

In order, therefore to guard against so great an evil, it has been the policy of all the American states, which have, individually, framed their state Constitutions since the revolution, and of the people of the United States, when they framed the Federal Constitution, to define with precision the objects of the legislative power, and to restrain its exercise within marked and settled boundaries. If any act of Congress, or of the Legislature of a state, violates those constitutional provisions, it is unquestionably void; though, I admit, that as the authority to declare it void is of a delicate and awful nature, the court will never resort to that authority, but in a clear and urgent case. *If, on the other hand, the Legislature of the Union, or the Legislature of any member of the Union, shall pass a law, within the general scope of their constitutional power, the court cannot pronounce it to be void, merely because it is, in their judgment contrary to the principles of natural justice. The ideas of natural justice are regulated by no fixed standard: the ablest and the purest men have differed upon the subject; and all that the court could properly say, in such an event, would be, that the Legislature (possessed of an equal right of opinion) had passed an act which, in the opinion of the judges, was inconsistent with the abstract principles of natural justice.*[350] [italics mine]

But Iredell, alas, missed the point. Chase was not invoking "abstract ideals" or advocating an unlimited field of operation for "natural justice." Just like Iredell, Chase believed that courts should set aside laws only in "a clear and urgent case." When Chase suggested that this could be done on the basis of principles inherent in "free republican governments," he believed that one could clearly circumscribe those principles by experience, authority, and history. While men might have disagreed for centuries about the meaning of abstract "natural justice," Chase believed that a more concrete meaning could be given to the "nature" of "free republican governments." Moreover, Chase also agreed with Iredell that the essence of the Court's determination, even if it was being guided by principles of "free republican governments," was the consent of the governed. Thus, if the Justices threw out state or federal legislation on the grounds that they transgressed these fundamental principles, they would simply have been implementing popular sovereignty in the manner defended by Hamilton in *Federalist* 78.

Chase's language in *Calder v. Bull* makes sense only if we assume him to have said that the people understood that when they set up a "free republican government" certain inherent supraconstitutional principles would govern it whether or not they were expressly set forth in a written constitution. Thus, for example, for Chase, it was an inherent principle of free republican governments that there could be no *ex post facto* criminal laws. Once the framers chose to erect a republic, that principle would have been operative whether or not the Constitution explicitly included such a principle in the text.

For Iredell, perhaps, there could be no such thing as unwritten constitutional principles of free republican governments that could guide an American court in making determinations of constitutional validity. It must be admitted that there were others, at the time of framing of the 1787 document, who believed that the new state or federal government's powers would be strictly limited to what the written Constitutions specified.[351] Nevertheless, most contemporaries appear to have believed in the practice of judicial preservation of liberty as outlined by Chase. And most of the framers understood that all the necessary principles of government could never be spelled out in a single written document. It was for this reason that many Federalists believed that the drafting of a Bill of Rights, for example, was a dangerous and futile exercise. There was a profound risk that rights not enumerated but habitually understood and enjoyed by the American people might later come to be lost if a Bill of Rights were strictly construed. As Gordon Wood has explained:

> [T]oo precise an enumeration of the people's rights was dangerous "because it would be implying, in the strongest manner, that every right not included in the exception might be impaired

by the government without usurpation "; [instead, some Federalists believed, it was better to rely on the courts, which] as "in all well-regulated communities," would protect the common law liberties of the people and determine "the extent of legislative powers" even in the absence of a specific bill of rights. "No power," said Theophilus Parsons of Massachusetts, "was given to Congress to infringe on any one of the natural rights of the people by this Constitution; and, should they attempt it without constitutional authority, the act would be a nullity and could not be enforced." "If the United States go beyond their powers," said Oliver Ellsworth, "if they make a law which the Constitution does not authorize, it is void; and the judicial power, the national judges, who, to secure their impartiality, are to be made independent, will declare it to be void."[352]

It was thus Chase's views, not Iredell's, that were in the mainstream of late eighteenth-century American jurisprudence.[353] It is surely significant that Iredell was alone on the Court in his express criticism of Chase on this point. In fact, compared to other early federal judges, Iredell was frequently off on a path of his own.[354] As already seen, Iredell was out of step with other judges of the time with regard to the need for the judiciary to be stern in upholding the responsibilities of the individual to the community when the stability of republican government was threatened.[355]

The principles of "free republican governments," the natural law limitations on constitutional power which Chase and most of his contempories endorsed and which Chase set forth in *Calder*, are not really broad principles of individual "natural *rights*." They seem to have more to do with the basic protection of private property. Thus, some modern thinkers such as Stephen Macedo and Richard Epstein have been able to construct powerful critiques of twentieth-century jurisprudence because the Supreme Court's current tendency to disregard private property flies in the face of these basic eighteenth-century notions.[356] These scholars, and perhaps an increasing number like them, recognize that the protection of private property under the Constitution not only flows from natural law, but also is enshrined in the Fifth

Amendment's guarantee of due process, and perhaps involved in the interpretation of the Ninth Amendment as well.

This reading of the Fifth Amendment, as guaranteeing a certain treatment for private property, may be a legitimate example of "substantive due process." As we will see in the next chapter, however, it has been more common in the recent past for "substantive due process" to serve as the illegitimate foundation of the liberal rights derived from penumbras, emanations, and whatnots by the Warren and Burger Courts. The most outrageous examples are found in the so-called "right to privacy" cases, *Griswold*,[357] *Eisenstadt*,[358] and *Roe v. Wade*.[359] But one must distinguish between substantive due process as practiced by the Warren and Burger Courts, and natural law jurisprudence as limned by Chase and favored by the framers in the early republic.

Recall, once again, that Chase did not rest his opinion in *Calder* explicitly on the Fifth Amendment's due process clause, but rather on the nature of "our free republican governments." As we have seen, these basic principles of governance also were invoked in the profound struggle over the idea of the federal common law of crimes, an issue that arose roughly contemporaneously with *Calder v. Bull*. Although, curiously, Chase was himself initially out of the mainstream on the common law of crimes issue, the natural law foundation for the common law of crimes was similar to that which Chase invoked in *Calder*.

The idea of the common law of crimes jurisdiction was that *any* government, by its nature, needed certain powers which statutes might not yet have covered and the common law of crimes could provide. Among those for the United States, as we have seen, were the power to punish individual citizens who made war on nations with which we were at peace, the power to punish those who sought to extort money from diplomats, or the power to punish those who sought to bribe federal officials. The near consensus among the federal judges who passed on the common law of crimes strongly supports the notion that supraconstitutional natural law principles were a vital part of early American federal jurisprudence.[360] The religious basis that underlies the common law of crimes is probably also present in the "nature of 'our free republican governments,' " since the operation of natural law is traditionally attributable to nature's God.

CHASE AND HIS IMPEACHMENT TRIAL

The inescapable intertwining of law with religion, which Chase demonstrated in his remarks to John Fries, which he developed in his jury charges, which we saw in jury charges by other Justices, and which lay at the bottom of the notion of the federal common law of crimes or of the principles of "our free republican governments," is also to be found at Chase's impeachment trial before the Senate. Chase was impeached—that is, formally charged with high crimes and misdemeanors—by the Jeffersonian-controlled House of Representatives in 1805. As is true for any impeachment of federal officials, following the bringing of charges by the House, a trial was to take place before the Senate. The charges against Chase were hardly crimes, although the advocates of the Chase impeachment may have honestly believed that his conduct was less than the "good behavior" the Constitution requires of judges. Instead, Chase was impeached for his intemperate criticism of the Jeffersonians that he made in the course of an 1803 Baltimore grand jury charge, and for his allegedly zealous solicitude, when he rode circuit in 1800, for a conviction in the Fries and Callender cases.

When Samuel Chase appeared before the Senate to answer the impeachment charges brought against him by the House of Representatives, he suggested that he also stood before God, the "searcher of hearts," who, Chase said, was always with him. Before the senators sitting in judgment of him, the Supreme Court Justice prayed that God would lead them, as right-thinking men, to understand that even if Chase were occasionally intemperate, he never knowingly did anything to compromise his office or betray his judicial oath. Similarly, the manager of the prosecution against Chase, John Randolph, closed his indictment of Chase with a prayer of thanks to God that Chase's conduct had not been worse.[361] Thus, in this highly politically charged proceeding, in a case, in effect, that pitted the conservative Federalist

123

judicial theories about deference and circumscription of juries against the radical Jeffersonian views that allowed juries virtually free reign to make up new laws for each case, both sides grounded their arguments in appeals to the deity.

CONCLUSION: RELIGION AND PROPERTY

The experiences of Samuel Chase and his embrace of a religious basis for his judicial behavior may have been the most dramatic of that displayed by any early federal judge, since they led to his trial and acquittal before the Senate itself. As we have seen, however, there was an astonishing number of other pronouncements by United States Supreme Court Justices riding circuit, and several other legal doctrines indicating the intertwined nature of law, morality, and religion in the early republic. Reviewing the early circuit court cases, and, in particular the experiences of Samuel Chase, both on and off the bench, one finds strong evidence of natural law theories. One also finds a recognition that natural law and civil order are, essentially, gifts of God. Finally, one finds that judges appear to believe that worship of the divine being is something that can and should be accommodated by a court of law. There is too clear evidence that at least one of the federal judges, Chase, believed that the saving of eternal souls, in a Christian manner, was part of his courtroom obligations. It was also apparently common practice publicly to invoke the assistance of divine powers before difficult decisions had to be made.[362]

Thus the experience of the first federal judges during the Constitution's infancy lead one to conclude that there was no wall of separation between church and state in the manner imagined by Thomas Jefferson (a point developed further in Chapter Four). For the moment it is enough to confirm our earlier suggestion that in the framers' time it was generally recognized that there could be no law without morality, and no morality without religion. Since the 1960s, too many Justices of the United States Supreme Court have all but forgotten these early principles, as they have, consciously or unconsciously, sought to implement a jurisprudence in which currently perceived public policy needs take the place of tradition, deference, and religion. What we now have, in short, is a jurisprudence conducted by Burke's despised "Oeconomists, sophisters, and calculators." It is a jurisprudence that, lamentably, does not build on a shared American commitment to law and morality, or the natural law principles of "our free republican governments." Instead, because it focuses on individual rights and neglects individual duties and responsibilities, much of the current Supreme Court jurisprudence virtually tears us asunder. Some of the particulars of this pernicious jurisprudence were sketched in the previous chapter, and the origins and development of these doctrines are more fully explored in the next one.

A subsidiary theme revealed in the materials reviewed here is the linking of natural law with the protection of property. We have observed this theme in sources such as Madison's *Federalist* 10 and Chase's opinion in *Calder v. Bull.* A later Supreme Court Justice was to go even further along the path Chase trod and find a violation of *ex post facto* constitutional prohibitions in a property case. Thus, in *Fletcher v. Peck* (1810)[363] Chief Justice John Marshall invalidated a Georgia State statute that rescinded land grants given out by a previous Georgia legislature. In determining the constitutionality of such action, in broad natural law language, Marshall said he would be guided by the "reasoning spirit of the Constititution" as much as by the text itself.[364] He proceeded to declare the Georgia statute that rescinded the grants to be a prohibited *ex post facto* law, and thus unconstitutional. Hadley Arkes suggests that Marshall's views on the illegitimate nature of *ex post facto* laws reflects a general agreement among the framers on the fundamental and unquestionable principle of natural law that the *ex post facto* clause simply expressed.[365]

The same principles were in circulation in 1795, when Supreme Court Associate Justice William Paterson wrote in *Van Horne's Lessee v. Dorrance,*[366] commenting on the principles expressed and inherent in the Pennsylvania constitution:

> . . . [I]t is evident that the right of acquiring and possessing property, and having it protected, is one of the natural, inherent, and

unalienable rights of man. Men have a sense of property: Property is necessary to their subsistence, and correspondent to their natural wants and desires. Its security was one of the objects that induced them to unite in society. No man would become a member of a community, in which he could not enjoy the fruits of his honest labour and industry. The preservation of property then is a primary object of the social compact, and, by the late Constitution of Pennsylvania, was made a fundamental law. Every person ought to contribute his proportion for public purposes and public exigencies but no one can be called upon to surrender or sacrifice his whole property, real and personal, for the good of the community, without receiving a recompence in value. This would be laying a burden upon an individual, which ought to be sustained by the society at large. The English history does not furnish an instance of that kind. The parliament, with all their boasted omnipotence, never committed such an outrage on private property and if they had, it would have served only to display the dangerous nature of unlimited authority. It would have been an exercise of power and not of right. Such an act would be a monster in legislation, and shock all mankind. The legislature [in the case at hand], therefore, had no authority to make an act divesting one citizen of his freehold, and vesting it in another, without a just compensation. It is inconsistent with the principles of reason, justice, and moral rectitude, it is incompatible with the comfort, peace, and happiness of mankind, it is contrary to the principles of social alliance in every free government and lastly, it is contrary both to the letter and spirit of the Constitution.[367]

"Where is the security, where the inviolability of property," asked Paterson, "if the legislature, by a private act, affecting particular persons only, can take land from one citizen, who acquired it legally, and vest it in another?"[368]

Summary of the Argument

If we seek to understand the original linkage of law with morality and morality with religion, we ought to look at the *Federalist*, the first federal jury charges, and events involving the earliest federal judges, particularly Samuel Chase. *Federalist* 78 and early jury charges justify judicial review of legislative actions on the ground that the judiciary will merely be administering the popular will. This implies that there is a single understanding of constitutional provisions. Although *Federalist* 10 appears to suggest that there will be differing views of the good in American society, it implies that there will be a single national interest. The single national interest will emerge, the framers believed, through the working of divine intervention. The dependence of the American legal order on religion and Divine Providence is also revealed by the jury charges of the first federal judges regarding the law of nations, condemning the principles of the French Revolution, embracing a federal common law of crimes, upholding a federal law of seditious libel, and administering federal treason law. Tying all of this together is a belief that there could be no law without morality, and no morality without religion. Our understanding of the religious nature of American law is also enhanced by a consideration of the role of natural law in early constitutional adjudication. The jurisprudence of Samuel Chase, and even the remarks at his impeachment trial, make clear the religious basis of American constitutional law. In the early years of the republic, then, there was no wall of separation between church and state; and it is wrong now for constitutional law to leave behind religion and responsibility, and to turn things over to the economists, calculators, and sophisters. It may be similarly wrong for us to ignore the natural law basis of property rights, and to permit wholesale redistribution efforts to be undertaken. We no longer face the threats of foreign intrigue the framers did, nor are our state and federal governments as fragile as theirs. We no longer need a

127

federal law of seditious libel, nor even a federal common law of crimes, and treason is rarely prosecuted in our courts. Nevertheless, as we will see in Chapters Four and Five, if we want to reduce the chance that the current strains in American society will severely rend our social fabric, we ought to recapture something of the framers' understanding of the interlocking natures of law, morality, and religion, and the importance of the protection of private property to the securing of liberty.

Chapter Three

WHAT WENT WRONG

Now that we have developed the understanding of the Constitution manifested by the framers, it is time to examine the principal jurisprudential steps that eroded or turned away from that understanding. We begin by commenting on two famous, or as they are usually regarded, *infamous*, Supreme Court cases, the first from the nineteenth and the second from the early twentieth century. These two judicial landmarks have become notorious as the duo that most legal academics have questioned most rigorously— *Dred Scott v. Sandford* and *Lochner v. New York*. The treatment of the *Lochner* case is followed by an exploration of the aftermath of that case in the Supreme Court's decisions during the New Deal. We are particularly concerned with Franklin Roosevelt's criticism of the Court and his threat to control it by packing it with sympathetic Justices. This in turn is followed by a discussion of the school prayer and flag salute cases, from the 1940s, 1950s, and 1960s. These cases have received the most criticism from those who believe (correctly) that the original understanding permitted a greater infusion of religion or patriotism into the public schools than the current Supreme Court majority accepts. We then turn to the most activist Supreme Court in our history, that of former Chief Justice Earl Warren, and examine the "great trilogy" of judicial expansionist decisions by that Court—*Reynolds v. Sims*,

129

the "one-man one-vote" legislative reapportionment case, *Miranda v. Arizona*, the "Miranda warnings" case, and *Brown v. Board of Education*, the most important of the school desegregation cases. Finally, we review the most important activist decisions of the Burger Court, in particular the *Roe v. Wade* abortion-rights decision.

A. Scott v. Sandford: Then and Now

The opinion usually singled out as the worst instance of the Supreme Court run amuck is the *Dred Scott* (1857) case.[369] This was the first time a congressional statute had been found unconstitutional since *Marbury v. Madison* (1803), and, indeed, only the second time in our history that the U. S. Supreme Court had exercised its power of judicial review to nullify a federal statute. The opinion by Chief Justice Roger Taney, in which he was joined by a substantial 7–2 majority of his Court, held that even free blacks were not "citizens" of the United States, and, further, that Congress had no power to forbid slavery in the then-existing territories of the United States.[370]

Almost no modern constitutional scholar, on the Left or Right, has had a good word to say about the *Dred Scott* opinion. It is frequently credited with accelerating the Civil War. It is dismissed by most as seeking to raise racial apartheid to the level of a constitutional principle.[371] And it has been condemned by some conservatives, such as Robert Bork, as opening the Pandora's box of substantive due process[372] that led ineluctably to *Griswold v. Connecticut* (1965)[373] and *Roe v. Wade* (1973),[374] the two most important cases which found an implied "right of privacy" in the Constitution. *Griswold* prevented states from prohibiting the use of contraceptives by married persons, and *Roe* barred states from preventing first trimester abortions.

Curiously, as a product of its time, the *Dred Scott* case has recently been best understood by a man of the Left, Bruce Ackerman. Yale law professor Ackerman's otherwise often alarming *We the People* (1991)[375] quite correctly analyzed Taney's opinion as a product of nineteenth-century thought about the nature of property in general and about the protection of ownership interest in human beings in particular. Indeed, in its elevation of property rights to the pinnacle of constitutional values, Taney's opinion is probably not very far from the framers' notions of property described in the previous chapter.

Nevertheless, whatever the correctness of Taney's opinion as to then-prevailing conceptions of property, as a matter of constitutional law the opinion was wrong, but not for the reasons the Left or even the Right has usually suggested. The opinion was wrong simply because either from lack of historical understanding, or from a noble but tragic desire to preserve the Union, Taney failed to follow in one part of his opinion the conservative rules of constitutional interpretation he appears to have understood in the other.

In the first part of his *Dred Scott* opinion Taney decided that even free blacks could not be regarded as citizens of the United States. He reached this conclusion because at the time of the framing of the Constitution, and shortly thereafter, public opinion and governmental measures assumed that nonwhite Americans were not full participating partners in the polity. In most if not all places, even free blacks were not permitted to serve in the militia, they were not allowed to be naturalized as citizens, and they were forbidden from marrying whites. They were under special municipal restrictions that curtailed, *inter alia*, their rights of assembly, and in all but one of the states they were prohibited from voting. All of this was done, Taney frankly pointed out, because blacks were perceived at the time of the framing of the Constitution as an inferior and subject race.

Perhaps in an effort to indicate that he was not the benighted racist subsequent generations have thought him, Taney acknowledged in *Dred Scott* that in his own time public opinion was more enlightened on the question of whether blacks were capable of exercising civic responsibilities in the same manner as whites.[376] Still, he claimed that his task as a constitutional interpreter was only to seek to arrive at the understanding of the document and its terms *as of the time the instrument was accepted as United States fundamental law.*[377] In this, at least according to the principles of constitutional interpretation that it has been argued here ought to govern, namely following the original understanding, Taney was assuredly correct.

In the second part of his opinion, however, where Taney dealt with the question of whether Congress has the power to forbid slavery in the territories, Taney failed to follow his own advice. Taney there declared that the Fifth Amendment's prohibition on depriving any person of his "life, liberty, or property" without due process must be construed as meaning that Congress could not take away the Southerner's purported right to take his slave property into a federal territory. This meant to Taney that the carefully crafted Missouri Compromise of 1820, which mandated, among other things, that some territories would be kept free of slavery, was unconstitutional. One of the primary attributes of living in the United States, Taney indicated, was being permitted to take your property anywhere. For Congress to declare that one's property in one's slaves could not be taken into a territory without losing it, Taney said, "could hardly be dignified with the name of due process."[378]

In reaching this result Taney took great pains to eschew any natural law arguments restricting slavery based on the law of nations (and English common law). "There is no law of nations," said Taney, "standing between the People of the United States and their Government, and interfering with their relation to each other."[379] In other words, no law of nations came between a property holder and his slave property. But there Taney would appear to have been wrong. At the time of the framing of the Constitution, and shortly thereafter, as we saw in the previous chapter, the natural law and law of nations foundations for the United States Constitution—which were indicated, for example, in *Calder v. Bull* and in the common law of crimes cases—were quite clear to contemporaries. Indeed, property itself was thought to be a concept that derived, ultimately, from natural law, as the words of Justice Paterson quoted in the last chapter suggest.

At the time of the framing of the Constitution the intellectual and spiritual leader of the Southern states, if not of the nation itself, was Virginia. Even in that state, in the late eighteenth century, there had developed a slavery jurisprudence that circumscribed the harshest applications of slavery doctrines through adherence to the basic natural law principle of a presumption against slavery and in favor of human liberty. Thus, in several important opinions, Virginia slave holders' wishes to manumit their slaves in their wills were implemented, even though at the time the testators died such manumission was not permitted by statute.[380]

Similarly, in an important decision rendered twenty years before *Dred Scott* by a court in the most philosophically respected of the Northern states, the most learned of the Massachusetts Supreme Judicial Court justices, Lemuel Shaw, addressed the constraints on slavery law in America. In his opinion in the case, *Commonwealth v. Aves* (1836),[381] Shaw made clear that his Massachusetts court accepted the principle of the English common law that the law of slavery, being against natural law, ought to be narrowly construed. As he explained, "[S]lavery is considered as unlawful and inadmissible in both [England and Massachusetts], and this because [it is] contrary to natural right and to laws designed for the security of personal liberty ... [S]lavery is of such a nature, that it is incapable of being introduced on any reasons moral or political, but only by positive law; and, it is so odious, that nothing can be suffered to support it but positive law."[382] Thus, for Shaw, in order for slavery to be accorded any legal validity at all, it needed the clear mandate of legislative enactment or custom to support it.

Combined, these cases, and others like them, suggest that there was a vital natural law tradition which, Taney's rejection of the anthropomorphic metaphor notwithstanding, did indeed stand between a slave holder and his property, and restrict the reach of slave law. This natural law tradition was clearly recognized in the late eighteenth century both in America and in England. If the second part of Taney's opinion had applied his first part's jurisprudential principle of original understanding, Taney probably would have held that the Fifth Amendment gave no absolute protection to slave property in the territories or anywhere else. Slavery thus would have been restricted by natural law and would have required express provisions or clear custom in order to support it. The Constitution gave no express support to slavery in the territories, and there was no clear customary guide. Thus, applying the principles of constitutional interpretation we limned in Chapter One, contrary to Taney's holding, Congress's prohibition of slavery in the territories could withstand judicial constitutional scrutiny, and the Missouri Compromise should not have been found unconstitutional.

Mr. Justice Curtis, one of the two dissenters, went so far as to cite Shaw's opinion in *Commonwealth v. Aves*, and seems to have had no trouble in understanding the limitations imposed on slavery by the law of nations.[383] Indeed Mr. Justice Curtis made clear *his* belief that the relevant law to be applied in the case, the law of the state of Missouri, was "the common law," and "the common law, as Blackstone says (4 Com., 67), adopts, in its full exent, the law of nations, and holds it to be a part of the law of the land."[384] Curtis went even further, and explicitly contradicted Taney on his reading of the Fifth Amendment. "Slavery, being contrary to natural right," Curtis observed, "is created only by municipal law."[385] Curtis took this fundamental principle of the law of nations to mean that unless there was a clear constitutional provision or congressional statute creating the status of slavery in the territories, there was nothing to stop Congress from there prohibiting it.[386] Similar points were made by the other dissenting Justice, McLean. For example, McLean quoted at some length the opinion of Lord Mansfield:

> The state of slavery is of such a nature that it is incapable of being introduced on any reasons, moral or political, but only by positive law, which preserves its force long after the reasons, occasion, and time itself, from whence it was created is erased from the memory; it is of a nature that nothing can be suffered to support it but positive law.[387]

McLean concluded that slavery was exclusively a state issue, but that until states were formed, there was no municipal law that restricted Congress's ability to bar slavery in the territories. By the rules of natural law and the law of nations, then, there could be no law of slavery in the territories without the support of express law, and this meant that Congress was free to prohibit it in the territories.

Taney's opinion in *Dred Scott* is thus highly vulnerable to criticism. With regard to the law of slavery, he departed from the principle of original understanding, and he paid insufficient heed to the validity of natural law and law of nations arguments. Nevertheless, it is still wrong to characterize Taney as a perpetrator of apartheid. Taney's opinion is about what the federal government had or had not done, or could or could not do. Taney did not seek to limit the right of any state to abolish slavery or to make whatever allowance it wished with regard to the participation of all of its population in the state franchise and state government. Even if Taney thought Congress had no power to prohibit slavery in the territories, this had no effect on what a *state* could do, so that if a majority of the population of a territory, upon admission as a state, decided to abolish slavery, it could still have been done.

Taney's opinion in *Dred Scott*, then, instead of perpetuating slavery, might well have been a judicial acceptance of the popular sovereignty plank of the Democratic party, as expressed by Stephen Douglas in the Lincoln-Douglas debates. Douglas thought that each state or territory ought to be able to decide the question of slavery for itself.[388] Taney appeared willing to let each state make that decision, although he was unwilling to let Congress decide the question for the territories. It should be stressed as well that Taney had freed his own slaves, and he "saw nothing positive about the institution of slavery itself."[389]

Since Taney could certainly read the natural law arguments advanced by the two dissenters, it appears likely that Taney deliberately chose to depart from the original understanding in his decision with regard to the Missouri Compromise because he was trying to keep the Union from splintering apart. He appears to have believed that weakening the power of the national government, and preserving the power of the states to make slavery determinations, was the means to achieve this end. His opinion did have the virtue of enunciating correct constitutional interpretive theory, namely original understanding, but he misapplied it with regard to slavery. As a result, Taney gave the due process clause a bad name for many modern constitutional theorists.[390]

Taney consciously or, perhaps unconsciously, moved away from the framers' understanding of natural law, under the pressure of his beliefs about concocting a political compromise to head off incipient national disaster. It should probably also be observed that Taney was not way out of line in recognizing that at some level politics played a role in constitutional interpretation; but alas, he got his politics wrong because he got his constitutional interpretation wrong. The politics at the time of the framing of the Constitution, or more correctly, the *political theory* dominant at the time of the Constitution, involved adherence to natural law views that limited the reach of slavery.[391] That politics, instead of withering away, as it did in the threatened South in the years leading up to the Civil War, flourished in the North, and eventually took control of the Northern war aims. We ignore the original constitutional understanding and the accompanying political theory of the framers at our national peril.

Dred Scott continues to generate controversy and to obscure constitutional understanding. In one of the most bizarre recent developments of our judicial politics, for example, the only black member of the United States Senate, Carol Moseley-Braun of Illinois, appears to have begun a one-person program to prevent even discussing the *Dred Scott* case. She has done so on the grounds that "as a descendant of a slave" she finds "it very difficult . . . to hear a defense, even an intellectual argument that would suggest that there is a rationale—an intellectual rationale, a legal rationale—for slavery that can be discussed in this [Senate] chamber at this time."[392]

The *Dred Scott* case came up in the questioning of now Supreme Court Associate Justice Ruth Bader Ginsburg at her Senate confirmation hearings before the Senate Judiciary Committee, of which Senator Moseley-Braun is a member. Senator Orrin Hatch, in questioning Ginsburg on her approach to the constitutionality of abortion regulation, likened *Dred Scott*'s insensitive approach

136

to property rights, which relegated blacks to second class status, to the *Roe v. Wade* Court's according a property right to pregnant women, which was similarly insensitive to the rights of fetuses. This was a perfectly valid and telling point. Still, after Moseley Braun went on to state that "It's very difficult for me to sit here and to even to quietly listen [sic] to a debate that would analogize *Dred Scott* and *Roe v. Wade*,"[393] Hatch apparently felt himself constrained to apologize to Moseley-Braun.[394]

Moseley-Braun may have misunderstood what Hatch was arguing. Thus, she may have wrongly been accusing Hatch of defending *Dred Scott*'s legal principle that there was a Fifth Amendment right to contract for property in slaves. Actually, Hatch had only spoken about contract rights in the context of another case, *Lochner v. New York*, to which we will turn next.[395] On the other hand, Moseley-Braun's own words, just quoted, certainly lend themselves to the interpretation that she feels it is inappropriate to dare to compare the slavery case with the abortion case, and this is the way her remarks were construed in the press.

Senator Hatch had earlier stated that "I thought the . . . *Dred Scott* case is the all time worst case in the history of the country." This led columnist Richard Grenier to observe, "at Senator Braun's level of rationality she seemingly could have heard a member say, 'This man's so rotten he's as bad as Adolph Hitler,' only to proclaim sonorously: 'I find it difficult to sit on this committee and hear a defense of Adolph Hitler.' "[396]

One hopes that our leaders in the Senate and elsewhere will heed the advice of some enlightened press commentary on the Hatch/Moseley-Braun interchange. The *New York Times*, attempting to be even-handed, first fulsomely praised Moseley-Braun for single-handedly getting the Senate to reverse a decision to renew the design patent of the United Daughters of the Confederacy's Confederate flag insignia. According to the *Times*, granting the patent would have been an example of "the unthinking way the white majority can offend minority Americans." Still, the *Times* called Moseley-Braun's condemnation of Hatch's likening *Roe v. Wade* to *Dred Scott* "a somewhat less inspired performance."[397]

The *Chicago Tribune* was a bit sterner with Moseley-Braun, although it also praised her actions with regard to the Daughters of the Confederacy. The *Tribune* called what Moseley-Braun did to Hatch "misus[ing] her moral authority." The paper then observed that Moseley-Braun, instead of debating Hatch's comparison of *Dred Scott* with *Roe*, "tried simply to silence it." Having apparently understood that Moseley-Braun misconstrued what Hatch was saying, the *Tribune* said, "Moseley-Braun was utterly wrong to suggest that there was anything racially insensitive about [Hatch's] analogy."[398]

The *Washington Times* was commendably even more blunt. It noted, "A new kind of prejudice stalks our consciousness. To speak up invites being called a 'racist.' To talk back encourages the slur of bigotry." It continued: "Mrs. Moseley-Braun's outrage [at Hatch's comparison] was misplaced, cheap and missed the point. (If Hitler is cited as a vicious anti-Semite, should a Jew complain for being reminded of the Holocaust?)."[399]

We should not, then, allow misplaced ideas about "sensitivity" to censor crucial discussion of constitutional law.[400] Moseley-Braun's apparent restrictions of constitutional discourse are too much like the antebellum South's own suppression of abolitionist literature to be tolerated in a society committed to free expression. This irony was best captured by columnist Stephen Chapman. He first protested Moseley-Braun's "preening display of outrage," which he believed was "partly meant to inform her fellow senators that, because she is black and they are white, all invocations of slavery for political ends must henceforth have her approval."[401] Chapman proceeded to condemn those who would suppress discussions of slavery as analogous to abortion, and he observed:

> Opposition to abortion, like the abolitionist movement, grew out of a perception that a group being denied legal rights was inescapably human and entitled to certain protections. In both cases the assertion was disputed by those who would suffer hardship if it were recognized . . . Both slave holders and female abortion-rights

138

supporters said the objects of concern were not people but property, to be used or disposed of at the sole discretion of the owner.[402]

One can hardly learn from the mistakes of *Dred Scott* if it cannot even any longer be discussed. It should be discussed and analzyed paying particular attention to its betrayal of our natural law heritage. The treatment of property, natural law, the due process clause, and the proper constitutional interpretative strategy in *Dred Scott* still have profound lessons for us.

B. *Lochner v. New York*

A different sort of natural law argument from that advanced and rejected in *Dred Scott*, but one perhaps nearly equally important to the natural law beliefs of the framing generation, lay at the core of the second major case to be reviewed, *Lochner v. New York* (1905).[403] *Lochner* was a case involving maximum hours laws for bakers. The great question in the case was whether a state such as New York could, by limiting hours bakers could work, dictate the terms of the employment contract in the baking trade. Prior Supremë Court cases were not clear on the issue. Several state court decisions and one United States Supreme Court opinion[404] had suggested that the state's interfering with the employment contract was an impermissible abridgement of the parties' contractual freedoms (freedoms, it will be remembered, which were important in the framing of the Constitution itself).

This idea of a constitutionally guaranteed "freedom of contract" flows naturally from the heightened status of property concepts in the Constitution and in our natural law tradition. After all, the freedom to contract is simply the freedom to exchange property with another person, and the alienability of property is a fundamental feature of the concept of property itself. Even so, other opinions of the Supreme Court had made clear that under certain exceptional circumstances the state could regulate contracts, pursuant to its "police power." Normally, however, freedom of contract prevailed. The *Lochner* court majority explained that this contractual freedom, evidenced in the Constitution's contracts clause—which forbids any state from interfering with preexisting contracts[405]—could also be seen to be protected as a fundamental freedom in the Fourteenth Amendment's "due process" clause.[406]

The argument that the Fourteenth Amendment's "due process" clause forbids this kind of economic regulation was essentially the same argument that Taney had made in *Dred Scott*. In *Dred Scott*, of course, instead of the Fourteenth Amendment's "due process" clause, which prevented the *states* from acting, the Fifth Amendment's "due process" clause, which restrained the *federal* government, was at issue.[407] Taney had said that any abridgement of a slave holder's property rights in the territories could not be dignified with the name of "due process." The plaintiffs in *Lochner*—who sought to prevent the state from interfering with their contracts with their employees—were making the same statement with regard to their and their employees' rights to settle employment terms on their own.

Nevertheless, before *Lochner*, the United States Supreme Court had held, in *Holden v. Hardy* (1898),[408] that a Utah law which regulated hours for miners was constitutional. In the Court's view, it was appropriate to exercise the state's police power to protect miners, since their trade was a particularly dangerous one, and since their bargaining power was relatively much less than that of the mine owners. The paradigm situation of bargaining between equals, which was the assumption behind freedom of contract, was thus absent.

Those defending the special legislation for bakers at issue in *Lochner* argued that, as in the case of the *Holden v. Hardy* miners, the trade of a baker was a particularly dangerous one. Bakers had to labor at unusual hours and were exposed to the risk of breathing noxious flour fumes. The *Lochner* majority was unpersuaded that the case of bakers could be analogized to that of miners, however. The majority reasoned that the trade of bakers was no more hazardous than many others, and that if the state's police power could regulate contracts for bakers, it could be used to regulate the contracts of any working men. There would then be little or nothing left of the constitutionally sacrosanct property right of individuals to contract for their own economic advantage.

A strong dissent to the majority's determination that the state was without power to regulate employment contracts was filed in the case by Justice Oliver Wendell Holmes, Jr. This dissenting opinion was to become one of Holmes's most famous pronouncements. It was to make him the darling of self-styled progressive or liberal constitutional theorists.[409] The Constitution, said the dissenting Holmes in *Lochner*, does not enact any philosophical theory, whether it be that of the organic state (presumably the view of those who would regulate relations between working men and employer) or Mr. Herbert Spencer's *Social Statics* (the Social Darwinist view implied by Holmes to be that of the majority).[410] Thus Holmes argued that the majority, in insisting on a constitutionally protected freedom of contract, was, in actuality, simply expressing its own policy preferences. The majority was not, in Holmes's opinion, following any neutral constitutional scheme.

It is now commonly accepted that Holmes was brilliantly right in his *Lochner* dissent. Even Robert Bork, one of our most articulate conservative judicial theorists, appears to agree with Holmes's *Lochner* dissent, and implies that the *Lochner* majority's invalidating the economic regulation at issue amounted to the Court's trying to "legislate at will."[411] The general unanimous approval of Holmes's *Lochner* dissent, unfortunately, has led to Holmes's views being invoked to support all sorts of social planning by the economists, sophisters, and calculators in the bureaucracies of federal and state governments.

A moment's reflection on the time of the framers, however, suggests that Holmes could not have been more wrong, and that conservatives such as Bork should hesitate before embracing his thought. If the history of the founding era shows anything, it is that the framers did most certainly have a philosophy of government in mind. At the core of that philosophy was the principle that property deserves special protection, and that the state may

141

not tinker with property rights without compensation.[412] Thus the fundamental property right of exchange through contracts ought to be enforced, and the national government ought to stand ready to ensure that a stable commercial environment, in which private contracting can flourish, is provided.

Thus, the *Lochner* majority's theory appears to have been much closer to original understanding than was Holmes's theory-neutral Constitution. In the *Lochner* majority's opinion one can hear echoes of what Samuel Chase said in *Calder v. Bull* about essentially natural law principles that protected property rights and prevented the government from arbitrarily taking one person's property and giving it to another.[413] This was similarly echoed in Justice Paterson's remarks in *Van Horne's Lessees*.[414] In short, *Dred Scott*'s holding may have been wrong because Taney forgot the lesson of original understanding, property, and natural law, but in *Lochner* the majority remembered the lesson and Holmes conveniently forgot it.

Taking this view of the *Lochner* case and its historical roots in natural law theory, then, I find myself differing on the merits of the *Lochner* decision from some of my conservative fellows, not only Judge Bork, but also Eugene Hickock and Gary McDowell. In an important recently published book, *Justice vs. Law* (1993),[415] Hickock and McDowell argue that *Lochner*'s "inherent problem" is "precisely the same as the problem of Taney's opinion in *Dred Scott*."[416] The force of this criticism is significant, because they regard *Dred Scott* as "the most vile of all the decisions ever handed down by the Supreme Court of the United States."[417] While they don't condemn *Lochner* so strongly, they do believe that *Lochner* supported "a theory of judging that was at odds with the idea of a written Constitution of limited and enumerated powers," and that, *Lochner* unleashed "a full-scale attack on the idea of limited, popular, constitutional government. Like its even more unseemly ancestor, *Dred Scott*," Hickock and McDowell argue, "*Lochner* helped set in motion the mechanics of government by judiciary."[418] Hickock and McDowell's book is an elegant and powerful critique of the modern Supreme Court's tendency to do sociology rather than law, but their evaluation of

Lochner misses the mark. As already indicated, *Lochner*, in context, can be seen to be solidly grounded in a specific and historically defined American natural law tradition of the protection of private property. Again, the real problem with *Dred Scott* is that it ignored this natural law tradition, while *Lochner* embraced it. *Lochner* was not a frontal assault on popular sovereignty, it was simply a restatement of the framers' belief that popular sovereignty, at some level, was secured by natural law and the right to property. Holmes was wrong when he forgot that the Constitution's framers did embrace a particular theory of political economy, that of natural law.

C. The New Deal Cases

Even though Holmes's *Lochner* dissent impressed most legal academics, the Supreme Court continued to look with a jaundiced eye on much economic planning and governmental interference with private contracting behavior. In 1935, for example, in another famous decision, *Schechter Poultry*,[419] a majority of the Supreme Court, in *Lochner*-like fashion, declared their antipathy toward "the organic state." Here the Court held unconstitutional the heart of President Franklin D. Roosevelt's New Deal, the National Industrial Recovery Act (NIRA). The NIRA had authorized local industries, in organic cooperation with government, to set up their own "codes of fair competition." These "codes" included mandatory wage and hour restrictions, mandatory collective bargaining, mandatory labor grievance procedures, massive required record keeping, and a plethora of other interdictions. Pursuant to the statutory scheme, any failure of any business person to adhere to any of these prohibitions or procedures could be punished as a crime, with attendant fine or imprisonment.[420]

In *Schechter*, the United States Supreme Court held, not surprisingly, that Congress could not constitutionally delegate its law-making power to private parties, as the NIRA did. Reaffirming nineteenth-century jurisprudence,[421] the Court also said that insofar as the codes allowed the federal government to regulate manufacturing that took place within an individual state, the NIRA went beyond the bounds of constitutionally authorized regulation of interstate commerce. Manufacturing or, as in the case at bar, chicken slaughtering and evisceration, was not commerce, the Court explained. Regulation of such an activity could not be justified on the theory that it *indirectly affected* interstate commerce. These two grounds for reversing the decision being clear—too much delegation and no interstate commerce—the majority did not find it necessary to reach the freedom of contract ground (the issue in *Lochner*), on which the plaintiffs also relied in seeking to overturn the NIRA.

Nevertheless, it was on freedom-of-contract grounds that the Court, one year later, found unconstitutional a New York statute that specified a minimum wage to be paid to women workers.[422] In a somewhat confused manner the Court had earlier upheld a statute limiting the number of hours women could work. This was in *Muller v. Oregon* (1908),[423] and the legislation was sustained on the theory that the state police power could be used to protect women's health in order to protect their central role as child bearers. In *Adkins v. Children's Hospital* (1923),[424] moreover, the Court had indicated that while maximum hours legislation for women might be constitutional, freedom of contract meant that minimum wage legislation for them was not.

American public opinion, however, orchestrated by President Franklin D. Roosevelt, was beginning to turn dramatically against the Court. The president charged that the Supreme Court was applying a "horse and buggy" definition of interstate commerce.[425] On March 9, 1937, after FDR's landslide 1936 victory, and before the Supreme Court had had a chance to rule on the measures of his so-called "Second New Deal," which radically changed the relationship between the federal government and individuals, and radically undercut the ambit of state sovereignty, the president let loose a mighty blast against the Court:

> When the Congress has sought to stabilize national agriculture, to improve the conditions of labor, to safeguard business against

unfair competition, to protect our national resources, and in many other ways to serve our clearly national needs, the majority of the Court has been assuming the power to pass on the wisdom of these acts of Congress—and to approve or disapprove the public policy written into these laws.

We have, therefore, reached the point as a Nation where we must take action to save the Constitution from the Court and the Court from itself. We must find a way to take an appeal from the Supreme Court to the Constitution itself. We want a Supreme Court which will do justice under the Constitution—not over it. In our courts we want a government of laws and not of men.[426]

FDR, of course, wanted no such thing. He didn't want a government of laws not of men, nor did he want "justice." He wanted a Supreme Court that would abandon its role as a check on the legislature and executive, and simply allow his administration to do what it wanted. In this speech FDR, in effect, denied that he believed the Court could exercise its judicial review function. Lest there be any doubt about what kind of Court he wanted (a more pliable one), at the time that FDR gave this speech his "Court-packing" plan, which would have allowed him to appoint enough Justices to put a majority of his own choosing immediately in place, was working its way through Congress.[427]

FDR had a substantial number of allies in the American legal academy. Rallying around Holmes's *Lochner* dissent, academic legal opinion, following the new politically correct course charted by press critics of the "Nine Old Men" (to use two journalists' way of describing the *Schechter* court)[428] encouraged the rejection of the Court's views of the centrality of freedom of contract and Congress's interstate commerce powers. By calling for an end to a "horse and buggy" definition of interstate commerce, of course, FDR had signalled his willingness to abandon the notion of original understanding, on which we have argued early constitutional interpretation was based. FDR, indeed, in seeking to implement measures such as the NIRA, had embarked on a path toward abandoning the rule of law in constitutional adjudication, and toward substituting in its place a Constitution more attuned to the passions of the majority. This was precisely the sort of Constitution the framers thought they had avoided, but as popular academic opinion strongly supported Roosevelt's views, the modern notion of a "living Constitution" was born, and the framers' idea of constitutional government according to the rule of law was seriously undermined.

We have tended to understand FDR's role as seeking to clean up the "wrong-headed" *Lochner* jurisprudence on the Court, as seeking to prevent the Court from unfairly obstructing progress. The truth is rather different. FDR and his academic allies had a new conception of the Constitution, one that radically rearranged the tenets of federalism and the economic freedoms of individuals. FDR's views were very different from the original understanding, to which the *Lochner* majority was much closer.

Some years before, the fictional character, Mr. Dooley, had suggested that the Supreme Court "follows th' iliction returns,"[429] and shortly after FDR's landslide victory in 1936, the Court, in what has frequently been referred to as the "switch in time that saved nine" did an about-face. In *West Coast Hotel v. Parrish* (1937),[430] a majority of the Court held that notions of freedom of contract no longer would bar minimum wage laws for women. Then, in *National Labor Relations Board v. Jones & Laughlin Steel Corp.* (1937)[431] the Court declared that Congress, pursuant to the interstate commerce clause, had the power to pass labor legislation that mandated collective bargaining, even for manufacturing plants.

In *Jones & Laughlin*, the Court frankly acknowledged that the *E.C. Knight* view (which had been accepted two years before in *Schechter*) that manufacturing was not commerce was simply no longer tenable. The Court did not bother to explain how, in just two years, it could so change its mind, nor did it explain why the view that manufacturing was not commerce was wrong. In accepting the relatively radical Wagner Act's[432] mandatory imposition of collective bargaining and unionization on all businesses with even an indirect connection to interstate commerce, the *Jones & Laughlin* Court completely buried the notion of a paramount individual employer/employee freedom of contract. The views of the *Lochner* majority were, so to speak, history.

On another judicial front, by allowing an administrative agency, the NLRB, pursuant to the Wagner Act, to impose money judgments for civil violations of the act, the Court brushed aside a powerful argument that this Wagner Act provision violated the Seventh Amendment's guarantee of a jury trial in civil suits. Samuel Chase and his Antifederalist colleagues who, in the ratification debates period (1787–1789) feared that the federal government would eventually fatally undermine the precious right of trial by jury, must have been spinning in their graves.

In rejecting *Jones & Laughlin*'s argument that the Seventh Amendment required a jury trial before fines could be imposed against a private party, the Supreme Court declared that an NLRB administrative proceeding was unknown at common law at the time of framing of the Seventh Amendment, and so the Seventh Amendment couldn't possibly apply. At one level this made some sense, since the text of the amendment itself *was* limited to suits "at common law." Still, when the *Jones & Lauglin* Court held that manufacturing was commerce, it had been willing to take the most expansive view of "interstate commerce" in order to accommodate the Constitution to the reality of modern vertically-integrated enterprise. The Court had further been willing to erode traditional understandings of freedom of contract in order to accommodate the needs of working men whose bargaining powers were purportedly unequal to that of powerful capitalists. *Yet the Court was unwilling to grant capitalists the same favor and construe the Bill of Rights according to its clear spirit of erecting a jury trial barrier between a zealous government (or administrative) prosecutor and a private victim.*

During the debates over ratification of the Constitution worry about jury trials in federal courts was perhaps *the* premier complaint of the Antifederalist opponents of the new Constitution. The passage of the Bill of Rights and even the 1789 Judiciary Act, as we now know, was a direct response to this complaint. The course more in keeping with the historical understanding of the need for jury trials, then, would seem to have been for the Supreme Court to rule for *Jones & Laughlin* on this point.[433]

With *Jones & Laughlin*, *West Coast Hotel v. Parrish*, and other cases like them, prodded by a popular president, Holmes's *Lochner* dissent had finally spawned a whole new ideology of the law, which went by the name of "legal realism."[434] To the legal realists the progressive policy goals of the New Deal were much more important than the framers' original intention, or any original understanding of the nature of the American polity. If the Constitution had been originally about the sanctity of private property and individual contracts, the "New Deal Constitution," the document as interpreted by the Court following its decisions in *West Coast Hotel* and *Jones & Laughlin*, was about something rather different.

Once the Court had announced its view newly favorable to the presidential and congressional initiatives, the "Court-packing plan" was no longer necessary, and it was never passed. Moreover, even without new legislation, FDR was soon able to "pack" the Court. After he had had an opportunity to name seven new Justices (Hugo Black, Stanley Reed, Felix Frankfurter, William O. Douglas, Frank Murphy, Robert H. Jackson, and Wiley Rutledge) more sympathetic to his views, the Constitution suddenly allowed much more government intervention, regulation, and coercion, pursuant to an essentially redistributive model. The former sanctity of freedom of contract was obliterated, and the views of what amounted to interstate commerce and thus what could be federally regulated "had expanded . . . so [far] that almost any activity could be so defined."[435]

Eventually, by late 1993, President Clinton's proposed health care plan, which would allow the federal government to intrude into virtually every sector of state and local government and life, was simply assumed by almost everyone to be constitutional. At this writing the details of the plan are uncertain, but one prominent feature seems to be prohibiting individuals from entering into their own choice of contracts (or no contracts) for health care insurance. This sort of interference with individual freedom of contract on this scale is surely unprecedented, and would have

148

sent the *Lochner* majority into conniptions. As David B. Rivkin, Jr., pointed out in a recent "Rule of Law" column in the *Wall Street Journal*, the national government's mandating health care for all individuals was hardly the kind of activity on the part of the federal government that the framers contemplated.[436] We have hit a sort of constitutional apocalypse, and one almost hopes that the Four Horsemen of the New Deal Court would arise from their graves, ride screaming into the nation's capital, and save Washington from itself.

But to return to the late 1930s: within just a few years of *Jones & Lauglin*, this major change in constitutional ideology, this profound departure from the original understanding of constitutional political economy, led to a series of decisions that reversed the original understanding of the nature of American society itself. This was true both with regard to preserving a significant sphere of legal and cultural autonomy for the individual states, and with regard to the content of the legal rules that began to be imposed on the states. Probably the most important and dramatic such area involved public education.

The Supreme Court became emboldened by the type of thinking Holmes displayed in his *Lochner* dissent—thinking that gave virtual license to the contemporary Court to impose its own philosophy on the state governments in a manner frankly contrary to the original spirit of the Constitution itself. Beginning with the New Deal "switches" on interstate commerce, freedom of contract, and the right to trial by jury, the Supreme Court proceeded to make much more new constitutional law. As we shall soon see, with regard to school prayer and school desegration, and in many other areas, as far as the original understanding of the relevant constitutional provisions ought to govern, the Supreme Court was clearly functioning unconstitutionally.

D. The School Prayer and Flag Salute Cases and the Doctrine of Selective Incorporation

The school prayer cases were foreshadowed by the so-called "flag salute" cases, in which plaintiffs, on religious grounds, objected to students being compelled to stand and recite the pledge of allegiance. In *West Virginia State Board of Education v. Barnette* (1943),[437] by a vote of 6–3, and reversing a decision of its own made just three years earlier,[438] the Supreme Court held that the states could *not* require students to salute the flag. According to the Court's majority, forcing students to salute the flag in effect compelled citizens to express beliefs and thus violated their First Amendment freedom of speech. In *Barnette* the Court thus sought to place its decision on "freedom of speech" grounds rather than on "establishment of religion" grounds. Still, the real issue in the case was to what extent a state government could legislate in a manner that offended particular religious beliefs.

There is no evidence that the founding generation regularly performed any group ceremonies such as the pledge of allegiance. There were few, if any, free state-sponsored public schools at the time of the First Amendment's drafting. The flag salute itself was not widely performed in American public schools until the twentieth century. Nevertheless, it is doubtful that the founding generation would have believed that the pledge of allegiance was in conflict with the First Amendment. Oaths or affirmations of allegiance to the Constitution or to the state constitutions for federal officers were commonplace at the time, as were invocations to the deity at the beginning of legislative and judicial sessions. Witnesses in courts were routinely sworn "so help you almighty God" to tell the truth, and condemned prisoners were advised on how to preserve their immortal souls in the proper Christian manner.[439]

With all of this attention to allegiance to the Constitution and to religion on public occasions, and with the widely perceived notion that the law itself depended on a moral basis furnished by religion, religion was accepted as a vital part of public life in the

150

framers' time. Adherence to religion was thought to be consistent rather than inconsistent with patriotism. A religion that forbade patriotic expression, such as the flag salute was later to become, might have been constitutionally protected with regard to its exercise. Still, even if it had been accepted at the time that the First Amendment applied to state governments, it seems doubtful that the First Amendment could have been invoked to grant the practitioners of such a religion a special exemption from state-sponsored religious or patriotic exercises. It is even less likely that the framers would have believed that any religiously based objections to the ceremony on the part of any individual should have forbade such public ceremonies at all.[440]

These latter arguments were spelled out in a cogent dissent to *Barnette* by Felix Frankfurter, as indicated earlier a Roosevelt appointee, a former Harvard Law School professor, and one of the most intellectually gifted and sophisticated Justices to sit on the United States Supreme Court in the modern era. While Roosevelt may have appointed Frankfurter because he shared FDR's progressive views with regard to the manner in which legislatures might reshape the American economy, soon after Frankfurter joined the Court, he found himself at odds with "the younger progressive [Roosevelt-appointed] justices like Hugo Black, William O. Douglas, Frank Murphy, and Wiley Rutldge."[441] Unlike them Frankfurter began to manifest a true conservative's belief that it was not the job of the Court to make social policy for the people. Rather it was the job of the Justice to allow the popularly elected legislatures to reflect the will of their constituents, so long as they did not transgress established constitutional boundaries.

Frankfurter's views in this regard were probably most clearly expressed in his *Barnette* dissent. This dissent was an extremely powerful statement not only of Frankfurter's views on the self-restraint the Court ought to exercise, but also of his embrace of the theory that his actions as a Justice ought to be circumscribed by the original understanding of the Constitution. At the outset of his dissent, Frankfurter noted that as a Jew he belonged to one of the most persecuted minorities in history. He explained that he was thus sensitive to the possibility of religious discrimination.[442] Still, he proceeded to make clear that he believed that where a majority of citizens wished to inculcate values of patriotism and religion in their public schools through exercises such as the flag salute and/or Bible readings, it was permissible. The implementation of the will of such majorities, Frankfurter explained, was constitutionally protected, and, it would appear, was laudable as an effort toward the requisite cultivating of virtue in the citizenry. Although Frankfurter's views were not only in dissent then, but remain unpopular in the academy, they deserve study as a means of helping to recapture the correct constitutional understanding, and extended treatment here.

The exposition of Frankfurter's conservative judicial theory in his *Barnette* dissent began by his quotation of Oliver Wendell Holmes's dictum that "legislatures are ultimate guardians of the liberties and welfare of the people in quite as great a degree as the courts."[443] Frankfurter went on to stress that "responsibility for legislation lies with legislatures," that unlike the Supreme Court, legislatures were directly "answerable" to the people. "[T]his Court's only and very narrow function," he stated, "is to determine whether within the broad [constitutional] grant of authority vested in legislatures they have exercised a judgment for which reasonable justification can be offered."

Here Frankfurter was embracing the work of the late nineteenth-century constitutional scholar James B. Thayer.[444] Thayer's doctrine was that if the legislature reasonably believed that the course of action it had taken was in pursuance of constitutional goals, it was not for the Court to substitute *its* legislative judgment based on the furthering of *other* constitutional goals. It appears, however, that more than democratic theory, and more than judicial restraint as such motivated Frankfurter. He also embraced the tenets of original understanding. The framers, Frankfurter acknowledged, could have involved the courts in the legislative process had they chosen to do so, since they had before them models such as "New York's Council of Revision." That council had been functioning since 1777, and its job was to review " 'all bills which [had] passed the senate and assembly . . .

before they become laws.' " The New York judges constituted a majority of that council, and it was their job to scrutinize the legislature's work before it could become law.[445]

Frankfurter explained that the framers chose not to replicate the practice of New York's Council of Revision. Even though it ran against the wishes of James Madison himself,[446] the framers chose not to allow the Supreme Court to become involved in the legislative process. Original understanding, then, suggested that Frankfurter defer to the framers' decision. Thus Frankfurter concluded that judicial invalidation of legislation pursuant to judicial review should be exercised only sparingly because "it serves to prevent the full play of the democratic process."[447] In *Barnette*, West Virginia had required "all pupils to share in the salute to the flag as part of school training in citizenship." There was no effort "to punish disobedient children or visit penal consequences on their parents." Rather the great question in the case was "the right of the State to compel participation in this exercise by those who choose to attend the public schools."[448]

The plaintiffs in the case, Jehovah's Witnesses, had sought to end the state practice of compelling their children to participate in the flag salute on the grounds that it represented the worship of icons forbidden by their religion. Frankfurter stated that compelling the flag salute *would* impermissibly violate the First Amendment's establishment clause "if the avowed or intrinsic legislative purpose is either to promote or to discourage some religious community or creed." But "it by no means follows that legislative power is wanting whenever a general non-discriminatory civil regulation in fact touches conscientious scruples or religious beliefs of an individual or a group."[449] A state could choose to exempt those with religious scruples about the flag salute if it chose to do so, Frankfurter indicated. But that was a matter for the state's legislative judgment, and not for the United States Supreme Court's.[450]

Frankfurter took particular pains to reject the plaintiff's argument that the state should be permitted to legislate in the face of religious scruples only with regard to matters of great importance:

153

Conscientious scruples, all would admit, cannot stand against every legislative compulsion to do positive acts in conflict with such scruples. We have been told that such compulsions override religious scruples only as to major concerns of the state. But the determination of what is major and what is minor itself raises questions of policy. For the way in which men equally guided by reason appraise importance goes to the very heart of policy. Judges should be very diffident in setting their judgment against that of a state in determining what is and what is not a major concern, what means are appropriate to proper ends, and what is the total social cost in striking the balance of imponderables.[451]

In his *Barnette* dissent, then, Frankfurter explicitly rejected the kind of "balancing test" approach that dominates most constitutional jurisprudence these days,[452] correctly acknowledging that such balancing was legislative and not judicial in nature. Alas, just such a balancing test, one that now requires the state to demonstrate a "compelling state interest" before it can overcome an individual's religious scruples, is now required by federal statute.

Following his rejection of such a "compelling state interest" requirement, Frankfurter stated that the history of the late eighteenth century and the writings of the framers did not furnish "justification for a claim by [religious] dissidents of exceptional immunity from civic measures of general applicability, measures not in fact disguised assaults upon such dissident views."[453] The great defenders of religious liberty in the founding era, Frankfurter explained, simply sought to "remove political support from every religious establishment. They put on an equality the different religious sects—Episcopalians, Presbyterians, Catholics, Baptists, Methodists, Quakers, Huguenots—which, as dissenters, had been under the heel of the various orthodoxies that prevailed in different colonies."[454] But even Jefferson, the great champion of religious freedom, according to Frankfurter, knew that religious minorities could disrupt society. Speaking of Jefferson and the other members of the founding generation, Frankfurter stated, "It never would have occurred to them to write into the Constitution the subordination of the general civil authority of the state to sectarian scruples."[455]

This history lesson of Frankfurter's has been neglected in the last thirty years, as self-actualization First Amendment jurisprudence has triumphed, and as the "liberalism" typified by the modern Democratic party "has infiltrated and taken over our church-state [jurisprudential] corpus."[456] The effect of this takeover, of course, is to repudiate Frankfurter's sensible views and to render virtually impermissible any governmental efforts at promoting morality, civic virtue, and the good life generally.[457] The depth of the entrenchment of the "self-actualization" perspective in constitutional law is shown by the hysteria generated among constitutional scholars and the liberal media by the Supreme Court's commonsensical decision rendered by Justice Scalia in *Employment Division v. Smith* (1990).[458]

In *Smith*, Scalia upheld the state of Oregon's denial of unemployment benefits on the grounds of "misconduct," where such misconduct was the criminal use of the hallucinogenic drug peyote. The plaintiffs in the case, falsely it would appear,[459] claimed that they had ingested the peyote sacramentally as members of the "Native American Church."[460] They claimed that to deny them unemployment benefits on this ground violated their constitutional guarantee of religious freedom.

Scalia, wisely following Frankfurter's logic[461] held in *Smith* that "an individual's religious beliefs [do not] excuse him from compliance with an otherwise valid law prohibiting conduct that the State is free to regulate."[462] The liberal academy, *una voce*, was horrified. Several conservative religious groups found themselves allied with individualistic liberals on this one issue, and great pressure was soon brought to bear on Congress. Then, as one of the proudest accomplishments of the first year of the Clinton admistration the so-called "Religious Freedom Restoration Act" was passed, explicitly to overrule Scalia's opinion in *Smith*. The new act required the courts to throw out state or federal laws that burden an individual's purportedly religiously motivated conduct "unless [the law in question] is a narrowly tailored means of achieving a compelling state interest."[463]

In other words, amid much hoopla, Congress and the administration forced the courts to engage in an O'Connor-like "balancing test" on such religious matters, as it had been doing, after *Barnette* and until *Smith*.[464] Instead of upholding Justice Scalia's return to Frankfurter's clear and proper standard, the federal government rendered matters uncertain, in the service of self-actualization. It is a bit beyond the scope of our analysis here, but perhaps one ought to wonder about the Religious Freedom Restoration Act's constitutionality, given that the act itself, insofar as it departs from the original understanding as understood by Frankfurter, may represent an exercise of powers dealing with religion that was forbidden to the federal government.[465]

To return to Frankfurter, the thrust of his analysis in his *Barnette* dissent was that the framers of the First Amendment did not intend to allow any dissenting sect to have the privilege of vetoing measures of general applicability. As Frankfurter put it, "The constitutional protection of religious freedom terminated disabilities, it did not create new privileges. It gave religious equality, not civil immunity."[466] Frankfurter also appeared eager to maintain that the essence of the First Amendment was "freedom from conformity to religious dogma, not freedom from conformity to law because of religious dogma."[467] Nevertheless, and most important for our purposes, *it did not appear that Frankfurter's concept of freedom from religious dogma necessarily extended to the prohibition of all religious exercises in state-sponsored institutions, even public schools.*

First of all, Frankfurter indicated that "The prohibition against any religious establishment by the government placed denominations on an equal footing—it assured freedom from support by the government to any mode of worship and the freedom of individuals to support any mode of worship."[468] But when Frankfurter spoke of the prohibition on the government's supporting any "mode of worship," he did not seem to mean that the government could not support "worship" of the Almighty itself, so long as it was done in a nonsectarian manner.

Thus, Frankfurter maintained that "The essence of the religious freedom guaranteed by our Constitution is therefore this: no religion shall either receive the state's support or incur its hostility." He further stated that "Religion is outside the sphere of political government."[469] Nevertheless, Frankfurter did not seem to imply that the state had to divorce itself from the moral and spiritual life or concerns of its citizens. As Frankfurter explained:

> This does not mean that all matters on which religious organizations or beliefs may pronounce are outside the sphere of government. Were this so, instead of the separation of church and state, there would be the subordination of the state on any matter deemed within the sovereignty of the religious conscience. Much that is the concern of temporal authority affects the spiritual interests of men. But it is not enough to strike down a nondiscriminatory law that it may hurt or offend some dissident view.[470]

Frankfurter went so far as to state that "It is only in a theocratic state that ecclesiastical doctrines measure legal right or wrong." And: "An act compelling profession of allegiance to a religion, no matter how subtly or tenuously promoted, is bad."[471]

Of utmost importance, however, Frankfurter pointed out that "an act promoting good citizenship and national allegiance is within the domain of governmental authority."[472] This was as true of acts promoting good citizenship as it was of acts requiring compulsory vaccination, food inspection regulations, the obligation to bear arms, appearance as a witness in judicial proceedings, or compulsory medical treatment.[473] Frankfurter yielded to no Justice in his belief that governmental support should not favor any particular sect.[474] Still, the logic of his opinion strongly suggests that nonsectarian state or local measures that aid in the formation of good citizenship are permissible, even if they touch on spiritual matters which might be regarded as religious.

Accordingly, in his *Barnette* dissent, Frankfurter appeared to suggest that it would be inappropriate for the Supreme Court to intervene in the "controversial issue of compulsory Bible-reading in public schools."[475] Frankfurter noted that state policy was in great conflict over the issue, and further that "The requirement of Bible-reading has been justified by various state courts as an appropriate means of inculcating ethical precepts and familiarizing pupils with the most lasting expression of great English literature."[476] "Is this Court," he asked, "to overthrow such variant state educational policies by denying states the right to entertain such convictions in regard to their school systems, because of a belief that the King James version is in fact a sectarian text to which parents of the Catholic and Jewish faiths and of some Protestant persuasions may rightly object to having their children exposed?"[477]

Similarly, Frankfurter expressed his belief that the Supreme Court ought not to "enter the old controversy between science and religion." He thought that it would be wrong for the Court to take a position choosing between favoring "The religious consciences of some parents [who] may be offended by subjecting their children to the Biblical account of creation," or offending other parents "by prohibiting a teaching of biology that contradicts such Biblical account."[478]

Frankfurter clearly implied that it was not for the highest federal Court to override state legislative judgments on this issue when he asked:

> Is it really a fair construction of such a fundamental concept as the right freely to exercise one's religion that a state cannot choose to require all children who attend public school to make the same gesture of allegiance to the symbol of our national life because it may offend the conscience of some children, but that it may compel all children to attend public school to listen to the King James version although it may offend the consciences of their parents?[479]

Frankfurter closed his dissent in *Barnette* by noting that the Court, in finding a compulsory flag salute unconstitutional, was reversing its own recent ruling on the issue that was a bare three years old. Moreover, the Court was also reversing the decisions of a host of learned Supreme Court Justices upholding compulsory flag salutes, including Chief Justice Charles Evans Hughes, and Justices Benjamin Cardozo and Louis Brandeis.[480] The invocation of Cardozo and Brandeis in this connection would have been particularly forceful, since as Frankurter's predecessors in what was frequently referred to as the "Jewish" seat on the Court, both Cardozo and Brandeis were similarly sensitized to the horrors of religious persecution.

Frankfurter stressed that "even though legislation relates to civil liberties, our duty of deference to those who have the responsibility for making the laws is no less relevant or less exacting."[481] He cautioned his brethren—in vain—that "The attitude of judicial humility which these considerations enjoin is not an abdication of the judicial function," but rather "a due observance of its limits." The decision in the case at bar—finding the flag salute unconstitutional—Frankfurter concluded, was not in line with the Court's primary role of "passing on the proper distribution of political power as between the states and the central government." Instead, he said, "To strike down a law like this is to deny a power to all government."[482]

Frankfurter's concern with legislative steps that any government might take to instill good citizenship would seem to support nonsectarian recognition that a citizen's obligations are reinforced by and, in the final analysis, dependent on, morality and religion. As we have seen,[483] and as we will further explore,[484] this was the belief of the framers of the Constitution. Frankfurter's wise views of the limits on the Court's role in this area should have been followed by the *Barnette* Court and deserve reintroduction into Supreme Court jurisprudence, if not by the Court itself, then by constitutional amendment.

The year after Frankfurter's death, in *Abington School District v. Schempp* (1963),[485] the Supreme Court held that Pennsylvania's law requiring that ten verses of the Bible be read at the opening of each public school day violated the First Amendment's establishment clause. This followed by one year the Court's lamentable decision in *Engel v. Vitale* (1962),[486] which forbad nonsectarian school prayer (and in which Frankfurter did not participate). We have, then, no opinion from Frankfurter giving his explicit views on nonsectarian school prayer. Nevertheless, the logic of his comments on compulsory Bible reading suggests a basis for believing that he would have dissented from the Supreme Court decisions in 1962 and 1963 forbidding public school devotional Bible reading and nonsectarian public school prayer.

Frankfurter's idea of preserving virtue in the citizenry as an essential of republican government was a staple for the founding era as well.[487] Frankfurter's thought on this issue—permitting the state and local governments to determine for themselves the manner in which to inculcate the moral and spiritual strength required for good citizenship in their public school students— ought to be returned to the place of prominence it deserves. Alas, to perform this feat of appropriate constitutional reinterpretation will be difficult, given the Court's, the academy's, the media's, and even the public's current rejection of Frankfurter's views, and the current infatuation with the self-actualization brand of First Amendment theory. The Supreme Court decisions and their approbation in the media have had a pernicious educational effect on the public, teaching us to think more about our individual rights than our responsibilities to each other, and making the building of community in America much more difficult. Not only should the Court move back toward a jurisprudence where responsibility and civic virtue are more important than self-actualization, but our educational institutions and our press need to relearn the lessons of the philosophy that animated the Founders. We have to start someplace in this endeavor, however, and getting the public to understand how the Supreme Court's jurisprudence went wrong and ought to be changed is as good a place as any.

SELECTIVE INCORPORATION THEORY

At this point, then, we might spend some time backtracking a bit—to flesh out how the Supreme Court became sidetracked on the issue of what state and local governments ought to be permitted to do with regard to determining the manner in which to inculcate notions of morality and virtue in the citizenry. The Supreme Court is now profoundly in error in its application of First Amendment theory. This error initially manifested itself most blatantly in the flag salute and school prayer cases. The error stems not only from an attitude about what the First Amendment ought to do, but also from the Court's acceptance of the so-called "incorporation" or "selective incorporation" doctrine, which is a much broader doctrinal rubric than First Amendment theory.

According to the once controversial "selective incorporation" doctrine, "the United States Supreme Court has held that most, but not all, guarantees of the federal Bill of Rights limit state and local governments as well as the federal government, because of the passage of the 'Due Process' Clause of the Fourteenth Amendment."[488] In other words, the Fourteenth Amendment's provision that no state shall "deprive any person of life, liberty, or property, without due process of law . . .," according to the modern Supreme Court, means that many of the prohibitions against action by the United States executive or legislature in the first eight amendments ought to be read as applying against state and local government as well. This includes, so the argument goes, prohibitions on making laws with regard to freedom of the press, establishing religion, prohibitions on unreasonable searches and seizures, the prohibition against self-incrimination, or the prohibition on cruel and unusual punishments.

The selective incorporation doctrine—selective because the Supreme Court has never said that the entire Bill of Rights is incorporated through the Fourteenth Amendment—is an invitation to unbridled judicial discretion, and must be ranked as one of the boldest and most astonishing acts of judicial usurpation in the history of the United States Supreme Court.

It clearly is judicial usurpation if one believes in implementing the original understanding, because the history of the Fourteenth Amendment demonstrates that it did not seek to perform a fundamental alteration in the character of the federal judiciary, or fundamentally to restrict the ambit of the operation of state authority. The amendment was not understood as giving federal

161

judges the power selectively to restrain the ability of the states to govern. The amendment, instead, was precisely targeted at the problem of ensuring justice to the newly freed Southern blacks. The "due process" clause was meant to ensure that the states did not arbitrarily remove the status of the freedmen by ignoring the accepted means of legal procedure. The amendment, that is, was drafted to guarantee the freedmen the exercise of their basic civil and political rights, such as the right to hold property, the right to contract, and the right to bring proceedings in the state courts to enforce their property and contract rights. The Fourteenth Amendment was not intended to be a blueprint for the wholesale restructuring of the relationship between the individual and the states.[489]

The Bill of Rights—the first Ten Amendments—it must be remembered, was originally enacted because many people believed that the federal government created under the Constitution of 1787 had the potential to expand its powers, and, eventually, to obliterate the state governments. Thus the Bill of Rights erected clear restraints around the federal government to minimize the chances of this happening.[490] The prime purpose of the Bill of Rights was to ensure a maximum amount of discretion on the part of the state governments and people, consistent with the national needs for internal and external defense and the enhancement of national commercial standing. Equally clearly, the Fourteenth Amendment was part of an effort to deny the state governments any further license to wrest from their newly freed black citizens their basic rights. It is a perversion of history, however, to convert the Bill of Rights into a club to beat back and restrict general state sovereignty. Where state sovereignty is wrongly used arbitrarily to discriminate against the persons the amendment was designed to protect, the freed slaves, one could construct an argument for some selective incorporation. But it violates our most basic principle of original understanding to use the Fourteenth Amendment fundamentally to restructure our federal system.

Nevertheless, since about 1925 the Supreme Court has been virtually ignoring these problems of the original understanding of the Bill of Rights and the Fourteenth Amendment. In that year the Supreme Court appears to have held that the First Amendment's fundamental protections to the rights of speech and press ought to be applied against the states as well.[491] In 1940, in *Cantwell v. Connecticut*,[492] the Supreme Court first applied the First Amendment's "free exercise" of religion clause to the states.[493] It was not until 1947, however, in *Everson v. Board of Education of Ewing Township*, that the Supreme Court first applied the First Amendment's "establishment clause" to the states through the Fourteenth Amendment's due process clause.[494] It was not until 1962, only a little more than thirty years ago, in the case of *Engel v. Vitale*,[495] that the Supreme Court went so far as to forbid nonsectarian state-sponsored public school prayer. In *Engel*, and earlier, in *Everson*, the Supreme Court compounded its basic error regarding selective incorporation of the First Amendment by enacting into constitutional jurisprudence a misreading of the First Amendment itself.

This misreading, clearest perhaps in *Engel*, changed the previous direction of First Amendment religion clause jurisprudence, typified by Frankfurter's dissent in *Barnette*. Pursuant to that earlier understanding, the Court had merely forbidden state aid to any particular religion. In *Engel*, the Court construed the establishment clause to forbid state aid to all religions or religion in general, and went beyond the requirement of neutrality toward particular sects. There is little if any historical basis to support the proposition that states should be prohibited from giving aid generally to religion (expanded upon in the next chapter). Indeed, if anything the First Amendment's establishment clause was designed to allow the states to determine what to do in matters of religion on their own, free from federal government interference.

The historical basis that the Supreme Court did use in *Engel*, in order to strike down nonsectarian school prayer, was not a careful reading of the climate at the time of the adoption of the First Amendment. Instead, it relied on particular writings of Thomas Jefferson and James Madison.

Jefferson was the author of the metaphor that there ought to be a "wall of separation" between church and state, but when his use

163

of the metaphor is put in context, it is not quite the foundation of secular humanism made out by its twentieth-century users. The phrase "wall of separation" appears in Jefferson's letter to a Committee of the Danbury [Connecticut] Baptist Association (Messrs. Nehemia Dodge and Others), dated January 1, 1802. In full Jefferson wrote:

GENTLEMEN,

The affectionate sentiments of esteem and approbation which you are so good to express towards me, on behalf of the Danbury Baptist Association, give me the highest satisfaction. My duties dictate a faithful and zealous pursuit of the interests of my constituents, and in proportion as they are persuaded of my fidelity to those duties, the discharge of them becomes more and more pleasing.

Believing with you that religion is a matter which lies solely between man and his God, that he owes account to none other for his faith or his worship, that the legislative powers of government reach actions only, and not opinions, I contemplate with sovereign reverence that act of the whole American people [the First Amendment to the Constitution] which declared that their legislature should "make no law respecting an establishment of religion, or prohibiting the free exercise thereof," thus building a wall of separation between church and State. Adhering to this expression of the supeme will of the nation in behalf of the rights of conscience, I shall see with sincere satisfaction the progress of those sentiments which tend to restore to man all his natural rights, convinced he has no natural right in opposition to his social duties.

I reciprocate your kind prayers for the protection and blessing of the common Father and Creator of man, and tender you for yourselves and your religious association, assurances of my high respect and esteem.[496]

Even in this letter, Jefferson appears to be not quite the enemy of general morality and religion his latter-day adherents have become. He does, indeed, speak of "a wall of separation between church and state" supposedly erected by the First Amendment, but Jefferson is careful to acknowledge the preeminence of social duties, the secondary role of natural rights, *and*, of all things, a belief in a single supreme male creator. It should be noted that Jefferson writes the letter presumably as part of his official duties as president, perhaps to reassure the Danbury Baptists of his good intentions and sound morality. Thus, in this 1802 letter, Jefferson actually anticipates Felix Frankfurter in declaring that an individual's "natural right" could not be invoked in opposition to "his social duties," and Jefferson appears to perform an official function that he closes with a prayer.

In 1785, James Madison had written a "Memorial and Remonstrance against Religious Assessments," in which he argued that a "true religion did not need the support of law; that no person either believer or nonbeliever, should be taxed to support a religious institution of any kind; that the best interest of a society required that the minds of men always be wholly free; and that cruel persecutions were the inevitable result of government-established religions."[497] The Court in *Engel* glossed over it, but in fact Madison was writing *before* the establishment of the federal government. Moreover, Madison's remarks really go more toward the establishment of a particular sect (and compelling its financial support) than toward the support of religion generally.

Whatever Jefferson was aiming at in his obscure 1802 letter, it is not consonant with Jefferson's fundamental suspicion of judicial discretion to allow the federal courts to dictate the standards of what the states and localities can do with regard to the spiritual instruction of their youth. According to Jefferson's famous 1820 comments:

> [The] judiciary of the United States is the subtle corps of sappers and miners constantly working under ground to undermine the foundations of our confederated fabric. They are construing our Constitution from a co-ordination of a general and special government to a general and supreme one alone.[498]

Whatever Jefferson's religious sympathies, to convert the irascible defender of state rights and privileges into a supporter of a free-ranging federal judiciary goes much too far.

Moreover, as indicated, Madison's comments appear to have been more directed at the question of what ought to be the proper policy in Virginia regarding the establishment of a particular sect than what ought to be the proper role of the federal courts in regulating state education. Madison and Jefferson's thought is thus slim support for interpreting the First Amendment to give the federal courts license to forbid nonsectarian prayer, much less devotional Bible reading, in the public schools.

The considerable historical difficulties in the way of the Supreme Court's interpretation of the establishment clause have been forcefully stated in dissent from time to time, most notably by Chief Justice Rehnquist. In his dissent in *Wallace v. Jaffree* (1985),[499] the Chief Justice eloquently sifted the historical evidence to argue that *Everson v. Board of Education* (1947) and its progeny were simply wrong. This was plain, Rehnquist pointed out, because the Constitution imposes no "wall of separation" between church and state, because the establishment clause merely forbids the federal government's establishment of a particular sect as the nationally favored church, and because there is no constitutional requirement that the state be neutral between religion and "irreligion." Rehnquist was, of course, right.[500]

The arguments of the dissenters such as Rehnquist and before him Potter Stewart have not, however, prevented the Court from declaring, by judicial fiat, that not only is nonsectarian school prayer unconstitutional, so too is the reading of verses from the Bible at the opening of each school day.[501] Similarly prohibited is the provision of a "moment of silence" at the beginning of a school day for the express purpose of facilitating "meditation or prayer."[502] The latest atrocity of this nature is the opinion in the *Weisman* case in which a majority, relying on Jefferson's thought, held that a rabbi could not be permitted to give a nonsectarian prayer at a compulsory middle-school graduation ceremony.[503] (More will be said about the Supreme Court's approach to the establishment clause in the following chapter, when the manner in which we ought to return to the original understanding is suggested.)

For the moment, it is enough to observe that on this issue the American public appears to have been able to understand constitutional directives better than the Supreme Court. The public has never supported Supreme Court jurisprudence in this area. At one time, apparently, fully 76 percent of Americans polled on the issue favored a constitutional amendment to permit school prayer, and 150 such amendments have been offered by 111 members of Congress, although none has yet succeeded,[504] perhaps because Congress's liberal majority, unlike its constituents, does not appear to favor such an amendment. Nevertheless, it is more than a little puzzling why the Supreme Court's modern secular interpretation of the First Amendment's religion clause continues, given the strong historical evidence and public opinion against it.

Perhaps the turn toward secularization of the First Amendment, exemplified by current First Amendment doctrine that local, state, and federal governments must not favor religion over "irreligion,"[505] is a product of our usual media ethic of self-actualization. Perhaps this current jurisprudence flows also from the understandable fears of religious persecution of the type practiced immediately before and during World War II, when the Nazis nearly succeeded in exterminating European Jewry. It must be more than a coincidence that many in favor of barring all state exercise of even nonsectarian religion have been Jewish.[506] Still, this strand of constitutional theory appears to depart rather radically from the more conservative traditional jurisprudence espoused in Frankfurter's *Barnette* dissent.

It must be said, however, that the aspiration of this brand of modern constitutional theory is a noble and valid one—to protect the rights of every individual in America to practice the religion of his or her choice, without the state coercing anyone to participate in any religious exercise that offends his or her conscience. That there are Jewish roots to this highly individualistic

167

theory is suggested not only by the long history of the importance of the individual and the individual conscience in traditional Jewish thought, but also by the Jewish backgrounds of many of the most prominent modern liberal scholars.[507]

Many leaders of the American Civil Liberties Union—the high priests of individualism, secularism, and noncoercion in American constitutional thought—and many plaintiffs in establishment clause cases,[508] have been Jewish. Indeed, it has even been suggested that for "[m]ost American Jews" the greatest source of values is not Judaism itself, but "the dominant secular liberal culture." According to Dennis Prager, a leading conservative Jewish theorist:

> . . . many Jews believe that all they need to do in order to formulate a Jewish position is: 1) Note that "Judaism teaches compassion." 2) Take the liberal position, which is the one that always seems to be the most compassionate. 3) Label that position "Jewish."[509]

Perhaps the style of modern American self-actualization constitutional jurisprudence—which is here a sort of jurisprudence of tolerance—with its abhorrence of coercion of individuals, flows naturally from the experience of the holocaust, and from the desire that it never be allowed to happen again. But the coercion rationale for opposing state-sanctioned nonsectarian prayer or religious exercise ought to be recognized as not everywhere valid. As Felix Frankfurter's dissent in *Barnette* demonstrates, there are other values besides total freedom from coercion in education that deserve constitutional protection. All education is, in some sense coercion, and if nonsectarian prayer has a role in moral education, then its value ought to be recognized, and, it would seem, constitutionally protected.

It is time to realize that not every school prayer carries with it the threat of religious persecution. If, as the framers believed, it is impossible to inculcate morality without religion, and if the paramount problem facing many public school students today is an almost total absence of meaningful moral guidance, perhaps our

168

current rejection of religion in the public sphere has gone too far.[510] The plague of teenage pregnancies among unwed mothers, and the results of that plague—dysfunctional families, unsupervised youth, the temptations of the life of the street, drug use, violent crime, and death itself—are plainly moral and not economic problems.[511] They demand moral solutions, and moral solutions, the Federalists tried to teach us, will not come without attention to religion.

The desire to protect the individual's freedom in the secular strand of current First Amendment theory is often coupled with a disturbing absolutism[512] and an inability to see that constitutional principles must be evaluated against a background of original purposes and beliefs: To wit, individualism has its limits in constitutional law, there are other purposes that a constitutional system must serve, and, ultimately, freedom of religion is not the same thing as freedom *from* religion. When the ACLU champions the cause of Nazis marching in Skokie, a town where many holocaust survivors lived,[513] and when a rabbi is prevented from delivering a nonsectarian prayer in Rhode Island,[514] perhaps it can be recognized that secular individualism has reached its limits.

I can remember, as a Jewish child in the fifties in a public school in Virginia where a Christian prayer opened the school day, feeling oddly left out, and feeling that the Jesus invoked as savior was not mine.[515] It was, of course, a not particularly pleasant feeling. When the Supreme Court threw out public school prayer, it must have done so in the belief that no one should, because of the faith of his or her ancestors, have to feel like an outsider in American society. If nonsectarian prayer returns to the schools, the children of agnostics and atheists will experience the unease that I did. There are worse things than youthful unease, however. Perhaps it is significant that there has been "a growing number of [conservative religious] Jews who wonder whether the recitation of an innocuous prayer in the school or a moment of silence really hurt the Jewish interest."[516] Moreover, feelings of exclusion and oddity are—alas—a normal part of growing up. And not even a majority of the Justices on the Supreme Court can banish them.

The use of balancing tests in religious jurisprudence is as

suspicious as it is in any other area of the Constitution, but it makes some sense to trade the unease of a few youthful unbelievers (or their parents) to save the very lives of others. If religion and morality in the public schools might repair some of the damage of some broken families—and perhaps even prevent the forming of others—isn't the return of morality and religion to the public schools fully justified? Could this be what a growing number of American believers of many faiths are increasingly coming to understand? And doesn't the correspondence of this belief with the original understanding of the Constitution make it all but irresistable?

E. The "Great Trilogy" of the Warren Court

The jurisprudential revolution that began with the Court's opinions in the *West Coast Hotel v. Parrish* and *NLRB v. Jones & Laughlin Steel* cases, and continued with the flag salute and school prayer cases, accelerated to even more alarming levels during the tenure of the great liberal activist Chief Justice, Earl Warren. He wrote the majority opinions for a mighty trilogy of cases, involving politics, criminal law, and school desegregation.

REYNOLDS V. SIMS

The landmark case in politics was *Reynolds v. Sims* (1964).[517] In an opinion written by the Chief Justice, the Court decided, by a vote of 8 to 1, that the only valid basis for apportionment of either branch of a state legislature was population. It might well be argued that *Baker v. Carr* (1962),[518] the first case opening the federal courts to challenges to the drafting of state legislative districts, is the most important of the reapportionment cases. Indeed Chief Justice Warren was reported to have called *Baker* "the most vital decision" during his time on the Court. He also is said to have stated that the "apportionment revolution" that *Baker v. Carr* initiated was "the most important achievement of

170

his Court."[519] Nevertheless, *Reynolds* is here treated as the most important of the reapportionment cases because Warren wrote the majority opinion in *Reynolds*, because *Reynolds* is the case that is usually remembered for establishing the "one person, one vote" principle, and because it was part of the six cases decided in June 1964 involving the legislatures of Alabama, New York, Maryland, Virginia, Delaware, and Colorado, which six cases together "effectively declared the apportionment of every state legislature unconstitutional."[520] It is also noteworthy because of Justice Harlan's lone and powerful dissent.

According to the Chief Justice's opinion in *Reynolds*, "Legislators represent people, not trees or acres. Legislators are elected by voters, not farms or cities or economic interests."[521] This meant that states could not do as the Constitution itself did, that is have one house that represented population (like the U.S. House of Representatives), and another house that represented the traditional political divisions of the polity (like the U.S. Senate). Thus hundreds of years of tradition in which one branch of state legislatures, which corresponded to the Senate, and in which representation had traditionally been allocated on the basis of counties or other political subdivisions, could no longer continue.

The *Reynolds* majority appears to have believed that state legislatures had been grossly malapportioned in order to preserve rule by entrenched incumbents or elites, and untying the Gordian knot by the "one person one vote" rule was the only way to proceed. The majority based its opinion on the Fourteenth Amendment's equal protection clause, which provided that no state shall deprive any person of the "equal protection of the laws." It was the belief of the majority that unequal representation for equal populations, even if it was limited to only one branch of the legislature, was unequal protection as well.

Justice Harlan's dissent makes clear that there were two profound problems with the majority opinion. The first, in keeping with the principle of original understanding, was that there was no historical basis for suggesting that the framers of the Fourteenth Amendment believed that they were giving the Supreme Court authority to order state reapportionment. There was no evidence that the Fourteenth Amendment's framers intended for the federal courts to trifle with the representational basis of the bicameral houses of state legislators. The framers of the Fourteenth Amendment, as already indicated,[522] intended it to protect the civil rights—for example, the right to vote—of the newly freed blacks. Further, the second section of the Fourteenth Amendment itself explicitly provided a remedy for states refusing to recognize the right of the freed slaves to participate in the political process—a reduction in the state's representation in Congress.[523] According to one of the oldest legal maxims, *expressio unius est exclusio alterius* (to set forth one is to exclude the others).[524] This venerable principle, when applied to the case, meant that the only manner in which the federal government could deal with perceived state recalcitrance on reapportionment was through altering a state's congressional representation.

The second problem with the majority's opinion, according to Harlan, and flowing from the majority's departure from the historical understanding of the Fourteenth Amendment in order to promote radical reform of state legislatures, was that the majority was going far beyond the federal judicial role. The majority was, in short, doing fundamental damage to what might be regarded as the most important principle of the federal Constitution itself, dual sovereignty, or federalism. According to the principles of federalism, which were instrumental in securing the passage of the Constitution itself, the federal government was supposed to be restricted to concerns properly of national scope, and the states were left free to operate in all other political spheres.

A review of the writings of the Antifederalists, the opponents of the Constitution in 1787–89, makes clear their fear that the federal government, and, in particular, the federal courts, might obliterate or reduce to insignificance the state governments.[525] Indeed, it was to counter that fear that Federalists such as James Madison threw their support behind the Bill of Rights—the First Ten Amendments—passed in 1791.[526] Justice Harlan was concerned that the majority in *Reynolds* "cut deeply into the fabric of American federalism,"[527] and, as did Justice Frankfurter in his *Barnette* dissent, Harlan cautioned "against judicial activism to cure perceived social ills."[528] Harlan quite correctly stated, "The Constitution is not a panacea for every blot upon the public welfare, nor should this Court, ordained as a judicial body, be thought of as a general haven for reform movements."[529]

Harlan's magisterial dissent in *Reynolds* obviously did not persuade Chief Justice Warren or his majority, which appears to have been motivated by an extremely egalitarian philosophy[530] that went considerably beyond that of the framers. The framers, at least if Samuel Chase and James Wilson can be taken as typical,[531] were concerned about the wisdom of universal suffrage and believed that only those with a significant property stake in the community could be counted on to vote wisely and in the best interests of all. To allow the federal government to meddle in state government to the extent of dictating apportionment on the basis of one man, one vote would have seemed more than a little surprising, as disturbing, in fact, as the abstract follies of the French Revolution.

Baker v. Carr and *Reynolds* reversed the constitutional jurisprudence established in Justice Frankfurter's majority opinion in *Colegrave v. Green* (1946),[532] decided sixteen years before *Baker v. Carr*. In *Colegrave* the four-person judicial majority refused to invalidate state apportionment decisions giving Illinois both the largest and the smallest congressional districts in the nation. Illinois had refused to do congressional apportionment based on population, and the plaintiffs thought that this violated the Constitution's equal protection clause. Justice Frankfurter explained that apportionment was a matter exclusively for the state authorities. For the federal courts to meddle in this area, Frankfurter explained in an important metaphor, would be improperly to involve itself in the "political thicket."[533] This was the same notion he had expressed in his dissent in *Barnette*—that the federal courts should not excessively meddle in state politics.

Sixteen years later *Baker v. Carr* simply overruled *Colegrave* by holding that apportionment was an "equal protection issue." Frankfurter wrote a cogent dissent in *Baker*, reiterating at length what he had said in his *Colegrave* majority opinion. In it Frankfurter railed against the Court's repudiation of his *Colegrave* opinion and against the *Baker* majority's "massive repudiation of the experience of our whole past in asserting destructively novel judicial power demands."[534] In retrospect it seems astonishing that the nation was willing relatively quiescently to accept the Supreme Court's amazing about-face on the federalizing of state reapportionment, to accept that the Court could dictate what amounted to the virtual restructuring of most of the state legislatures. Perhaps the explanation is that such a restructuring on the basis of population benefited the Democratic party, which still enjoyed the support of a majority of voters and at the time controlled the presidency and the Congress.

Perhaps too it is no coincidence that since then the Republicans have been substantially outnumbered in the House of Representatives and have only controlled the Senate for the briefest of periods, even though Republican victories in presidential elections have been fairly common. Could it be that the Warren Court's efforts at promoting democracy have only perpetuated Democratic incumbency?

MIRANDA V. ARIZONA

The second of the Warren Court's great trilogy was a case also infused with a kind of egalitarianism, but in the most unlikely of contexts. This was the notorious *Miranda v. Arizona* (1966),[535] 5–4 decision. Warren's opinion in *Miranda* required state and local police, upon arrest of a suspect, and prior to interrogation, to inform him that "You have the right to remain silent, anything you say can and will be held against you in a court of law; you have the right to an attorney, and if you cannot afford one, one will be appointed for you. . . ."[536]

In his opinion for the majority in *Miranda* Chief Justice Warren found that this warning was needed from the police because to interrogate a suspect without informing him of his constitutional rights was itself a violation of those rights. Of course, the "rights" protected by the warning requirement in *Miranda* were themselves a product of the Warren Court judicial discretion

174

using "selective incorporation" into the Fourteenth Amendment from the Fifth[537] and Sixth Amendments.[538]

If these earlier Warren Court opinions, applying "selective incorporation" of the Fifth and Sixth Amendments into the Fourteenth, were dubious acts running against the notions of original understanding, then *Miranda* only served to compound the error. It piled original misunderstanding upon original misunderstanding, to become, as it were, judicial usurpation on stilts. It was not that the Warren Court majority did not act from noble motives. The majority was probably worried about police brutality, particularly against minorities in the South. This was the era of the great civil rights marches in the South, and an era when Southern sheriffs with bull horns, dogs, and rubber hoses entered popular mythology as stock villains.

In order to discourage such official misconduct, the Court decided that it would let defendants in such tainted proceedings escape conviction. Thus the Court ruled in *Miranda* that if suspects had been interrogated without being given their requisite warnings as to their rights, any fruits of that interrogation, such as confessions or further leads, could not be used in evidence at their trials. Because "the constable blundered," in other words, the suspect would go free.[539]

The majority appears to have reasoned that allowing an occasional guilty suspect his freedom was better than risking false confessions obtained through trickery, torture, or worse. Summarizing the facts before it in the several cases decided at the same time as *Miranda*, the majority opinion stated:

> In each of these cases, the defendant was thrust into an unfamiliar atmosphere and run through menacing police interrogation procedures. The potentiality for compulsion is forcefully apparent, for example, in *Miranda*, where the indigent Mexican defendant was a seriously disturbed individual with pronounced sexual fantasies, and in *Stewart* [a companion case], in which the defendant was an indigent Los Angeles Negro who had dropped out of school in the sixth grade. To be sure, the records do not evince overt physical

175

coercion or patent psychological ploys. The fact remains that in none of these cases did the officers undertake to afford appropriate safeguards at the outset of the interrogation to insure that the [confession] statements were truly the product of free choice.

. . . The current practice of incommunicado interrogation is at odds with one of our Nation's most cherished principles—that the individual may not be compelled to incriminate himself. Unless adequate protective devices are employed to dispel the compulsion inherent in custodial surroundings, no statement obtained from the defendant can truly be the product of his free choice.[540]

Justice Harlan, again in dissent, this time writing for himself and Justices Stewart and White, reiterated his concern that the Court, through its exercises in selective incorporation, was venturing into territory where it had no legitimate business. As Frankfurter had done in his *Barnette* dissent, and as Frankfurter had done in his *Colgrave* majority opinion, Harlan explained that the *Miranda* majority was unwisely inserting the federal courts where they did not belong. As Harlan stated, "Viewed as a choice based on pure policy, these new rules [dictated by the majority] prove to be a highly debatable, if not one-sided, appraisal of the competing interests, imposed over widespread objection, at the very time when judicial restraint is most called for by the circumstances."[541] Harlan continued by suggesting:

What the Court largely ignores is that its rules impair, if they will not eventually serve wholly to frustrate, an instrument of law enforcement [confessions secured through custodial interrogation] that has long and quite reasonably been thought worth the price paid for it. There can be little doubt that the Court's new code would markedly decrease the number of confessions . . .

How much harm this decision will inflict on law enforcement cannot fairly be predicted with accuracy. . . . We do know that some crimes cannot be solved without confessions, that ample expert testimony attests to their importance in crime control, and that the Court is taking a real risk with society's welfare in imposing its new regime on the country. The social costs of crime are too great to call the new rules anything but a hazardous experimentation.[542]

Harlan thus stressed that the *Miranda* majority was hardly capable of promulgating a wise code of procedure for police, as this was a task for legislators advised by law enforcement professionals, and not for the heavy-handed efforts of courts.[543] If carefully articulated police procedures were to be spelled out, Harlan suggested, it ought to be done by a body more capable of weighing the competing concerns of law enforcement and civil rights of suspects, such as the state legislatures.[544]

Led by the Chief Justice himself, the Warren Court majority was not troubled by assuming this legislative role. The majority apparently found it easy to see where fair procedures lay, and it did not hesitate so to direct the police. This attitude came in for Harlan's sharpest criticism in his *Miranda* dissent. Harlan showed that the facts in the case were clear. It was a cruel rape of an eighteen-year-old girl, and there was an eyewitness identification of Miranda by his brutalized victim. This fingering of the suspect came immediately before Miranda's interrogation. Harlan lamented that Miranda's oral and written confessions, which Harlan did not view as the products of coercion, were now inadmissible:

> One is entitled to feel astonished that the Constitution can be read to produce this result. These confessions were obtained during brief, daytime questioning conducted by two officers and unmarked by any traditional indicia of coercion. They assured a conviction for a brutal and unsettling crime, for which the police had and quite possibly could obtain little evidence other than the victim's identifications, evidence which is frequently unreliable. There was, in sum, a legitimate purpose, no perceptible unfairness, and certainly little risk of injustice in the interrogation. Yet the resulting confessions, and the responsible course of police practice they represent, are to be sacrificed to the Court's own finespun conception of fairness which I seriously doubt is shared by many thinking citizens in this country.[545]

Here too, alas, Harlan's sentiments went unheeded. In a line of decisions flowing in the same jurisprudential stream as *Miranda*, the Warren and Burger Courts went on to elaborate a jurisprudence of the "exclusionary rule." In case after case the Court made clear that if any evidence had been obtained through interrogations, searches, or other procedures that did not comply with the increasingly burdensome strictures the federal courts were imposing on state law enforcement officers, such evidence could not be used against defendants. An increasing number of convictions began to be overturned.

The beginning of this particular strain of criminal procedural jurisprudence was an earlier Warren Court decision, *Mapp v. Ohio* (1961).[546] In *Mapp*, five Justices decided on the "selective incorporation" of the exclusionary rule. The Court held in *Mapp* that the already existing exclusionary rule, which applied to federal government officials because of the Fourth Amendment's prohibition on unreasonable searches and seizures conducted by the federal government, ought to be incorporated into the Fourteenth Amendment, against state officials as well. In dissent, Harlan, joined by Justice Frankfurter and Justice Whittaker, protested against the use of the incorporation doctrine and the extension of the exclusionary rule to the states.

Miranda, Mapp, and the Warren Court's other criminal procedure cases thus illustrate the same problem of the federal courts intruding into the traditional territory of state governments as does *Reynolds v. Sims*, and ought to have been regarded as unacceptable simply on those grounds. We appear to have been virtually alone among Western industrialized nations in employing such a finespun set of rules of criminal procedure, and in thus hamstringing law enforcement officials.[547]

Following decades of criticism on this issue, the Supreme Court has recently begun a retreat from the "exclusionary rule," or "fruit of the poisonous tree" doctrine, as it is also called. In perhaps the most significant steps, the Court has recently ruled that unconstitutionally seized evidence will not be suppressed if, "hypothetically, the police would have 'inevitably discovered' the evidence even if the unconstitutional search had not occurred."[548] In addition to this "harmless error" rule, the Court has also indicated some receptiveness to ruling that even though the search violates the fine-spun constitutional strictures of its criminal procedure jurisprudence, evidence will not be excluded in cases where it can be demonstrated that the police involved believed in "good faith" that they had complied with the Constitution.[549] At long last Harlan's views may be on the way to being vindicated.

The criminal procedure cases of the Warren Court were among those that initially aroused the most hostility and led to the "Impeach Earl Warren" bumper stickers. Criminal procedure reforms by the Court appear to have generated little public reaction, however, for police forces have either internalized changes such as the *Miranda* warnings, or recent decisions have neutralized their deleterious effects. These days the problem for law enforcement appears to be simply coping with the increasing violence and sophistication of organized gang activity, particularly in cases dealing with drugs, and with the chronically inadequate supply of funding for law enforcement efforts. New federal anticrime measures such as the Racketeer-Influenced and Corrupt Organizatons Act (RICO) give prosecutors needed tools such as the ability to confiscate ill-gotten gains or assets used in criminal activities, and the issue appears to have shifted from procedural hamstringing to supplying sufficient manpower. As a matter of substantive law, *Miranda* and its progeny may not now be so troublesome as Harlan feared, although the broad-ranging judicial policy-making procedure he excoriated in his dissent in that case and in *Reynolds* remains profoundly troubling.

BROWN V. BOARD OF EDUCATION AND ITS AFTERMATH

Although the lasting substantive effect of *Miranda* has proven to be insubstantial, this has not been true of the last of the great trilogy of Warren Court cases, *Brown v. Board of Education of Topeka* (1954).[550] *Brown* was the first of the trilogy to be decided, but it is here treated last in recognition of its supreme status. For many years, if American laymen knew of any one Supreme Court case, it was *Brown*. In recent years, however, an equal number may be aware of *Roe v. Wade*, of which more shortly. In *Brown* the issue was whether the late nineteenth-century rule of *Plessy v. Ferguson* (1896),[551] which allowed "separate but equal" public

179

facilities for the white and black races, ought to be allowed to stand. The constitutional provision to be interpreted was the Fourteenth Amendment's "equal protection" clause, which forbids the denying of any person "the equal protection of the laws."

As indicated earlier, the "equal protection" clause of the Fourteenth Amendment, when passed, was obviously designed to aid the newly emancipated slaves, but it may have meant little more than that the freedmen were to have the same ability to use the courts to enforce their property and contract rights as did whites.[552] As one recent commentator, Michael Kent Curtis, has explained, the Fourteenth Amendment was passed in order to ensure that the Civil Rights Act of 1866 could not be invalidated. The civil rights protected by the 1866 act were "the right to own property and make contracts and to appear as a witness in court to protect those rights. Equality with respect to civil rights meant equal status in the legal relations of the private economy, coupled with the right to enforce that equal status."[553] Nevertheless, by the time of *Plessy* it had become clear that the equal protection clause could be taken to mean something more. It had become a requirement that when the government affirmatively provided a public service to any of its citizens, it could not discriminate in the provision of those services on the basis of race.

On the other hand, *Plessy*, as indicated, stood for the proposition that providing equal services to persons of different races did not necessarily mean providing them in the same place at the same time. By the time of *Plessy*, the practice of racially segregated public schools was widespread in both the North and South. Particularly in the South racially segregated schools were soon joined by racially segregated drinking fountains and racially segregated seating on buses and other forms of public transportation. In *Plessy* itself the issue was the constitutionality of a Louisiana statute that required railroads to provide "equal but separate accommodations for the white and colored races." The statute was upheld, and the "separate but equal" rule entered into constitutional law.

By the time of *Brown*, the *Plessy* rule, attacked through a coordinated series of lawsuits brought by the legal arm of the NAACP, among others, had begun to erode. The most prominent of these decisions, which chipped away at the *Plessy* rule, was the Court's opinion in *Sweatt v. Painter* (1950)[554] holding that students could not be separated by race and placed in different state-operated law schools. The *Sweatt* Court explained that part of what made law schools what they were was the ability to interact with all class-mates and graduates beginning in law schools and continuing for the rest of a lawyer's professional career. If law students were segregated by race, of course, this could not happen.

This point was further developed in *Sweatt*'s companion case of *McLaurin v. Oklahoma State Regents for Higher Education* (1950),[555] a Fourteenth Amendment equal protection challenge to Oklahoma's policy of complying with a federal court order to admit blacks to its state law school. Oklahoma authorities had also sought to comply with an Oklahoma statute which mandated graduate education "upon a segregated basis." Pursuant to Oklahoma's policy, the black plaintiff in the case, a law student at the University of Oklahoma School of Law, had been required to sit in a classroom row marked "reserved for Negroes." He had been required to study at a separate desk in the library and to eat at a separate table in the cafeteria. Continuing the reasoning in *Sweatt*, the *McLaurin* Court ruled that such segregation imposed on McLaurin violated the Fourteenth Amendment. He was enti-tled, pursuant to the "equal protection" clause, to "receive the same treatment . . . as students of other races."[556]

Taken together, *Sweatt* and *McLaurin* stand for the proposi-tion that as far as law school education is concerned, much of what constitutes a satisfactory professional education is the stu-dents' ability to interact with all of their fellows—black or white. All must be permitted, on an integrated basis, to engage in the spirited argumentation and disputation that characterize law school classrooms. Marking out and separating students by race in separate schools or separate geographical parts of classrooms or facilities impermissibly obstructs and frustrates the essential inter-change among colleagues in the legal educational mission.

Following the victories at the professional school level in *Sweatt* and *McLaurin*, the stage was set for *Brown* itself, a challenge to

181

separation by race in the public primary and secondary schools; a challenge orchestrated by the Legal Defense Fund, the legal arm of the NAACP, then led by Thurgood Marshall. Marshall was eventually to become the first black Justice on the Supreme Court, and, of course, the man whom Clarence Thomas replaced.[557] Through the machinations of the new Chief Justice, Earl Warren, the opinion of the Court was unanimous in *Brown*. Warren crafted an opinion that skirted doctrinal difficulties, and avoided sensitive questions of appropriate remedies, in order to convince other members of the Court not to dissent. Warren believed that on the sensitive public issue of public school integration it was important to present the country with a unified Court.[558] This was no mean feat for the new Chief Justice, because, strictly speaking, as a matter of principled constitutional law, the *Brown* opinion is almost certainly indefensible.

Warren infused his *Brown* opinion with a number of suspect propositions concerning the importance of history and the original understanding of the Constitution to the Court's decision-making. For example, contrary to what is asserted generally in this book, Warren claimed that "We cannot turn the clock back to 1868, when the amendment was adopted, or even to 1896 when *Plessy . . .* was written."[559] He indicated that it was futile to search for the one true meaning of the Fourteenth Amendment, partly because, in his opinion, the historical record of the meaning of the amendment's language was unclear, and partly because the field of public education had become important in ways not contemplated by the framers of the amendment.[560]

Warren simply skipped over the evidence that the Fourteenth Amendment did have a clear and limited purpose—to secure the provision of equal access to the courts for the enforcement of the newly freed slaves' property and contract rights. Instead, Warren declared that the Fourteenth Amendment had now to be construed as guaranteeing that if a state government undertakes to provide a service—public education—to any of its citizens, it must provide such a service without discriminating on the basis of race. Then, remarkably, Warren went on to hold that equality could never be achieved in the setting of an elementary school where the races were separated.

Citing the law school cases, *Sweatt* and *McLaurin*, Warren claimed that separating black schoolchildren from white was harmful to the black children, because it generated a fatal feeling of inferiority:

> To separate them from others of similar age and qualifications solely because of their race generates a feeling of inferiority as to their status in the community that may affect their hearts and minds in a way unlikely ever to be undone.[561]

To support this proposition Warren turned not to law, or to the pedagogy of the law school classroom that drove the decisions in *Sweatt* and *McLaurin*, but to the emerging field of social psychology. To support his language about the "hearts and minds" of the black schoolchildren, Warren cited, in *Brown*'s infamous Footnote 11, the work of several social psychologists. These academics claimed that their research demonstrated that forced segregation produced psychological distress and impaired learning abilities for black children.[562]

Brown fails as good constitutional law because it ignores the original understanding of the Fourteenth Amendment. Other grave difficulties also afflict the opinion. Without the *psychological* claim that forced segregation denies equal protection, *Brown* makes no sense. If the case is about providing equal educational opportunity, the psychological data is crucial.

One federal district court judge later ruled, on the basis of psychological authority *contrary* to that in *Brown*, that segregation could be upheld on the basis of its psychological *benefits* to black children. That judge was reversed by a federal court of appeals, and the Supreme Court refused to review the case.[563] Equal or stronger data from social psychologists than that used in *Brown* might actually suggest that blacks could find it easier to learn and progress educationally in a single-race environment, where they were free from racial tensions and strife, and where black pride could be used to enhance the educational experience. But for whatever reason, the Supreme Court was not prepared to retreat from its order to end segregated public schools.

It appears, then, that what the Court was really up to in *Brown* was to promote a racial assimilationist ideal that it apparently was unable or unwilling to support as a matter of constitutional law, but which seemed to the Court wise policy.[564] Perhaps the ruling in *Brown*—that states could not maintain school systems in which the law directed that students be separated by race—might have been supportable if the Court had been willing to embrace the general ideal of a "color-blind" Constitution (developed in the following chapter). There *is* a powerful argument to be made that such a rationale for *Brown* makes sense, even as a matter of following the original understanding. Thus, Justice Hugo Black, in 1966, remarked that "In my judgment the holding in *Brown* against racial discrimination was compelled by the purpose of the framers of the Thirteenth, Fourteenth, and Fifteenth Amendments completely to outlaw discrimination against people because of their race or color."[565] The only problem with this view of the Thirteenth, Fourteenth, and Fifteenth Amendments, as suggested earlier, is that "the legislative history of the Fourteenth Amendment 'rather clearly' demonstrated 'that it was not expected in 1866 to apply to segregation.' "[566]

One might surmount this problem of original intention with a sophisticated argument about how "original understanding" ought to proceed at a great level of generality. Thus, even if the framers of the Fourteenth Amendment did not mean to outlaw official segregation, if they did have a broad principle of racial equality in mind, then as social circumstances changed the application of that principle might change. According to this view, then, by 1954 officially segregated schools might come within the ambit of the framers' broad principle of racial equality and thus be prohibited. As the great constitutional scholar Alexander Bickel explained in making this point, there was "an awareness on the part of [the framers of the Fourteenth Amendment] that it was a *Constitution* they were writing, which led to a choice of language capable of growth," and Bickel continued, "the record of history, properly understood, left the way open to, in fact, invited, a decision based on the moral and material state of the nation in 1954, not 1866."[567]

But this rationale involving broad general principles and changed circumstances would permit almost unlimited malleability to constitutional decision-making, and would give Justices an intolerable amount of discretion.[568] It would fly in the face of the judicial conservatism of Frankfurter. But a "living Constitution," one of infinite malleability *was* the document that was being invoked in *Brown*, and—it must be stressed—for whatever reason, the Court was not willing even to embrace the theory of a color-blind Constitution in the case. In any event, what followed *Brown* became even more problematic.

Brown was followed by the so-called *Brown II* (1955) decision in which the Court ordered the dismantling of state-mandated segregated school systems "with all deliberate speed."[569] It was also followed by the even more controversial *Green v. County School Board of New Kent* (1968).[570] In *Green*, the Court decided that a school district's ending racial discrimination in school assignments was not enough to comply with the mandate of *Brown*. It held that "freedom of choice" plans were not acceptable, and that compliance with *Brown*, "at least in formerly state-segregated . . . systems, could . . . only be demonstrated by the production of schools with racial mixes reflecting that to be found in the school age population."[571] This meant that instead of approaching school assignments in a color-blind manner, school administrators in systems which had formerly discriminated on the basis of race were now forced to *continue* to make school assignments on the basis of race. If *Brown* might have been supportable on the theory of a "color-blind" Constitution, no such rationale was available for *Green*. It was purely indefensible as principled constitutional law.

As Texas law professor Lino Graglia has recently pointed out, this "crucial move" by the Court in *Green* "changed the *Brown* prohibition of segregation and all racial discrimination by government into a requirement of integration and racial discrimination by government."[572] Graglia has shown that in a series of decisions finding that "compulsory racial discrimination" was required in employment as well as education cases, the Supreme Court completely perverted the language of the nation's civil rights laws. These laws prohibited making employment decisions on the basis of race. But the Court, anxious to ensure employment of minorities in proportion to their numbers in the general population, *contrary to the text of the laws and to representations made at their passage with regard to their color-blind character*, construed the civil rights laws to prohibit making employment decisions without taking race into account.[573]

Senator Hubert Humphrey, a key backer of one of the civil rights laws involved, Title VII of the 1964 Civil Rights Act, claimed that "[T]itle VII does not require an employer to achieve any sort of racial balance in his work force by giving preferential treatment to any individual or group." Humphrey "even promised on the floor of the Senate that he would physically eat the paper the bill was written on if it were ever used to require corrective hiring preferences."[574] Humphrey died before he could be forced to take his unsavory meal. He and his fellow sponsors of the bill tried to make it clear in Title VII that "Nothing contained in this title shall be interpreted to require any employer . . . to grant preferential treatment to any individual or to any group because of race, color, religon, sex or national origin of such individual or group on account of an imbalance. . . ."[575] But this inconvenient text, and its clear embrace of the notion of a "color-blind" Constitution was dismissed by the Supreme Court in a series of decisions giving permission for racial discrimination to achieve racial balance. The Court's theory seems to have been, the clear statutory language to the contrary, that two wrongs can make a right.

The key Supreme Court case in this regard was *Griggs v. Duke Power Co.* (1971),[576] in which the Court held that ostensibly neutral testing practices for employees were unlawful if they operated to maintain the effects of past discrimination. The defendants' lack of intent racially to discriminate in administering the tests was held to be irrelevant. The Court went on to hold in *Griggs* that where tests had a "disparate impact" upon minorities, the employer had the burden of proving that "business necessity" justified the testing practices. Placing the burden on employers led many to believe that the only way in which they could avoid costly and uncertain lawsuits was to impose racial quotas. Although the Supreme Court reversed *Griggs*'s holding on the burden of proof in *Ward's Cove Packing Co. v. Atonio* (1989),[577] the Civil Rights Act of 1991 reversed *Ward's Cove*, placing the burden back on employers, and making quotas once again virtually inevitable. Just as the so-called Religious Freedom Restoration Act overturned a return to sound jurisprudence on the part of the Court, and proceeded to codify error, so too did the so-called Civil Rights Act of 1991 fly in the face of sensible "color-blind" constitutional decision-making.

The culmination of all of this, as far as education was concerned, was a decision rendered the same year as *Griggs*, 1971. This was the even more controversial "school-busing" decision, another case concerned with official racial discrimination to achieve racial balance. *Swann v. Charlotte-Mecklenburg Board of Education* (1971),[578] the most important desegregation case since *Brown*, was a unanimous opinion by the new Chief Justice, Warren Burger. In *Swann* the Court held that in ordering compliance with *Brown*'s constitutional command to desegregate schools, it was an appropriate remedy to use mathematical formulas to achieve racial balance across the entire geographic area of a school system. Pursuant to implementing the mathematical formulas, the *Swann* Court held, it was permissible to force students to ride school buses in order to achieve racial balance. This would be permitted even if the forced busing ended, for the system in question, the nation's traditional practice of neighborhood-based public schools.

Said the Chief Justice in *Swann*, "Desegregation plans cannot be limited to the walk-in school."[579] Thus, in the service of achieving their goal of racial balance which the Supreme Court appeared to believe necessary for assimilationist education, the members of the Court, in effect, ended the ideal of neighborhood schools for most of the nation's urban centers. Professor Graglia, perhaps the foremost critic of the Court's school busing

187

decisions, called *Swann* "the *Dred Scott* of the twentieth century, the outstanding example of improper judicial behavior resulting in a decision of disastrous consequences."[580]

Brown, Griggs, and *Swann* are firm signposts of the beginning of an extraordinary era in which the opinions of social scientists and modern social planners became far more important than the constitutional understanding of the framers or of long-standing practices pursuant to that understanding. It was not long before the dubious logic of *Brown* was even more dubiously extended to forbid tracking according to scores on aptitude tests in the District of Columbia schools. The U. S. Court of Appeals for the District of Columbia ordered the end of tracking, because such tracking resulted in disproportionate numbers of minority students in the lower academic tracks.[581]

Brown is now the most sacred decision in the pantheon of great Supreme Court cases, and even conservatives appear constrained to praise it. Thus Robert Bork, in a book whose principal purpose is to embrace judicial restraint and condemn the use of the courts to formulate policy in an extraconstitutional manner, nevertheless appeared to agree with the holding in *Brown.* Bork calls *Brown* "a great and correct decision,"[582] although he concedes that the *Brown* decision was "supported by a very weak opinion." In its place Bork tries to construct a different rationale, still reading the Fourteenth Amendment broadly to condemn desegregated schools. This is probably the weakest part of Bork's analysis of constitutional law. As did Earl Warren's opinion in *Brown,* Bork's effort flies in the face of the understanding of the Fourteenth Amendment's text at the time it was passed.[583]

But whatever the correctness of *Brown*'s legal and constitutional reasoning, it is undeniable that *Brown* had salutary effects in ending some racial discrimination. It is also properly credited with facilitating the passage of the Civil Rights Act of 1964 and the Voting Rights Act of 1965, among other measures.[584] *Brown* also led to an era, particularly in the South, which saw the end of legally sanctioned segregation in public accommodation, and may well have contributed to a greater willingness on the part of Americans to move toward the *Brown* Court's assimilationist ideal. In addition, it cannot be denied that state-sponsored seg-regation by race was an evil abomination that had to end if traditional American values of liberty and political equality were to continue to be taken seriously.

Nevertheless, if *Brown* was, after all, a social experiment of dubious constitutionality, honesty requires that we acknowledge that it has had its tragic aspects as well. Probably the most disturb-ing of these, and something that should serve as a caution for those who would advocate judges' functioning as social policy makers, is that the decision ultimately may have badly harmed those it was originally designed to protect. Putting aside the problem that the Fourteenth Amendment was probably *not* framed with any regard to public education, much less with an inflexible requirement for racially integrated public education, or enforced racial discrimination to achieve racial balance in the workforce,[585] the Court's assimilationist vision may have been disastrously short-sighted. *Brown* appears to have been written to better the education of black schoolchildren, particularly black schoolchildren of modest means. The attempt to integrate public education in large urban school districts, and to bring better education to disadvantaged minorities, has failed, and *Brown* and its progeny are partly to blame.

As Lino Graglia has stated, forced busing has managed "to increase, not decrease, racial separation, first in the public schools and then in the cities."[586] Perhaps, then, the *Brown* and *Swann* Courts ought to bear some of the responsibility for the ruin of inner city public education, and, one suspects, for the concomitant pain and suffering of many lower-class urban black families.

The authors of *Brown*, even if they were competent to assess the psychological studies on which they relied, do not appear to have had the competence to assess the sociological implications of the decision. They responded only to an attractive assimilationist ideology. They were unable to see that their direction to end dual school systems in the nation's urban centers would, very soon, result in unitary school systems populated principally by the mi-nority the Court had sought to assimilate. These unitary school

189

systems were eventually to become much more expensive and much less educationally successful than what they had replaced.[587]

Indeed, the real problem is probably one of class, not race. It is a problem perhaps of social psychology, but not in the way the Warren Court thought. White middle-class parents probably feared that their own children would either be threatened by working-class or welfare minority children, or that the level of education offered their children would suffer as teachers' time was consumed in attempting to bring poor children up to the level of their more privileged classmates. White children, in the 1960s and 1970s, left urban public school systems in droves. Alternatively, dismayed that their children would be spending long periods of time riding buses across vast and increasingly dangerous urban areas because of the courts' misguided orders that such measures be undertaken in order to achieve more racial balance, members of the middle class with school-age children fled and continue to flee to safer havens of private schools or of the suburbs.[588]

Paradoxically, as the idea of racial integration and affirmative action became more politically and culturally fashionable, the best of the black students were sought after by private schools, and as these most frequently came from the wealthiest and most stable minority families, those left behind in the urban systems were increasingly from the most unstable of homes and the hardest to teach.

Just as the black middle class was increasingly able to find its way into exclusive private schools, or to move to the suburbs as racially restrictive covenants were declared unenforceable,[589] so too did middle-class blacks find it increasingly easier to assume more prestigious positions in American industry, commerce, and education. The result of the exodus of such middle and upper income blacks from urban areas was to remove much of the pool of talent for local economic, moral, and political leadership. Increasingly minority areas plunged into a spiral of welfare dependency, teen pregnancy, youthful crime, chaos, and despair.

By the 1990s, as revealed in the Los Angeles gang wars and the riots following the acquittal in the state trial of the policemen who

190

arrested Rodney King, urban minority life had come to resemble nothing more than Hobbes's state of nature where life was nasty, brutish, and short. Jared Taylor argues that in the areas populated by the urban underclass the writ of law has receded, "leaving behind . . . anarchy and misery." Our nation, he notes, "endures unspeakable third-world squalor because it has crept upon us gradually, because the middle class can live beyond its reach, and because it is largely a product of good intentions."[590]

Pat Buchanan, writing of the decline of the inner cities with some poignancy, as he describes what happened to his childhood hometown of Washington, D.C., is more blunt:

> In 1948, one in eight black children was born out of wedlock; in our major cities, today, it is closer to five in eight. The black family that survived segregation, depression, and war collapsed under the Great Society. The greatest cost of the Welfare State is not to be measured in dollars; and it has not been paid by taxpayers. Begun with good intentions, the Great Society ended with the worst of results. While hundreds of billions have been piled upon the national debt, we have created in America's great cities a permanent, sullen, resentful underclass, utterly dependent upon federal charity for food, shelter, and medical care with little hope of escape.[591]

In such an environment it is no wonder that an increasingly bureaucratized, more highly unionized, and much less responsive educational establishment was increasingly unable to deliver decent teaching to the remaining unlucky inhabitants of the inner cities. The children of the black urban poor had been effectively denied the educational opportunity *Brown* had promised. Even a biographer of Thurgood Marshall, the man traditionally credited with the integrationist strategy of the *Brown* litigation, concluded in 1987 that blacks might have been better served by concentrating on equalizing the funds spent on black and white schools. This might have worked out better than attempting, as the *Brown* Court did, to solve the problem by peremptorily seeking to unify the two systems.[592] Perhaps if there had been a mandate to equalize expenditures, the eventual crushing expenses of maintaining separate but equal school systems would have led, through economics, to unified and integrated systems. This might well have happened when the white and black populations were more economically equal in other regards as well, and when blacks and whites were in a better position to realize the noble assimilationist goal.

F. *Roe v. Wade*

Remarkable as *Brown*, *Swann*, *Griggs*, and their progeny were as examples of stretching constitutional provisions and of social planning by the Supreme Court, the prize for making up constitutional doctrine out of whole cloth probably still belongs to the Burger Court's fantastic decision in *Roe v. Wade*.[593] The crucial passage in the opinion, by Justice Harry Blackmun, was as follows:

> [A woman's] right of privacy, whether it be founded in the Fourteenth Amendment's [due process clause's] concept of personal liberty and restrictions upon state action, as we feel it is, or, as the District Court determined, in the Ninth Amendment's reservation of rights to the people, is broad enough to encompass a woman's decision whether or not to terminate her pregnancy. The detriment that the State would impose upon the pregnant woman by denying this choice altogether is apparent. Specific and direct harm medically diagnosable even in early pregnancy may be involved. Maternity, or additional off-spring, may force upon the woman a distressful life and future. Psychological harm may be imminent. Mental and physical health may be taxed by child care. There is also the distress, for all concerned, associated with the unwanted child, and there is the problem of bringing a child into a family already unable, psychologically and otherwise to care for it. In other cases, as in this one, the additional difficulties and continuing stigma of unwed motherhood may be involved.

With these words Justice Blackmun established a purported constitutional foundation for treating unwanted pregnancies as "distressful," psychologically harmful, and stigmatizing. His legal focus, at least in the first trimester of a pregnancy, was solely on the alleged needs and convenience of the mother.

Justice Harry Blackmun's majority opinion thus appears clearly sympathetic to the policy arguments of the advocates of abortion or "freedom of choice," as it is euphemistically called. Blackmun's *Roe* opinion is thus implicitly contemptuous of the arguments of the advocates of an embryo's right to life. *Roe v. Wade*, in outlawing first trimester pregnancy regulation, simply swept aside what until then had been recognized for more than a century as perfectly permissible. Blackmun's opinion, as then Associate Justice Rehnquist's dissent stressed, ignored the principle of original understanding. Blackmun's opinion departed even from prior substantive "due process" decisions, which had required that rights protected be only those that were "fundamental" or "implicit in the concept of ordered liberty."[594] As Rehnquist explained:

The fact that a majority of the States reflecting, after all, the majority sentiment in those States, have had restrictions on abortions for at least a century is a strong indication, it seems to me, that the asserted right to an abortion is not "so rooted in the traditions and conscience of our people as to be ranked as fundamental." . . . Even today, when society's views on abortion are changing, the very existence of the debate is evidence that the "right" to an abortion is not so universally accepted as the appellant would have us believe.

To reach its result, the [majority] has had to find within the scope of the Fourteenth Amendment a right that was apparently completely unknown to the drafters of the Amendment. As early as 1821 the first state law dealing directly with abortion was enacted by the Connecticut Legislature. . . . By the time of the adoption of the Fourteenth Amendment in 1868, there were at least 36 laws enacted by state or territorial legislatures limiting abortion. While many states have amended or updated their laws, 21 of the laws on the books in 1868 [the year of the adoption of the Fourteenth Amendment] remain in effect today. . . .

There apparently was no question concerning the validity of this provision or of any of the other state statutes when the Fourteenth Amendment was adopted. The only conclusion possible from this

193

history is that the drafters did not intend to have the Fourteenth Amendment withdraw from the States the power to legislate with respect to this matter.[595]

Justice Blackmun's departure in this instance from the original understanding of the Fourteenth Amendment, his clear preference for one set of social policies over another, and his concomitant finding that the Fourteenth Amendment's due process clause guaranteed pregnant women and their doctors freedom to perform abortions in the first trimester of their pregnancies have all proven to be completely indefensible as a matter of constitutional law. As Harvard Law Professor Mary Ann Glendon pointed out, as previously indicated, in her seminal *Abortion and Divorce in Western Law* (1987):[596]

> As time passes, not only does the *Roe* decision appear to be collapsing from within, but the opinions of leading constitutional law writers, many of them not opposed to abortion in principle, have been marshalled against it. Archibald Cox, Alexander Bickel, John Hart Ely, Harry Wellington, Richard Epstein, and Paul Freund have all been highly critical. Furthermore, at least two of *Roe's* prominent defenders [Lawrence Tribe and Michael Perry], would, I believe, also be opposed to it if they consistently applied their own theories of constitutional hermeneutics to that case.

Even Ruth Bader Ginsburg, President Clinton's first nominee to the Supreme Court, a champion of gender equality and women's rights, recognized that there were grave difficulties with *Roe v. Wade.* In a speech delivered in 1993, which some prochoice advocates used to question the appropriateness of Ginsburg's nomination,[597] Judge Ginsburg criticized *Roe* for making abortion more of a political controversy than it should have been. She questioned *Roe* for short-circuiting the political developments that were leading state legislatures in a direction more favorable to freedom of choice.[598] In fairness to Ginsburg, she had made quite clear before her nomination that she supported constitutional grounding for a purported right to have an abortion, although her argument was on equal protection grounds rather than on *Roe*'s right to privacy rationale. Ginsburg's equal protection rationale is probably even more radical than *Roe*'s approach, but her criticism of *Roe* was still valid, even if her own arguments for constitutional protection for abortion are problematic.[599]

In any event, to suggest, as the majority in *Roe* did, that the Fourteenth Amendment's due process clause had to be interpreted as carrying with it a substantive right to choose to terminate a pregnancy in the first trimester was to engage in the same sort of discredited decision-making that liberals had excoriated in *Dred Scott* and *Lochner*.[600] It was the same approach Roger Taney had supposedly employed in *Dred Scott* when he found that "due process" guaranteed the right to hold slaves in the territories, and that the majority had employed in *Lochner* to find that "due process" prohibited a state from regulating the wages or working conditions of bakers.[601]

Harry Blackmun had spent a considerable amount of time, before ascending the Supreme Court bench, as counsel to the Mayo Clinic, one of the country's premier medical facilities, and perhaps he came to believe that he was uniquely qualified to address what he may have regarded as an essentially medical, rather than a legal issue.[602] So it was that Blackmun interpreted the Fourteenth Amendment to require that the constitutionality of abortion legislation turn on what trimester of a woman's pregnancy was involved. Embracing the suspect "balancing test" method, Blackmun explained that the interests of the mother in exercising dominion over her own body had to be balanced against both the state's interest in protecting her life and the life of her offspring, and the fetus's own due process rights to life. The latter two, Blackmun confidently explained, could not even come into being in the first trimester of pregnancy.

Since abortion was not a significant risk to the health of the mother during the first trimester, the state could have no legitimate interest in protecting her health by prohibiting abortion. As Blackmun put it, using language perhaps more fitting for a medical than a legal argument:

With respect to the State's important and legitimate interest in the health of the mother, the "compelling point," in the light of present medical knowledge, is at approximately the end of the first trimester. This is so because of the now-established medical fact that until the end of the first trimester mortality in abortion may be less than mortality in normal childbirth. It follows that, from and after this point, a State may regulate the abortion procedure to the extent that the regulation reasonably related to the preservation and protection of maternal health.[603]

As Blackmun indicated, pursuant to then current medical technology, the fetus could not be said to be viable outside the womb in the first trimester. Blackmun apparently reasoned that the state had no business attemping to protect the fetus's life during these months, since it was not yet a person. For Blackmun, then, fetal viability may have been the test of fetal personhood, and thus the fetus could have no constitutional rights until relatively late in the pregnancy.[604] In the second trimester, Blackmun stated, termination of a pregnancy could be more hazardous to the health of the mother, and so the state could legitimately seek to regulate the practice in order to protect her health. At some point late in the second trimester or early in the third the fetus itself might reach potential viability outside the womb, and when that happened, Blackmun appeared to reason, the fetus would achieve the status of person protected under the Constitution. At that point, though not before, Blackmun clearly indicated the state could regulate abortion in the interest of protecting the "potential" life of the fetus. As Blackmun stated:

With respect to the State's important and legitimate interest in potential life, the "compelling" point is at viability. This is so because the fetus then presumably has the capability of meaningful life outside the mother's womb. State regulation protective of fetal life after viability thus has both logical and biological justifications. If the State is interested in protecting fetal life after viability, it may go so far as to proscribe abortion during that period, except when it is necessary to preserve the life or health of the mother.[605]

196

Curiously, Blackmun never explained his implicit suggestion that the fetus's "potential" life, which would inevitably be lost in the abortion procedure, had to be subordinated to the life of the mother. Perhaps Blackmun managed to finesse this by never actually declaring the fetus a "person," even when it was viable outside the womb, but only referring to the fetus as a "potential life." Thus, according to Blackmun's opinion, it was permissible, indeed required, for the state to decide, even in the third trimester when the mother's life was threatened, that if the abortion could save her life, it was to be done.

Blackmun's three trimester analysis of abortion law might have made some sense, if constitutional law were simply a reflection of medical knowledge, given the state of medical knowledge at the time. But once technology reached the point of being able to breed test-tube babies outside the womb nearly from conception, it destroyed the internal logic of Blackmun's tests, and would have called for the creation of completely different legal rules. Such were the hazards of linking jurisprudence to contemporary ideas about medical technology. Blackmun's trimester approach remained as something of an embarrassment even to abortion rights defenders,[606] and (as indicated in the first chapter), was quietly repudiated by the Supreme Court itself in the 1991 *Planned Parenthood v. Casey* decision. That case adhered to *Roe*'s constitutional fiction that there was a constitutional right to choose to have an abortion. The *Casey* decision abandoned the trimester standard, and adopted the even more amorphous "undue burden" on the woman standard as a test for permissible regulation.

CONCLUSION

Chief Justice Earl Warren's great trilogy of *Reynolds, Miranda*, and *Brown*, and Justice Harry Blackmun's extraordinary *Roe v. Wade* opinion, probably represented the apogee of the Supreme Court's acting as a legislature and not as a court. More precisely, they were the low point in any history of Supreme Court decision-making that accords with the original understanding of

197

the Constitution. The Supreme Court in the 1950s, 1960s, and 1970s built on the experience of the post–1937 Supreme Court. That New Deal Court had been cowed into adjusting the interstate commerce clause, the Fifth Amendment, and the Seventh Amendment of the Constitution to accord with Franklin Roosevelt's politics. The Warren and Burger Court majorities turned the Constitution in general, and the Fourteenth Amendment in particular, into a vehicle for what a majority of the Justices believed to be progressive social policy. This represented an abandonment of several hundred years of Anglo-American jurisprudence. It severely threatened an untimely end to an American tradition to which Frankfurter referred in his *Barnette* dissent, and which Harlan epitomized in his *Reynolds* and *Miranda* dissents. This was the previously dominant conservative judicial tradition of judicial deference, in which it had been the job of the courts to preserve the best in the past and the job of the legislatures to create positive policy for the future.

By the late 1980s, developments in the constitutional jurisprudence of race, religion, and abortion had all but put an end to the idea of this tradition—the essence really of the rule of law—governing on the Supreme Court. There were, in short, few if any who continued to believe that the Court merely found law, and it was a commonplace that the Court was functioning merely as another political institution. This explains the hard-fought battles over the nominations of Robert Bork and Clarence Thomas. Both of those nominees to the Court professed to believe that it was not the job of the Court to find new rights in the Constitution, and they were thus perceived as threatening to undo the "progressive" judicial reforms of the past four decades.

Yet (as indicated in Chapter Two) if the theory of popular sovereignty upon which the institution of judicial review was bottomed in *Federalist* 78 means anything, it means that it is the job of the judges to follow the dictates of the people expressed in the Constitution and in the statutes. It should not be the judges' profession to circumscribe the legislatures of the state or federal government by inventing new constitutional prohibitions or policies, or by undermining the dual-sovereignty theory of the Constitution itself. There are many areas in the last few decades where the Court has improperly embarked on remaking social policy for the entire nation. We cannot explore all of them here, but we can mark out at least three for our further consideration, and for suggesting how the Court might be returned to the correct judicial track, closer to the original understanding. How, then, might an alternative jurisprudence be fashioned in the three currently most problematic areas of race, religion, and abortion? How might we craft an alternative jurisprudence that might have some chance of returning the Court to its proper role and help recapture the original understanding of the Constitution?

Summary of the Argument

In *Dred Scott* Chief Justice Taney failed to follow the correct canons of judicial interpretation, because he failed to understand that natural law was a vital part of our jurisprudential tradition. Still, Taney was not a racist, and it is silly to forbid public discussions of *Dred Scott*, as Senator Carol Mosely-Braun recently tried to do. The case still has much to teach us about natural law, property, and the risks when the Court ignores them. In *Lochner*, by contrast, the majority was correct to embrace "freedom of contract" through the "due process" clause, and Holmes's dissent was wrong to reject the original understanding. During the time of the New Deal, the Supreme Court initially stuck to the original understanding with regard to property rights and Congress's power, but then, under pressure from FDR, abandoned that original understanding, as is particularly evident in the *Jones & Laughlin* case. Once the Court had abandoned original understanding as a constitutional guide in the later New Deal cases, an avalanche of unconstitutional decisions followed. These included the *Barnette* case, which forbade compulsory flag salutes in the public schools, and the school prayer decisions, which were wrong as a matter of history *and* as a matter of policy. These decisions are in particular error because they unconstitutionally selectively incorporated prohibitions against the federal government into the Fourteenth Amendment and applied them against state and local governments. Frankfurter's *Barnette* dissent is a better exposition of proper principles of constitutional interpretation. Sadly, Frankfurter's strictures have tended to be ignored, and instead the Supreme Court, particularly under Earl Warren, continued to act unconstitutionally by making law rather than simply interpreting it. Questionable Supreme Court cases decided by the Warren Court included *Reynolds v. Sims*, which improperly overturned established state practices regarding bicameral legislatures, *Miranda v. Arizona*, which improperly interfered with state police procedures, and *Brown v. Board of Education*, which inappropriately frustrated state and local educational efforts. The errors of the Warren Court were then compounded by the Burger Court's desegration, school busing, and affirmative action decisions, and by the abortion decision, *Roe v. Wade*. All of these errors amounted to a virtual abandonment of original understanding jurisprudence, and to an abandonment of the traditional judicial role of preserving the best of the past and leaving the future to the legislatures. Next: How might we get back to proper jurisprudence in constitutional cases involving race, religion, and abortion?

Chapter Four

SETTING IT RIGHT

How then, might one construct an alternative jurisprudence of constitutional law that more satisfactorily would come to grips with the currently most insoluble issues for constitutional law involving race, religion, and abortion? How might the missteps or usurpations of prior Supreme Court majorities on the Warren, Burger, and Rehnquist Courts be corrected? How might new results be reached that are more in keeping with the beliefs of the framers, which were influenced by the natural law and based on religion, and in line with the often-suppressed conservative strain in our constitutional heritage? In this chapter each of these three key problem areas is taken up in turn.

A. Race

RACIAL PREFERENCES IN THE COURTS

Modern Americans, as individuals, like to think that they have overcome racial prejudice. The dominant opinion in the national media and on our campuses notwithstanding, the objective data does seem to indicate that racism is no longer a major impediment to progress for minority groups.[607] Nevertheless, to an extraordinary extent, much of the latest constitutional jurisprudence on the topic of race, or at least with regard to American blacks and Hispanics, has embraced the academically fashionable or politically correct view that positive action must be taken to correct the results of past discrimination against these races.[608] Further, most academic quarters also agree that this positive action should include federally mandated local programs that ensure members of purportedly disadvantaged minority groups have political, and, in some cases, economic representation in accordance with the proportion of their population. This appears to be the view, for example, of the University of Pennsylvania law professor, Lani Guinier, whom President Clinton nominated to be assistant attorney general for civil rights.[609] Ms. Guinier's nomination was withdrawn when the president apparently concluded that her views, insofar as they repudiated the core American concept of majority rule, were too far removed from the beliefs of most Americans. Her views, however, were probably well within the mainstream of the current legal academy.

This academic view, moreover, has spilled over into the courts and into the federal legislature. Thus, the Voting Rights Act of 1965 has been construed in a manner suggesting that state and federal legislative districts must be created which give minorities representation in the legislature in similar extent to their percentage of the population. The logic of the voting rights act with regard to minority representation has even been extended to the election of judges.[610] This last is particularly troubling since, as has been repeatedly argued here, the essence of judging ought to be to follow the preexisting rules of the law, not to alter legal doctrines "equitably" in order to redress grievances of particular segments of the population.

In his famous *Democracy in America*, Alexis de Tocqueville, the most astute observer of nineteenth-century American society, predicted that with the election of judges would come the eventual demise of the protection from anarchy that the American rule of law offered.[611] It is bad enough that many states have made their judiciaries elective, thus suggesting that judging must some-

204

how pass continuing popular ratification. But to further suggest that the judges themselves must reflect the racial composition of the electorate is very nearly to give up on the idea of the rule of law itself and to invite the "fatal consequences" for the American republic of which Tocqueville warned.[612]

There is, however, some reason to hope that the United States Supreme Court understands the evil of racially based classifications. Various provisions of state and municipal laws setting aside business for contractors solely on the basis of the race of the contracting companies' owners have recently been disallowed by the Supreme Court. In *Richmond v. J. A. Croson Co.* (1989),[613] the Court held that the "strict scrutiny" standard applied in determining the constitutionality of affirmative action plans based on race. It then applied that standard to find that the minority "set-aside" plan in Richmond, Virginia, was unconstitutional. That plan had required prime contractors to subcontract at least 30 percent of the dollar amount of any contracts to minority business enterprises.

The "strict scrutiny" standard, which we have already encountered in the questionable *Griswold* concurring opinion by Justice Harlan,[614] is a "balancing test" of a kind so often favored by Justice O'Connor, who wrote the majority opinion in *Croson* (and who, it will be remembered, was the author of the "undue burden" standard in abortion cases).[615] As applied in *Richmond v. Croson*, "strict scrutiny" requires that minority set-aside plans "demonstrate a compelling interest that requires a showing of past discrimination [by the particular locality's officials], not mere reliance on [general] societal discrimination for their justification." The decision also requires municipalities seeking to implement minority set-aside programs to "choose means that are narrowly tailored to vindicate [the compelling interest] and [to] take into account factors such as the necessity of the relief and the efficiency of alternative remedies [for past discrimination], the duration of the remedy, the flexibility of the remedy and/or the availability of waivers, the relationship of the numerical goals to minorities within the relevant labor market, and the likely effect on innocent parties."[616] As this list of factors to be taken into account, and

205

the inherently slippery nature of the balancing test approach suggests,[617] *Richmond* leaves the law of minority set-asides in an extremely uncertain state.

The practice of minority set-asides—whatever its shaky constitutionality—remains common. Even more questionably, by a bare 5–4 majority in 1990, one year after the Richmond set-aside case, the Supreme Court allowed the FCC to award coveted permits to operate broadcasting stations on the basis of the race or sex of the applicant. Such minority set-aside policies are a blatant invitation for fraud, and it is now apparently common for nonminority businesspersons to organize minority members into a "front" for the purposes of taking advantage of set-aside policies.[618] Instead of actually spreading wealth to disadvantaged minority members, then, a set-aside program may simply have the effect of enriching those who practice chicanery and artifice.[619] The principled position on this issue was articulated by the four dissenters in the FCC case, *Metro Broadcasting, Inc. v. FCC* (1990).[620] Commenting on the FCC's policy of favoring racial minorities in order to achieve greater diversity in programming content, they wrote, "The Constitution provides that the Government may not allocate benefits and burdens among individuals based on the assumption that race or ethnicity determines how they act or think."[621]

Finally, and in an awesome reversal of many generations of understanding, the Supreme Court has even restricted the practice of peremptory challenges on juries, to hold that jurors may not be removed pursuant to peremptory challenges on the basis of race. A peremptory challenge formerly allowed parties the right to strike a certain number of jurors for any arbitrary reason they desired. The purpose of such challenges was to give the parties, and, in particular, criminal defendants, the best opportunity to be tried by a jury that they believed to be fair and unbiased.[622]

These reversals of long-standing practices may well injure the very minority members they were designed to protect. Gerrymandering representation to favor particular races will result in removing pressure on other representatives to respond to the needs of their minority constituents, and will have the effect of further ghettoizing the areas represented. As nonminority members realize that elected representatives in minority-dominant areas will serve the needs of a particular minority group, the nonminority members may decide to leave the area. This will result in further Balkanizing of American politics and society along racial and minority lines, at a time when our need is for greater harmony and assimilation.

Minority set-aside programs will likely continue to promote fraud, as minority members are sought out for nominal participation to take advantage of preferential policies. Thus, set-asides will likely not have the redistributionist impact that their authors desire, and will create resentment and ill-will among honest and disappointed nonminority contractors or applicants.

The practice of forbidding peremptory challenges based on race, as Justice Thomas forcefully argued in his concurring opinion in *Georgia v. McCollum* (1992),[623] may actually result in further discrimination against minority members because they will no longer be permitted to exclude possibly prejudiced nonminority jurors.[624] As he explained, " . . . I am certain that black criminal defendants will rue the day that this court ventured down this road that inexorably will lead to the elimination of peremptory strikes."[625]

All of these race-based approaches are essentially glorified affirmative action programs. As such, they can ultimately be expected to result in the same kind of continued suspicion of minorities by nonminorities and self-doubt among minorities that Stephen Carter chronicled so effectively in his *Reflections of an Affirmative Action Baby* (1991), and Shelby Steele criticized so forcefully in his *The Content of Our Character: A New Vision of Race in America* (1990).

Carter's condemnation of affirmative action as "racial justice on the cheap"[626] stresses that it normally helps those minorities least in need (members of the black middle class).[627] It also removes pressure to undertake the more difficult and more expensive tasks of raising the standard of living and the opportunities for the truly disadvantaged minority members of the lower classes.[628] Carter argues that the prevalent practice of lowering entrance requirements and standards for particular professions or professional schools for minorities is itself a racist undertaking. He argues that lowered standards are dangerous and demeaning to the minority members they seek to benefit. Programs that search out and offer opportunities for training to minority members, for example at the nursery school, primary and secondary school, and perhaps even the college level, ought to be encouraged as the only legitimate forms of "affirmative action," but to go further is unwarranted.[629] As Carter explains, "[I]f we can gain for ourselves a fair and equal chance to show what we can do—what the affirmative action literature likes to call a level playing field—then it is something of an insult to our intellectual capacities to insist on more."[630]

Carter is particularly contemptuous of the currently popular "diversity" rationale for applying differential criteria to graduate school and college admissions for minority members. The rationale is that they can present an alternative viewpoint that will enrich the experience of all members of the university or professional communities. As did the dissenters in *Metro Broadcasting*, Carter denies "that race is a good proxy for viewpoint,"[631] or that there is a single black perspective.[632] Those who maintain that black members of the academy or professions have valuable contributions to offer because of their backgrounds of disadvantage or oppression, he argues, are little better than bigots who would suggest that blacks have a higher disposition to commit crime than do whites.[633] In words echoing the sentiments of the late Martin Luther King, Carter suggests: "We [blacks] must learn once more to love and cherish individuals for who they are, not for what they represent; and having learned it once more ourselves, we can once more teach it to a doubting world."[634] A "sensible way to start," Carter concludes, "is to say that with all the various instances in which race might be relevant, either to the government or to individuals, it will not be used as an indicator of merit—no one will be more valued than anyone else because of skin color."[635]

In his landmark and prize-winning[636] 1990 book, Shelby

Steele treated themes similar to Carter's, and even picked his title from the words of Martin Luther King. Steele argued forcefully that blacks hurt themselves by treating matters of race as of more importance than human universals. According to Steele, the best solution to the "demoralization and poverty that continue to widen the gap between blacks and whites in America" is for blacks to embrace a program to encourage "individual initiative, self-sufficiency, [and] strong families."[637] Race-based remedies and approaches, according to Steele, have the pernicious effects of encouraging blacks to avoid individual responsibility for their lives, and of encouraging blacks to be dependent on the largesse of whites.[638] Probably worst of all, affirmative action programs, which apply differential admissions standards or qualitative tests for blacks and whites, do blacks more harm than good.[639] This is because they not only create hostility toward blacks on the part of whites (against whom such programs discriminate) but they also create debilitating self-doubts in the very blacks such programs are designed to aid. They suggest to both blacks and whites that blacks don't have the wherewithal to succeed on their own.[640] Instead of race-based remedies or quotas, Steele states that

> What is needed now is a new spirit of pragmatism in racial matters where blacks are seen simply as American citizens who deserve complete fairness and in some cases developmental assistance, but in no case special entitlements based on color. We need deracinated social policies that attack poverty rather than *black* poverty, and that instill those values that make for self-reliance. The white message to blacks must be: America hurt you badly and that is wrong, but entitlements only prolong the hurt while development overcomes it.[641]

Or as Steele explains in the concluding portion of his book, summarizing his argument:

> To retrieve our individuality and find opportunity, blacks today must—consciously or unconsciously—disregard the prevailing victim-focused black identity. Though it espouses black pride, it is actually a repressive identity that generates a victimized self-

image, curbs individualism and initiative, diminishes our sense of possibility, and contributes to our demoralization and inertia. It is a skin that needs shedding.[642]

Carter and Steele, and a few other minority spokesmen like them, such as Glen Loury, Thomas Sowell, and Clarence Thomas, who criticize the forms of affirmative action and racial preference often advocated by mainstream black leaders, have points of view that are rarely aired in the mainstream media. Stephen Carter has observed, "The spectrum of permissible views in serious public political life is far narrower in the United States than in the democracies of Western Europe."[643] Still, there is increasing evidence that the "black dissenters," as they have been called,[644] better represent the views of the American black community. Thus Stephen Carter maintains that there is "consistent polling data demonstrating that a plurality, and perhaps a majority, of black Americans oppose racial preferences."[645]

The inherent problems in these racial preference-based approaches lead ineluctably to the conclusion that the now neglected theory of a "color-blind Constitution" should be moved back to the center stage of constitutional adjudication.[646] The notion that the Constitution is color-blind should be used to reverse or curtail these misconceived societal experiments in affirmative action and racial preference. It should be stressed that a "color-blind Constitution" does not necessarily imply that we have attained the ideal of a "color-blind society." Interpreting the Constitution as "color blind" should not prevent us from condemning or preventing official discrimination on the basis of race. Nor should it stop us from undertaking to ensure that educational opportunities are offered equally to citizens without regard to race.[647]

But blacks and other minority members would be best aided by ensuring that they are treated the same as anyone else. The doctrinal support for this approach was eloquently stated by the first Justice Harlan in his dissent in *Plessy v. Ferguson*, the case that found "separate but equal" constitutional. Said Harlan, "The Constitution is color-blind, and neither knows nor tolerates classes among citizens."[648] There is plenty of constitutional principle to support this view.

The body of the Constitution never expressly states that there must not be different treatment for persons of different races, but this is precisely the idea of the Civil War and Reconstruction amendments. These are the Thirteenth Amendment (1865) (which forbids slavery or involuntary servitude except for commission of a crime), the Fourteenth (1868) (which guarantees citizenship and equal protection of the laws to all state citizens), and the Fifteenth (1870) (which expressly provides that "The right of citizens of the United States to vote shall not be denied or abridged by the United States or by any State on account of race, color, or previous condition of servitude.").

Moreover, even if there were no express amendment language, the implications from our natural law tradition are clear. We have already seen how ideas about natural law restricted the institution of black slavery.[649] The clearest general statement of our traditional natural law principles is in the Declaration of Independence, and it is also suggestive. The first "self-evident truth" mentioned in the Declaration's opening paragraph is that "all men are created equal," and the second is that all men "are endowed by their Creator with certain inalienable rights, that among these are Life, Liberty, and the pursuit of Happiness." The Declaration makes no distinctions between persons of different races, just as natural law does not. Natural law expects that all will be equal before the law, and, indeed, the application of the rule of law indiscriminately is a core natural law principle. If, as has been argued repeatedly here, the Constitution is undergirded with a reverence for natural law and natural law's Creator, it is easy to see that He has all but declared racial classifications suspect and a color-blind Constitution inescapable.

The notion of support for a return to the jurisprudence of a "color-blind" Constitution can also be found in Justice Scalia's concurrence in *Richmond v. J.A. Croson Co.* (1989),[650] and is beginning to be heard once again in the popular media. As Scalia's opinion suggests, with a color-blind Constitution one would not need "balancing tests" and "strict scrutiny," and official racial discrimination of a type practiced by Richmond in its set-aside program would simply be barred. We would have returned to constitutional determination by categories rather than balancing.[651]

In a recent piece in the *National Review*, law professor Lino Graglia argued forcefully that

A more promising approach [than affirmative action plans] to social stability, surely, is to maintain a system of law, government, and public policy that uniformly insists on the total irrelevance, at least for official or public purposes, of claimed membership in any particular racial group. It may be naive idealism to believe that racial peace can be achieved through official inculcation of the view that racial distinctions are odious and pointless, but it is at least an ideal worth pursuing. We can be certain, on the other hand, that racial peace will not be found through policies that enhance racial consciousness, presume the existence of widespread and near-ineradicable racial animosity, and insist that racial distinctions are of central importance.[652]

Once a race-blind jurisprudence returns to the Supreme Court, the Court would also be wise to reverse related doctrines, such as that of the notorious *Missouri v. Jenkins* (1990)[653] case. In that decision, the Supreme Court held that lower federal courts had the power to order the levying of taxes in order to see that desegregation remedies were carried out. The ill-fated plan of the Kansas City School District, conceived to lure whites back into an inner-city school system, involved the expenditure of many millions of dollars, and had utterly failed to win voter approval. The United States Supreme Court affirmed the lower court's determination that it could overrule the fiscal preferences of the voters. The Court, in effect, set spending for a desegregation plan as the polity's highest priority, and imposed a property tax to fund the plan. While the plan resulted in the erection of some magnificent edifices, it appears to have failed in its goal to restore racial balance to Kansas City's schools.[654] It is one of the most egregious examples of judicial usurpation of the role of other branches. A truly color-blind Constitution ought to forbid student allocation or transfer based solely on race, and spending funds to alter racial balances in the schools.

A color-blind constitutional strategy does not mean, of course, that other strategies for ensuring quality education to all students, such as equalizing per pupil expenditures within particular districts, or even equalizing per pupil expenditures on a statewide basis, are impermissible. The idea of a color-blind Constitution means only that governmental programs which discriminate on the basis of any race are intolerable. The end of expenditures to promote racial balance, moreover, should bring about the end of the threat of judicial taxation.

The costs of maintaining a constitutional system in which race plays a prominent part, in which special deference is accorded to members of a particular race, ostensibly to make up for past discrimination, have been considerable and will continue to mount. There is no way that past injustices committed by a previously dominant race to a previously subservient race can be corrected by persons living in the present.[655] Centuries of exploitation can never be wiped away, and the impossibility of redressing past harms can only lead to perpetual claims of reparations. The guilt such claims have induced on the part of many liberals is the source, one suspects, of our current jurisprudence of race, with its special consideration for racial minorities. It is hard to imagine how this guilt can be totally assuaged, or the logic of reparations satisfied, without a wholesale redistribution of wealth and power in American society.

The logic of reparations leading to radical restructuring and redistribution appears to be admitted, and even desired, among the more candid left-leaning American legal writers. Their jurisprudence accords little weight to traditional concepts of private property and less to the existing system of governmental and social hierarchies.[656] But even apart from the fact that such wholesale redistribution raises constitutional problems of its own, there is no assurance that such massive social change would result

213

in an overall increase in welfare. It is by no means clear that if there were a massive shift in wealth from the richest to the poorest sectors of society that the same incentives for production could be maintained. The recent experience of socialist Eastern Europe, where just such redistribution was sought, certainly suggests caution in implementing such a scheme.

RACE AND THE JURY: THE RODNEY KING PROBLEM

Given the intractability of the problem of past discrimination, and the unfeasibility or impossibility of solving it, it is no wonder that the piecemeal nature of our current strategy of racial appeasement leads to further demands, despair, and even violence. The most visible recent example of this was the Los Angeles riots following the acquittal in the state trial of most of the white policemen involved in the subduing of the black criminal suspect Rodney King. An all-white jury acquitted most of the officers, and a mostly black mob terrorized Los Angeles for days, looting and ruining thousands of businesses, and causing billions of dollars in damages.[657]

Many black leaders and their followers assumed that an all-white jury—and one chosen from a suburban county where many white L.A. policemen lived—could not be objective in a case where white defendants were accused by a black man. They thus assumed that the acquittals had resulted from an unfair trial. Emotions were further exacerbated by the incessant broadcasting of part of a videotape of a portion of King's turbulent arrest.

The Rodney King tape, while dramatic, and while appearing to present a brutal subduing of King, told only a small part of the story of the encounter. It failed to illustrate, for example, how the arresting officers, after a lengthy car chase at more than 100 miles per hour, might have perceived danger from King, and might have believed that the strongest measures were necessary to subdue him. Reports indicated that King appeared mentally deranged and refused to comply with orders to surrender (like his two black companions, who were not at all injured by the police).

214

King was a large and strong man to begin with, but he resisted, with extraordinary ease, the first physical efforts to subdue him. His apparently superhuman strength and his erratic behavior led the officers to believe that he was exhibiting the symptoms of the drug P.C.P. This convinced the arresting officers that the strongest measures were necessary, as did King's continued resistance to arrest. Measures that might quickly have restrained him, such as the chokehold, had been forbidden by L.A. police rules, so that all that was left was to administer glancing blows until King submitted, as he eventually did. None of these matters was conveyed by the edited videotape, but taken together, these exculpatory factors certainly could have led a reasonable jury to the conclusion that the officers did not act criminally and used only necessary force.[658]

The Rodney King imbroglio showed a sad failure on the part of officials and the public to remember the core assumptions of criminal jury trials—that defendants are to be presumed innocent, and that only the jury determines whether there was proof of criminality beyond a reasonable doubt. Even the president of the United States indicated shock and disapproval with the verdict acquitting the officers who allegedly so brutally had beaten King. An ill-advised federal prosecution (persecution?) for what was essentially a state law infraction was immediately launched. It is difficult to believe that respect for the rule of law and its component parts, including the sanctity of a jury verdict in a criminal case, counted for as much in this new federal proceeding as naked racial appeasement.

The convictions of two of the four officers secured in the federal trial, while pacifying to a certain degree the residents of South Central Los Angeles, ought to be regarded as travesties of justice and violations of the clear spirit of the double jeopardy clause. The memory of the carnage following the acquittals in the first (state) trial must surely have weighed on the minds of some members of the jury in the second (federal) trial. In that second trial, all of the jurors were citizens of the county of Los Angeles itself, and had at least indirect personal experience of the aftermath of the first trial. Moreover, the use of one of the four defendants' videotaped testimony from the state trial in the federal trial (in which latter trial he chose not to testify) as surely violated the Fifth Amendment's prohibition against self-incrimination. That particular defendant was acquitted, so the case cannot be appealed on that ground, although other irregularities and the "double jeopardy argument" might still lead to a successful federal appeal of the convictions in the second trial. At this writing (late 1993) the two defendants have already begun serving their federal sentences, and the outcome of any appeals remain uncertain.

We may not be far from the day when courts find that the Constitution assures every defendant of a minority race representatives from his or her race on a jury. Perhaps we have reached the point when a verdict in any state criminal trial that fails to satisfy minority representatives will be followed by a federal "civil rights trial."[659] If this is true, we have effectively abandoned the notion that objective legal determinations by laymen are possible, and we have also abandoned the important principle of double jeopardy.

As the debates over the ratification of the Constitution show, the institution of the American trial by jury was thought to be an essential safeguard from oppression by the government or from powerful individuals. The safeguard was to come from the jury's commitment to dispense justice without regard to the power or the influence of the parties involved. Juries would not act arbitrarily, but would serve as antidotes to the arbitrary use of power. In order for the jury to fulfill this function, the jury, no less than the judges, was bound to follow the law. The jury was *not* to substitute an arbitrariness of its own. To do so would have been as profound an evil for a regime of the rule of law as oppression by the government prosecutors.

It was often said, particularly in the early days of the republic, that the jury was to be the judge of fact *and* law in criminal cases. Thus, a jury acquittal in a criminal case could not be set aside by a judge. Still, the *power* on the part of juries, in effect to ignore the law, was not recognized as conferring a *right* to do so. Indeed, the juries' power to judge of *law* was *not* intended to allow it to make new law itself, but existed to counter the possibility that the prosecution might have acted arbitrarily, ignoring the law. The most astute early observer of this dilemma, Supreme Court Justice Samuel Chase, noted that if the jury failed to follow the law anarchy and chaos would result.[660] Chase was impeached for his views on the jury, but his acquittal probably helped preserve his principles as a basic set of American jurisprudential maxims.

We continue to maintain that the jury possesses the power to determine the law for itself. This power is usually referred to in the literature as "jury nullification." But even though the jury has this *power*, it still does not have the *right* to ignore the law. In recent years it has been held that the jury should not even be permitted to be advised by defense counsel that the power exists, that it has been exercised repeatedly in American history, or that the facts of the current case suggest that jury nullification might be called for.[661] We thus make the delicate presumption that the jury will follow the law, and this is why we take such care over jury instructions from the judge. If there are individual acts of injustices by particular juries this is the price we pay for believing in popular sovereignty, for believing the concomitant corollary that defendants are entitled to a jury chosen from the laity, and for believing that a popular check against arbitrary prosecutorial actions is necessary.

Our commitment to stand by jury verdicts in the case of criminal acquittals is an essential feature of the integrity of the constitutional system. To manipulate the federal prosecutorial process in order to pander to a debased form of racial politics, as federal officials did in bringing King's alleged assailants to a second trial in federal court, is seriously to undermine the integrity of the law itself.

There was, it is true, a constitutional argument that the second trial of the Rodney King defendants did not constitute a case of double jeopardy forbidden by the Constitution, but the case was a weak one.[662] The Constitution explicitly provides, in keeping with our ancient common law commitment to honor jury verdicts, that no person can be tried twice in a criminal proceeding arising out of the same acts.[663] Nevertheless, in the nineteenth century it was held that if the same acts violated the laws of two different sovereignties—such as two different states—then each jurisdiction could separately try the alleged violator.[664] This decision arose because it was feared that at a time of great sectional strife and division over the slavery issue, a Northern state might seek, in effect, to immunize its citizens from violating the slave laws of Southern states by trying them for such crimes, and administering only nominal punishments.

Whatever the wisdom of such a weakening of the double-jeopardy rule, and whatever its policy merits to minimize sectional strife, it was a serious encroachment on the constitutionally guaranteed freedom from prosecutorial persecution. In the years since the nineteenth-century sectional strife cases, it has been repeatedly held by the Supreme Court that the state and federal sovereignties are permitted to try criminals for the same acts, which supposedly result in different crimes.[665] The policy was probably a bad one in the nineteenth century, and has become a worse one now. Certainly, in the Rodney King case, at least, our supposed inability to solve our racial strife threatens completely to undermine the system of trial by jury itself.

Politicians now apparently feel that they have license to attack jury verdicts on racial grounds. Some even come close to believing that their constituents are under no restraint to obey the laws of private property or breach of the peace, as Congresswoman Maxine Waters appears to have indicated at her press conference following the riots produced by the original acquittals in the King case.[666] Much of the blame can be laid at the door of federal officials, from the president on down. Indeed, and ironically, President Bush's very appointment of Clarence Thomas to the Supreme Court sends the not so subtle message that the rule of law now gives way to racial reparations. It is time to move on from a policy of racial appeasement, which can never be successful. It is time to return to a commitment to even-handed justice, to the concept of a color-blind Constitution, for which we have some chance of success.

TOWARDS A "COLOR-BLIND" CONSTITUTION:
SHAW V. RENO

There has been one recent and encouraging sign from the Supreme Court that the notion of a "color-blind Constitution"
might be due for a revival. This might mean that an era of attempted racial appeasement may be drawing to a close, and that
legislation expressly designed to favor one race over another may
be disallowed. The sign came in *Shaw v. Reno* (1993),[667] in an
opinion, *mirabile dictu*, by Justice Sandra Day O'Connor. The
opinion gets only two cheers, because it garnered a slim 5–4
majority, and also because Justice O'Connor, as she is wont to do,
couched the decision in terms of the sort of balancing test the
future application of which is by definition uncertain. Be that as it
may, there is language in the case that ought to gladden the hearts
of writers such as Shelby Steele and Stephen Carter, who have
railed against racial stereotyping and the evils of affirmative action.

At issue in *Shaw v. Reno* was the creation by the State of North
Carolina, pursuant to federal mandate,[668] of two congressional
voting districts designed to produce black majorities that would
send black representatives to the federal legislature. The districts
were blatant gerrymanders. The first district "is somewhat hook
shaped. Centered in the northeast portion of the Sate, it moves
southward until it tapers to a narrow band; then, with finger-like
extensions, it reaches far into the southern-most part of the State
near the South Carolina border. [This district] has been compared to a 'Rorschach ink-blot test . . ."[669] The prize piece of
work, however, was the second proposed majority-black district
which was

> even more unusually shaped. It is approximately 160 miles long
> and, for much of its length, no wider than the I–85 corridor. It
> winds in snake-like fashion through tobacco country, financial
> centers, and manufacturing areas "until it gobbles in enough
> enclaves of black neighborhoods. ". . . One state legislator has
> remarked that "if you drove down the interstate with both car
> doors open, you'd kill most of the people in the district."[670]

219

Justice O'Connor further noted that "The district even has inspired poetry [sic]: 'Ask not for whom the line is drawn; it is drawn to avoid thee.' "[671]

The plaintiffs in *Shaw*, five white residents of Durham County, North Carolina, argued that the "State had created an unconstitutional racial gerrymander." Justice O'Connor and her colleagues *did not* hold on the basis of the facts presented to them that the plaintiffs ought to win their case. Still, they did make clear that where a state deliberately creates congressional districts along racial lines "in which a majority of black voters was concentrated arbitrarily—without regard to any other considerations, such as compactness, contiguousness, geographical boundaries, or political subdivisions"—"to assure the election of . . . black representatives to Congress" such state action is a "racial classification" in violatation of the Fourteenth Amendment's equal protection clause. Such state action, said the Court, "is presumptively invalid and can be upheld only upon an extraordinary justification."[672]

This was, alas, something less than a ringing endorsement of a "color-blind" Constitution. Plaintiffs had argued that "the deliberate segregation of voters into separate districts on the basis of race violated their constitutional right to participate in a 'color-blind' electoral process."[673] Justice O'Connor recognized this argument as the invocation "of the ideal of a 'color-blind' Constitution,"[674] but she refused fully to accept it. Instead, she observed, "This Court never has held that race-conscious state decisionmaking is impermissible in all circumstances."[675]

Even so, there was much in O'Connor's opinion that could form the basis of a holding that the Constitution is or ought to be construed as "color-blind." Borrowing from a variety of earlier Supreme Court pronouncements, O'Connor stated that "Classifications of citizens solely on the basis of race 'are by their very nature odious to a free people whose institutions are founded upon the doctrine of equality.' "[676] Making an argument similar to those advanced by Shelby Steele and Stephen Carter, O'Connor noted that such racial classifications "threaten to stigmatize individuals by reason of their membership in a racial group and to

220

incite racial hostility."[677] Quoting Justice William Brennan, one of the most liberal members ever to sit on the Supreme Court, O'Connor stressed that even ostensibly benign racial classifications can have their malignant side. "Even in the pursuit of remedial objectives," she observed, "an explicit policy of assignment by race may serve to stimulate our society's latent race-consciousness, suggesting the utility and propriety of basing decisions on a factor that ideally bears no relationship to an individual's worth or needs."[678]

O'Connor was unwilling to go so far as completely to undo racial classifications by governmental authorities, however. She contented herself with the observation that "the Fourteenth Amendment requires state legislation that expressly distinguishes among citizens because of their race to be narrowly tailored to further a compelling governmental interest."[679] Precisely what "compelling governmental interest" would justify a racial classification was left murky. Indeed, Justice O'Connor appeared to go further than the "compelling interest" test when she stated that "A racial classification, regardless of purported motivation, is presumptively invalid and can be upheld only upon an extraordinary justification."[680] Perhaps, however, "compelling interest" and "extraordinary justification" mean the same thing. Perhaps they are simply a means of maintaining discretion for a Justice or judge applying the type of balancing test of which Justice O'Connor is so fond. After all, the use of such a balancing test normally advances a standard that virtually dictates the outcome in the case even before it is applied. Once a "compelling interest" is required of governments, after all, it is almost never produced.[681]

In any event, Justice O'Connor did hold squarely that the Court's previous precedents were enough to support plaintiffs' contention that "redistricting legislation that is so bizarre on its face that it is 'unexplainable on grounds other than race,' [citation omitted] demands the same close scrutiny that we give other state laws that classify citizens by race."[682] There was similarly enough authority to support plaintiffs' contention that "district lines obviously drawn for the purpose of separating voters by race require careful scrutiny under the Equal Protection Clause regardless of the [possibly benign] motivations underlying their adoption." While O'Connor did little to elucidate the meaning of the terms "careful scrutiny," "close scrutiny," "compelling interest," or "extraordinary justification," she did hint that the Supreme Court had previously recognized "a significant state interest in eradicating the effects of past racial discrimination."[683] She cautioned, though, that "the State must have a "strong basis in evidence for [concluding] that remedial action [is] necessary."[684]

Apparently "a long history of official racial discrimination in [a state's] political system and . . . pervasive racial bloc voting" by a dominant race might constitute such a "strong basis."[685] Where "the deliberate creation of majority-minority districts is the most precise way—indeed the only effective way—to overcome the effects of racially polarized voting"[686] it might meet the "compelling interest" or "extraordinary justification" test. In such a case of a history of official racial discrimination, where racial redistricting is the only way to overcome racially polarized voting, then, racial redistricting might survive the "careful scrutiny" or "close scrutiny" required under the Fourteenth Amendment.

O'Connor refused to say for certain, however, how her balancing act was to be performed. She left the decision of how to resolve the case to the courts below, who were directed to take another look. Further, she noted that three of her brother Justices, White, Stevens, and Rehnquist, had "specifically concluded that race-based districting, as a response to racially polarized voting, is constitutionally permissible only when the State 'employs sound districting principles,' and only when the affected racial group's 'residential patterns afford the opportunity of creating districts in which they will be in the majority.' "[687] O'Connor thus seemed to be suggesting that whether or not racial classifications would be permitted in redistricting, they could not support the kind of bizarre gerrymandering for racial purposes which existed in the case at bar.

It is hard to read Justice O'Connor's rather tortured opinion and not come away believing that she was very uncomfortable with the idea of racial classifications used for any purpose. As she stated with great eloquence, again in words that could have been used by Steele or Carter, or any adherent to the notion of a color-blind Constitution:

> Racial classifications of any sort pose the risk of lasting harm to our society. They reinforce the belief, held by too many for too much of our history, that individuals should be judged by the color of their skin. Racial classifications with respect to voting carry particular dangers. Racial gerrymandering, even for remedial purposes, may Balkanize us into competing racial factions; it threatens to carry us further from the goal of a political system in which race no longer matters—a goal that the Fourteenth and Fifteenth Amendments embody, and to which the Nation continues to aspire. It is for these reasons that race-based districting by our state legislatures demands close judicial scrutiny.[688]

One can only add that Justice O'Connor's conclusion endorsing "close judicial scrutiny" hardly follows from her premises about the risks of racial classifications. The goal of a political system in which race no longer matters demands more than the elusive or incoherent balancing test involving "close judicial scrutiny" of "race-based" state decisions. *It demands the categorical abolition of "race-based" state decisions.* Given the impossibility of remedying past racial discrimination by actions taken in the present, as indicated earlier,[689] the "compelling justification" for race-based classifications evaporates. There is no need for an essentially arbitrary judicial balancing test, and race-based measures ought to be unconstitutional. On the day the Supreme Court makes this holding we will have come as close as we ever will to the "equal protection" goal of the Fourteenth Amendment.[690]

In the meantime, as Justice O'Connor herself poignantly observed, to the extent that we allow race-based redistricting, in order to encourage the election of more minority representatives in Congress and elsewhere, we "may exacerbate the very patterns of racial bloc voting that majority-minority districting is sometimes said to counteract."[691] The worst effect of all of this,

O'Connor noted, in a manner similar to the arguments made earlier,[692] will be a weakening of our system of representation itself:

> When a district obviously is created solely to effectuate the perceived common interests of one racial group, elected officials are more likely to believe that their primary obligation is to represent only the members of that group, rather than their constituency as a whole. This is altogether antithetical to our system of representative democracy. As Justice Douglas [another extraordinarily liberal Supreme Court Justice] explained . . . nearly 30 years ago:
>
> > Here the individual is important, not his race, his creed, or his color. The principle of equality is at war with the notion that District A must be represented by a Negro, as it is with the notion that District B must be represented by a Caucasian, District C by a Jew, District D by a Catholic, and so on . . . That system, by whatever name it is called, is a divisive force in a community, emphasizing differences between candidates and voters that are irrelevant in the constitutional sense . . .
> >
> > When racial or religious lines are drawn by the State, the multiracial multireligious communities that our Constitution seeks to weld together as one become separatist; antagonisms that relate to race or religion rather than to political issues are generated; communities seek not the best representative but the best racial or religious partisan. Since that system is at war with the democratic ideal, it should find no footing here.[693]

If we seek to recapture the original understanding of constitutional government and representation that was important to the original framers in 1787 or even the framers of the Fourteenth and Fifteenth Amendments, then, it is hard to read Justice O'Connor's or Justices Douglas and Brennan's eloquent remarks as an endorsement of "close scrutiny," or "compelling interest," or any other balancing tests. Justice O'Connor's opinion in *Shaw v. Reno* should be taken as a well-reasoned repudiation of classifications undertaken on a racial basis. Belying the logic of the balancing test she sought to implement, her opinion in *Shaw v.*

Reno is a powerful restatement of the natural law constitutional ideal, embedded in the Fourteenth Amendment. That ideal— also Martin Luther King, Jr.'s—is that we ought to respond to each other according to the content of our characters rather than according to the color of our skins.[694]

B. Religion

In the last chapter we discussed the problematic Jeffersonian notion of a "wall of separation" between church and state. We concluded that Justice Frankfurter's approach, in his dissent in *West Virginia v. Barnette*, was more in keeping with the original understanding. In this approach, nonsectarian school prayer and Bible reading were matters for the exercise of the discretion of the state governments. In this chapter we amplify that argument, and discuss recent criticism of the Court's First Amendment "establishment clause" jurisprudence.

The First Amendment has two clauses dealing with religion. The first, the "establishment clause," provides that "Congress shall make no law respecting an establishment of religion." The second, the "free exercise" clause, forbids Congress from "prohibiting the free exercise" of religion.[695] Most First Amendment jurisprudence in the area of religion has not concerned these restrictions on Congress, however, but the efforts of state and local governments. This is a consequence of the Supreme Court's belief that the Fourteenth Amendment's first section[696] selectively incorporates parts of the Bill of Rights in determining the essential freedoms it protects.

This "selective incorporation" jurisprudence (as argued in the preceding chapter) is itself an unprincipled usurpation of law-making power. It is one of the most egregious examples of the Court's upsetting the delicate balance of dual sovereignties the 1789 Constitution sought to establish. It ought to be reexamined and rejected, as effectively obliterating federalism. But given that "selective incorporation" has become one of the most firmly entrenched of constitutional doctrines, the chances of this

225

happening are remote at best. At this point, then, it may be wise simply to move on and accept the notion that the First Amendment, which speaks only in terms of prohibitions on "Congress," can be construed also to apply to state and local authorities.

The currently accepted standard for evaluating the constitutionality of the acts of state, local, or federal governments regarding the establishment of religion is drawn from *Lemon v. Kurtzman* (1971).[697] It is, as Jeffrey Rosen, the astute and acerbic legal writer for the *New Republic* has put it, "the aptly named *Lemon* test." This doctrine prohibits, as unconstitutional efforts at the establishment of religion, government actions that

(1) have no secular purpose;
(2) have a "primary effect" of advancing or inhibiting religion; or
(3) foster an "excessive entanglement" between government and religion.[698]

The *Lemon* test standards are among the vaguest in constitutional jurisprudence and have two exceptionally pernicious effects. The first is that the standards are so elusive that they permit almost completely inconsistent results. Thus:

> Under *Lemon*, [state subsidized] bus trips from home to religious school are constitutional, but [state subsidized] bus trips from religious schools to local museums are unconstitutional. . . . [Subsidized] Standardized tests are O.K., but [subsidized] teacher-prepared tests are not. Government can provide parochial schools with books but not maps . . . The Court has invoked *Lemon* to strike down a nativity scene [on public property] surrounded by poinsettias and to uphold a nativity scene [on public property] surrounded by elephants, Teddy bears, Santa's workshop and a talking wishing well. This is the Court's idea of equal time for atheists; practitioners call it the "three plastic animals rule."[699]

The second pernicious effect of *Lemon* is that the "primary effect" standard seems to require that governments actually dis-

226

criminate against religious schools, and bar them from receiving some aid that is available to public or secular schools.[700] Thus, the *Lemon* rule regarding the establishment clause actually results in a violation of the "free exercise" clause. Under the *Lemon* standards, the only permissible result seems to be a public ideology of secularism. As Rabbi Jacob Neusner recently observed, probably with the "three plastic animals rule" in mind:

> At this time, militant secularists rule, driving the last vestiges of religious affirmation out of the public square: Santa Claus but no creche, "Jingle Bells" but not "Silent Night," Hanukkah dreidles but not Hanukkah candles.[701]

One way out of this *Lemon* dilemma, proposed by the *New Republic's* Rosen, is to substitute a rule of "neutrality" for *Lemon's* three unadministerable standards. That rule, according to Rosen, would not mean erecting the "wall of separation" between church and state. It would simply mean that whenever government provided any aid to education, it could provide it equally to religious and secular institutions. Rosen believes that this would dissipate the "false tension" between the two clauses of the First Amendment, and would remove the absurdity of present results under the *Lemon* standard.

Rosen claims that a rule of "neutrality" would find unconstitutional required prayer in the public schools (since government is supposed to be "neutral" on religion), but would not bar "moments of silence" in which students could decide to pray, if they so chose. Similarly, "All government-sponsored creches, menorahs and the like would be unconstitutional, with or without talking plastic garnishes." Finally, "students would be able to use state aid—including vouchers—in religious or secular private schools, without Talmudic surveillance from the justices at every turn."[702]

Rosen's "neutrality" approach has the virtue of being clearer, at least on the surface, than the convoluted *Lemon* tests, but it would be prone to murkiness when applied in practice. For example, is a public school "moment of silence" desired only by those

227

seeking to pray permissible? If everyone understands that religious schools offer greater discipline and vouchers are disproportionately used to gain entry into religious schools, does that amount to more than "neutrality" with regard to state aid to religion?

Given these difficulties, there is great appeal to the equally straightforward standard apparently advocated by Justice Frankfurter in his *Barnette* dissent, and endorsed most recently by Justices Rehnquist, Scalia, White, and Thomas. According to this standard, while governments may not promote the interests of any particular sect, the establishment clause should *not* be read as prohibiting government sponsorship or encouraging of religion in general. According to this reading of the amendment, while government must not interfere with the "free exercise" of religion, it is under no obligation to guarantee anyone "freedom *from* religion."

Curiously, otherwise shrewd observers like Rosen reject this doctrinal solution, claiming that the Rehnquist, Scalia, White, and Thomas approach has been "swaddled in historical claims that have been thoroughly discredited by scholars." According to Rosen, "Of all the historical claims Rehnquist has floated to mask his conservative political agenda, his claims about religion have been the most thoroughly disproved." Rosen further asserts, painting with a nice wide brush, that "no serious scholar has challenged [these] conclusions [of Rehnquist's critics]."[703] I may not be above levity or whimsicality (neither is Rosen), but I hope I am a serious enough scholar to meet Rosen's tests. And I most certainly think that the Rehnquist critics on whom Rosen relies, Douglas Laycock and Leonard Levy, scholars on whom Justice Souter similarly relied in his important concurring opinion in *Weisman*, can be rebutted. Rosen, adopting Laycock and Levy's analysis, declares that "Rehnquist, Scalia, White and Thomas have refused to answer the overwhelming evidence against them."[704] They could, and should.

All that Rehnquist, Scalia, White, and Thomas need do is to turn to perhaps the greatest authority on the original understanding of the First Amendment's religion clauses, Joseph Story. Story was Associate Justice of the Supreme Court from 1811–1845, and Dane Professor of Law at Harvard University. He was the author of many legal treatises and some of the most important opinions of the Supreme Court. He is now acknowledged to have been "the most commanding legal figure of his age."[705]

Joseph Story began a long career of public service as a Jeffersonian representative in the Massachusetts legislature from 1805–1811, and served in the United States Congress from 1808–1809. He was appointed Associate Justice at the young age of thirty-two by President Madison in 1811. In 1833, at the height of his intellectual powers, Story wrote his commanding three-volume *Commentaries on the Constitution of the United States*, the most important constitutional commentary of the first half of the nineteenth century. Story himself abridged this tome in one volume "For the Use of Colleges and High Schools."[706]

The editors of a 1987 reprint of Story's one-volume abridgement note that Story was uniquely qualified as interpreter of the original understanding of the Constitution. These editors, two distinguished constitutional law scholars at the University of Illinois, Ronald D. Rotunda and John E. Nowak, observed that "This man of such unique abilities [Story] lived at precisely the best time for him to reflect upon and explain [the original constitutional] principles."[707] They continued:

> Story's explanation of the constitutional principles is the explanation of a Supreme Court Justice and scholar who knew their origins and the problems encountered in making the new Republic function under those principles. Although Story was born three years after the Declaration of Independence was signed, he had personal knowledge of the origins of the Constitution. It must be remembered that his family was active in the Revolution, and he was a close associate of men who had been both the intellectual and political leaders of the revolution. The Constitution was drafted when he was only eight years old; the first ten amendments to the Constitution, which form the Bill of Rights, were ratified only twenty years before Story took his oath of office as a Supreme Court Justice. For all practical purposes, he was present at the creation of our constitutional system of government.[708]

Even the University of Chicago's Cass Sunstein, a leading left-liberal constitutional theorist, observes that Story was "probably the leading early commentator on the Constitution."[709]

What Story had to say about the meaning of the First Amendment, it would seem, is thus entitled to great weight. In the one-volume abridgement, whose text is identical to that of the three-volume masterpiece,[710] Story wrote that "the right of a society or government to interfere in matters of religion will hardly be contested by any persons, who believe that piety, religion, and morality are intimately connected with the well being of the state, and indispensable to the administration of civil justice."[711] It was clear that Story was one of those persons of whom he spoke, someone who was concerned with statecraft and its use of piety, religion, and morality. Story went on to suggest, in words reminiscent of those used by Samuel Chase in the second trial of John Fries,[712] just what "great doctrines of religion" the state ought to help promulgate:

... the being, and attributes, and providence of one Almighty God; the responsibility to him for all actions, founded upon moral freedom and accountability; a future state of rewards and punishments; the cultivation of all the personal, social, and benevolent virtues;—these never can be a matter of indifference in any well ordered community. It is, indeed, difficult to conceive, how any civilized society can well exist without them.[713]

We have tried to do just that, and our civilization shows many signs of crumbling.

Further explicating what he believed to be the sensible duty of government in matters of religion, Story stated that "it is impossible for those, who believe in the truth of Christianity, as a divine revelation, to doubt that it is the especial duty of government to foster, and encourage it among all the citizens and subjects." Lest it be thought that the "free exercise" clause of the First Amendment forbids this sort of "interference in religion," Story made clear that the government's duty to foster and encourage Christianity was "a point wholly distinct from that of the right of

230

private judgment in matters of religion, and of the freedom of public worship according to the dictates of one's own conscience."[714]

Story conceded that "The real difficulty lies in ascertaining the limits, to which government may rightfully go in fostering and encouraging religion."[715] Still, he made it clear that

> Probably at the time of the adoption of the Constitution, and of the [First Amendment] the general, if not the universal, sentiment in America was, that Christianity ought to receive encouragement from the state, so far as it is not incompatible with the private rights of conscience, and the freedom of religious worship. An attempt to level all religions, and to make it a matter of state policy to hold all in utter indifference, would have created universal disapprobation, if not universal indignation.[716]

So much, then, for Jefferson's vaunted wall of separation between church and state, and so much for those who would read the First Amendment to forbid the state from adopting any posture but that of self-actualization and secular humanism.

Story went on to wonder whether "any free government can be permanent, where the public worship of God, and the support of religion, constitute no part of the policy or duty of the state in any assignable shape."[717] Returning to an earlier point, however, Story observed that "the duty of supporting religion, and especially the Christian religion" did not include "the right to force the consciences of other men, or to punish them for worshipping god in the manner, which they believe, their accountability to him requires." Story further allowed that "The rights of conscience are, indeed, beyond the just reach of any human power. They are given by God, and cannot be encroached upon by human authority, without a criminal disobedience of the precepts of natural, as well as of revealed religion."[718]

Nevertheless, and Jeffrey Rosen notwithstanding, Story went on in a manner that clearly supports the opinions in First Amendment cases of Justices Rehnquist, Scalia, Thomas, and White. Story indicated that both the First Amendment's strictures

231

against government coercion of the "rights of conscience" and the duty of obedience to the precepts of natural and revealed religion did not mean that the state could not promote religion in general and Christianity in particular. In terms that seem quite shocking in our age when a politician can find himself in deep trouble by declaring that this remains "a Christian nation,"[719] Story explained that

> The real object of the [First] amendment was, not to countenance, much less to advance Mahometanism, or Judaism, or infidelity, by prostrating Christianity; but to exclude all rivalry among Christian sects, and to prevent any national ecclesiastical establishment, which should give to an hierarchy the exclusive patronage of the national government.[720]

By forbidding the establishment of a national hierarchy, such as a set of federal bishops or prelates, Story indicated, the First Amendment was intended to "cut off the means of religious persecution, . . . and the power of subverting the rights of conscience in matters of religion." These rights of conscience, Story explained, "had been trampled upon almost from the days of the Apostles to the present age."[721] Because various Christian groups, among them Episcopalians, Presbyterians, Congregationalists, and Quakers were "the predominant sect" in some states, and because in others "there was a close numerical rivalry among contending sects," Story suggested, "it was impossible that there should not arise perpetual strife and perpetual jealousy on the subject of ecclesiastical ascendancy, if the national government were left free to create a religious establishment."[722]

The logic of Story's analysis makes plain *that even if the federal government was forbidden from establishing a national hierarchy, this did not mean that the federal government was prohibited from taking measures to secure Christianity in general,* particularly given that the First Amendment was not believed by Story to protect non-Christian worshipers at the expense of Christians. Story went on to comment that "the whole power over the subject of religion is left exclusively to the state governments, to

232

be acted upon according to their own sense of justice, and the state Constitutions[.]"[723] By this Story meant that the state governments had the power to promote the interests of any particular sect over others if they so chose, but this would have no effect on the conduct of the national government.

Story's closing remarks on religion were in seeming contrast to what he had earlier said about the groups the First Amendment was designed to protect. He observed that whatever the policies promoted by the *state* governments, "the Catholic and the Protestant, the Calvinist and the Arminian, the Jew and the Infidel, may sit down at the common table of the *national* councils, without any inquisition into their faith, or mode of worship."[724] With this last ecumenical flourish, however, Story probably meant to indicate no more than that the First Amendment forbade any religious tests for federal office, and not that the federal government was estopped from adopting a religious or even a Christian cast.

The implication of what Story had to say about the First Amendment's establishment clause, and its free exercise clause, and in particular Story's belief in the individual state's possessing the "whole power over the subject of religion," is clear. It is impossible to believe that a state or local government's choosing to institute religious or even Christian convocations on public occasions, or even a state's choice to promote prayer in the public schools, would have struck Justice Story as a violation of the First Amendment. If the original understanding of that amendment is to govern, it simply cannot be invoked to forbid school prayer, much less a nonsectarian blessing at a state-sponsored middle school convocation.

How, then, could it be that whatever persuaded Story failed to persuade Justice Souter, writing in *Weisman?* What, then, are the arguments of Justice Souter, relying on the scholars Laycock and Levy, that were so persuasive to Rosen, and are they convincing?

Justice Souter's historical argument turns almost entirely on the drafting history of the provision that eventually became the First Amendment: Souter begins "when James Madison arrived at the first Congress," with Madison's text of proposed consti-

233

tutional amendments. Madison's proposed amendment with regard to religion was that "*the civil rights of none shall be abridged on account of religious belief or worship, nor shall any national religion be established, nor shall the full and equal rights of conscience be in any manner, or on any pretext, infringed.*"[725] Souter doesn't say so, but this language would not have expressly prohibited any state aid to religion in general. Madison's freedom of religion draft amendment would seem calculated only to prevent discrimination that would favor a particular sect.

Nevertheless, Souter makes much of the fact that "Madison's language did not last long," and was soon changed, by a Select Committee of the House. The new House Select Committee's proposed amendment read that "*no religion shall be established by law, nor shall the equal rights of conscience be infringed.*"[726] This language, too, would seem more logically directed at preventing the favoring of a particular sect than at barring all aid to religious practices.

Still, the House Select Committee proposal was further amended by the House acting as a Committee of the Whole. Pursuant to a proposal by Samuel Livermore, the Committee of the Whole changed the Select Committee's language to read "*Congress shall make no laws touching religion, or infringing the rights of conscience.*"[727] Had this proposal been accepted as the First Amendment, of course, Souter and those who would draw a firm Jeffersonian "wall of separation" between church and state[728] would have the best of the argument. It would be difficult to imagine language better calculated to forbid any governmental involvement with religion than "Congress shall make no laws touching religion. . . ."

Nevertheless, *this clear language of Congressman Livermore's, suggesting that the government was not supposed to be involved with religion in any way was itself rejected.* Instead, language "derived from a proposal by Fisher Ames of Massachusetts" was substituted. This new language was "*Congress shall make no law establishing Religion, or prohibiting the free exercise thereof, nor shall the rights of conscience be infringed.*"[729] Souter concedes that the adoption of this language might suggest that "the Representatives had thought Livermore's proposal [which drove a clear wedge between all religion and the government] too expansive." Souter also notes Leonard Levy's suggestion that Congress simply worried that Livermore's "language would not 'satisfy the demands of those who wanted something said specifically against establishments of religion.' "[730]

Souter appears to concede that all of this speculation as to motives is no more than that. Still, Souter makes much of the fact that "the House rejected the *original* Select Committee's version, which arguably ensured only that 'no religion' enjoyed an official preference over others, and deliberately chose instead a prohibition extending to laws establishing 'religion' in general."[731] Souter appears to infer from this that the House's aim was to reject all federal involvement with religion whatever. But, again, if this is what the House meant to do, Livermore's language—"Congress shall make no laws *touching* religion"— was better calculated to do it than was Fisher Ames's— "Congress shall make no law *establishing* Religion." Given that the phrase "established church" in England has always referred to a particular sect, it is difficult to understand the language the House sent on to the Senate—"Congress shall make no law *establishing* Religion"—as being concerned with anything but the federal government's establishment of a particular sect. It certainly was *not* intended to mandate state *neutrality* toward religion in general.

Souter's speculation regarding the meaning of Fisher Ames's language—that it was intended to prevent aid to religion in general—seems particularly far-fetched considering Fisher Ames's beliefs. Fisher Ames was a member of the so-called "High Federalists," a group committed to elite leadership for the new nation, and a group which appears to have believed in the importance of morality and religion in government. Moreover, it is highly doubtful, contrary to Souter's implicit suggestion, that Fisher Ames meant to remove the possibility that any of the original thirteen constituent states could aid religion, as the Supreme Court now construes the First Amendment to do. If Ames was concerned about any interference with religion, it should be remembered that it was strictly at the federal rather than at the state level.

Souter moves on to consider the history of the language of the provision that eventually became the First Amendment as it traveled through the Senate, and then the House's response to the Senate. He suggests that this legislative history supports the argument that "the framers meant the Establishment Clause's prohibition to encompass nonpreferential aid to religion."[732] But Souter's own legislative history of what went on in the House, in rejecting Livermore's clear language, seriously undercuts this assertion.

In any event, Souter observes that "the Senate considered a number of provisions that would have permitted" nonpreferential aid to religions, and did eventually adopt one of them. He notes that the Senate "briefly entertained" a text that provided that "Congress shall make no law establishing One Religious Sect or Society in preference to others, nor shall the rights of conscience be infringed."[733] Had this language been the text of the First Amendment, of course, the "nonpreferentialists" would have had conclusive proof of *their* views. Rehnquist, Thomas, Scalia, and White would have won, and Souter et. al. would then have had to concede defeat. Just as Souter would have clearly prevailed if Livermore's proposal had been the text enacted, so would he clearly have been wrong had this Senate proposal been the final text. But alas, the Senate eventually rejected that language, and adopted the text of the House's [Fisher Ames's] proposal, but without the clause protecting the "rights of conscience."[734]

Since we have no record of the Senate debates involved, Souter observes that "we cannot know what prompted" the Senate simply to adopt the House language. Nevertheless, it appears that "six days later, the Senate went half circle and adopted its narrowest language yet."[735] This was a provision that "Congress shall make no law establishing articles of faith or a mode of worship, or prohibiting the free exercise of religion."[736] This language is a bit obscure, and could be read to forbid any involvement with religion, or could be read simply to prohibit a particular sect's being established by the federal government.

In any event, in the consideration in the House that followed this latest version from the Senate, the House rejected the Senate language, and the matter was left to a Joint Conference Committee to resolve.[737] The views of the House conferees apparently won out, and the final language became "Congress shall make no law respecting an establishment of religion, or prohibiting the free exercise thereof."[738] Souter declares, "What is remarkable is that, unlike the earliest House drafts or the final Senate proposal, the prevailing language is not limited to laws respecting an establishment of 'a religion,' 'a national religion,' 'one religious sect,' or specific 'articles of faith.' "[739] He further stresses, "The framers repeatedly considered and deliberately rejected such narrow language and instead extended their prohibition to state support for 'religion' in general."[740]

As Souter's own research reveals, however, we cannot know the meaning of the framers' "repeated rejections" of particular language. Of much more importance, we do have evidence that if the framers had wanted to make clear that there could be no governmental involvement promoting religion they had language available—Livermore's—that would have done precisely that. Given the availability of the Livermore approach—forbidding any action "touching" religion—I think that Souter and the scholars on whom he relies incorrectly make too much of the rejection of language involving individual sects, or creeds, and too little of the explicit rejection of language involving acts "touching religion."

Finally, it seems quite significant that Fisher Ames's language, "Congress shall make no law *establishing* Religion . . . ," was rejected in favor of the final language, "Congress shall make no law *respecting an establishment* of religion." The language eventually adopted, *contrary to what Souter suggests*, in its use of the phrase "an establishment of religion," seems more specific—more directed against the adoption of a particular sect—than does "establishing religion." "Establishing religion"—the language that was rejected—seems more directed at religion *in general*.

237

The meaning of the language eventually adopted that prohibits Congress from making "an establishment of religion" is still unclear—it could mean any particular sect, which I think likely, or it could be twisted to mean *all* religion. But given the Fisher Ames language that was rejected—forbidding "establishing religion"—this seems an inappropriate reading. Moreover, if the final language was supposed to mean a prohibition against all encouragement of religion, there was explicit language better calculated to achieve this aim—that of Congressman Livermore—which was rejected. Thus it appears that the non-preferentialist meaning for the clause ought to be preferred. The final language of the First Amendment, its legislative history strongly suggests, should be read as *not* prohibiting aid to religion in general. *Thus, Souter's effort at legislative history, contrary to the assertions of Rosen, supports the nonpreferentialist reading of the clause by Rehnquist, Scalia, White, and Thomas.*[741]

The arguments of Souter, and the scholars on whom he relies, principally Laycock and Levy, are thus far from convincing. Indeed, their linguistic exegesis leads to the opposite conclusion from that which they suggested. It is, of course, possible that the change in the language from the draft versions of the amendment to the final text had no substantive significance. A close reading of the legislative history, however, appears to give plenty of support to Justice Story's interpretation that the clause as eventually accepted is properly understood as not permitting the favoring of any particular sect. Instead, Story's reading of the establishment clause, that, in short, the First Amendment was *not* intended to bar encouragement of religion in general, seems correct.[742]

It should be borne in mind, however, that the latest learning on the desires of the framers suggests that it is probably an illegitimate interpretive exercise to try to determine their subjective *intention* with regard to the use of particular language. The common law tradition in which they were participants stressed that words of legislators (and by implication Constitution makers) were to be interpreted not according to the intention of particular drafters, but rather according to the understanding of contemporaries, particularly the ratifiers.[743] Thus, those who

238

wish to be faithful to the dictates of the Constitution should base their interpretive strategy on "original understanding," rather than "original intention."[744]

I find this "original understanding" argument to be persuasive. If one seeks the "original understanding" of the First Amendment, then, one must look not only to the text of the document itself, but to the context in which it was drafted. Such an exercise seriously undercuts the implications of the work of Souter, Laycock, and Levy with regard to the First Amendment's impact on state and local governments' involvement with religion, and their argument that the framers wanted neutrality toward all religion. It is clear that whether the framers of the First Amendment meant to exclude the federal government from all participation in any kind of encouragement of any religion, they recognized that state governments *were* involved in religious promotion, and they do not appear to have had any desire to curtail those activities.

The earliest federal judges, it will be remembered, made clear their belief that there could be no law without morality and no morality without religion.[745] In accordance with this belief the state governments were purposely left free to inculcate basic morality and religion, as the language of the First Amendment was directed only at *congressional* acts. It simply is inconceivable that any framer of the First Amendment could have believed that he was dictating that no state could permit prayer to be used on public occasions, and equally inconceivable that he would have chosen to use the First Amendment as a means to bar prayer or moments of silence in the schools that would be training young people in the obligations of republican citizenship. If close textual analysis, consideration of original intention *and* original understanding can tell us anything, what they suggest is that it was wrong for the Supreme Court to incorporate into the Fourteenth Amendment's due process clause anything from the First Amendment regarding the prohibition of an establishment of religion.

It may be a while before the Supreme Court returns to this view, but hairline cracks in the judicially created spite wall of separation between religion and the state erected in *Weisman* and its antecedents may be developing. The criticism of *Weisman* has energizied media critics of the Court, who see the decision as the work of a "renegade" group of unelected judicial lawmakers reversing traditional practice in the republic.[746] Some even seemed to have called for civil disobedience to the rule barring prayers at graduation ceremonies.[747] One can occasionally read in the *Wall Street Journal* that the practice of beginning school days with a prayer refuses to die.[748] More telling, the Supreme Court itself may be pulling back from the *Weisman* decision. In June of 1993, for example, the Supreme Court let stand a federal court of appeals decision permitting student-initiated prayer at a public high school graduation ceremony.[749] The Supreme Court also ruled 9–0 that "public school systems that open their schools to after-hours use by community groups must permit religious groups to use the buildings on the same terms."[750]

The Court has not yet returned to recognizing the historic importance of religion in instilling good citizenship—the basis of earlier American public-sponsored prayer. But the Court has begun to allow religious exercises on public property or at public events on the basis of the First Amendment's *guarantee of free speech*. In *Lamb's Chapel v. Center Moriches School District* (1993), the use of the public schools case, an evangelical Christian church had sought to use a room in Center Moriches High School in eastern Long Island after hours to show a series of films with a "Christian perspective" on family life.

Justice White (one of the four dissenters in *Weisman*), writing for the majority in *Lamb's Chapel*, held that the Center Moriches school district's refusal to allow the group to screen its films was "plainly invalid" under prior Supreme Court precedents. For White, the refusal was discrimination against speech on the basis of the point of view presented. Since other speakers had been permitted to use school facilities to express their views on family life, the school district could not discriminate against a religious group simply because it sought to address the subject based on its religious convictions. The Court concluded, in effect, that the case was not really about the integration of religion with the public schools, but rather, as the *New York Times* Supreme Court reporter Linda Greenhouse explained, about "equal-access use

240

of the schools," something that presented no constitutional problem.[751]

In *Lamb's Chapel* the Court once again reaffirmed its *Lemon* test, which the "equal-access use" supposedly passed. This was not without some spirited comment from Justice Scalia (joined by Justice Thomas), who concurred in the result, allowing the religious group to use school facilities, but wrote separately in order to protest basing the decision on *Lemon*. Said Scalia, "Like some ghoul in a late-night horror movie that repeatedly sits up in its grave and shuffles abroad after being repeatedly killed and buried, *Lemon* stalks our establishment clause jurisprudence once again, frightening the little children and school attorneys of Center Moriches."[752] Perhaps in time the Court will finally garner the courage to drive the wooden stake through the *Lemon* ghoul's heart, cut off its head, and return the interpretation of the establishment clause to its benign original understanding. In order for the Court fully to do this, however, it may also have to reject as unconstitutional the recently passed Religious Freedom Restoration Act (RFRA).[753] The RFRA, after all, unwisely promotes individual self-actualization in a manner that undermines the traditional values of the community, and, in effect, establishes religion by spelling out a standard for a court to determine its existence. There is little support for the *Lemon* test, and it may soon go. But given the coalition of diverse groups that pushed for the RFRA, the Court, shy of political controversy, may hesitate before overturning it.[754]

E. Abortion

Abortion is the most intractable of the current constitutional conundrums, because at bottom it involves the most profound, essentially religious beliefs. Stated most simply, one's point of view on abortion turns ultimately on whether or not one believes that an embryo is a person.[755] If one does, as the prolife movement has made clear, then abortion is murder and indefensible. If one doesn't, then there seems no denying that the woman carrying the embryo ought to be able to determine what to do with it, just as she ought to be capable of making any determination regarding surgery to be performed on any other part of her body.[756] The determination of "personhood" appears to be a theological one, since science can offer no clear indication of when an embryo passes from the animal to the human, or when, as classical religious thinkers would have it, the embryo acquires a soul.

Our legal history has not been uniform on the issue. At common law, the question of whether abortion was permitted turned on whether the embryo had begun to move within the womb, the so-called "quickening" of the fetus. The classic statement is in Sir William Blackstone's *Commentaries on the Laws of England* (1765). In Volume I, in the course of his discussion of "The Rights of Persons" (Book I, Chapter I), Blackstone notes, "The right of personal security consists in a person's legal and uninterrupted enjoyment of his life, his limbs, his body, his health, and his reputation."[757] Blackstone then proceeds to explain:

Life is the immediate gift of God, a right inherent by nature in every individual; and it begins in contemplation of law as soon as an infant is able to stir in the mother's womb. For if a woman is quick with child, and by a potion, or otherwise killeth it in her womb; or if any one beat her, whereby the child dieth in her body, and she is delivered of a dead child; this, though not murder, was by the antient law homicide or manslaughter. But at present it is not looked upon in quite so atrocious a light, though it remains a very hideous misdemeanor.[758]

English "Abortion law became more stringent in 1803, when abortion was criminalized. Punishment for abortion before quickening was set at exile, whipping, or imprisonment. Post-quickening abortion was sanctionable with death."[759]

Abortion was not prohibited by state statute in many American states until well into the nineteenth century, but it was uniformly barred until the second half of the twentieth century, when some states began to relax abortion restrictions. It looked as if the matter would be decided on a state-by-state basis until the Supreme Court's surprising decision in the 1973 *Roe v. Wade* case.[760] Since that case, with its uneasy trimester compromise solution to the abortion problem, the federal courts have been virtually inundated with abortion cases. The results have been hopelessly inconsistent and unsatisfactory, bringing the Supreme Court into more disrepute than it has experienced since the *Dred Scott* case, almost one hundred and forty years ago.

Even though the whole thrust of the analysis offered here has been to confirm the Federalists' understanding that there can be no law without morality and no morality with religion, there are limits to what a religiously based jurisprudence ought to try to do, at least where that jurisprudence is invoked at the federal level. If Story's comments on the First Amendment teach us anything, they teach caution with regard to the imposition of the views of any particular religious domination. It is not for the federal government, for example, even if it can generally promote religion, to take a position on transubstantiation, or the loosening of the strictures on the faithful by Vatican II.

The treatment of abortion is one area where it might be best for the Supreme Court to hesitate to invoke a religiously based jurisprudence. Religion and a religiously based jurisprudence can clearly play a part in the public sphere on matters for which there is a broad history of nonsectarian consensus, such as school convocations, or even school prayer, at least where this is decided at the local level. But on the essentially religious question of when an embryo or a fetus becomes a person there is no broad national nonsectarian consensus. National polls and election results curiously seem to point both ways on whether the public favors a right to abortion or an embryo's right to life.

Seventy-three percent (73%) of Americans polled in June 1990 by Louis Harris and Associates, Inc., when asked the question, "Do you favor or oppose giving a woman, with the advice of her physician, the right to choose to have an abortion?" responded "in favor of that right."[761] Still, in February 1991, when the gallup organization asked, "Which of these statements best deScribes your feelings about abortion?" 36.8 percent said, "Abortion is Just as Bad as Killing a Person Who has already Been Born, it is Murder"; 11.5 percent said, "Abortion is Murder, but it is

Not as Bad as Killing Someone Who has Already Been Born"; and 28.3 percent said, "Abortion is Not Murder, but it Does Involve the Taking of Human Life."[762] Astonishingly, then, 73 percent of Americans appear to favor a woman's right to have an abortion, but 77 percent believe that abortion is either murder or the taking of a human life. The Wirthlin poll, conducted in November 1990, found that 60 percent of the respondents "agreed that every unborn child has a basic right to life, although 83 percent of the same respondents said that abortion should be available under certain conditions."[763]

As we have repeatedly maintained here,[764] the Supreme Court should not reach decisions without a firm grounding in the original understanding of the Constitution's framers, or, in exceptional cases, in clear custom which serves as a proxy for the original understanding.[765] Such "clear customs" would probably be those that have been followed and accepted for most if not all of our national history, and would be those most reflective of the natural law roots of our jurisprudence. They would be matters similar to those of which Chase spoke in *Calder v. Bull*, principles such as the government must not take one person's property simply to give it to another, or must not allow one person to be both judge and party in the same case.[766] This notion of "clear custom" jurisprudence, it will be observed, has much in common with Justice Antonin Scalia's notable essay on "specific traditions" implemented in connection with the due process clause. To understand what customs we ought to enforce with regard to asserted rights, it is useful to consider the debate between Justice Scalia and Justice Brennan on this point.

In the bizarre case of *Michael H. v. Gerald D.* (1989),[767] the natural father of a daughter born to a woman married to another man sought to claim a "due process" liberty interest in securing visitation rights for his daughter. The state of California, however, had a statutory scheme which conclusively presumed that a child born to a married woman was, for all legal purposes, to be considered the child of the woman and her husband, unless either the woman or the husband sought to rebut the presumption. Justice Scalia, writing for a four-person plurality, held that without a specific tradition according protection to the interests of adulterous fathers, there could be no due process interest to be protected. Scalia reasoned that the only liberty interests that could be invoked as protected by the due process clause were those "so rooted in the traditions and conscience of our people as to be ranked as fundamental."[768] Scalia indicated that protecting the visitation or other parental rights for adulterous fathers was not such a fundamental interest.

Several of the other Justices had trouble with Scalia's narrowa reading of substantive due process rights. They claimed that Scalia was wrong to "consult[] the most specific tradition available," and that the issue should have been whether there was a long-standing tradition protecting "parenthood," or "the family." Of course, applying such a "general" reading of tradition, given the particular facts of the case, a due process right for the particular plaintiff might have been found.[769] But Scalia quite correctly pointed out that at the general level of tradition that his critics, Justices O'Connor and Brennan, wanted to embrace, there would be virtual license for Justices to "decide as they think best." According to Scalia, "a rule of law that binds neither by text nor by any particular, identifiable tradition is no rule of law at all."[770]

Justice Brennan, at whom Scalia was probably aiming his barbs about judicial discretion, replied that the concept of tradition "can be as malleable and as elusive as 'liberty' itself," and Brennan denied that "tradition places a discernible border around the Constitution."[771] Instead, Brennan argued, quoting a prior opinion by Justice White, "What the deeply rooted traditions of the country are is arguable."[772] Brennan went on to contend that if the Court were to have adopted Scalia's narrow view of tradition (which Brennan claims can't be known anyway) the Supreme Court could never have found protection for a variety of purported rights. These included "the use of contraceptives by unmarried couples,"[773] "or even by married couples,"[774] "the freedom from corporal punishment in schools,"[775] "the freedom from an arbitrary transfer from a prison to a psychiatric institution,"[776] "and even the right to raise one's natural but illegiti-

245

mate children."[777] Just so. All of these are examples of the kind of judicial license that the federal courts probably should never have been able to exercise. Left off of Brennan's list, apparently by design, is the most outrageous exercise of such license, the finding of a "due process" liberty that covers the choice of a pregnant woman to have an abortion.[778]

Thus the jurisprudence of tradition, or clear custom—the sensible construction of the due process clause—suggests that Justice Scalia's conclusion in his dissent in *Casey*,[779] that the Supreme Court has no place in the abortion debate, is correct. Not only is the implication inescapable from Scalia's opinion in *Michael H.*, but when the Court seeks to legitimize the views of one side in an essentially political or cultural struggle, and when neither side can claim a clear historical or constitutional validity to its position, the implication of *Dred Scott* itself is that the Court would do best to let the issues be resolved in other political arenas.[780] Because consensus would more likely be achieved at a state level, abortion is a matter that is best left to the state governments. It is with the states that the Constitution's framers would have chosen to place it, since at the time of the Constitution's framing all matters of family law, such as marriage, divorce, and child custody, were recognized as concerns of the state, not the federal government.

Because the framers of the Fourteenth Amendment were concerned with protecting the civil rights of the newly freed slaves, it is doubtful that they believed they were doing anything that would affect the most basic questions of domestic law, as the abortion dispute does. The Fourteenth Amendment, therefore, can offer no warrant for federalizing abortion, much less penumbras from the Fourth, Fifth, or Ninth Amendments.

The logic of the position sketched here would seem to call for the federal government to remain neutral on the question of the legality of abortion as practiced in the individual states. Neutrality is impossible, however, with regard to what is done in government hospitals or with federal funds granted to health care providers. The question of what to do about abortion will also be an important one in the coming battle over whether to institute a national system for health care. The issue sharply divides the nation, and there is a lack of consensus over whether the embryo is a person whose right to life might be protected from federal governmental interference under the due process clause of the Fifth Amendment. Perhaps it might be argued that, according to natural law thinking, we would do well to err on the side of protecting human life, and thus ban federally funded abortions. Unfortunately, if the embryo is *not* a person, then a natural law theorist might argue that we should err on the side of protecting the natural human liberty of the mother to choose to terminate a pregnancy, thus asserting control over her own life. Here natural law, based ultimately on religious precepts, is of no more help than religion itself. The matter, it seems, ought to be for Congress or the executive to resolve through the usual political processes, without Court interference.

But if the federal government decides *not* to allow funds to be used for abortions, either in state clinics receiving federal funds, or in hospitals under direct federal government control, the federal courts should not reverse those decisions. Thus, the Supreme Court's recent decision in *Rust v. Sullivan* (1991),[781] which upheld the so-called "gag-rule" banning federally funded clinics from offering counseling on termination of pregnancies, was correct.[782] Critics of the decision wanted to paint it as a First Amendment violation, as the government censoring the speech of doctors or clinic workers accepting federal funds. It was, of course, no such thing.

Even if there is a federally protected right against legislation *forbidding* abortion, it does not follow that there is a positive duty for the federal government either to facilitate abortion through counseling, or, *a fortiori*, to use federal funds to pay for abortions. When federal funds are used to support clinics where abortions are not performed, but where referrals are made to clinics owned, operated, and staffed by the same persons, the federal government is indirectly in the business of providing abortions. If the federal government is under no duty to provide abortions, it is permissible to indicate that no federal money ought to be used indirectly to provide them either.

247

It is not a First Amendment violation to forbid abortion counseling funded by federal assistance. The choice to accept federal funding is a voluntary one, and any choice involving governmental work may involve some limitation on the free exercise of particular constitutional rights. For generations, for example, statutes have been held constitutional that forbid federal workers from partisan political activity on the job even though the Constitution protects such rights in the abstract. Similarly, if one were hired to publish the Federal Register, the listing of all federal regulations, one could not claim a First Amendment right to fill the official regulations with one's own editorial comments or political harangues, even though one's First Amendment rights might thereby seem to be infringed.

The next troubling abortion issue for the Courts may be the so-called "Freedom of Choice" bill currently before Congress. Various versions of that bill seek to overrule the *Planned Parenthood v. Casey* decision insofar as it put limits on the purported constitutional right to an abortion announced in *Roe v. Wade*. The "Freedom of Choice" Act might thus deny states the powers to impose restrictions such as twenty-four-hour waiting periods, to require abortion clinics to counsel on fetal development and alternatives to abortion, or to require parental notification or consent before performing abortions on teenagers. The proposed federal statute might also require even religious hospitals that receive federal funding to give up the right to refuse to perform abortions on moral grounds.[783] Some drafts of the proposed statute provide that "A state may not restrict the right to abortion even after the fetus can survive on its own if the abortion is 'necessary to protect the life or health of the woman.' " These bills apparently define "health" to include "all factors—physical, emotional, psychological, familial and the woman's age— relevant to the well being of the patient." This means that the statute, if enacted, may have to be read as saying that "a woman may not abort a viable fetus, unless she really wants to."[784]

Particularly insofar as the Freedom of Choice bill could permit abortions for viable fetuses, it would seem to run counter to the part of *Roe v. Wade* that discovered a Fourteenth Amendment

248

interest in the life of the unborn, that the state could choose to protect. On this ground alone the Freedom of Choice bill could not survive constitutional challenge. One hopes that the Court may have the courage, if a Freedom of Choice Act is ever passed and challenged, to declare that this traditional matter of what is, after all, domestic law does not belong in the federal domain. The right to choose an abortion, if one exists, is not among the pantheon of civil rights contemplated by the framers of the Fourteenth Amendment. If the notions of original understanding advanced here make any sense at all, the Supreme Court should determine that there is no constitutional basis for the federal government's dictating to the states what they can or cannot do about abortion. Indeed, as we have already seen,[785] insofar as the Clinton health plan seeks to move into areas of domestic policy traditionally the realm of the states—including abortion apparently—that whole scheme ought to be facing a grave constitutional challenge if it is ever passed, and if we take the original concept of our federalism seriously.

In any event, if the Freedom of Choice Act should ever be passed, a courageous Court, concerned with preserving some shred of federalism and state police power to protect the rights of all of its citizens born and unborn, ought to declare the Freedom of Choice Act unconstitutional. This ought to be done even if it means acknowledging that *Roe v. Wade* was fatally flawed. But given the atrocity of the *Casey* decision which reaffirmed *Roe,* and given that a position in favor of *Roe* and the Freedom of Choice Act is likely to be a litmus test for any Clinton nominee, such a Supreme Court decision is not likely to come in the near term. If this matter is to be restored to the states, it will probably have to be done by constitutional amendment. (This and other such matters are addressed in the concluding chapter.)

There is one other argument involving the constitutionality of abortion provisions that should be raised in passing. If one analyzes the problem as a matter of determining when the embryo is a "person," with attendant rights guaranteed by the Fifth and Fourteenth Amendments, there is no resolving the constitutional dilemma created between balancing the rights of the embryo and the rights of the mother. Thus the matter seems best left to the individual state legislatures, as already indicated. A second argument appears to be emerging in the literature, however, most notably with Oxford and New York University law professor Ronald Dworkin's new book, *Life's Dominion* (1993).[786] I say "emerging in the literature," but what I really mean is emerging in the relatively left-flowing mainstream of the American academy. The argument of which Dworkin suddenly makes so much has always been at the center of prolife rhetoric and thought.[787]

Professor Dworkin suggests that the struggle over abortion is not really about when the embryo becomes a "person," but rather about the sanctity, sacred nature, or intrinsic value of individual human life.[788] Remarkably, Dworkin then goes on to argue that the "sanctity" argument applies to the life of the mother as well, and appears to suggest that we can weigh differing quantities of sanctity in individual lives, so that there is still a "balancing" exercise to be done, weighing the sanctity of embryonic life against that of the mother. Dworkin uses a complex argument to make this point, involving his concept of "frustration" of human life. He maintains that it is worse to terminate, or apparently fundamentally to impair, a human life where there has been considerable creative human investment in that life, than it is to terminate a life—say that of the embryo—where there has been no such investment.[789]

Dworkin then proceeds to suggest that most of us would agree on certain areas where the sanctity of the mother's life takes precedence. One such area, for Dworkin, is cases of rape or incest, where the mother's very bodily integrity has been forcibly breached, where her personality has been dismissed, and where she has been forced to submit to the overbearing will of another.[790] He appears to take a similar position in cases where the mother's life is threatened by her pregnancy, seeming to suggest that the sanctity of the embryo's life cannot prevail over the certain death of the mother.[791]

Dworkin's argument about the sanctity of human life, however, appears to cut in a way other than he intends. If human life really is a sacred gift of God, and if a primal command of God to

250

man is to protect and honor God's gifts, then—except in the case of an actual threat to the life of the mother—it is difficult to understand why any balancing act is involved at all. The "balancing act" appears to be smuggled in with Dworkin's idiosyncratic notion that the sanctity of individual life depends on the amount of creative investment in it. But sanctity is no more amenable to carving up by degrees than is pregnancy itself. One cannot be a little pregnant, and one's life is probably not more sacred than any one else's. Life is life, and less than life is something else.

Thus, it would seem that the sanctity of even embryonic life ought to trump any mere psychological trauma to the mother. If the miracle of life is God-given, and if the command of God is to preserve it, even in the case of rape or incest, there should be no arguments permitting abortion.

Earlier we contended that it was clear to the framers and ratifiers of the Constitution that, as Justice Story argued, the state and federal governments were permitted to encourage religion, though the federal government was not to do so through the promotion of any particular sect. If the command to preserve human life can be recognized as a primal religious matter, it would seem that there ought to be constitutional support for banning all abortions, except where the life of the mother is threatened by a continued pregnancy. One might even argue that any state or federal legislation that permitted abortions for any reason other than a threat to the life of the mother was an antireligious measure of a sort that ought to be barred under the First Amendment, as, in effect, an impermissible interference with a great religious precept.

The First Amendment would clearly bar the state or federal governments from prohibiting children, say, from praying before any particular age. Perhaps, then, no state or federal government ought to be permitted to allow embryonic children to be terminated before they even have a chance to participate in the fulfillment of the commands of the deity.

But today, we are probably too secular a state to allow this sort of argument barring abortion to carry the day, at least at the national level. Still, it is not without merit, and it, or something

251

like it, surely explains the zealotry of Operation Rescue and other organizations committed to protecting the lives of the unborn as sacred. Given that the First Amendment ought to be construed as permitting states to determine policy in this area, any state could bar abortion (except perhaps in the case of a clear threat to the life of the mother) on sanctity grounds.

Indeed, Dworkin notwithstanding, the logic of the idea of the sanctity of human life would probably lead most people ineluctably toward a prolife and anti-abortion position. This was the logic of Ronald Reagan's stated position on the issue—nine years before Dworkin's book—in 1984. Reagan suggested that just as the antislavery forces did, prolife forces should appeal

to the hearts and minds of their countrymen, to the truth of human dignity under God. From their example, we know that respect for the sacred value of human life is too deeply ingrained in the hearts of our people to remain forever suppressed. . . . The real question today is not when human life begins, but, *What is the value of human life?* . . . The real question . . . for all of us is whether that tiny human life has a God-given right to be protected by the law—the same right we have. . . . Every legislator, every doctor, and every citizen needs to recognize that the real issue is whether to affirm and protect the sanctity of all human life, or to embrace a social ethic where some human lives are valued and others are not. As a nation, we must choose between the sanctity of life ethic and the "quality of life" ethic. . . . I am convinced that Americans do not want to play God with the value of human life. It is not for us to decide who is worthy to live and who is not. . . . [As] Malcolm Muggeridge [writes]: "Either life is always and in all circumstances sacred, or intrinsically of no account; it is inconceivable that it should be in some cases the one, and in some the other." . . . Prayer and action are needed to uphold the sanctity of human life. . . . [W]e cannot survive as a free nation when some men decide that others are not fit to live and should be abandoned to abortion or infanticide. . . . [T]here is no cause more important for preserving . . . freedom than affirming the transcendent right to life of all human beings, the right without which no other rights have any meaning.[792]

252

I find the logic of this position persuasive. Until very recently, like most law school academics and American intellectuals, I reflexively tended toward a prochoice position. Works by American legal academics or members of the chattering classes seem to be overwhelmingly prochoice.[793] The exception that proves the rule is Harvard Law Professor Mary Ann Glendon's *Abortion and Divorce in Western Law* (1987).[794] Glendon makes the compelling argument that American law ought to discourage abortion even in the early stages of pregnancy, so long as we follow the French example and provide "comparatively generous financial support for married as well as unwed mothers."[795] I agree with Glendon. As one's faith grows stronger (as seems to happen toward the onset of middle age and when one raises children), the idea of a right to an abortion becomes increasingly incomprehensible. This phenomenon should be on the rise as the baby boom generation, the great bulge in our demographical body (like some great mongoose moving through the digestive system of a cobra), enters middle age.

Like many others, if I had a free hand in public policy, and if I were advising state governments, I would ban abortions except to protect the life (not the mental health) of the mother. (That is the extent to which I find Dworkin's argument impressive.) Like Glendon, in fairness to mothers and to their children, I would want to see that sufficient resources of society were provided in order to ensure that unwanted and unplanned children were raised in a supportive environment. But since I am not charged with such utopian planning, I have not had to make the decision whether the supportive environment would be achieved by grants in aid, through encouraging adoption and foster parenting, or through state institutions, each of which has its attractive and unattractive aspects. In part in order to avoid this dilemma, I am content, for the present, to leave the constitutional argument where it was earlier in this section, with the Constitution having nothing to say one way or the other about what the states can do in the area of abortion.

We used to be content to preserve the states as fifty separate social laboratories to work out and offer competing views about

253

how our polity ought to function. Even Justice O'Connor, who appears to have been complicit in removing the issue of husband notification from the ken of state legislatures in *Casey*,[796] once took the position that "when we are concerned with extremely sensitive issues, such as the one involved here [abortion], 'the appropriate forum for their resolution in a democracy is the [state] legislature.' "[797] A classic judicial statement on the states' role in this regard was the second Justice Harlan's, in 1957:

> It has often been said that one of the great strengths of our federal system is that we have, in the forty-eight States, forty-eight experimental social laboratories. "State statutory law reflects predominantly this capacity of a legislature to introduce novel techniques of social control. The federal system has the immense advantage of providing forty-eight separate centers for such experimentation."[798]

Harlan noted an earlier case's observation that

> the marriage relationship, being a matter as to which numerous divergent views are held in modern society, is peculiarly the sort of problem that ought to be left open for experimentation in the more or less isolated social laboratories which the 48 states have been supposed to constitute.[799]

The same ought to be said about the essentially domestic problem of abortion.

A similar conclusion seems to be reached in the provocative work by Robert A. Burt, *The Constitution in Conflict* (1992).[800] Burt believes that pregnant women should have a right to travel interstate to a jurisdiction that might permit abortion, but he wants "a patchwork of differing abortion regimes [to be allowed to] develop among the states."[801] Some day the states ought to get religion, as it were, and ban abortion. To make it possible for that day to dawn, we should now leave the abortion issue to the states.

254

Summary of the Argument

Race. Most Americans now believe that they are free from racial prejudice, and the data on employment discrimination appear to support this view. Nevertheless American law is currently dominated by doctrines that permit remedies to make up for past racial discrimination. Unfortunately these policies hurt the very people they are designed to help, as Stephen Carter and Shelby Steele make clear. A better solution for dealing with the issue of race in America is to return to the notion, expressed in the Civil War and Reconstruction amendments, and in our natural law tradition, of a color-blind Constitution. The costs of maintaining a constitutional system that accords special treatment on the basis of race are mounting and far outweigh the benefits. This is true with regard to both races. A particularly egregious example of our misconceived racial policies are the events which grew out of the arrest of Rodney King. Fortunately there is some reason to hope that the Supreme Court has begun to move once again toward color-blind jurisprudence.

Religion. As we learned in Chapter Three, the First Amendment was *not* intended to apply to the states, but even if it were, the current standard for deciding whether there is a violation of the First Amendment's establishment clause, the "Lemon test," makes little sense. A "neutrality" test has also been proposed, but the most persuasive early nineteenth-century commentator, Justice Joseph Story, believed that it was the duty of the government to promote religion, though not that of any particular sect. Contrary to what Justice Souter suggested in *Weisman*, the legislative history of the First Amendment, and its original understanding, also suggest that the government is free to promote religion, though not any particular sect. There are some signs that the Court is beginning to understand this.

Abortion. The question of when an embryo becomes a person is a theological issue, our legal history has not been uniform on the point, there is no public consensus, and there is no "clear custom." The Supreme Court should thus leave policy in this area to the states. There will inevitably be some federal involvement, but the political process, and not the Courts should determine the policy to be applied. There is no First Amendment right to give or receive abortion counseling in federally funded clinics. The proposed Freedom of Choice bill is unconstitutional. There is an alternative method for analyzing the constitutionality of abortion, involving the sanctity of human life. Contrary to the suggestion of Ronald Dworkin, that argument cuts in favor of governmental banning of abortion. It is a persuasive argument, but the current state of American society suggests limited receptivity to the argument at the national level. For the time being it seems wisest to rely on fifty separate social laboratories to work out a solution to the abortion issue.

Chapter Five:

LAW, POLITICS, AND RECAPTURING

THE CONSTITUTION

A. Introduction: Altering the Supreme Court

At some level, the justification for much of the constitutional change surveyed in this book is that the rule of law is a myth. Put somewhat differently, the claim of those who would alter the Constitution by finding in it new or unenumerated "rights" or "entitlements" is that judges will inevitably have to legislate, because the meaning of constitutional provisions is obscure or contradictory. When constitutional issues come before the Court, they argue, judges must derive new meanings for the Constitution consonant with changed social or economic circumstances. A corollary to this belief is that not only constitutional law, but *all legal interpretation* is simply a species of politics—that the inescapable task of judges is to make *ex cathedra* pronouncements on appropriate social policies, balancing and choosing between the claims of competing interest groups.

At least since the time of the nomination of Robert Bork, the view that the Supreme Court ought to respond to particular interest groups, in the manner once believed appropriate for legislatures, has been dominant. This view—the notion that constitutional law is only contemporary politics writ large—has led to the unacceptable state of constitutional law which we have reviewed. Before concluding our assessment of current constitutional practice, and reflecting on the politicized nature of the current Supreme Court, it may be appropriate to suggest one structural reform, not needing a constitutional amendment, which might somewhat ameliorate the problem. We now have nine members on the Supreme Court, and this comparatively large number has helped lead presidents, the Senate, and the media in recent years to think of the Supreme Court not as a court, but rather as a superlegislature. Accordingly it has become fashionable to think of Supreme Court Justices as representing particular constituencies. Thus, it was virtually unthinkable for George Bush to appoint a white male to the seat vacated by Thurgood Marshall, and Bill Clinton apparently succumbed to considerable pressure to nominate another woman and a Jew (to restore the "Jewish seat") to the Court with his first nomination, that of Ruth Bader Ginsburg.

There is, of course, a laudable psychological effect on formerly powerless or discriminated-against ethnic or racial groups when their members are able to see one of their number raised to a high station. They feel that participation in the normal political process can bring rewards, and thus they should not become fatally alienated from society. Nevertheless, to claim that the Supreme Court cannot adequately perform its functions of judicial review involving particular ethnic groups, or involving particular matters of gender or sexual orientation, without input from Justices who happen to possess these particular ascriptive criteria is to suggest that there is no objective content to the rule of law itself.

The whole basis of judicial review as limned in *Federalist* 78, *United States v. Callender*, and *Marbury v. Madison*, it bears emphasizing, was that there was a single constitutional meaning that could be discerned by reflective unbiased interpreters of wisdom and integrity. Just as no single ethnic or sexual group has a monopoly on wisdom and integrity, so too no group possesses special insight into constitutional interpretation. To suggest

258

otherwise, and to suggest that the Court needs Justices chosen on a basis other than their understanding of the historical meaning and traditional purpose of the Constitution is wrong. It makes Justices into political servants of special interest groups rather than allowing them to be what the framers contemplated: the agents of popular sovereignty. It makes Justices law-givers rather than law-finders; it goes against what Hamilton, Chase, and Marshall contemplated, and it amounts to taking the Constitution away from the people.

To make the Justices nine Platonic guardians, charged with reformulating our jurisprudence to accord with their notions of appropriate social policy, as Learned Hand remarked many years ago, is to undermine popular sovereignty itself:

> [I]t certainly does not accord with the underlying presuppositions of popular government to vest in a chamber, unaccountable to anyone but itself, the power to suppress social experiments which it does not approve. For myself it would be most irksome to be ruled by a bevy of Platonic Guardians, even if I knew how to choose them, which I assuredly do not. If they were in charge, I should miss the stimulus of living in a society where I have, at least theoretically, some part in the direction of public affairs.[802]

In order to prevent the large number of Justices from being an excuse to make the Court a representative body, the Congress (into whose hands the Constitution places the regulation of the number of Justices) ought to reduce the number of Justices on the Court. This number should be large enough to guarantee enough reflection to arrive at correct constitutional interpretation, but too small to allow special interests to argue for representation.

The Supreme Court survived quite nicely with only six Justices until 1807, when a seventh was added. The eighth and ninth Justices were added in 1837. Perhaps it is time we contemplated pulling back to five, six, or seven. With a smaller number of Justices, the Court might be able to cease improperly regarding itself as more like a legislature or a council of revision than as a body devoted to the maintenance of established rules and traditions. Once this is accomplished the Supreme Court might be able to regain the respect Justices Souter, O'Connor, and Kennedy vainly sought to achieve in their *Casey* plurality opinion,[803] which itself was another naked exercise in social policy-making.[804] The Supreme Court would instead be free to return to its role as a guarantor of the Constitution itself, and thus return to serving the people rather than dominating them.

B. Critical Legal Studies

The Court is not likely to regain the respect of the people unless it ceases to be perceived as practicing politics. A smaller number of Justices might help in that endeavor, but to get the Court out of the policy-making business will be no easy task. That the Supreme Court has been practicing politics for at least two generations has been an inescapable reality for any modern American jurisprudential thinker. Since most of the academic theorists have approved of the Court's ostensible egalitarian goals, the temptation to build a legal philosophy supporting such judicial politics has been all but inescapable for them. One academic group, with some notoriety, has carried this practice to its logical end. The claim that there really is no such thing as the rule of law, that instead all law is politics, appears to be the core insight of one of the most influential movements in the late twentieth-century legal academy, Critical Legal Studies.

Critical Legal Studies (CLS) has been something of a scourge of conservative legal thinkers, who have bemoaned the iconoclastic nature of its thought. A former dean at Duke, the highly respected Paul Carrington, suggested that the cynical debunking of legal tradition of CLS's practitioners belonged not in law schools, but perhaps in some other university departments, maybe sociology or political science.[805] The more woolly-headed aspects of the Crits' program, such as admission to law schools by lottery but with affirmative action programs for the children of minorities or the lower classes, or forcing all law professors to spend some time as janitors while law school janitors were mercilessly made to preside in law school classrooms, have been properly held up to ridicule, and have cost Critical Legal Studies much credibility outside the academy.[806] Still, as we reach the end of our examination of the current state of American constitutional jurisprudence, we might pause for a moment to give, as it were, the same two cheers for the Critical Legal Studies movement that we gave for Justice O'Connor's opinion in *Shaw v. Reno*.[807] CLS does have something to teach conservatives, the friends of the original understanding of the Constitution.

The very best of the work in Critical Legal Studies, or by fellow-travelers such as Roberto Unger, is immensely valuable to conservatives for what it reveals about law as a part of larger belief systems. In Unger's first (and for legal conservatives, at least) still his best book, *Knowledge and Politics* (1975), he demonstrated that legal, political, and scientific thought about the human condition were inextricably linked. In fairness, of course, this "demonstration" of Unger's had also been anticipated by earlier writers on epistemology and social or natural science, most notably by Carl Becker (*The Heavenly City of the Eighteenth Century Philosophers* (1932)) and Thomas Kuhn (*The Structure of Scientific Revolutions* (2nd ed. 1971)). Still, it was notable that a law professor was prepared to tackle such deep thought.

Unger explained that we were living in a period when ideas, first formulated in the seventeenth century, had reached virtually universal acceptance, even though they were inherently flawed. These included such presumably unassailable tenets of American intellectual life as the inevitable separation of the realm of reason and the realm of personal preference, the inevitable separation of public and private spheres, and the inevitable separation of secular from religious concerns.

From Unger's insights about the artificial "antinomies," as he called them, of reason/desire, public/private, and Man/God, soon flowed the belief of some CLS figures[808] that we ought to make plans for leftist utopias. Freed from the trappings of conventional legal thought, they argued, we might acquire truer knowledge and recognize that some desires are intrinsically more reasonable than others because they might lead us to closer fellowship with one another. Eventually, the argument runs, when we come to our senses and throw off modern "false consciousness," we will discover that we cannot really continue to separate our public from our private lives. When we really understand the manner in which we are all in kinship with one another, when our private beings merge with our public ones, we will also understand that we are all a vital part of the nature of God, and the barriers between the secular and the religious will begin to crumble as life becomes richer and more rewarding.[809]

The insight that modern society has unwisely and artificially separated us from aspects of ourselves is just as profoundly important for conservatives as it is for radicals, however. The development of large-scale capitalism, with its acceptance of the values of the secular marketplace, was as alarming a development for true conservatives such as Edmund Burke (and recent thinkers such as Russell Kirk) as it is now for Critical Legal Studies scholars. Indeed, there is a remarkable similarity between the perception of modern distress articulated by Roberto Unger, on the far left, and that put forth by conservative guru William J. Bennett, on the virtuous right.

In a recent piece in the *Wall Street Journal*, Bennett began by noting the cultural anarchy into which our republic has fallen:

[S]ince 1960, there has been a 560% increase in violent crime. There has also been more than a 400% increase in illegitimate births, a quadrupling of divorces, a tripling of the percentage of children living in single-parent homes, more than a 200% increase in the teenage suicide rate, and a drop of 75 points in the average of SAT scores of high school students. Today 30% of all births and 68% of black births are illegitimate.

The U.S. ranks near the top in the industrialized world in its rates of abortion, divorce, and unwed births. We lead the industrialized world in murder, rape and violent crime. And in elementary and secondary education, we are at or near the bottom in achievement scores.[810]

Adopting a position similar to that of this book, Bennett observed, "In my view the real crisis of our time is spiritual . . . an undue concern for external affairs and worldly things . . . an absence of zeal for divine things."[811] As Terry Eastland and Bennett had done in a 1979 book, Bennett noted the incongruity of the claim that we want to achieve a "color-blind" society while "we continue to count by race."[812] Finally he lamented that we claim to want to encourage "virtue and honor among the young," while we "shun the language of morality."

Bennett argues (as did the last chapter) and as did Story and the Federalists, that "we need to return religion to its proper place [in American life]. Religion, after all provides us with moral bearings."[813] If we were to come up with a blueprint for what the United States might look like if we implemented the constitutional strategy suggested in this book, the reversal of the trends Bennett notes would certainly be high on the list. The return of morality and religion to central places in American classrooms ought ineluctably to lead to an end to the spiritual crisis Bennett rightly condemns.[814]

Bennett did not address the change in constitutional law that will be necessary in order to resolve the nation's spiritual crisis. That is our concern, and the work of scholars such as Unger does make more clear the possibility of an alternative system of jurisprudential thought to that which the Supreme Court has manifested since the New Deal. Such an alternative jurisprudence recognizes the legitimacy, indeed, the real inevitability, of grounding law in a positive system of beliefs about Man and God. This is work that conservatives ought to embrace with some relish. Indeed, if there is an error in Unger's work which conservatives ought to recognize, it is his implicit suggestion that ideas about integrating law with morality and morality with religion were going out of favor in the seventeenth century. As we have learned, even at the time of the ratification and first implementation of the United States Constitution, its framers and its first judges understood that it was folly to separate legality and spirituality completely.

C. The Conservative Politics of Law:
Race, Religion, and Abortion Redux

It is a staple of modern conservative thought that law ought to be viewed not simply as an instrumental tool to gratify individualistic desires, but rather as a means of maintaining a governmental structure that will shield us from our baser instincts and allow us more easily to develop virtue and serve our fellows and our God. Many contemporary commentators on the American moral crisis may slight the fact, but if American spirituality is to be healed the law must play an important part. The precise part the law ought to play in morality, and the part that morality ought to play in law in conservative theory, is best described in Russell Kirk's six basic "canons of conservative thought." Kirk's canons echo several of the same themes as William Bennett's modern lament. Kirk's six canons are:

(1) Belief in a transcendent order, or body of natural law, which rules society as well as conscience. Political problems, at bottom, are religious and moral problems . . . True politics is the art of apprehending and applying the Justice which ought to prevail in a community of souls.

(2) Affection for the proliferating variety and mystery of human existence, as opposed to the narrowing uniformity, egalitarianism, and utilitarian aims of most radical systems . . .

(3) Conviction that civilized society requires orders and classes, as against the notion of a "classless society." . . . Ultimate equality in the judgment of God, and equality before courts of law, are recognized by conservatives; but equality of condition, they think, means equality in servitude and boredom.

(4) Persuasion that freedom and property are closely linked:

separate property from private possession, and Leviathan becomes master of all. Economic leveling, [conservatives] maintain, is not economic progress.

(5) Faith in prescription and distrust of "sophisters, calculators, and economists" who would reconstruct society upon abstract designs.

(6) Recognition that change may not be salutary reform: hasty innovation may be a devouring conflagration rather than a torch of progress. Society must alter, for prudent change in the means of social preservation; but a statesman must take Providence into his calculations, and a statesman's chief virtue, according to Plato and Burke, is prudence.[815]

The reader, it is hoped, will have discerned that these principles have served as firm anchors in our analysis of constitutional development. They serve also as signposts towards a more satisfactory American society. The details of that society, of course, must be worked out over time, and with the Burkean prudence Kirk recommends. Radical change, such as reestablishing state churches or seditious libel law, are not called for. But a profound spiritual strengthening is.

In furthering a jurisprudence of altruism and a divine purpose to human strivings in constructing a system of government, in a sense, of course, law becomes a reflection of politics, just as Critical Legal Studies has always maintained. But where conservatives differ from modern-day liberals or from CLS scholars is in the content of the politics of law. For us law does not offer only neutrality toward equally valid personal moralities, nor does law dictate a redistributionist or socialistic ethic. Our version of the rule of law (as the CLS scholars have some merit in contending) is an essentially political (as well as a religious and an epistemological) one. Still, the conservative's version of the rule of law can lay more claim to validity according to the original understanding of our constitutional tradition than can the alternative visions of the leftists or the liberals in the legal academy.

The conservative's notion of the rule of law recognizes that our legal system embraces certain political ideals. In that sense—and only in that sense —the conservative's vision of the law and the Constitution are a reflection of politics. The conservative's politics of law, unlike the liberal's, does not give judges a policy-making role. The conservative vision does not regard its judges as clothed with the discretion to ignore old legal rules and make new ones. As did Burke, the conservative vision recognizes that society changes, and that prudential alteration in the law and Constitution are necessary. The appropriate source of this change, however, is not to be the judges but wise legislators enacting statutes or the people acting to amend their Constitution.

Most of the outlines of this conservative and essentially British political[816] conception were in place at the time of the framing of the 1787 Constitution. This conservative jurisprudence furnishes a base to appreciate and recapture the social order the framers' generation thought that they were founding. Originally we did not have the currently dominant conception of our polity, the constitutional philosophy of self-actualization,[817] wherein individual rights are at the center of politics, and wherein individuals habitually think of themselves as waging a ceaseless war against the government and their fellows.

The original conception of the United States presumed a more organic social order, with "duty" more important than rights (as we saw in Chapter Two). As one recent study of jury charges in the first decade of the republic put it:

> During the decade in which the Bill of Rights was added to the Constitution, one might think that the philosophical theme of these grand jury charges would be individual liberty; it was not. The theme which pervades these charges is *duty*.[818]

To the same effect were the late eighteenth-century comments of Justice Samuel Chase complaining that "men of property, education, and knowledge" too often declined serving on juries: "Americans are unworthy of the *Rights* and the security they enjoy, under their Government [and] Laws, who will not take a *part* in those *public Duties*, that are necessary for their *support, protection, and preservation*."[819]

266

That early conception of the nature of law and society acknowledged what we now routinely refuse to admit: that social orders are inevitable in any complex society. As a result, different social classes—with distinctions based on wealth, education, experience, and cosmopolitanism—are also inevitable.[820]

This does not mean, of course, that one class is supposed to be perpetually at the mercy of any other, whether it is the richest oppressing the poorest or the poorest continually seeking to confiscate and redistribute the wealth of the richest. Rather all classes are expected to understand that each owes reciprocal duties to the others, and that each has a vital contribution to make to the welfare of all. Thus, for example, the richest class ought to regard itself as having a social duty to ensure that the poorest classes are not without the basic human needs of food, shelter, medical care, and some leisure. The poorest classes ought to understand that their participation in the political sphere or the marketplace should not jeopardize enjoyment of wealth by any class in society.

In addition, as the young Thomas Jefferson appears to have understood, the wealthy are under an obligation to see that the talented among the lower classes are afforded an opportunity to rise in social station. We should recognize this obligation today, and go beyond Jefferson to apply his insight without regard to race, gender, ethnic group, as well as original class status, in order that all may benefit from the leadership of the most able. In Jefferson's *Notes*,[821] he wrote of the need to rake "geniuses from the rubbish," by which he meant the obligation of the state to provide educational advancement for its brightest youths of whatever social class. Jefferson did not suggest that this ought to extend broadly across race or gender, but his logic, particularly today, leads to that interpretation. The hedonistic individualism of the last four decades of the twentieth century, in other words, ought to be replaced by a philosophy more in keeping with the precepts of the founding generation, a philosophy of altruism and community, where social duties are given at least equal prominence with individual rights.

Moreover, we should give up the idea, just beginning to penetrate the national consciousness, that it is the job of the federal government to renew American virtue. The structure of government that the framers' erected for us left the spiritual care of the American citizenry almost exclusively in the hands of state and local authorities. That is where it still belongs, because communities of moral endeavor can best take root at the local level. Local peculiarities of history, tradition, geography, and economy will shape moral striving in a manner that cannot be dictated by a federal bureaucracy. Indeed, there is much to be said for the proposition that even local politics should not be shaped by federal overseers. Thus the Warren Court's centralizing ideology in its "one man, one vote" decisions needs revision (as argued in Chapter Three). Perhaps local authorities would better be able to do their task of inculcating morality, virtue, and spirituality in the citizenry if they were freer to develop political forms that took more account of history, tradition, and local peculiarities than the Warren Court's majority was prepared to allow them.

For almost sixty years we have conceptualized constitutional law as if it were a tool for redressing grievances of insular minorities, of race, gender, or ethnic groups.[822] We should seek to reconceptualize constitutional law as a means not of fragmenting or Balkanizing our politics along these lines, but rather of integrating social classes and the disparate American races and ethnic groups into a communitarian ideal. To a certain extent, of course, we are a pluralistic society, but we stand in great danger, greater than ever before, of losing our identity as a country or as a national community.

The communitarian nature of our basic beliefs has been obscured by almost three generations of constitutional interpretation. These basic beliefs, those of the founding generation, might well be understood as actually being closer to the ideals of the Renaissance or even the Middle Ages than to the European Enlightenment of the late eighteenth century. We ought to conceive our social order not as an agglomeration of fragmented individuals, but rather as the medievalists and Shakespeare did—as a great chain of being in which each of us has a particular place from which our lives draw meaning because of our relationship to others in the chain.

The revisions in constitutional doctrine suggested here—having to do with race, religion, and abortion—are all designed as first steps towards bringing us back to this ideal, that social duties have more prominence than individual rights. They are all conceived with a desire to return us to a position in which a spiritual renewal can take place.

As William Bennett implied, and as Justice O'Connor also appears to have realized, the concept of a "color-blind Constitution" ought to be invoked to end further Balkanization of our society, and to renew our commitment to a shared purpose in American life. Once again allowing our government to promote religion in the public sphere on a nonsectarian basis ought to sharpen our awareness of this shared purpose of life, and its religious dimensions. With this understanding—an understanding that *must* be communicated to America's youth, and especially to the poor—will come a better appreciation of the role that morality must play in human endeavor. Justice Story, Justice Chase, and their fellow members of the early founding generations were correct in believing that one cannot separate morality from religion—particularly true for the young. If the collapse of the social order in our poorest areas is due to a plethora of undisciplined children sired by irresponsible fathers and raised by immature and deprived mothers, as we are beginning to understand, then the problem is one of morals, not merely a problem of economics.[823]

Trying to cure our urban ills by ever greater influxes of cash will fail, as it has failed for the last generation. We will do better to try to cure them by teaching morality and religion. Once morality and religion return to the classroom, so too might Justice Story's insights about the necessity of teaching that we bear responsibility for our conduct in this world toward others for which there will be an accounting in the next. Quite likely, the lower illegitimacy rate that prevailed in the period before the secularizing sixties might have owed something to the teaching of this morality in

269

public schools and more responsible families, that is, before the Supreme Court yanked the religious underpinnings of morality from public education.

Finally, returning the question of abortion to the states for discussion and resolution, in a legal atmosphere where it is once again permissible to discuss religious obligation openly, ought further to promote an awareness of our legal, moral, and spiritual duties to our fellows, including the unborn.[824]

D. The Preservation of Popular Sovereignty, Religion, and the Role of the Judiciary

What, you might well ask, has all of this to do with popular sovereignty, the theory the framers offered to justify acceptance of the new Constitution in 1787? How does it help us in our goal to allow the people to recapture the Constitution? Isn't all this communitarian language, all this talk of inevitable social classes and reciprocal social duties, contrary to the spirit of American democracy? Could it really have been consistent with the framers' intentions? Or, if the framers had conceived of government as necessitating elites, weren't they betraying the popular sovereignty they purported to be acting for? These important questions must be asked of any constitutional theory, whether it calls itself "organic" or "original understanding" or "a living Constitution," and they must be answered satisfactorily if the interpretive strategy advanced is to be broadly acceptable.

Starting with the framers, then, could it be said that they really did believe in popular sovereignty? Did Hamilton and the other High Federalists' belief that America ought to be ruled by the "better sort," by "the good the wise and the rich," reveal their cloven hooves?[825] Probably not. Any serious theorist of government for even the tiny nation of 3 million souls which we were at the beginning would understand that the entire population could not actively participate in the ongoing governance process. All that could be promised to the people was the occasional exercise

270

of the franchise by those with sufficient interest in the community, though they would also be expected willingly to pay their taxes and to refrain from destructive criticism or armed attack on the government they elected. The only choice of the framers, given the models they had at hand, was to give us a republic, an aristocracy, or a monarchy, and (as we learned in Chapter One) they chose a republic, *not* a democracy. Once monarchy and aristocracy were rejected, popular sovereignty, expressed through a republican form of government, was the only possibility.

The task of American political theorists then became simply working out a means for erecting a representative ("republican") form of government in which the government would work in the best interests of the people, and in which, it was hoped, virtue could predominate. Those who framed the federal government apparently left the fostering of virtue to the states, and tried to use other means to deal with a possible lack of virtue at the federal level. Jeffersonian and Jacksonian theorists would later argue against the essentially elitist views of the Founders,[826] but the framers' elitism represents perhaps the inevitable solution to a perennial problem of how to secure what's best for the people when the mass of the people is physically incapable of governing itself or even easily expressing its needs. Indeed, the structure of the federal government, with its system of checks and balances, including judicial review, was set up, as Madison pointed out in the famous passage from *Federalist* 51, to save the people and their governors from themselves, or at least from their worst tendencies. "If men were angels," Madison noted, "no government would be necessary." Since they were not, however, and since it was impossible to have angels govern men, both external controls (implementing popular sovereignty through the exercise of the franchise) and internal controls (checks and balances through separation of powers) were necessary.[827]

The Jeffersonians and the Jacksonians had a more sanguine view of human nature than Madison and believed to a greater extent in the utopian perfectibility of man. The *Federalist*'s belief, expressed by Madison, in the individual's perennial shortcomings formed a more sensible basis for the structure erected.[828] The

271

Federalists assumed that individual members of the government would inevitably fail in virtue and succumb to self-interest. To counter this inevitability they created a structure of dual sovereignty and a tripartite division of the federal government that would seek to meld the interests of the individuals to that of their offices, while still checking their excesses. In this manner—by checking popular sovereignty and its officials at certain points— the Federalists offered the best chance to make popular sovereignty actually work.

Finally, there was what might be described as a mystical or spiritual dimension to the theory of popular sovereignty as expressed in the *Federalist*. The American people were expected to fulfill their Christian or spiritual duties to each other and their Creator—duties central to early republican philosophy.[829] In order to do this, they must have understood, as John Fries learned from Samuel Chase,[830] that Americans had a duty to keep not only their private contracts and pay their debts, but also to keep their social contract, and to defer to their elected government in its operations. As Samuel Chase put it, "The *real patriot* is the man whose *ruling passion* is the *love of his country*, which consists in due obedience to Government, and its Laws; in a reverence for *public Liberty*, and a discharge of all *social duties*."[831] It was the moral and spiritual as well as political duty of governmental officials to act in the interest of the people. It was the duty of the people not to interfere with official actions, either by rebellion or by licentious criticism, as the seditious libel cases showed.[832]

Paradoxically, then, popular sovereignty was originally to be secured, not by a maximum of direct democracy (as has lately come to be American political theory), but by a religiously inspired deference, a spirit of altruistic self-sacrifice, the cultivation of a natural aristocracy, and a system of checks and balances and dual sovereignty. Even with the structural correctives in place, it was believed that only if individual Americans expressed self-control and virtue, would God likely see that the American people as a whole prospered. Again Samuel Chase's Jury Charge Book is instructive:

272

[P]ermit me, Gentlemen, most earnestly to recommend to you, by the love of your Country, and a regard to its dearest rights, to exert your *utmost* endeavors to support your Federal Government, and the present administration thereof; and to maintain inviolate the Union of the States, on which, under God, your *safety* depends. . . . Let us prepare our minds to meet, with fortitude and perseverance the event of War [with France], the scourge of Nations; and let us place our *whole* confidence in the Justice of our Cause; and the protection of the great Ruler of the Universe! America united has everything to *hope*, but divided, without the special interposition of Providence, she has everything to fear."[833]

For such a scheme to succeed, of course, there had to be a considerable amount of piety and faith on all sides, and there had to be a governmental structure that would ameliorate lapses in both.

A crucial part of this structure of checks and balances was set forth by Alexander Hamilton in *Federalist* 78, by Samuel Chase in his Jury Charge Book and in *Callender*, and by John Marshall in *Marbury v. Madison*. This was the role of the judiciary in declaring that either the executive or legislature had gone too far, that such acts were unconstitutional and stood in need of correction. Popular sovereignty demanded no less. The converse of this principle was equally important, however, and bears emphasizing. If the sovereign people had, upon reflection, promulgated the original Constitution, then for judges to stray from the original understanding was impermissible. Judges were not to alter the Constitution's meaning on the basis of the unreflective political demands of even the majority of the American people. To do so would be to betray the Constitution's original promise of popular sovereignty existing pursuant to the rule of law.

To argue for a "living Constitution," then, or to argue that judges ought to alter the meaning of that document in accordance with their perceptions of changed political conditions ought to be regarded as constitutionally impermissible, as a sort of jurisprudential treason. The argument of *Federalist* Nos. 78, 79, and 80, the numbers concerned with the workings of the new

273

federal judiciary,[834] was that the provisions for lifetime tenure, secure compensation, and appointive rather than elective selection for federal judges were to insulate them from popular opinions. To suggest that judges ought to change the law in light of changing opinions would seem pernicious indeed.

From this, and from all the rest that has been offered here, it should be understood that a communitarian theory closest to our roots will not be the essentially democratic secular order that such "neorepublican" legal academics as Frank Michaelman of Harvard and Cass Sunstein of Chicago appear to favor.[835] Indeed, to a great extent these two seem to believe that our eighteenth-century republican theorists simply presaged the New Deal, with its focus on redistribution of wealth and diminishment of traditional centers of political power and social legitimacy.

Insofar as classical eighteenth-century American republicanism emphasized altruism over individualism there is merit to embracing the term "republicanism" today, but the secular-democratic trappings with which Sunstein and Michaelman would overlay it ought to be jettisoned. The original American republic, as it was conceived by the first American practitioners of constitutional law, was a place where the essentially conservative framers understood that a social hierarchy was inevitable, where some deference was indispensable, and where religion was essential.

At this time in our history it seems important to observe that the essential religious component of American public life should not exclude those who practice any particular religion. The flap that greeted Gov. Kirk Fordice's recent remarks that America was a "Christian nation"[836] is instructive in this regard. In a 1993 symposium in which Governor Fordice was a participant he stressed that it was wrong of the national media to impute an exclusionist cast to his comments, and, in particular, his refusal to amend his comments to suggest that we were a "*Judeo*-Christian nation." As Fordice elaborated in the symposium:

> The Christian background of, and influence upon, the founding of our nation are incontrovertible by any serious scholar, but so is the absolute protection that the Founding Fathers provided when

274

they barred Congress from prohibiting the free exercise of any religion. Perhaps that beautiful tolerance for other religions is the ultimate tribute to early Christian influence in America, and I subscribe to it absolutely as I do all tenets of the Constitution.[837]

Another participant at that symposium, Rabbi Jacob Neusner, Distinguished Professor of Religious Studies at the University of South Florida, Tampa, sought to look beyond Fordice's "Christian nation" comments to understand the essential religious beliefs and political goals that they implied. Rabbi Neusner argued that as we understand those beliefs today, the words "Christian nation" might obscure more than they clarify since

> nearly the whole message set forth by the Christian Right can find its counterpart, point by point, in Judaism or Islam: belief in the sanctity of the human person, created in God's image; belief in God's will rather than secular "values"; belief that right and wrong come to us from revelation . . .
>
> Why not use the formulation "America is a nation that fears God"? And cannot our meaning be borne by language that says, "This country is founded on the belief that we are subject to the Justice and mercy of a caring, loving God, to whom we are responsible?"[838]

Rabbi Neusner's formulation, it will be observed, does not differ much from that put forward by Joseph Story, shortly after the passage of the First Amendment itself.[839] It could serve as an excellent summary of the essential religious foundation the American constitutional government requires.[840] Still another participant in the symposium, Ralph E. Reed, Jr., the executive director of Christian Coalition, remarked, quoting Alexis de Tocqueville: "Despotism may be able to do without faith, but democracy cannot. Religion is needed . . . in democratic republics most of all."[841]

One other aspect of "neorepublicanism," particularly as practiced by Sunstein, needs further comment. Sunstein, like those New Dealers from whom he draws inspiration, believes that government ought to engage in the redistribution of property or

275

property rights in accordance with a philosophy of egalitarianism. Sunstein justifies this—as did the New Dealers—by his belief that property itself is a social construction, a creation of government, a creature of the man-made social order, and thus can legitimately be manipulated, transferred, or dissolved by the temporal authorities. The original theory of our republican framers, however, was that property was something that preceded government. Their belief—that of Locke—as expressed by Jefferson's Declaration, was that governments were formed to protect preexisting property rights (as well as those of the person) more fully. Property was something that existed in the presocial state of nature, it was a human conception, yes, but one implanted by God, one ordained by him as an inalienable right. To sport with the citizen's property rights, as the New Deal did, as Sunstein's philosophy would authorize, and—alas— as we today unthinkingly constantly do, would have horrified Chase, Jefferson, and Madison. This is why it has been argued here (in Chapter Three) that *Lochner* was closer to the original understanding than Holmes's dissent, and why the New Deal Court's "switch in time" in *Jones & Laughlin* and cases like it can be seen to be a betrayal of our traditions.

A real effort to recapture the Constitution, then, demands a renewal of our early regard for private property as the inviolable guarantor of liberty and a vital instrument for securing the citizen's very personality. This aspect of the framers' intention has been developed by others, most notably Richard Epstein and Stephen Macedo.[842] Here we thought it better to concentrate on several issues—race, religion, and abortion—which have more recently gone constitutionally awry. The New Deal cases regarding property have been entrenched for almost sixty years, and reversing them will be a formidable task. Our constitutional misjudgements regarding race, religion, and abortion are of more recent vintage, the public is still engaged in discussing them, and the time seems ripe for a reexamination. Thus it is primarily with regard to these three topics that we have sought to recapture something of our original understanding of American constitutionalism and our true republican traditions.

Much of the early American republican constitutional philosophy was simply an outgrowth of English thought. But by the time of the framing of the 1787 Constitution, American ideas had taken on a distinctive character. Thus, like the English, we conceded the need for hierarchies in the society and deference among social orders. But we assumed that hierarchical status would be based on merit rather than birth, and we were committed to greater social mobility and fluidity among classes than were our English ancestors. We were more ready to tolerate the displacements brought on by allowing economic opportunity across classes. And, from the beginning, we allowed the market more freedom to distribute goods and services. We were thus less willing than the British to tolerate governmental interference with economic progress and social mobility.

We did not embrace the British vision of a tripartite constitutional government with omnipotent legislative power. Instead, we believed that the security of the social order could be guaranteed only by limiting the power of government itself. Finally, we early departed from the idea of a state church supported by taxation of all. Nevertheless, we clung to the notion that a Christian set of beliefs was indispensable for proper participation in good citizenship.

E. Hierarchy, Deference, and Elites

To recapitulate: unlike the British, we have had, since the Declaration of Independence in 1776, a commitment to popular sovereignty as the basis of our government. In England the legitimate government, since 1688, had been composed of three orders of society—Crown, Aristocracy, and Commons. In the United States government was legitimate only if all three branches flowed directly or indirectly from the people. There is a profound difference, however, between a direct democracy and a republican government (even one founded on notions of popular sovereignty) which aspires to implement the rule of law.

The rule of law, with its commitment to even-handed application of preexisting precedents and practices, is not supposed to be an instrument for arbitrary redistribution of wealth. Further (as indicated in the first chapter), a republican form of government, where the sovereign people act indirectly, through their representatives, necessitates some sort of hierarchy for interpretative and law-making purposes. The judicial and the legislative functions cannot be exclusively performed by the people themselves, though they can have some input into the process through casting their ballots or serving on juries.

Moreover, *Federalist 78*, with its acknowledgement that fit persons for the judiciary will be few and far between, recognizes,[843] though we refuse to acknowledge it today, the necessity for public deference to the peoples' representatives and to the judges appointed to serve in the courts. Thus, from the beginning, it has been acknowledged that in America we must produce a set of persons or class fit to command that deference. The most obvious members of that class, as Tocqueville remarked, are the members of the legal profession itself.[844] Other, more recent astute observers of American cultural history, such as Nelson Aldrich in *Old Money*, and Richard Brookhiser in *The Way of the Wasp*, have recognized that it is not just members of the legal profession in America who have been bred to assume the roles of responsibility necessary to a republic.

Some of the more thoughtful possessors of "old money" in the Northeast have founded private schools and universities devoted to training a leadership class. These educational institutions are today committed to reaching down the social scale, as Jefferson recommended, to ensure that the class that commands will be furnished with fresh stock and possess some of the character of popular representation indispensable for American political success. We usually choose to ignore the salutary and focus only on the pernicious elements of the existence of a class structure in America. Still, the Way of the Wasp in America has been to seek to cultivate a leadership class to serve as role models—to exemplify the kind of altruistic virtue and self-sacrifice without which, according to the ancients, a republic could not endure.

278

Unlike the British, we have, from almost the beginning, encouraged this leadership class to play a role in commerce and manufacturing. Perhaps it is more accurate to say that a much greater number of the original members of this class or their immediate ancestors came from manufacturing and commercial backgrounds.[845] It is thus not remarkable that American law has been linked more commonly to the market and to market forces than to the preservation of special privileges for a land-based aristocracy. Nevertheless, what makes us essentially American includes a good deal of essentially British conservative class-based hierarchical and elitist attitudes, at least when it comes to the practice of the American bench and bar.

To try to suggest that one can implement a system of constitutional jurisprudence without this kind of elitist base, as most of the American legal academy has been doing for almost sixty years, is to engage in folly. Without such an essentially aristocratic elite, and without that elite's commitment to altruism and to the maintenance of legal rules pursuant to an ethic of community and self-sacrifice, the United States is in danger of degenerating into anarchy or dictatorship. The weakening of authority generally in contemporary American society, the near disappearance of deference, and the prevalence of a debased sort of Jeffersonian egalitarianism have brought us close to the point of collapse.

The Madisonian vision of competing interest groups has been acknowledged from the beginning of the American experience, but a societal commitment to an ethic of aristocratic altruism has roots that are quite as deep. As Madison recognized, in *Federalist* 10, interest groups seek to implement their own goals, which are not necessarily in the best interests of the society itself.

With the increasingly democratic character of our recent politics, the ethic of community that eighteenth- and nineteenth-century American aristocratic leaders helped establish has dangerously eroded. Still, the public hunger for something beyond mere selfish individualism will not be completely denied. The American Left, committed as it has been (like the Left in the French Revolution) to abstract democratic theory and individualism has often failed to grasp this public need. Thus, the Left and its allies in much of the American media have sought to challenge and fight each recent public manifestation of a desire to move beyond selfish individualism and reestablish communitarian values in American constitutional law.

F. Amending the Constitution

Nowhere has the liberal-left's failure to grasp the inevitable public hunger for community been more evident than in recent public debates over constitutional amendments. The egalitarian, self-actualizing, individualistic Left's most recent effort at constitutional amendment was the proposed Equal Rights Amendment (ERA). The ERA, which provides in pertinent part that "equality of rights under the law shall not be denied or abridged by the United States or by any State on account of sex," was conceived as a protection for individuals and founded on a theory of equal rights.[846] It did not become constitutional law. Its proponents failed to convince enough state legislators (the governments closest to the people) that the ERA would not result in an abandonment of established and respected traditions. Apparently there is still some support for the notion that individualistic egalitarianism may not be all there is in the law. The tradition that women and men are different, that women may have needs that might require the allocation of legal rights or responsibilities different from those of men—their capacity for childbirth, for example, or their strength and endurance—still may hold some sway.

Curiously, though the Left was unable to pass the ERA, it has frustrated conservative efforts to amend the Constitution in behalf of the traditional values the ERA appeared to threaten. Thus conservatives have been unable to pass the proposed flag desecration amendment, a school prayer amendment, or amendments designed to overturn *Roe v. Wade*. In the case of the conservatives, of course, the problem has not been the state legislatures, but Congress itself. Still dominated by the Left, Congress has refused to make it possible for the amendments even to be considered in the state legislatures.

The liberal-left's tactic in these cases (similar to the Right's successful tactic in defeating the ERA) has always been to present the proposed constitutional amendments as innovations hostile to the traditions of the Bill of Rights. Thus the flag desecration amendment and the school prayer amendments were said to be dangerous attempts to repeal cherished First Amendment protections.

When, for example, the proposed flag desecration amendment—a measure which would have made it constitutionally permissible to punish flag desecration as a crime—was before the House's Committee on the Judiciary in 1989, the University of Chicago Law School's dean, Geoffrey R. Stone, expressed strong opposition.[847] Dean Stone cautioned that the procedure of the constitutional amendment to protect the flag would be "unwise in the extreme," for it would be "tampering" with the Constitution "to adjust for what must fairly be understood as matters of only secondary importance in the overall scheme of American government." He continued:

> We have not in the past, and we should not in the present, submit to the temptation to invoke the solemn processes of constitutional amendment to override a decision of the Supreme Court just because it offends—or even deeply offends—a substantial majority of our citizens. Such a process would clutter, trivialize, and, indeed, denigrate the Constitution and the broad principles for which it stands.[848]

In 1985, after the Senate Judiciary Committee favorably reported to the Senate a draft amendment on voluntary school prayer,[849] Walter Dellinger, a professor at Duke Law School, asked the committee, in effect, to reject "this and all similar amendments" because it might pose a danger to the American tradition of freedom of religion.[850]

The anti-abortion amendments have been said to be in opposi-

281

tion to a traditional right to privacy existing either in the Fourteenth Amendment or penumbras from the First, Fourth, and Ninth Amendments.[851]

Nevertheless, the constitutional history reviewed here suggests that the conservative right has a counterargument—that its amendments are only undertaken to restore a previously existing proper state of American constitutional law. No framer could have conceived of the First Amendment as permitting the burning of the American flag as a means of protected expression. Nor would any of the original advocates of the First Amendment have believed that the First Amendment's religion clauses were a ban on local governments who sought to promote nonsectarian public prayer. It is similarly inconceivable that even the radical framers of the Fourteenth Amendment could have understood that they were making a constitutional declaration that pregnant women had a right to terminate embryonic human life. One can agree or disagree with regard to each of these conservative amendment efforts, but one ought to acknowledge that instead of being nefarious attacks on the Bill of Rights they are valid exercises in attempting to return the legal system closer to its republican roots.

G. Recapturing the Constitution by Amendment

It is time that the American public take steps to recapture its Constitution; and a renewed effort at an amendment to permit prayer in the schools, an amendment to return the issue of abortion to the states, and an amendment to ensure a color-blind Constitution might be proper places to start. Our goal ought to be to restore a sense of social responsibility, legitimate hierarchy and authority, and deference and duty to American law in order to counter the anarchic influence of the currently dominant philosophy of individualism. There might be many other areas of law we could treat, especially those regarding property and redistribution. But those topics must be left for another time and place. For our purposes here, the school prayer amendment might help to restore a sense of morality and altruism in public endeavors, and to underscore our tradition of the divine natural law roots of American law and life. An amendment renewing the debate over abortion in the states should, eventually, similarly lead to an appreciation of the sanctity of human life, and a heightened appreciation of our duty to the unborn and to each other. This ought to lead to an appreciation of the need to provide the social support to build more security in American families and to work to salvage that endangered institution. A color-blind constitutional amendment could also foster the American community by ending one of the most divisive issues in American society. It would further serve to emphasize the conservative natural law ideal of equality before the law.

A school prayer amendment could be worded in such a way as simply to restate the creed of many of the framers' generation and reaffirm our commitment to areas of religion in public life still embraced by the Court:

> Whereas there can be no law without morality, and no morality without religion, therefore the right of the people to hear nonsectarian prayers on public occasions, or of children in public schools to enjoy similar rights, or of federal, state or local governments to place non-sectarian religious mottoes on seals, coins, or currency shall not be abridged.

Given the sharp divisions in public opinion, an anti-abortion jurisdiction amendment ought properly to be neutral on abortion, and, as Justice Scalia has suggested, it should take the federal government out of the area and return it to the states:

> The United States Constitution shall not be construed by the federal or state courts or by the federal legislature or executive to grant a right to terminate a pregnancy before birth. Whether any such right or rights shall be permitted is exclusively within the determination of the individual states.

283

Our third and final amendment returns to the first Justice Harlan's understanding of the "color-blind" Constitution:

> Neither the federal, state, or local governments shall be permitted to discriminate against or favor individuals or groups on the basis of race or ethnic origin.

With one stroke that amendment would end such contemporary evils as race-norming, racial quotas, minority set-asides, gerrymandering to achieve racial representation, and denying peremptory challenges on the basis of race. But because it is targeted only at governments, it would still permit private individuals or corporations, if they were so inclined, to institute affirmative action programs to aid in developing talent among members of previously disadvantaged groups. The amendment would also not affect congressional efforts, such as the civil rights laws, to prevent individual acts of racial discrimination based on Congress's power to regulate interstate commerce. It would, however, strongly suggest that the civil rights laws be read according to their actual texts, and no longer as a means of discrimination *in favor* of a particular race.

The amendment cornucopia that is proposed here may strike some as dangerously trifling with fundamental law. Indeed, this was the most prominent argument made against the flag desecration amendment—that the Bill of Rights had stood us well for two hundred years, that it was the height of hubris to think that it could be improved, and that to alter it in any way—for example, to punish acts of desecration involving the flag—would be fundamentally to endanger our most precious freedoms.[852] There is, perhaps, no great need to push for a flag desecration amendment, but neither is there much validity in the argument against it. The notion that the people's will should be checked if they seek to amend their Constitution is worse than nonsense. It is an insult to popular sovereignty itself. It is time that the American people understand that the amendment process is as much a vital part of constitutional law as the workings of the federal courts or the pronouncements of the federal legislature. At the time of the ratification debates on the Constitution, for example, even its advocates understood that the document they had drafted was not perfect, and the amendment process was going to be necessary to refine and correct excesses or omissions. The great national war hero, future first president, and proponent of the 1787 Constitution, George Washington observed that the possibility of amending the Constitution was universally accepted. "That the proposed Constitution will admit of amendments is acknowledged by its warmest advocates," he wrote in a letter in 1788, and expressed his surprise that the Constitution's opponents sought to defeat it unless a Bill of Rights were added. Washington stated, "it should be remembered that a constitutional door is open for such amendments as shall be thought necessary by nine States." Thus he made clear his belief that the whole constitutional project should not be scuttled while proposed amendments were thrashed out *before* ratification.[853]

Lately, however, probably because the most prominent amendment movements come from the conservative side of the political spectrum (the right to life, school prayer, and flag desecration amendments) and because liberal opinion dominates the academy and the media, the amendment process has been discouraged. Indeed, Lawrence Tribe, in his testimony on the flag desecration amendment before the United States Senate Judiciary Committee in 1989, all but suggested that the amendment process was too dangerous to be trusted to popular opinion.[854]

It is of course true that the framers wanted to construct a document whose meaning was not to be altered because of the temporary public excitement of a majority, and that judicial review itself was designed to resist that excitement as manifested in the legislature.[855] Nevertheless, to suggest that popular movements are somehow ill-advised when they advocate amendments is to make a mockery out of republican constitutional government itself. Intriguingly, while this obvious fact may have escaped some constitutional liberals,[856] to his credit, one of the most prominent left-leaning thinkers, Bruce Ackerman, in an exercise something like this book, has actually advocated a popular constitutional amendment movement. Ackerman's proposed amendments would give any constitutional conservative pause if not apoplexy. In his *We the People*, Ackerman advocates a series of constitutional amendments spelling out not rights but entitlements for each citizen. Implementing Ackerman's proposed Bill of Entitlements would require just the sort of wholesale redistribution which the Constitution was designed to prevent. Moreover, even Ackerman doesn't go as far as he might in placing faith in popular sovereignty. One of his proposed amendments would actually make the others unamendable![857]

The American people ought to understand again that it is *their* Constitution the Supreme Court has been expounding for all these years. If they are to appreciate that popular sovereignty really is the governing philosophy of this nation, it is difficult to imagine an exercise better suited to accomplishing these ends than to participate in a national referendum on the document itself through consideration of several key amendments.

A national exercise in constitutional amendment would be unnecessary if the Supreme Court were to return closer to the original understanding of many constitutional provisions, in the manner suggested in the last chapter. Perhaps reducing the number of members of the Court might help it to recapture its original modest but important role in American society. Given that power is never easily relinquished, however, and given that the Supreme Court has, for the last sixty years, been exercising a power that does not rightfully belong to it, the Court is unlikely to surrender it. It seems, then, to be time for the American people themselves, acting through Congress and their state legislatures, to take the Constitution back into their own hands.

The passage of amendments is never easy, as the experience with the ERA demonstrates. Nevertheless, if a conservative series of amendments can somehow find its way out of Congress and into the states, which are closer to our republican roots, they should stand a better chance of passage. That the time is ripe for such pressure on Congress and for such a conservative amendment exercise is indicated by the recent success of the term limits movement, the phenomenal rise of a conservative voice in talk radio, and the best-selling status of books by conservatives such as

Rush Limbaugh. The people appear to be poised to act, and all that is lacking is a coherent and concrete program. These three amendments, aiming at a moral, spiritual, and constitutional renewal ought to be a good beginning.

CONCLUSION

Two hundred and eighteen years ago Thomas Jefferson's draft of the Declaration of Independence, borrowed from the abstract theory of John Locke, set forth a utopian ideal for America to which we are rhetorically, if not always actually committed. It was of a nation in which all were equally endowed with inalienable rights, to life, liberty, and the pursuit of happiness, and in which the government protected those Divine gifts. It took only about ten years' experience with state legislatures trying to perfect American liberties for America's leading citizens to realize that there was more to governing than promoting the individual liberty that the Declaration appeared to promise.

The Federal Constitution of 1787 was designed to protect property. Its chief proponents and implementers, the Federalists, and the administrations of Washington and Adams, believed that property and person could not be secured without a sharpening of individual moral responsibility. If the Declaration was about Liberty, than the federal Constitution was about Security and Responsibility.

The give and take between the Jeffersonian democratic advocates of liberty and the Federalist republican conservators of property and responsibility has oscillated through the rest of our history. It has not been our task to chronicle each and every oscillation, but we have seen how since about 1937 a debased form of Jeffersonian ideals has been in the ascendance, particularly in the federal courts.

The Federalist notions of responsibility, of piety, of community, and, above all, of the rule of law and the inviolability of person and property is due for a major renaissance. Perhaps it is the genius of American life that we have managed to survive over two hundred years with such fundamentally different conceptions of the good polity in uneasy tension. One, the Jeffersonian, now all but threatens to obliterate our society itself, having for so long dominated the judiciary and allied itself with the practitioners of dubious social science in the academy. The balance must be redressed before the anarchy and chaos of our central cities spread over our whole country, and the American experiment in popular sovereignty collapses.

We must once again embrace the Burkean wisdom of tradition, religion, self-reliance, and prudence, relearn the old lessons, and reject the folly offered by the sociologists, psychologists, and other assorted social therapists so eagerly embraced by the Warren and Burger Courts. The Supreme Court, the institution that led us into our present wilderness of the spirit, could just as easily lead us out. If it is unwilling, then the people, through constitutional amendments, or through pressure on their representatives and the executive to provide for different or fewer Justices, should show the way. It is time to recapture the Constitution and the country.

Summary of the Argument

We are now too often told that what the Supreme Court does is simply politics writ large. This was not the view of the framers. One way of discouraging this view of constitutional law might be to reduce the number of Justices on the United States Supreme Court. There is a need, even if we can counter the concept of constitutional law as politics, to return the spiritual dimension to constitutional law and American society. This is a concern of Critical Legal Studies and of American conservatives such as William Bennett. On the other hand, in one sense law *is* politics, but that sense is properly a Burkean conservative one, as suggested by Russell Kirk's six canons of conservative thought. This conservative politics of law includes, among other things, legitimate hierarchies, duties as more important than rights, less oppression, less redistribution, social mobility, and morality and religion as fundamental political concerns. The suggested treatment of race, religion, and abortion in the last chapter is in accordance with these ideas.

But how does one reconcile the American ideal of popular sovereignty with these ideas of hierarchy and duty? The framers' answer was that popular sovereignty *was* the core principle of the system, but a constitutional structure of hierarchies, checks and balances, dual sovereignty, and judicial review was necessary to protect that core. Popular sovereignty was also to be secured by religiously inspired duty and deference among the people. It was to be secured by judges who followed the original understanding, and not by judges who succumbed to ephemeral popular pressures. It was also to be secured by protecting property. Originally, republican theory was not about a maximum of democracy, but about securing order through deference, virtue, and religion, and through the cultivation of an American natural aristocracy. A debased form of Jeffersonian democracy now threatens our social order, and a means of countering this might be a popular movement for constitutional amendments. Amending the Constitution is difficult when opponents charge that amendments trifle with a fundamental governmental principle. The reply of conservatives ought to be that given the obduracy of current constitutional jurisprudence, amendments are necessary to restore the appropriate preexisting state of constitutional law. Three amendments that would help recapture the Constitution are a school prayer amendment, an amendment that would leave abortion decisions to the states, and a color-blind Constitution amendment. It would be easiest if the Supreme Court, by itself, returned to its role as an interpreter, and not a radical reorganizer of American constitutional law. Failing that, through constitutional amendment and pressure on their representatives, the American people ought to recapture the Constitution and the country.

NOTES

1. Gene R. Nichol, "constitutional Judgment," 91 *Michigan Law Review* 1107, 1109–1110 (1993) (Quoting from J.M. Balkin, "What Is a Post-modern Constitutionalism?" 90 *Michigan Law Review* 1966, 1967 (1992). For further development—that the modern Supreme Court has stopped doing constitutional law and is instead engaged in sociology—see Eugene W. Hickok and Gary L. McDowell, *Justice vs. Law: Courts and Politics in American Society* (New York: The Free Press, 1993).

2. See, e.g., Joseph Goldstein, *The Intelligible Constitution: The Supreme Court's Obligation to Maintain the Constitution as Something We the People Can Understand* (New York and Oxford: Oxford University Press, 1992) where it is argued that the modern Court has lost touch with the duty to expound the Constitution using clear principles and unambiguous reasoning.

3. Robert Bork, *The Tempting of America: The Political Seduction of the Law* (New York: The Free Press, 1990) p. 6.

4. Id., at 132.

5. Charles Fried, "Manners Makyth Man: The Prose Style of Justice Scalia," 16 *Harvard Journal of Law & Public Policy* 529, 531 (1993) (Fried argues that Justice Antonin Scalia, whose opinions are written with style, grace, and common sense, is the exception who proves the rule).

6. As Harvard Law Professor Morton J. Horwitz recently wrote, the October 1991 term of the United States Supreme Court witnessed the "sudden defeat of the originalist crusade begun by the Reagan Administration with the aim of overruling *Roe*. . . . [I]n *Casey*, the joint opinion of Justices O'Connor, Kennedy, and Souter presented a major rebuff to originalist ideas. . . ." Horwitz, "Forward: The Constitution of Change: Legal Fundamentality Without Fundamentalism," 107 Harvard Law Review 30, 117 (1993).

7. Id.
8. Robert Dawidoff, "The Jeffersonian Option" 21 *Political Theory* 434, 437 (1993).
9. For Jefferson's lack of a role in drafting the Constitution, for his initial opposition to it, and for information on who the principal drafters and champions of the document were see generally the two splendid new Library of America volumes edited by Bernard Bailyn, *The Debate on the Constitution* (New York: Library of America, 1993).
10. See, e.g., Thomas Jefferson to James Madison, March 15, 1789, reprinted in Thomas Jefferson, *Writings* (New York: Library of America, 1984) pp. 942, 943, where he states that "In the arguments in favor of a declaration of rights [the proposed Bill of Rights to be added as the first amendments to the Constitution], you omit one which has great weight with me; the legal check which it puts into the hands of the judiciary. This is a body, which, if rendered independent and kept strictly to their own department, merits great confidence for their learning and integrity."
11. See Chapter Three, infra, at text accompanying note 498, for his famous salvo at the federal judiciary. See also, e.g., Thomas Jefferson to Col. John Taylor, May 28, 1816, reproduced in J. Somerville and R. Santori, eds., *Social and Political Philosophy* (Garden City, New York: Anchor Books, 1963), pp. 251, 253, 254, where Jefferson notes implicitly that the national judiciary cannot be republican because it is "independent of the nation, their coercion by impeachment [presumably referring to the failed effort to remove Justice Samuel Chase] being found nugatory." For more on Jefferson's fear of the judiciary, and what is said to be his countervailing attempt to erect an elite corps of Virginia lawyers trained in the non-Christian old-Saxon uncorrupted common law, see A. G. Roeber, *Faithful Magistrates and Republican Lawyers: Creators of a Virginia Legal Culture 1680–1810* (Chapel Hill: University of North Carolina Press, 1981), p. 224.
12. It should be acknowledged that there is also afoot in some sectors of the academy a simplistic attempt to denigrate Jefferson on the ground that he kept slaves, and thus was a hypocritical proponent of the notion that, as the Declaration of Independence put it, "All men are created equal." See, e.g., Dawidoff, supra note 8, at 438:

> Jefferson's critics say that, like his opposing slavery but not being able to advocate its abolition, let alone deprive himself of the pleasures and comforts of ownership, his thinking is marred by something wishful and discrepant even unto hypocrisy. Jefferson was the first American limousine liberal, someone whose principles, especially where other people are concerned, did not interfere significantly with his own life and who was willing to enforce dangerous

Dear Reader:

Thank you for purchasing this Regnery book. Since 1947, we have published books on a wide variety of subjects. Often on the cutting edge of American and global affairs, our books are known for challenging the status quo. The book you purchased is no exception.

If you would like to know more about our books, please fill out this postcard and drop it in the mail. Thank you.

Sincerely,

[signature]

Alfred S. Regnery
President & Publisher

REGNERY
PUBLISHING, INC.
Established 1947

Name _____

Address _____

City _____ State ____ Zip ____

I would be interested in seeing a book about _____

I received this card in the book titled _____

BUSINESS REPLY MAIL

FIRST-CLASS MAIL   NO. 10176   WASHINGTON, DC

POSTAGE WILL BE PAID BY ADDRESSEE

**REGNERY
PUBLISHING, INC.**
Established 1947

422 First Street S.E. • Suite 300
Washington, D.C. 20078-1083

utopian fantasies in the name of a cherished good whose force in challenging his own privilege he was not equally impelled to face. [footnote omitted] ... Who after all was Jefferson kidding? He wrote of natural rights and equality, but look at him and look at his friends and slaves and milieu.

This blasting of Jefferson on these grounds is one of the most egregious examples of academics engaging in a refusal to consider the real context of history. To his credit Jefferson was consistent in his questioning of slavery, see e.g., his comments on the injustice of the institution in his *Notes on Virginia* and his wish that the 1776 Virginia Revisal of laws eliminate slavery. Those who have suggested that for his times Jefferson was a radical thinker, see, e.g., Richard K. Matthews, *The Radical Politics of Thomas Jefferson: A Revisionist View* (Lawrence: University Press of Kansas, 1984), seem to me to have the better argument. It is true that he wrote about what he believed to be lesser literary gifts on the part of black people, but he even ventured this opinion with trepidation, and suggested it was subject to change once more anthropological data accumulated. For these views of Jefferson, expressed in the *Notes*, see Jefferson, *Writings*, supra note 10, at 264–270.

13. Thomas Jefferson to Col. John Taylor, May 28, 1816, reproduced in *Writings*, supra note 10, at 1392–1393.
14. See, Jefferson, *Notes on the State of Virginia* (written in 1781 and 1782 and first published 1787), reproduced in Jefferson, *Writings*, supra note 10, at 121, 285–287.
15. See Jefferson, *Writings*, supra note 10, at 271–275.
16. Id., at 272.
17. Id., at 272–273.
18. See, e.g., Thomas Jefferson, *The Jefferson Bible: the Life and Morals of Jesus of Nazareth*, with an introduction by F. Forrester Church and an afterword by Jaroslav Pelican (Boston: Beacon Press, 1989), Charles B. Sanford, *The Religious Life of Thomas Jefferson* (Charlottesville: University Press of Virginia, 1984), Denise Lardner Carmody and John Tully Carmody, *The Republic of Many Mansions: Foundations of American Religious Thought* (New York: Paragon House, 1990), pp. 87–119. For one of the latest embraces of secular humanism on the Supreme Court see Lee v. Weisman, 112 S. Ct. 2649, 120 L. Ed. 2d 467, 495 (Souter J., concurring).
19. Note 14, supra.
20. See, e.g., Bork, supra note 3. Even that most activist of recent Justices, William J. Brennan, echoed Learned Hand in acknowledging that judges are "not Platonic guardians appointed to wield authority according to their

personal predelictions." William J. Brennan, Jr., "The Constitution of the United States: Contemporary Ratification," given as a speech for the Text and Teaching Symposium at Georgetown University (October 12, 1985), reprinted in Jack N. Rakove, editor, *Interpreting the Constitution* (Boston: Northeastern University Press, 1990), p. 25. For Learned Hand's remarks to this effect see Learned Hand, *The Bill of Rights: The Oliver Wendell Holmes Lectures* (Cambridge: Harvard University Press, 1958), p. 73.

21. Madison was later to become Jefferson's firmest supporter and sidekick, and to join him in attacking the Federalists.

22. James Madison, Alexander Hamilton, and John Jay, *The Federalist Papers* (Isaac Kramnick, editor) (Harmondsworth: Penguin Books, 1987), pp. 319–320.

23. For a sample charge that the Federalists' Constitution was, bluntly stated, "A most daring attempt to establish a despotic Aristocracy," see "Centinel" [Samuel Bryan] I, in the *Independent Gazetteer* (Philadelphia), October 5, 1787, reprinted in Bernard Bailyn, editor, *The Debate on the Constitution* (New York: Library of America, 1993), pp. 52–62, and for a sample observation that the proposed government would "in the first place, create a *Venetian* aristocracy, and, in the end, produce an *absolute monarchy*," see "A Democratic Federalist," *Pennsylvania Herald* (Philadelphia), October 17, 1787, reprinted in Id., at 70–76.

24. I Alfred H. Kelly, Winfred A. Harbison, and Herman Belz, *The American Constitution: Its Origins and Development* (New York: W.W. Norton & Co., 7th ed., 1991), p. xxiv.

25. See generally, Jeffrey Hart, *Acts of Recovery: Essays on Culture and Politics* (Hanover: University Press of New England, 1989).

26. Allan Bloom, *The Closing of the American Mind: How Higher Education Has Failed Democracy and Impoverished the Souls of Today's Students* (New York: Simon & Schuster, 1987).

27. For a similar recent attempt to uncover a lost "natural law" basis for American constitutional law see Hadley Arkes, *Beyond the Constitution* (Princeton: Princeton University Press, 1990).

28. C. S. Lewis, *Mere Christianity* (New York: Macmillan Co., 1958), p. 22. After one has taken a wrong turn, Lewis reminds us, the quickest path to progress is to retrace steps to the point where the wrong path was taken, then to proceed, perhaps in an entirely different direction, along the proper path.

29. Arkes, *supra* note 27, at 11.

30. Frank Donovan, editor, *The George Washington Papers* (New York: Dodd, Mead & Co., 1964), p. 258.

31. George Washington, "To The People of the United States," September 19, 1796, reprinted in II John Marshall, *The Life of George Washington* (New York: Walton Book Company, 1930), p. 479.

Notes

32. See, e.g., *Board of Education of the Westside Community Schools v. Mergens*, 496 U.S. 226, 263 (1990), *Young v. American Mini Theatres*, 427 U.S. 50, 64 (1976), *Police Department of Chicago v. Mosely*, 408 U.S. 92, 95 (1972).
33. Stephen L. Carter, "Does the First Amendment Protect More Than Free Speech?" 33 *William & Mary Law Review* 871, 874 (1992).
34. A representative sample of such theorists includes Thomas Emerson, *The System of Freedom of Expression* (New York: Random House, 1970), and Thomas Emerson, "Toward a General Theory of the First Amendment," 72 *Yale Law Journal* 877, 879–811 (1963) (individual self-fulfillment marked out as one of four goals of First Amendment); Martin Redish, *Freedom of Expression: A Critical Analysis* (Charlottesville, Va: Michie Co., 1984) (self-actualization a primary goal); C. Edwin Baker, "Scope of the First Amendment Freedom of Speech," 25 *University of California at Los Angeles Law Review* 964 (1978).
35. *Smith v. Board of School Commissioners of Mobile County*, 655 F.Supp. 939, 986–987 (S.D.Ala. 1987).
36. *Jaffree v. Board of School Commissioners*, 554 F.Supp. 1104, 1129 N.41 (S.D.Ala. 1983).
37. *Smith v. Board of School Commissioners of Mobile County*, 827 F.2d 684, 690 (11th Cir. 1987) ("The district court found that the home economics, history, and social studies textbooks [endorsed by Alabama officials] both advanced secular humanism and inhibited theistic religion. Our review of the record in this case reveals that these conclusions were in error"). Readers of the District Court and Court of Appeals opinions may understandably reach the conclusion that the District Court and the Court of Appeals took the same evidence and interpreted it differently, and that it is highly dubious whether the Court of Appeals properly gave the deference due to factual determinations by a trial judge.
38. Susan Baxter, "The Last Self-Help Article You'll Ever Need," 26 *Psychology Today* 70 (1993).
39. Id.
40. There is beginning to be a greater recognition of the wisdom of moving away from the rampant individualism in American law, particularly in the field of family law. For an important book that may have begun this trend see Mary Ann Glendon, *Abortion and Divorce in Western Law* (Cambridge: Harvard University Press, 1987). The most recent series of attacks on individualistic liberalism began somewhat earlier, and the case for a return to a communitarian rather than an individualistic ethos was made perhaps most poignantly in Robert Bellah, et. al., *Habits of the Heart: Individualism and Commitment in American Life* (Berkeley: University of California Press, 1985). For similar critiques of liberalism see Michael Sandel, *Liberalism and the Limits of Justice* (Cambridge and New York:

295

Cambridge University Press, 1982), and Roberto Unger, *Knowledge and Politics* (New York: The Free Press, 1975).

41. This idea will be developed somewhat more fully in Chapter Two.

42. See generally R. Kent Newmyer, *Supreme Court Justice Joseph Story: Statesman of the Old Republic* (Chapel Hill: University of North Carolina Press, 1985).

43. See Chapter Four infra, text accompanying notes 705–724.

44. *United States v. Trans-Missouri Freight Association* 166 U. S. 290 (1897).

45. *Allgeyer v. Louisiana* 165 U.S. 578 (1897).

46. *Lochner v. New York*, 198 U.S. 45 (1905). On *Lochner*, see Chapter Three infra, at text accompanying notes 403–418.

47. See James W. Ely, Jr., "Four Horsemen," in Kermit Hall, editor, *The Oxford Companion to the United States Supreme Court* (New York and Oxford: Oxford University Press, 1992), p. 309.

48. *Lochner v. New York*, 198 U.S. 45 (1905). On the *Lochner* case and the jurisprudence it typified see generally Stephen A. Siegel, "Lochner Era Jurisprudence and the American Constitutional Tradition," 70 *North Carolina Law Review* 1 (1991).

49. See generally Ackerman's very valuable and perhaps very dangerous, see text accompanying note 857. infra, Bruce Ackerman, *We the People: Foundations* (Cambridge: Harvard University Press, 1991).

50. See Chapter Five, infra, at text accompanying notes 805–809. For the charges against Critical Legal Studies, see, e.g., the comments of Robert Bork, in *The Tempting of America: The Political Seduction of the Law* (New York: Free Press, 1990), p. 207. (Critical Legal Studies, especially the variant practiced at Harvard, is described as "a nihilistic neo-Marxist movement that views all law as oppressive and political. It is nihilistic because its members typically demand the destruction of current doctrine and hierarchies as illegitimate, but they acknowledge that they have no notion of what is to replace this society."). Bork's comments rather badly mischaracterize what Critical Legal Studies is about. See generally Stephen B. Presser & Jamil S. Zainaldin, *Law and Jurisprudence in American History* (St. Paul: West Publishing Co., 2nd ed., 1989), pp. 939–1017, for a more balanced presentation, especially the comments of Robert Gordon, a leading Critical Legal Studies theorist, replying to the incorrect charge that Critical Legal Studies is "legal nihilism."

51. For a synoptic view of this writing see generally Russell Kirk, *The Conservative Mind: From Burke to Santayana*, (Chicago: Henry Regnery Co., 1953, 6th ed., 1978). For a more specific discussion of the impact of Burkean conservatism on the framers' generation, see Russell Kirk, *The Conservative Constitution* (Washington, D.C.: Regnery Gateway, 1990).

52. For an example of the risks of derision such an approach today runs, see Robert Gordon's reply to Paul Carrington, 35 *Journal of Legal Education*

1, where Gordon, a distinguished Stanford law professor, dismisses the "twin idiocies" of believing that there is only one meaning to constitutional provisions, and believing that they are completely indeterminate.

53. See, e.g., William H. Rehnquist, "The Notion of a Living Constitution," 54 *Texas Law Review* 693 (1976). Rehnquist astutely suggests that there are two senses in which one might use the notion of a "living Constitution," one which is probably in accord with the understanding of the framers, and one of which is not, and is therefore illegitimate. "Where the framers of the Constitution have used general language," Rehnquist explains, "they have given latitude to those who would later interpret the instrument to make that language applicable to cases that the framers might not have foreseen." In contrast to this legitimate interpretive power, however, Rehnquist maintains, the Court should not stretch to create new unenumerated rights, to make policy or to become, to quote from a brief cited by Rehnquist, "the voice and conscience of contemporary society."

54. Richard S. Myers, "Book Review," 42 *Journal of Legal Education* 619 (1992).

55. See generally Rakove, supra note 20, for the firestorm touched off in the 1980s by the "originalist" arguments of Meese and Bork.

56. Stephen Carter, *Reflections of an Affirmative Action Baby* (New York: Basic Books, 1991), pp. 146–147.

57. Id., at 154, quoting the black political scientist Thomas Sowell, and citing "Quoted in Henry Allen, 'Hot Disputes and Cool Sowell,' " *Washington Post*, October 1, 1981, p.C1.

58. Bradley cites Richard S. Kay, *Adherence to the Original Intentions in Constitutional Adjudication: Three Objections and Responses*, 82 *Northwestern University Law Review* 226 (1988); Richard S. Kay, "The Illegality of the Constitution," 4 *Constitutional Commentary* 57 (1987); Earl M. Maltz, "The Failure of Attacks on Constitutional Originalism," 4 *Constitutional Commentary* 43 (1987); Earl M. Maltz, "Foreward: The Appeal of Originalism," 1987 *Utah Law Review* 773; Earl M. Maltz, "Some New Thought on an Old Problem—The Role of the Intent of the Framers in Constitutional Theory," 63 *Boston University Law Review* (1983); and Christopher Wolfe, *The Rise of Modern Judicial Review: From Constitutional Interpretation to Judge-Made Law* (New York: Basic Books, 1986); Christopher Wolfe, "The Original Meaning of the Due Process Clause," in *The Bill of Rights: Original Meaning and Current Understanding* (Eugene V. Hickok, Jr. editor, (Charlottesville: University Press of Virginia, 1991), p. 213; Gerard V. Bradley, "Beguiled: Free Exercise Exemptions and the Siren Song of Liberalism," 20 *Hofstra Law Review* 245, 248–249 (1991).

59. Bradley, supra note 58, at 249, citations omitted.

60. See Edwin Meese III, "Interpreting the Constitution," address before the American Bar Association, Washington, D.C., July 9, 1985, in Rakove,

supra note 20, at 13–21; Robert H. Bork, "Neutral Principles and Some First Amendment Problems," in Rakove, supra note 20, at 197–226.

61. On the nature of this unbridled discretion see Hickok and McDowell, supra note 1.

62. For Bork's shortcomings in this regard, which he is said to share with Raoul Berger and Chief Justice William Rehnquist, see Arkes, supra note 27, at 14–16.

63. Chapter Five, supra, at text accompanying notes 805–809.

64. The most valuable among these is probably Gordon Wood, *The Creation of the American Republic 1776–1787* (Chapel Hill: University of North Carolina Press, 1969).

65. For the ravages of "political correctness" and its handmaiden, "diversity," on college campuses see generally Dinesh D'Souza, *Illiberal Education: The Politics of Race and Sex on Campus* (New York: Free Press, 1991), and for the particularly virulent strain beginning to infect the law schools see Paul Carrington, "Diversity!" 1992 *Utah Law Review* 1105.

66. For an exploration of what might still be learned from these figures, even if some of their views are unpalatable today, see Suzette Hemberger, "Dead Stepfathers," 85 *Northwestern University Law Review* 220 (1990).

67. For example, according to Senator Paul Simon, whose view is representative of Thomas's liberal foes, "What happened was not a careful search for the best in the nation . . . The president wanted a black conservative, someone far enough to the right to satisfy both his hard-core rightists and African-Americans, and apparently did it." Paul Simon, *Advice and Consent* (Washington, D.C.: National Press Books, 1992), p. 78.

68. The practice shows no signs of ceasing, as President Clinton's nomination of Ruth Bader Ginsburg, widely perceived as an attempt to please feminist and Jewish groups, demonstrates. See, e.g., editorial, "New Court Pick Fits Bill," *Christian Science Monitor*, June 16, 1993, p. 18; Blu Greenberg, "Ginsburg Nomination: Good Vibes," *New York Newsday*, June 22, 1993, p. 77.

69. See, e.g., Thomas's remarks discussed in the text accompanying notes 97–99, infra.

70. Terry Eastland, *Energy in the Executive: The Case for the Strong Presidency* (New York: Free Press, 1992), p. 238.

71. Id., at 236.

72. Id., at 236.

73. The success rate for nominating candidates for lower court judgeships with appropriate judicial philosophies, those favoring judicial restraint, has apparently been higher. During the Reagan-Bush years almost 75 percent of the federal district and court of appeals positions were filled with relatively conservative appointments, and they have resisted the temptation to continue the former tendency to use the federal courts to expand plaintiffs

rights and remake society pursuant to liberal self- actualization theory. See generally Eastland, supra, note 70, at 258–267. Nevertheless the lower federal courts are supposed to follow the Supreme Court, and if the republican presidents have failed to achieve their goals for the Supreme Court—and we argue here that they have—five lower court judges will not be able alone to recapture the original constitutional understanding.

74. *Planned Parenthood v. Casey*, 112 S.Ct. 2791 (1992).
75. *Lee v. Weisman*, 112 S.Ct. 2649 (1992).
76. On *Roe*, see generally Chapter Three, infra, at text accompanying notes 593–606.
77. Michael Stokes Paulsen, "Book Review," 10 *Constitutional Commentary* 221, 225–226 (1993).
78. See Chapter Four infra, at text accompanying notes 725–742.
79. With the decision in *Weisman*, the Court vacated and remanded the 5th Circuit decision which had held that public school commencement prayers might be permissible when initiated and carried out by students, rather than by school officials. *Jones v. Clear Creek Independent School Dist.*, 930 F.2d 416 (5th Cir. Tex. 1991), *vacated and remanded* 112 S.Ct. 3020 (1992). On remand, the 5th Circuit stuck by its decision to permit the prayer, *Jones v. Clear Creek Independent School Dist.*, 977 F.2d 963 (1992), *rehearing en banc denied* 983 F.2d 234 (1992), and this time the Supreme Court effectively acquiesced to the lower court's ruling by denying a second writ of certiorari. *Jones v. Clear Creek Independent School Dist.*, 124 L. Ed. 2d 697, 61 U.S.L.W. 3819 (U.S. 1993). The meaning of the 5th Circuit's refusal to back down in the face of *Weisman*, and the Supreme Court's decision not to rehear the case, is subject to hot debate. See, e.g., Michael deCourcy Hinds, "Robertson Trying to Put Prayer in School," *New York Times*, April 16, 1993, at A12; editorial, "Not a Prayer," *Boston Globe*, June 13, 1993, at 84.
80. See infra, Chapter Three, at text accompanying notes 437–516.
81. For the triumph of this spirit in the federal courts in Alabama see *Smith v. Board of School Commissioners of Mobile County*, 827 F.2d 684, 690 (11th Cir. 1987), discussed in the Introduction, text accompanying notes 35–37, supra.
82. For Edmund Burke's attack on the atheistic and rationalist spirit of the French Revolution see generally Russell Kirk, *The Conservative Mind from Burke to Eliot* (Washington and Chicago: Regnery Gateway, 7th ed., 1986), pp. 29–37. For a typical expression of Burke's sentiments, from his Edmund Burke, *Reflections on the Revolution in France* (London: Everyman Library edition, 1964, originally published 1790), pp. 83–84 is:

... We [English] are not the converts of Rousseau; we are not the disciples of Voltaire; Helvetius has made no progress amongst us.

Atheists are not our preachers; madmen are not our lawgivers. We know that we have made no discoveries; and we think that no discoveries are to be made, in morality; nor many in the great principles of government, nor in the ideas of liberty, which were understood long before we were born, altogether as well as they will be after the grave has heaped its mould upon our presumption, and the silent tomb shall have imposed its law on our pert loquacity. In England we have not yet been completely embowelled of our natural entrails: We still feel within us, and we cherish and cultivate, those inbred sentiments which are the faithful guardians, the active monitors of our duty, the true supporters of all liberal and manly morals. We have not been drawn and trussed, in order that we may be filled, like stuffed birds in a museum, with chaff and rags and paltry blurred shreds of paper about the rights of man. We preserve the whole of our feelings still native and entire, unsophisticated by pedantry and infidelity. We have real hearts of flesh and blood beating in our bosoms. We fear God; we look up with awe to kings; with affection to parliaments; with duty to magistrates; with reverence to priests; and with respect to nobility. Why? Because when such ideas are brought before our minds, it is *natural* to be so affected; because all other feelings are false and spurious, and tend to corrupt our minds, to vitiate our primary morals, to render us unfit for rational liberty; and by teaching us a servile, licentious, and abandoned insolence, to be our low sport for a few holidays, to make us perfectly fit for, and justly deserving of, slavery, through the whole course of our lives.

For Alexander Hamilton's attack—quite similar to Burke's—on the French Revolution, see his remarks, written under the name "Titus Manlius" [Alexander Hamilton], *The Stand*, April 7, 1798, reproduced in Cabot Lodge, editor, *Hamilton's Works* (New York and London: G.P. Putnam's Sons, 1886), Vol. VI, pp.257–81, and in Russell Kirk, editor, *The Portable Conservative Reader* (Harmondsworth: Penguin Books, 1982), p. 80. Hamilton there notes the impossibility of separating morality from religion: "Equal pains [in France] have been taken to deprave the morals as to extinguish the religion of the country, if indeed morality in a community can be separated from religion . . ." A bit later commenting on "The politician who loves liberty," Hamilton observes that "He knows that morality overthrown (and morality *must* fall with religion), the terrors of despotism can alone curb the impetuous passions of man, and confine him within the bounds of social duty."

83. For an introduction to conservative thinking on the failure of the Russians in this regard see, e.g., the excerpt from Max Eastman's *Reflections on the*

Failure of Socialism (San Diego: Viewpoint Books, 1955), in Roger Scruton, editor, *Conservative Texts* (New York: St. Martins Press, 1991), pp. 78–84. For a representative American conservative statement of the importance of operating "under God" and under "natural law" in our political tradition, see the excerpt from John Courtney Murray, *We Hold These Truths: Catholic Reflections on the American Proposition* (New York: Sheed and Ward, 1960), in Scruton, supra, at 218–222.

84. Most notably Justice Scalia, who wrote two powerful dissenting opinions in the two cases.

85. Terry Eastland, *Energy in the Executive: The Case for the Strong Presidency* (New York: Free Press, 1992), p. 252.

86. David Brock, *The Real Anita Hill: The Untold Story* (New York: Free Press, 1993).

87. See Robert Bork, *The Tempting of America: The Political Seduction of the Law* (New York: Free Press, 1990), pp. 267–343.

88. Eastland, supra note 85, at 250.

89. See David O'Brien, *Judicial Roulette: Report of the Twentieth Century Fund Task Force on Judicial Selection* (Washington, D.C.: Priority Press, 1988).

90. Cited in Paul Simon, *Advice and Consent* (Washington, D.C.: National Press Books, 1992), pp. 265–66.

91. Eastland, supra note 85, at 256.

92. See generally id., at 257.

93. *United States v. Dewey*, 37 F. Supp. 449 (1941).

94. This is the theme of Hadley Arkes, *Beyond the Constitution* (Princeton: Princeton University Press, 1990).

95. Arkes, supra note 94, at 10.

96. Arkes, supra note 94, at 11.

97. The Heritage Lectures No. 119, Heritage Foundation Reports (June 18, 1987).

98. See Chapter Four, infra.

99. Heritage Lecture No. 119, supra note 97. Two other short summaries of Thomas's belief in natural law, expressed in prenomination articles, appear in the recently published, Fred R. Shairo, editor, *Oxford Dictionary of American Legal Quotations* (New York and Oxford: Oxford University Press, 1993), pp. 314–315, and are reproduced below:

> The rule of law in America means nothing outside Constitutional government and Constitutionalism, and these are simply unintelligible without a higher law. Men cannot rule others by their consent unless their common humanity is understood in light of transcendent standards provided by the Declaration's "Laws of Nature and of Nature's God." Natural law provides a basis in human dignity by

which we can judge whether human beings are just or unjust, noble or ignoble. Clarence Thomas, "Affirmative Action: Cure or Contradiction?" *The Center Magazine*, Nov./Dec. 1987, at 20,21. "Natural rights and higher law arguments are the best defense of liberty and of limited government. Moreover, without recourse to higher law, we abandon our best defense of judicial review—a judiciary active in defending the Constitution, but judicious in its restraint and moderation. Rather than being a justification of the worst type of judicial activism, higher law is the only alternative to the willfulness of both run-amok majorities and run-amok judges. Clarence Thomas, "The Higher Law Background of the Privileges and Immunities Clause of the Fourteenth Amendment," 12 *Harvard Journal of Law & Policy* 63, 63–64 (1989).

100. United States Constitution, Art. IV, § 4 (guaranteeing a republican form of government to each state).

101. United States Constitution, Article IV, §4, cl. 1 (emphasis, but not capitalization supplied).

102. See generally Alexander Hamilton's explanation of the clause in *Federalist 21*, in James Madison, Alexander Hamilton, and John Jay, *The Federalist Papers* (Harmondsworth: Penguin Books, 1987), pp. 173–174.

103. On the history of the clause see generally William M. Wiecek, *The Guarantee Clause of the U.S. Constitution* (Ithaca: Cornell University Press, 1972).

104. See generally Kloppenberg, "The Virtues of Liberalism: Christianity, Republicanism, and Ethics in Early American Political Discourse," 74 *Journal of American History* 9 (1987); and Carrol Smith-Rosenberg, "Discovering the Subject of the 'Great Constitutional Discussion,' 1776–1789," 79 *Journal of American History* 841 (1992).

105. Quoted in Russell Kirk, supra note 82, at 75.

106. Hart, supra note 25, at 55.

107. Charles Francis Adams, editor, *Collected Works of John Adams* (Boston: Little, Brown, 1851), pp. 285–86, quoted in Kirk, supra note 82, at 98.

108. Jeffrey Hart, *Acts of Recovery: Essays on Culture and Politics* (Hanover and London: University Press of New England, 1989), p. 59.

109. I Adams, *Works*, supra note 107, at 462, quoted in Kirk, supra note 82, at 95.

110. Kirk, supra note 82, at 95–96.

111. Cf. I Adams, *Works*, supra note 107, at 462, quoted in Kirk, supra note 82, at 95.

112. See Thomas Jefferson, *Notes on Virginia*, discussed in the Introduction, supra, text accompanying notes 15–19.

113. On John Adams's manifestations of this philosophy see generally Kirk, supra note 82, at 98–110.
114. See, e.g., Frank I. Michaelman, "Foreword: Traces of Self- Government," 100 *Harvard Law Review* 4 (1986). In this piece, Michaelman criticizes the Supreme Court's 1985 decision upholding the air force ban on wearing visible religious items (in this case, a yarmulke) while in uniform. *Goldman v. Weinberger*, 106 S.Ct. 1310 (1985). That decision, the Court explained, was based on what it believed to be "Neutrality . . . and the rule of law." Michaelman, at 8, citing and paraphrasing Justice Stevens' concurring opinion in *Goldman*, at 1315–16. In Michaelman's *Forward* he attacks the notion of a Court bound by the rule of law, and argues instead for what he regards as a judicial philosophy embracing "republicanism," which philosophy would presumably permit an activist judiciary bound less by the rule of law than by a mandate to become a "bastion of (its own) self-government," Michaelman, at 74. In other words, Michaelman maintains that a "republican" Court can (and should) protect the rights of citizens to evolving individual freedoms (such as, perhaps, a purported constitutional right to live an openly homosexual life while in the military) by declaring its own freedom from, among other things, adherence to previous precedents. Whether or not such a judicial philosophy has anything to do with "republicanism" as understood by the framers, Michaelman's *Forward* was one of the earliest examples of a highly placed law professor taking "republicanism" seriously, and it contains a wealth of source material for further reading on historical and contemporary notions of "republicanism." Among other scholars attempting to explore just what the framers meant by "civic virtue" and "republicanism" are Suzanna Sherry (see, e.g., "Civic Virtue and the Feminine Voice in Constitutional Adjudication," 72 *Virginia Law Review* 543 (1986)) and Cass Sunstein (see, e.g., "Interest Groups in American Public Law," 38 *Stanford Law Review* 29 (1985)).
115. Kirk, supra note 82, at 103–104.
116. Reprinted in Stephen Presser and Jamil Zainaldin, *Law and Jurisprudence in American History* (St. Paul: West Publishing Co., 2nd ed., 1989), p. 109.
117. Jean-Jaques Rousseau, *The Social Contract* (Harmondsworth: Penguin Books, 1968, Maurice Cranston, trans. 1959), p. 82.
118. Thomas A. Smith, "Note, The Rule of Law and the States: A New Interpretation of the Guarantee Clause," 93 *Yale Law Journal* 561 (1984).
119. Supra, text accompanying note 93.
120. John Gresham, *The Firm* (New York: Doubleday, 1991), p. 58.
121. Mary Jordan, "More Attorneys Making a Motion for the Pursuit of Happiness," *Washington Post*, September 4, 1993, p. A3.

122. Ruth Marcus, "Gloom at the Top: Why Young Lawyers Bail Out," *Washington Post*, May 31, 1987, p. C1. See also Jane Halsema, "Law Firms Offer Second Path for Non-Partners," *San Diego Business Journal*, January 2, 1989, p. 22. ("Young lawyers traditionally started their careers by enduring 90-hour work weeks for as long as 10 years.") There was thus quite a substantial factual basis on which John Gresham could build to tell his tale of the system of bottom-line lawyering gone evil and mad.

123. On the lamentable decline of this ideal see generally, Anthony T. Kronman, *The Lost Lawyer: Failing Ideals of the Legal Profession*, (Cambridge: Harvard University Press, 1993).

124. See, e.g., Liza Mundy, "The pro bono hustle; Legal work performed without charge for a worthy cause," *Washington Monthly*, September 1989 ("more and more college students willingly sell themselves into indentured servitude, amassing huge student loan debts that will leave them little flexibility when they graduate. This is the reason that only 2 percent [of law students] will go into public service law. . . . 63.5 percent take their first job with a private firm . . . 15 percent—in many cases the best and the brightest—are lured into big firms with over 100 attorneys. . . .").

125. Marcus, supra note 122.

126. Illinois Legal Times Roundtable, "Associates Tell All," *Illinois Legal Times*, June 1991, p. 1. (Associate indicates that with student loan debts of $50,000 idealism had to take a back seat to finding a lucrative job).

127. See, e.g., Id.

128. Garry Wills, in *Inventing America: Jefferson's Declaration of Independence* (New York: Doubleday and Co., Inc., 1978), pp. 229–239, 317–318, explains that the words "sacred honor" derive from Jefferson's dependence on the Scottish Enlightenment philosopher Frances Hutcheson. Hutcheson's thought embraced the notion of the inalienable rights of man, but grounded the notion not in concepts of autonomous individualism, as do modern liberals, but rather in more "republican" notions of virtue and societal interdependence. Had Jefferson been more influenced by the individualism that seems inherent in Locke, Wills reasons, Jefferson would not have left out of his listing of "inalienable rights" the right to property. For Hutchinson, apparently, the right to own property was considered to be something of a boon which followed a life of civic virtue rather than a Lockean fundamental which proceeded it. All of this is implied in the use of the phrase "sacred honor."

129. Id., at 317.

130. See generally, Ellis Sandoz, *A Government of Laws: Political Theory, Religion, and the American Founding* (Baton Rouge: Louisiana State University Press, 1990). For some of the raw materials on which Sandoz relied see Ellis Sandoz, editor, *Political Sermons of the Founding Era*

1730–1805 (Liberty Press, 1991). Sandoz laments the tendency of moderns to neglect the important religious and specifically Christian element of early American political theory:

> The Christian anthropology [referring to a previous paragraph which distills general Christian understandings] somehow gets short shrift in recent political discussions, but it constitutes the deepest basis for ever asserting that there ought to be democracy or self-rule by the people. Democracy is a rule of, by, and for the people, and rule of, by, and for the people in its modern version partakes heavily of something that it has not necessarily had in many Christian countries and did not widely have in antiquity. In the modern period, ironically, is a notion that insofar as there is this ineradicable natural integrity that inheres in every single human being, then there is also the claim buttressed in a variety of ways that democracy is the natural political order.

Sandoz, *A Government of Laws*, supra, at 13–14. Sandoz continues:

> At the very center of [the shift of political power from the ruler to the ruled that culminated with the Age of Democratic Revolution in the eighteenth century] is a magnification of the dignity and worth of the individual human being, which is profoundly indebted to the philosophical and meditative traditions of the Christian West and, indeed, quite incomprehensible apart from them.

Id., at 14. And, finally, for our purposes:

> The American founders did not dream . . . that the protection of property and the erection of an extended commercial republic contradicted their dedication to individual liberty or to the continuation of a Christian commonwealth moored in toleration of a denominational diversity and disestablishment. Id., at 23.

131. See text accompanying note 99, supra.
132. Kirk, supra note 82, at 80, quoting "The Stand," Henry Cabot Lodge, editor, *The Collected Works of Alexander Hamilton* (New York: Putnam, 1886) vol. V, p. 410.
133. I William Blackstone, *Commentaries on the Law of England* (originally published at Oxford, 1765, Chicago: University of Chicago reprint, 1979), pp. 39–40.
134. Id., at 40–42.
135. Id., at 41.
136. Id., at 70 (emphasis in the original).
137. Ibid.
138. For the development of this theme in the work of Blackstone see Daniel J.

Boorstin, *The Mysterious Science of the Law* (Cambridge: Harvard University Press, 1941).

139. See generally Julian S. Waterman, "Thomas Jefferson and Blackstone's Commentaries," 27 *Illinois Law Review* 629, 632 (1933).

Somewhat later, however, Jefferson became queasy about the political and social implications of Blackstone's widespread acceptance. As Waterman notes, he wrote to Horatio G. Spofford on March 17, 1814:

> Blackstone and Hume have made Tories of all England, and are making Tories of those young Americans whose native feelings of independence do not place them above the wily sophistries of a Hume or a Blackstone.

Id., at 634–5.

Ironically, Jefferson also included the *Commentaries* on an updated reading list prepared in 1814, this time describing Blackstone's work as "the last perfect digest of both branches of law, common law and Chancery." Id., at 636.

140. Id., at 658–9.

141. Justices Jay, Wilson, Ellsworth, and Iredell, among others, all supported prosecutions brought under a federal common law jurisdiction. See generally Stephen B. Presser, *The Original Misunderstanding* (Durham: Carolina Academic Press, 1991), pp. 67–99 (text and notes), and Chapter Two infra, at text accompanying Notes 288–301.

142. Wilson stated this belief in his charge to the grand jury of the circuit court for the District of Virginia (1793), reprinted in Francis Wharton, editor, *State Trials of the United States During the Administrations of Washington and Adams* (Philadelphia: Carey and Hart, 1849) (hereafter "State Trials"), p. 62.

143. In *Under God* (Simon and Schuster, 1990), Garry Wills describes the inanity of some modern intellectuals who express surprise at what they perceive as a "sudden" rise of evangelical Christianity, and a politics based on those tenets, in the 1980s. Wills puts political evangelicalism— what the media call the "Religious Right"—in historical perspective by showing that an amalgam of Christianity and American republicanism has undergirded the nation and its political rhetoric since its founding. During times of war, Wills notes, American political rhetoric particularly seems to draw from the Bible as well as from the Declaration of Independence for its imagery, and no more so than during the Civil War. Id., at 208. Abraham Lincoln's recurrent biblical imagery, for example, favored the Book of Luke, and Lincoln, in effect, made of the Bible "an explicit guide to constitutional interpretation." Id., at 213. See also Wills, *Inventing America*, supra note 128, in the "Prologue," at xiv-xvi (describing

Lincoln's recurrent choice of imagery and reference—to the Bible and to the Declaration of Independence—as a natural marriage as well as wise political rhetoric, because it made manifest the coexistence of religion, morality, and political structure in America in a way that the Constitution, a product of political compromise, could not). For the full story on the Gettysburg Address see also Gary Wills, *Lincoln at Gettysburg: The Words that Remade America* (New York: Simon & Schuster, 1992).

144. For the influence of the English common law in general, and Magna Carta and the English "Ancient [Saxon] Constitution" in particular, see the recent essays collected in Ellis Sandoz, editor, *The Roots of Liberty: Magna Carta, Ancient Constitution, and the Anglo-American Tradition of Rule of Law* (Columbia, MO: University of Missouri Press, 1993).

145. Arkes, supra note 94, at 15.

146. Id., at 17.

147. Id., at 16–17.

148. Mary Ann Glendon, *Abortion and Divorce in Western Law* (Cambridge: Harvard University Press, 1987), p. 140.

149. For a splendid historical and critical article on balancing test jurisprudence see T. Alexander Aleinikoff, "Constitutional Law in the Age of Balancing," 96 *Yale Law Journal* 943 (1987).

150. Id., at 943–944.

151. *Schneider v. State*, 308 U.S. 147 (1939).

152. See, e.g., *Garcia v. San Antonio Metro. Transit Authority*, 469 U.S. 528, 562–63 (Powell, J. dissenting).

153. *United States v. Nixon*, 418 U.S. 683 (1974).

154. Aleinikoff, supra note 149, at 948.

155. Id., at 949.

156. *McCulloch v. Maryland*, 17 U.S. (4 Wheat) 316 (1817).

157. Aleinikoff, supra note 149, at 949.

158. *Planned Parenthood v. Casey*, 112 S. Ct. 2791, 2826–29 (1992), where the majority opinion lists and discusses the various findings of expert witness regarding the effects of the statute on abusive relationships.

159. *Griswold v. Connecticut*, 381 U. S. 479, 482–5 (1965).

160. Id., at 481.

161. Id., at 530.

162. See, e.g., Thomas Kauper, "Penumbras, Peripheries, Emanations, Things Fundamental and Forgotten: The *Griswold* Case," 64 *Michigan Law Review* 235, 253.

163. See William W. Van Alstyne, "Closing the Circle of Constitutional Review From *Griswold v. Connecticut* to *Roe v. Wade*: An Outline of a Decision Merely Overruling *Roe*," 1989 *Duke Law Journal* 1677, 1684.

164. *Poe v. Ullman* 367 U.S. 492, 539–545 (1961) (Harlan, J. dissenting).

165. *Griswold*, 381 U.S., at 500, citing *Palko v. Connecticut*, 302 U.S. 319, 325.
166. Id., at 501.
167. *Poe v. Ullman*, 367 U.S. 492, 542 (Harlan, J. dissenting).
168. Id., at 545.
169. Id., at 554.
170. Id., at 554–555.
171. The same metaphor is used by Aleinikoff, supra note 149, at 1004 ("Much of modern due process and equal protection law can be explained as the Court placing its finger on the scale on behalf of individuals and minorities. . . . Balancing has turned us away from the Constitution, supplying "reasonable policy-making in lieu of theoretical investigations of rights, principles and structures.")
172. Casey, supra note 158, at 2813–14.
173. Thomas Sowell, "Supreme Court Sinks Teeth into Self-Anointed," *Rocky Mountain News*, March 18, 1992, at 62.
174. Rowland Evans and Robert Novak, *Buffalo News*, September 5, 1992, at C3. See also the Associated Press release, "Federal Appeals Judge Criticizes 2 Jurists," the *Orlando Sentinel*, June 14, 1992, at A23.
175. See Justice Rehnquist's dissent in Casey,, 112 S.Ct., at 2865.
176. On the difficulties with *Roe*, see infra, Chapter Three, at text accompanying notes 593–606, and Chapter Four, at text accompanying notes 755–801.
177. 112 S.Ct. 2791, 1992 U.S. LEXIS 4751, *193:

    In one sense, the Court's approach [affirming *Roe*] is worlds apart from that of the Chief Justice and Justice Scalia [rejecting *Roe*]. And yet, in another sense the difference between the two approaches is short—the distance is but a single vote.

    I am 83 years old. I cannot remain on this Court forever, and when I do step down, the confirmation process for my successor may well focus on the issue before us today. That, I regret, may be exactly where the choice between the two worlds will be made.

178. For Tribe's current defense of Justice Blackmun's majority opinion in *Roe* see, e.g., Lawrence H. Tribe, *Abortion: The Clash of Absolutes* (New York: Norton, 1990), pp. 77–138. Tribe's conclusion in that work was that "As an interpretation of the Constitution *Roe* will remain controversial. But it has much to commend it and cannot fairly be dismissed as indefensible or flatly wrong." Id., at 138.
179. Tribe, "Foreword: Toward a Model of Roles in the Due Process of Life and Law," 87 *Harvard Law Review* 1, 7 (1973).
180. Glendon, supra note 148, at 44.
181. See generally Chapter 2, "The Civil Theology of Liberal Democracy:

Locke and His Predecessors," in Sandoz, *Government of Laws,* supra note 130, at 51–82.

182. For the Christian aspect in America see generally Chapter 5, "Reflections on Spiritual Aspects of the American Founding," in Sandoz, *Government of Laws,* supra note 130, at 125–162.

183. Cited in Id., at 142–3.

184. See, e.g., Glendon, supra note 148, at 123–124.

185. Arkes, supra note 94, at 12.

186. This is why Hillary Clinton's supposed belief in the tenets of the Children's Defense Fund's approach to families, which encourages the development of rights of family members against each other and the assertion of those rights through litigation, is so distressing. For the details on Ms. Clinton's views, and conservative concern with them see David Lauter, "Hillary-Bashing Becoming a Part of GOP Campaign," *Los Angeles Times,* August 19, 1992, p. A1. Family members need to be encouraged to cooperate to achieve common goals, and need to learn, often, to submerge what they believe to be their individual needs (self-actualization, perhaps?) to the good of the family unit. Such a view would discourage divorce (since the latest empirical findings, contrary to what was believed in the era of the apex of self-actualization, show that even if the parents are unhappy with the marriage their divorce harms their children more than if they had tried to work out their problems and remain in their marriage). For details of recent studies, and for the harm caused by single-parent families, see the seminal piece by Barbara Dafoe Whitehead, "Dan Quayle Was Right," *Atlantic,* April, 1993, p. 47. At least where there is no physical abuse, the reduction in thinking of children as possessed with rights to check the actions of their parents might result in a healthier respect for authority in the family, which could lead in turn to a greater respect for authority and structure in society. This could lead to reduced crime and distress, and a more stable environment in which families could be reconstituted and the chaos and anarchy in our inner cities diminish.

187. To similar effect see Glendon, supra note 148, at 52–53, 58, 62, 114–131.

188. I Blackstone, supra note 133, at 165.

189. See Chase's *Manuscript Jury Charge Book,* at 42–46, which is in the Vertical File of the Manuscript Division of the Maryland Historical Society, Baltimore. The Jury Charge Book records charges that Chase made to grand juries in 1798–1800, 1802–03, and 1805–06 (hereafter Jury Charge Book).

190. See Geoffrey Seed, *James Wilson,* (Millwood, N.Y.: KTO Press, 1978), p. 23, quoting Robert G. McCloskey, editor, *The Works of James Wilson* (Cambridge: Harvard University Press, 1967), pp. 406–7.

191. See Morton J. Horwitz, "Republicanism and Liberalism in American Constitutional Thought," 29 *William and Mary Law Review* 57, 58 (1987). A brief history of the road to the Sixteenth Amendment—the income tax amendment—can be found in Richard B. Bernstein with Jerome Agel, *Amending America: If We Love the Constitution So Much, Why Do We Keep Trying to Change It?* (Times Books, 1993), pp. 118–22.

192. See, e.g., Paul C. Roberts, "Debt, Lies, and Inflation," *National Review*, August 31, 1992, p. 31 (describing a disinformation campaign, promoted by Democrats and a sympathetic media, which so successfully painted the Reagan boom years as a period of economic disaster that it effectively derailed the reelection campaign of George Bush).

193. Mary Ann Glendon, "What's Wrong with the Elite Law Schools," *Wall Street Journal*, June 8, 1993, p. A14. "Legal academia is left of the mainstream," said Glendon's fellow Harvard law professor, Charles Fried, who was U. S. solicitor general under Reagan. Adam Pertman, "Legal Changes Explored to Redress Bias," *Boston Globe*, June 21, 1993, p. 1.

194. For a fine introduction to Burke's thought see Conor Cruise O'Brien, *The Great Melody: A Thematic Biography of Edmund Burke* (Chicago: The University of Chicago Press, 1992).

195. For the working out of the similarities between Edmund Burke's jurisprudential views and that of the framers, see Chapter VI, "Edmund Burke and the Constitution," in Russell Kirk, *The Conservative Constitution* (Washington, D.C.: Regnery Gateway, 1990).

196. For further indications of what Burkean jurisprudence comprises see Chapter Five, infra.

197. *Brown v. Board of Education*, 347 U.S. 483, 492 (1954).

198. See generally the Introduction to this book, supra, text accompanying note 28.

199. For a typical statement, see, e.g., "Samuel Spencer and William R. Davie Debate the Need for a Bill of Rights and the Jurisdiction of the Federal Courts," July 29, 1788, in Bernard Bailyn, *The Debate on the Constitution* (New York: Library of America, 1993), Vol II, pp. 888–96, in which Mr. Spencer presents the case for the states' need for a Bill of Rights to protect their judiciaries from federal usurpation, and Mr. Davie presents the opposing view—that only a federal judiciary that is generally paramount over local and state courts could hold the nation together.

200. Forrest McDonald has written that "it is meaningless to say that the framers intended this or that the framers intended that: their positions were diverse and, in many particularly incompatible. . . . Some of their differences were subject to compromise; others were not." Forrest McDonald, *Novus Ordo Seclorum: The Intellectual Origins of the Constitution* (Lawrence, KS: University Press of Kansas, 1985), p. 224, quoted

in Gerard V. Bradley, "Beguiled: Free Exercise Exemptions and the Siren Song of Liberalism," 20 *Hofstra Law Review* 245, 252 (1991).

201. See generally Presser, *The Original Misunderstanding*, supra note 141, at 27.

202. Id., at 82–86, and notes.

203. Max Farrand, editor, *Records of the Federal Convention of 1787* (1911; rev. ed. in 4 vols., 1937; rpr. New Haven: Yale University Press, 1966), vol. I, p. 125 (cited in Sandoz, *Government of Laws*, supra note 130, at 22).

204. See Bernstein, supra note 191, at 263–65, describing how the amendment process itself has become a "political football" used by citizens and legislators frustrated with their inability to further an agenda through legislative action or the judicial system. In part, this is the fault of the compromises implicit in the drafting of the Constitution, because the original intent of the use and scope of Article V was purposely left vague. Id., at 19–20.

205. See Herbert Wechsler, "Toward Neutral Principles of Constitutional Law," 73 *Harvard Law Review* 1, 16 (1959).

206. See generally Richard Epstein, *Takings: Private Property and the Power of Eminent Domain* (Cambridge: Harvard University Press, 1985). The quoted language is from a discussion of Epstein's views in Herman Schwartz, "Property Rights and the Constitution: Will the Ugly Duckling Become a Swan?" 37 *American University Law Review* 9, 13 (1987) (footnotes omitted), citing *Takings*, at 162, 163, 170–81.

207. See generally Chapter Three, infra, text accompanying Notes 469–487.

208. See generally, Morton J. Horwitz, *The Transformation of American Law 1780–1860* (Cambridge: Harvard University Press, 1977), pp. 6–9.

209. Gerard V. Bradley, "Beguiled: Free Exercise Exemptions and the Siren Song of Liberalism," 20 *Hofstra Law Review* 245, 303–304 (1991). The "burgeoning load" cited by Bradley is Gordon S. Wood, *The Creation of the American Republic: 1776–1787* (Chapel Hill: Univeristy of North Carolina Press, 1969), pp. 61–82; Russell Hittinger, "Liberalism and the American Natural Law Tradition," 25 *Wake Forest Law Review* 429, 445–49 (1990); Robert C. Palmer, "Liberties as Constitutional Provisions: 1776–1791," reprinted in William E. Nelson & Robert C. Palmer, *Liberty and Community: Constitution and Rights in the Early American Republic* (1987), pp. 55. Bradley, at 304 N.302.

210. Bradley, supra note 209, at 304.

211. Id., at 304, citing William E. Nelson, "Changing Conceptions of Judicial Review: The Evolution of Constitutional Theory in the States 1790–1860," 120 *University of Pennsylvania Law Review* 1166 (1972).

212. See, in particular, the very accessible Alexander Bickel, *The Supreme Court and the Idea of Progress* (New York: Harper and Row, 1970).

213. Id., at 175.

214. Ibid.
215. See, e.g., Sandoz, *Government of Laws*, supra, note 130, and James T. Kloppenberg, "The Virtues of Liberalism: Christianity, Republicanism, and Ethics in Early American Political Discourse" 74 *Journal of American History* 9 (1987).
216. See generally James McClellan, *Joseph Story and the American Constitution: A Study in Political and Legal Thought with Selected Writings* (Norman: Oklahoma University Press, 1971) and R. Kent Newmyer, *Supreme Court Justice Joseph Story: Statesman of the Old Republic* (Chapel Hill: University of North Carolina Press, 1985). On Story's importance as a commentator on the nexus between religion and government, see Chapter Four, infra, at text accompanying Notes 705–724.
217. See generally Felix Frankfurter & James Landes, *The Business of the Supreme Court* (New York: Macmillan, 1971); Ralph Lerner, "The Supreme Court as Republican Schoolmaster," 1967 *Supreme Court Review* 127.
218. See, e.g., Maeva Marcus, James R. Perry, et al, editors, *The Documentary History of the Supreme Court of the United States, 1789-1800: Appointments and Proceedings*, Vol. 1 (New York: Columbia Univ. Press, 1985); *The Justices on Circuit, 1789–1800*, Vol. 2 (New York: Columbia Univ. Press, 1988). Manuscript collections are still worthy of mining, however. Indeed, one of the best sources for understanding the nexus between law and religion in the early republic still exists only in manuscript, the Jury Charge Book of Samuel Chase, supra note 189.
219. The most significant numbers of *The Federalist* and contemporary arguments for and against the Constitution have recently been published as a splendid two-volume collection, Bernard Bailyn, editor, *The Debate on the Constitution* (New York: Library of America, 1993).
220. There are many editions of *The Federalist*. One of the best and most readily accessible is James Madison, Alexander Hamilton, and John Jay, *The Federalist Papers* (Harmondsworth: Penguin Books, 1987) (edited and with an introduction by Isaac Kramnick).
221. Introduction to the 1987 Penguin edition of *The Federalist*, supra note 220, at 11.
222. First published in New York, May 28, 1788, Vol. II, pp. 467–475 of the *Debates*, supra note 219, and pp. 436–442 of the Penguin edition of *The Federalist Papers*, supra note 220.
223. But see *Missouri v. Jenkins*, discussed in footnote 588, Chapter Three, infra.
224. U. S. Const. art. VI, § 1.
225. *Debates*, supra note 219, Vol. II, pp. 469–472, Penguin *Federalist*, supra note 220, at 438–440. For the implementation of Hamilton's arguments in federal case law see Samuel Chase's opinion in *U.S. v. Callender*, 25

Notes

Fed. Cas. 239 (C.C.D. Virginia, 1800), and John Marshall's opinion in *Marbury v. Madison*, 1 Cranch 137 (1803).

226. U.S. Const. art. III, § 1.

227. Most constitutional scholars have expressed an opinion on the question of the legitimacy of judicial review, although their analysis is often offered not really to solve the historical problem, but rather to buttress a point of view on the issue of whether the Court in recent decades has abused that power. *See*, e.g., Leonard W. Levy, *Original Intent and the Framers' Constitution* (New York: Macmillan, 1988). Levy, who stoutly maintains that the expansive readings of the Constitution in recent Supreme Court decisions is perfectly legitimate, describes some of the history of the debate over the legitimacy of judicial review in Chapters 5 and 6, pp. 89–126, and concludes that judicial review, then and now, exists by popular consent rather than by any design of the framers. A different vision is presented by Robert A. Burt, *The Constitution in Conflict* (Cambridge: Harvard University Press, 1992), who argues that Madison's vision of an egalitarian division of government, in which the federal branches are equal in their authority to interpret the Constitution, is preferable to the type of judicial review envisioned by Hamilton in *Federalist No. 78*. For further recent discussion see also Mark Tushnet, *Red, White, and Blue: A Critical Analysis of Constitutional Law* (Cambridge: Harvard University Press, 1988); and Shannon C. Stimson, *The American Revolution in the Law: Anglo-American Jurisprudence before John Marshall* (Princeton: Princeton University Press, 1990).

228. This public address is reproduced in Griffith J. McRee, *Life and Correspondence of James Iredell* (Vol. 1 and 2, combined, New York: Peter Smith, 1949), pp. 145–46.

229. *Calder v. Bull*, 3 Dallas 386 (1798).

230. Id., at 395.

231. Id., at 399.

232. *U. S. v. Matthew Lyon*, 15 Fed. Cas. 1183, 1185 (C.C.D. Vermont, 1798) (emphasis added).

233. 25 Fed. Cas. 239, 253–7 (C.C.D. Virginia, 1800).

234. Id., at 257.

235. Albert J. Beveridge, *The Life of John Marshall*, Vol. III, p. 39 (Boston: Houghton-Mifflin, 1919).

236. Id., at 40, n. 1. See also Russell Kirk, *The Conservative Mind* 96–98 (Chicago: Henry Regnery and Co., 1953), noting Marshall's use of some of the *Federalist*'s arguments, particularly those in No. 78.

237. Chase Jury Charge Book, supra note 189, at 11–12 (emphasis in the original).

238. Id., at 16–17. Similar language is repeated in the Chase Jury Charge Book, at 30–31.

313

239. On judicial review as an accepted and understood practice among American Whigs by the time of the Revolution see Robert Lowry Clinton, *Marbury v. Madison and Judicial Review* (Lawrence: Kansas University Press, 1989), pp. 18–19, and sources cited therein. For the last royal governor of Massachusetts's expressed doubts about the Americans and their theory that the courts could independently enforce fundamental rights, see Bernard Bailyn, *The Ordeal of Thomas Hutchinson* (Cambridge: Harvard University Press, 1974), pp. 99–107, reprinted in Stephen B. Presser and Jamil S. Zainaldin, *Law and Jurisprudence in American History* (St. Paul: West Publishing Co., 2nd ed., 1989), pp. 92–95.

240. *Debates*, supra note 219, Vol. I, pp. 404–411, Penguin *The Federalist*, supra note 220, pp. 122–128.

241. See, e.g., Gordon S. Wood, *The Creation of the American Republic, 1776–1787* (Chapel Hill: Univ. of North Carolina Press, 1969). Wood suggests that during the debates over the Constitution the Federalists were forced to justify the new Constitution by use of the rhetoric and the implicit rights-based ideology of the American Revolution. This often obscured rather than clarified the nature of the constitutional undertaking, as expressed for example, in the unashamedly aristocratic thought of some of the framers, such as John Adams. The result of Federalist trimming was the creation of a distinctly liberal tradition which "has mitigated and often obscured the real social antagonisms of American politics." Id., p. 562.

242. See, e.g., "Brutus I," an Antifederalist piece originally published in the *New York Journal*, October 18, 1787, reprinted in *Debates*, supra note 219, Vol. I, pp. 170–171.

243. *Debates*, supra note 219, Vol. I, pp. 408–411, Penguin *Federalist* supra note 220, pp. 126–128.

244. *Debates*, supra note 219, Vol. I, pp. 407, 409, Penguin *Federalist*, supra, pp. 125, 126.

245. *Debates*, supra note 219, Vol. I, p. 411, Penguin *Federalist*, supra note 220, p. 128.

246. *Debates*, supra note 219, Vol. I, p. 12.

247. *Debates*, supra note 219, Vol. I, p. 181.

248. *Debates*, supra note 219, Vol. II, p. 415.

249. *Debates*, supra note 219, Vol. I, p. 869.

250. Learned Hand, *The Bill of Rights: The Oliver Wendell Holmes Lectures, 1958* (Cambridge: Harvard University Press, 1958), p. 74.

251. *Debates*, supra note 219, Vol. II, pp. 404–405.

252. To the same effect see the "Ratification of the Federal Constitution of the Commonwealth of Massachusetts," February 6, 1788, which begins: "acknowledging with grateful hearts the goodness of the supreme ruler of the universe, in affording the people of the United States, in the course of his providence, an opportunity, deliberately and peaceably, without fraud

or surprise, of entering into an explicit and solemn compact with each other, by assenting to and ratifying a new Constitution. . . ." *Debates*, supra note 219, Vol. II, pp. 547–548. Identical language appears in the "Ratification of the State of New Hampshire," June 21, 1788, Id., at 550.

253. Maeva Marcus, editor, *Documentary History of the United States Supreme Court: Jury Charges 1789–1794* (New York: Columbia University Press, 1991) [hereafter "*Documentary History*"], p. 359.

254. Id., at 359.

255. Id., at 495.

256. David J. Katz, "Grand Jury Charges Delivered by Supreme Court Justices Riding Circuit During the 1790s," 14 *Cardozo Law Review* 1045, 1083 (1993).

257. Grand Jury Charge (C.D.D. Va., Nov. 23, 1798) (Cushing, J), in Documentary History, supra note 253, Vol. III, p. 305. Quoted in Katz, supra note 256, at 1083.

258. See generally Edmund Burke, *Reflections on the Revolution in France* (Conor Cruise O'Brien, editor, Harmondsworth: Penguin Books, 1969, originally published 1790).

259. *Documentary History*, supra note 253, Vol. III, p. 311.

260. *Documentary History*, supra note 253, Vol. III, p. 138.

261. Id., at 359 (emphasis in original).

262. Id., at 41.

263. Id., at 60.

264. *Documentary History*, supra note 253, Vol. III, p. 436 (quoting from the *United States Oracle* for May 24, 1800).

265. Paterson Unidentified Grand Jury Charge No. 4, *Documentary History*, supra note 253, Vol. III, pp. 462, 463, 464. Paterson's charge and others, as well as the belief of the Justices that they were "the first line of defense against the collapse of their new government," are discussed and analyzed in Katz, supra note 256, at 1061.

266. See generally Stephen B. Presser, *The Original Misunderstanding* (Durham: Carolina Academic Press, 1991).

267. *Documentary History*, supra note 253, Vol. III, p. 410.

268. Id. at 413. Chase was quoting from Matthew 7:18–20.

269. *Documentary History*, supra note 253, Vol. III, p. 416.

270. Chase Jury Charge Book, supra note 189, pp. 33–34. See to the same effect, Id., at page 53:

> I cannot suppose that I shall give offense to any person by recommending to you, my fellow-Citizens, in my *judicial* character, the practice of all *religious, moral & social* duties; or by delivering an opinion that there can be no *political* happiness without *liberty; no*

liberty without morality; and no morality without religion. . . .
[emphasis in original]

271. Id., at 34–35.
272. Id., at 35.
273. Id., at 38.
274. Id., at 38–39.
275. See, e.g. *The National Intelligencer*, Philadelphia, August 10, and August 12, 1803.
276. Chase Jury Charge Book, supra note 189, pp. 39–40.
277. Id., at 40–41.
278. Id., at 45.
279. Id., at 41.
280. Id., at 45.
281. Id., at 41–42. The "great many names" is presumably a reference to Locke's *Second Treatise on Civil Government* (1690), to Rousseau's *The Social Contract* (1762), and to Paine's *Common Sense* (1776) and *The Rights of Man* (1791, 1792).
282. Chase Jury Charge Book, supra note 189, at 43–44.
283. The dangers of a judiciary beholden to the whims of the legislature were noted by many in the debates in the press at the time of the federal Constitution and in the Constitutional Convention itself. Many feared that the proposed Constitution didn't go far enough in protecting the judiciary. For example, James Wilson offered a "Summation and Final Rebuttal" during the debates (Dec. 11, 1787), in which he noted that "the powers of the several parts of this government are not kept as distinct and independent as they ought to be." *Debates*, supra note 219, Vol. I, pp. 832, 842. See also, e.g., "Dissent of the Minority of the Pennsylvania Convention," *Pennsylvania Packet* (Philadelphia), December 18, 1787, in *Debates*, supra note 219, Vol. I, pp. 526, 534, 546. In response to these repeated criticisms, Madison argued that while complete separation would be unworkable because each branch could accumulate power independent of the checks and balances of the others, "[federal judges] are to be rendered totally independent, both of the people and the legislature, both with respect to their offices and salaries." *The Federalist* 47 (Jan. 30, 1788), in *Debates*, supra note 219, Vol. II, p. 121. In other words, judges were not to be removed (or have their positions abolished) merely because of a change in the political winds. For more on this subject see "Brutus" XI, *New York Journal*, Jan. 31, 1788, in *Debates*, supra note 219, Vol. II, pp. 129–135, and *Federalist 48* (Feb. 1, 1788), Id. at 136–41.
284. For the argument that the 1802 Judiciary Act was unconstitutional see, e.g., Stephen B. Presser, *"Et Tu Raoul? Or The Original Misunderstand-*

ing Misunderstood," 1991 *Brigham Young University Law Review* 1484–1486. For Marshall's reluctance to press the point see Stephen B. Presser, *The Original Misunderstanding: The English, The Americans, and the Dialectic of Federalist Jurisprudence* (Durham: Carolina Academic Press, 1991), pp. 162–164.

285. See, e.g., the most democratic, and radical, of the state constitutions at the time of the Revolution, the *Pennsylvania Constitution of 1776*, Chap. II, § 6, reproduced in part in Presser and Zainaldin, *Law and Jurisprudence*, supra note 239, at 109:

> Every freeman of the full age of twenty-one years, having resided in this state for the space of one whole year next before the day of election for representatives, and paid public taxes [which were payable only on property] during that time, shall enjoy the right of an elector: Provided always, That sons of freeholders [of property] of the age of twenty-one years shall be entitled to vote, although they have not paid taxes.

286. James Wilson, *The Works of James Wilson* (Robert G. McCloskey editor, 1967), pp. 409–411. See also Gordon Wood, supra note 241, at 167–69, and notes. Wood notes that, while the notion of representation in government was a key element in the political thought that fueled the Revolution, the individual right to vote was not yet considered a necessary key to proper representation. It must be admitted that Wilson's views on the franchise were not always consistent. Thus, when, at the Philadelphia Constitutional Convention, Madison argued for restricting suffrage to freeholders in federal elections, Wilson is supposed to have stated: "It would be very hard and disagreeable for the same persons at the same time, to vote for representatives in the State Legislatures and to be excluded from a vote for those in the National Legislature." Quoted in Max Farrand editor, *The Records of the Federal Convention of 1787* (New Haven: Yale University Press, 1911) (Aug. 7), Vol. II, p. 201, cited in Charles Page Smith, *James Wilson*, pp. 249–50 (Chapel Hill: University of North Carolina Press, 1956). Smith describes Wilson as one who believed that "government draw[s] its authority as directly as possible from the people." Id., at 257. In order to reconcile this statement of Wilson's with those in his law lectures, perhaps it could be said that Wilson may have believed in suffrage for freeholders only, but recognized that it would be inconsistent to allow the states the freedom to base suffrage on other grounds, or even try universal suffrage, if the federal franchise was based solely on property ownership.

287. See William Blackstone, *Commentaries on the Laws of England* (Chicago: University of Chicago Press, 1979) (originally published 1769), Vol. I, p. 165. For a thorough analysis of the opposing notions of liberty and

property in eighteenth-century England, see H. Dickenson, *Liberty and Property: Political Ideology in Eighteenth-Century Britain* (London: Weidenfeld and Nicolson, 1977).

288. For the nearly complete report of the struggle over the federal common law of crimes see Chapter 6 in my *The Original Misunderstanding,* supra note 284. It should also be supplemented with the recently published John D. Gordan III, "United States v. Joseph Ravara: 'Presumptuous Evidence,' 'Too Many Lawyers,' and a Federal Common Law of Crime," in Maeva Marcus, editor, *Origins of the Federal Judiciary: Essays on the Judiciary Act of 1789* (New York: Oxford University Press, 1992), pp. 106–172.

289. An act to establish the Judicial Courts of the United States, I Statute 73, 78–9, § 11 (Sept. 24, 1789).

290. *United States v. Henfield,* 11 Fed. Cas. 1099 (C.C.D.Pa., 1793).

291. Wilson's charge, to the grand jury that eventually indicted Henfield, is reproduced with the report of that case. 11 Fed. Cas., at 1107.

292. On this case, *United States v. Ravara,* see John D. Gordan III, supra note 288.

293. *United States v. Robert Worrall,* 28 Fed. Cas. 774 (C.C.D.Pa. 1798).

294. Ibid. Richard Peters, sitting on *Worral,* agreed with the jurors, stating the federal government could apply the common law when it was necessary to preserve itself:

> Whenever an offense aims at the subversion of any Federal institu-tion, or at the corruption of its public officers, it is an offense against the well-being of the United States; from its very nature, it is cognizable under their authority; and, consequently, it is within the jurisdiction of this court, by virtue of the 11th section of the Judicial Act.

28 F. Cas. at 779–80. Samuel Chase, sitting with Peters, objected to this application of common law to American jurisprudence, and became the first Federalist judge to issue the "heresy," from the Federalist perspec-tive, that there was no federal common law of crimes. Chase argued in his opinion in *Worral* that, unlike the states, the United States did not import the whole of English common law. 28 F. Cas. at 779. He acknowledged that the individual states had imported parts of the common law, but reasoned further that, since each state had its own common law, there was no reliable, national body of common law on which the federal courts could rely. Id.

295. For the story of Justice Chase's apparent change of heart see *Original Misunderstanding,* supra note 284 at 95–96.

296. *United States v. Hudson & Goodwin,* 11 U.S. (7 Cranch) 32 (1812). For

the details of the case, albeit in an otherwise excellent law review note that may be a bit too sympathetic to the Jeffersonians, see Gary D. Rowe, "Note, The Sound of Silence: *United States v. Hudson & Goodwin*, The Jeffersonian Ascendency, and the Abolition of Federal Common Law Crimes," 101 *Yale Law Journal* 919 (1992).

297. *Original Misunderstanding*, supra note 284, at 82.

298. *Bishop v. Wood*, 426 U.S. 341, 350 (1976) (Brennan, J. dissenting).

299. *Wheeldin v. Wheeler*, 373 U.S. 647, 653 (1963) (Brennan, J. dissenting).

300. Id., at 663.

301. *Bishop v. Wood*, 426 U.S. 341, 349 n.14 (1976) (Stevens, J. writing for the Court).

302. For the story of the American experience with seditious libel in the early years see *Original Misunderstanding*, supra note 284, at 118–124, 131–140, and sources there cited, and see also, principally for the most important primary sources, Presser and Zainaldin, supra note 239, at 200- 223.

303. Act for the Punishment of Certain Crimes, July 14, 1798, 1 Stat. 596, §3, reproduced in Presser & Zainadin, supra note 239, at 200.

304. Jefferson ultimately underwrote the efforts of Thomas Cooper and James Callender, two accused under the Alien and Sedition Acts. See Merrill Peterson, *Adams and Jefferson: A Revolutionary Dialogue* (Athens: University of Georgia Press, 1976) pp. 78, 98, 100. Once Jefferson was elected, he commuted Callender's sentence and remitted his fine. Cooper, more bluntly, was said to be "a paid hireling of the vice-president [Jefferson]." Id. at 98. Jefferson's support of press attacks on Adams led Adams to break off their friendship for many years. At the time Adams concluded that Jefferson's "patronage of Callender and a host of Republican libellers was not only a blot on his moral character but proof he was a captive of party." Id. at 100.

305. For the account of these journalistic activities, and press opposition to the Federalist administrations generally see Donald H. Stewart, *The Opposition Press of the Federalist Period* (Albany, New York: State University of New York Press, 1969).

306. See, e.g., John C. Miller, *Crisis in Freedom: The Alien and Sedition Acts* (Boston: Little Brown, 1951), or J. Smith *Freedom's Fetters: The Alien and Sedition Laws and American Civil Liberties* (Ithaca: Cornell University Press, 1956).

307. On Callender see J. Miller, supra note 306, at 210–220.

308. Miller, supra note 306, at 216.

309. Quoted in the report of the case, *United States v. Callender*, 25 Fed. Cas. 239 (C.C.D.Va. 1800), and reprinted in Presser & Zainaldin, supra note 239, at 210.

310. Miller, supra note 306, at 216–217.

311. For a recent useful scholarly analysis of the trial see Kathryn Preyer, *"United States v. Callender: Judge and Jury in a Republican Society"* in Marcus, supra note 288, at 173.

312. *Original Misunderstanding*, supra note 284, at 133–134, and sources there cited. See also Preyer, supra note 311, at 177–178.

313. N. Rosenberg, *Protecting the Best Men: An Interpretive History of the Law of Libel* (Chapel Hill: University of North Carolina Press, 1986) 296 n.29, quoting John P. Kennedy, *Memoirs of the Life of William Wirt* (Philadelphia: Lea and Blanchard, 1850), Vol. 1, pp. 81–84.

314. Julius Goebel, Jr., *A History of the Supreme Court of the United States: Antecedents and Beginnings to 1801* (New York: Macmillan, 1971), Vol. I, pp. 637–638, 638 n.107.

315. On the Federalists simply intending to respond to acts of mendacity, see, e.g., William Winslow Crosskey *Politics and the Constitution* (Chicago: Univeristy of Chicago Press, 1953), Vol. II, p. 767, where it is stated that the 1798 Act was a "natural reaction" to an "extremely indecent campaign of public mendacity." To the same effect see Goebel, supra note 314, at 633. If the attempt was to silence the Republican press it failed rather dramatically. In 1789, when the act was passed, there "were less than a score of Republican newspapers out of a total of two hundred; by 1800 there were at least fifty newspapers supporting Jefferson." Miller, supra note 306, at 221–222.

316. See, e.g., the remarks of Justice Chase to the jury in *United States v. Thomas Cooper*, 25 Fed. Cas. 631 (1800), "A republican government can only be destroyed in two ways; the introduction of luxury, or the licentiousness of the press. The latter is the more slow, but most sure and certain, means of bringing about the destruction of the government." Reprinted in Presser and Zainaldin, supra note 239, at 203.

317. For the details on the Whiskey Rebellion see Thomas P. Slaughter, *The Whiskey Rebellion: Frontier Epilogue to the American Revolution* (New York: Oxford University Press, 1986), and Leland D. Baldwin, *Whiskey Rebels: The Story of a Frontier Uprising* (Pittsburgh: University of Pittsburgh Press, rev. ed. 1968). See also the collection of essays, Steven R. Boyd, editor, *The Whiskey Rebellion: Past and Present Perspectives* (Westport, Conn.: Greenwood Press, 1985).

318. For these points see generally *Original Misunderstanding*, supra note 284, at 15, 30–34, and 202 n.68, and sources there cited.

319. U.S. Constitution, Article III, Section 3 (1): "Treason against the United States shall consist only in levying War against them, or in adhering to their Enemies, giving them Aid and Comfort."

320. See, e.g., the argument of defense counsel in the trial of the Whiskey rebels reproduced in Presser & Zainaldin, supra note 239, at 154- 155, and the similar arguments of defense counsel in the trial of John Fries,

reproduced in Presser & Zainaldin, supra note 239, at 161–162, and, finally, the arguments of Congressman Randolph at the Senate trial for impeachment of Justice Chase, reproduced in Presser & Zainaldin, supra note 239, at 243–244.

321. United States Constitution, Article III, Section 3.

322. See generally, *United States v. Insurgents*, 26 F.Cas. 499 (C.C.D.Pa. 1795).

323. On this point see *Original Misunderstanding*, supra note 284, at 15, 30, 31–32.

324. United States v. Fries, 9 F. Cas. 895, 897 (C.C.D. Pa. 1799).

325. See his opinion in *United States v. Worrall*, 28 Fed. Cas. 774 (C.C.D.Pa. 1798), reproduced in Presser & Zainaldin, supra note 239, at 194.

326. *Original Misunderstanding*, supra note 284, at 102–103.

327. See, e.g., Iredell's comments on separation of powers in *Ware v. Hylton*, 3 U.S. (Dallas) 199, 266 (1796):

> [Legislative discretion] is a discretion no more controllable (as I conceive) by a Court of Justice, than a judicial determination is by them, neither department having any right to encroach on the exclusive province of the other, in order to rectify any error in principle, which it may suppose the other has committed. It is sufficient for each to take care that it commits no error of its own.

328. See infra, text accompanying notes 350 to 355, reviewing Justice Iredell's opinion in *Calder v. Bull*.

329. Letter from James to Hannah Iredell, May 11, 1799, excerpted in *McRee*, supra note 228, at 573–74 (Peter Smith, 1949).

330. For Chase's manipulation in the *Callender* trial see supra, text accompanying notes 307 to 313.

331. *Original Misunderstanding*, supra note 284, at 108–109.

332. For a narrative of these events see *Original Misunderstanding*, supra note 284, at 109–111.

333. *Original Misunderstanding*, supra note 284, at 110–112.

334. 9 Fed. Cas., at 942.

335. John Sanderson, *Biography of the Signers to the Declaration of Independence* (Philadelphia: R.W. Pomeroy, 1827), Vol 9, p. 230.

336. Quoted in Presser & Zainaldin, supra note 239, at 177.

337. Id.

338. *Original Misunderstanding*, supra note 284, at 110.

339. U.S. Constitution, Amendment I ("Congress shall make no law respecting an establishment of religion, or prohibiting the free exercise thereof....").

340. *Calder v. Bull*, 3 U.S. 386, 1 L.Ed. 648, 3 Dallas 386 (1798).

341. For a rare listing of some state court decisions which take a perspective very similar to that expressed by Chase in *Calder v. Bull*, see Suzannah Sherry, "Natural Law in the States," 61 *University of Cinncinnati Law Review* 171 (1992).

342. 3 U.S., at 389.

343. 3 U.S., at 387–389 (emphasis supplied).

344. This seems to be the perspective adopted as well in Sherry, supra note 341. Professor Sherry's piece is an attempt to suggest the error of those, like the critics of Thomas, who claimed that natural law played no part in the jurisprudence of written constitutions.

345. This was the perspective taken, for example, in Robert H. Bork's recent *The Tempting of America: The Political Seduction of the Law* 31–32 (New York: Free Press, 1990), pp. 31–32.

346. The suggestion to the contrary in Bork, supra note 345, at 19–20, referring to Chase's opinion in *Calder*, which Bork calls "an extraordinary opinion," betrays a lack of familiarity with the dominant characteristics of jurisprudence in the late eighteenth century. See generally Sherry, supra note 341.

347. This is the meaning of Chase's language that "I will not go further than I feel myself bound to do; and if I ever exercise the jurisdiction I will not decide any law to be void, but in a very clear case." 3 U.S., at 395. See, to precisely the same effect, the language of Spencer Roane in *Currie's Administrators v. The Mutual Assurance Society*, 4 Hen. & M. (14 Va.) 315 (1809): "For my part, I will not outrage the character of any civilized people, by supposing them to have met in legislature, upon any other ground, than that of morality and justice. In this country, in particular, I will never forget, 'that no free government, or the blessing of liberty, can be preserved to any people, but by a firm adherence to justice, moderation, temperance, frugality and virtue, and by frequent recurrence to fundamental principles.' [cite to Virginia Bill of Rights, art. 15, omitted] *I must add, however, that when any legislative act is to be questioned, on the ground of conflicting with the superior acts of the people, or of invading the vested rights of individuals, the case ought to be palpable and clear:* in an equivocal or equiponderant case, it ought not easily to be admitted, that the immediate representatives of the people, representing as well the justice as the wisdom of the nation, have forgotten the great injunctions under which they are called to act. In such case, it ought rather to be believed, that the judging power is mistaken." (emphasis supplied)

348. This inference can be drawn from *Calder v. Bull* itself, where Chase determines the meaning of the term "ex post facto laws" by reference to Blackstone, Wooddeson (Blackstone's successor as Vinerian professor at Oxford), "the author of the Federalist," and the declarations of the Constitutional Conventions of Delaware, Massachusetts, Maryland, and

North Carolina, and Lord Raymond's reports, 3 U.S., at 391–392, and where he explains the purposes of the ex post facto clause by referring to four abuses committed by Parliament in the eighteenth century. 3 U.S., at 389.

349. In *Dr. Bonham's Case* (1610). For a discussion of the importance of this case—in which Coke refused to enforce an act of Parliament which made the Royal College of Physicians judge and party in the case of determining license fees which physicians were required to pay—to the American theory of judicial review see Bernard Bailyn, *Pamphlets of the American Revolution* (Cambridge: Harvard University Press, 1965), Vol. I, pp. 411–13. Bailyn's comments are reprinted in Presser & Zainaldin, supra note 239, at 67–69.

350. 3 U.S., at 398–399 (emphasis supplied).

351. On this point see generally Gordon Wood, supra note 241, and especially pages 259–305.

352. Wood, supra note 241, at 537–538.

353. On this point see in addition to the comments just quoted from Wood's book, supra note 241, Sherry, supra note 341.

354. I take this to be the meaning of Julius Goebel's comment that Iredell "usually had his own characteristic approach." Goebel, supra note 314, at 783. Indeed, it appears that in 1788 Iredell acknowledged the validity, even under the Constitution, of unexpressed constraints on governmental power as found in the common law, when he appeared to assume in a pamphlet that "the common law would remain as a sort of 'unwritten' substratum of the federal system. There is no question but that he acted upon this premise when he first became a Justice." Id., at 297.

355. I reach this conclusion based on the facts that Iredell, sitting on circuit with Richard Peters, was reluctant to impose a sanction on John Fries, who was convicted of treason as a result of his participation in the Northampton rebellion of 1799. It is also significant that Iredell's views on the scope of jury discretion were far broader than those of at least one of his colleagues on the court, William Paterson. At the Fries trial Iredell told the jury "[I]t is not for the court to say whether there was treasonable intention or act as charged in the indictment; that is for the jury to determine; we have only to state the law, we therefore should have no right to give our opinion on it." Quoted in *Original Misunderstanding*, supra note 284, at 107. This was in complete contrast to William Paterson's charge to the *Whiskey Rebels'* jury five years before. Ibid.

356. For Epstein's theories see Chapter One, supra, text accompanying note 206, discussing Richard Epstein, *Takings: Private Property and the Power of Eminent Domain* (Cambridge: Harvard University Press, 1985), and for an accessible introduction to Epstein's thought for business persons see Andrew Leigh, "Leaders & Success," *Investor's Business Daily*, p. 1,

Notes

October 11, 1991. For Macedo's writings see, e.g., Stephen Macedo, *Liberal Virtues: Citizenship, Virtue, and Community in Liberal Constitutionalism* (New York: Oxford University Press, 1990), and Stephen Macedo, "Morality and the Constitution: Toward a Synthesis for 'Earthbound' Interpreters," 61 *University of Cinncinnati Law Review* 29 (1992). For Senator Joseph Biden's comments on the importance of his questions regarding the influence of Macedo and Epstein on Clarence Thomas, and for Epstein's and Macedo's communications with Biden, see *Hearing of the Senate Judicial Committee, Morning Session,* September 16, 1991, Federal News Service, LEXIS.

357. *Griswold v. Connecticut,* 381 U.S. 479 (1965).

358. *Eisenstadt v. Baird,* 405 U.S. 438 (1972).

359. *Roe v. Wade,* 410 U.S. 113 (1973).

360. For similar proof that such principles were a foundation for state jurisprudence see Sherry, supra note 341.

361. For their arguments, see Presser & Zainaldin, supra note 239, at 231–246.

362. See, e.g., the remarks of Samuel Chase and John Randolph at the beginning of the Chase impeachment trial, text accompanying note 361, supra.

363. *Fletcher v. Peck,* 6 U.S. (6 Cranch) 87 (1810).

364. For the suggestion that Marshall certainly did go beyond the text, and that this is evidence of an "unwritten Constitution," see Tom Grey, "Do We Have an Unwriten Constitution?" 27 *Stanford Law Review* 703, 708 (1975).

365. See Hadley Arkes, *Beyond the Constitution* (Princeton: Princeton University Press, 1990), pp. 26–29.

366. *Van Horne's Lessee v. Dorrance,* 28 F.Cas. 1012, 2 Dal. 304 (C.C.D.Pa., 1795).

367. Id., at 1015.

368. Id., at 1016. Rejecting the Pennsylvania statute at hand, which transferred property from one group of citizens to another, and sought to grant compensation in other real estate, Paterson declared, in language that is too rich not at least to merit quoting in a footnote:

> If this be the legislation of a republican government, in which the preservation of property is made sacred by the Constitution, I ask, wherein it differs from the mandate of an Asiatic prince? Omnipotence in legislation is despotism. According to this doctrine, we have nothing that we can call our own, or are sure of for a moment we are all tenants at will, and hold our landed property at the mere pleasure of the legislature. Wretched situation, precarious tenure! And yet we boast of property and its security, of laws, of courts, of Constitutions, and call ourselves free!

Id., at 1018.
369. *Scott v. Sandford*, 19 How. (60 U.S.) 393 (1857).
370. These territories were later to become many of the Western and Midwestern states, including Oklahoma, Kansas, and Wisconsin.
371. See, e.g., J. Skelly Wright, "Professor Bickel, the Scholarly Tradition, and the Supreme Court," 84 *Harvard Law Review* 769, 797 (1971). (Wright excoriates Bickel for Bickel's argument that history can legitimize judicial decisions: "Should a different outcome on the Civil War battlefields really make us approve *Dred Scott?* If Taney's Court had made apartheid its overriding principle, and apartheid had actually come to pass in America, would the judicial result be any more defensible?") See also Robert Bork, *The Tempting of America: The Political Seduction of the Law* (New York: Free Press, 1990), p. 28. (In *Dred Scott*, "the politics and morality of the Judges combined to produce the worst Constitutional decision of the nineteenth century.")
372. See Bork, supra note 371, at 31 ("Though [Taney's] transformation of the due process clause from a procedural to a substantive requirement was a sham, it was a momentous sham, for this was the first appearance in American constitutional law of the concept of 'substantive due process,' and that concept has been used countless times since by judges who want to write their personal beliefs into a document that, most inconveniently, does not contain those beliefs").
373. 381 U.S. 479 (1965).
374. 410 U.S. 113 (1973).
375. Bruce Ackerman, *We the People: Foundations* (Cambridge: Harvard University Press, 1991). The book is alarming for its insistence that the Constitution can be altered by means other than the amendment process, and for its advocacy of a series of constitutional amendments that would legitimate the radical program of the American Left and make it unamendable in the future. See, e.g., Stephen Presser, "Locking in Liberalism," Tribune Books, *Chicago Tribune*, October 6, 1991, Section 14, page 5.
376. *Scott v. Sandford*, 60 U.S. (19 How.) 393, 407 (1957).
377. Id.
378. Id. at 450.
379. Id. at 451.
380. On this point see generally, Robert Cover, *Justice Accused: Antislavery and the Judicial Process* (New Haven: Yale University Press, 1975), pp. 67–75.
381. *Commonwealth v. Aves*, 35 Mass. (18 Pick.) 193 (1836).
382. Quoted in Stephen B. Presser & Jamil S. Zainaldin, *Law and Jurisprudence in American History* (St. Paul: West Publishing Co., 2nd ed., 1989), pp. 401–402.

383. 60 U.S., at 591 (opinion of Mr. Justice Curtis, dissenting).
384. Id., at 595.
385. Id., at 624.
386. Id., at 623–633.
387. Id., at 535, dissenting opinion of Mr. Justice McLean, quoting from Lord Mansfield's opinion in *Somersett's Case*, Lafft's Rep. 1; 20 Howell's State Trials 79.
388. See, e.g., "Mr. Douglas' Speech, First Lincoln-Douglas Debate, Ottawa, Illinois," reprinted in *Abraham Lincoln: Speeches and Writings 1832–1858* (New York: Library of America, 1989), pp. 495–497.
389. Walter Ehrlich, "Roger Brooke Taney," in Kermit Hall, editor, *The Oxford Companion to the Supreme Court of the United States* (New York: Oxford University Press, 1992) (hereinafter cited as "Oxford Companion"), pp. 857, 859. A relatively recent balanced treatment of Taney's life is Walker Lewis, *Without Fear or Favor: A Biography of Chief Justice Roger Brooke Taney* (Boston: Houghton, Mifflin, 1965).
390. See, e.g., Bork, supra note 371.
391. See generally Cover, supra note 380.
392. "Senate Judiciary Committee Hearings on the Confirmation of Ruth Bader Ginsburg as Associate Justice of the United States Supreme Court," July 22, 1993, as reported by the Federal News Service, on LEXIS.
393. Ibid.
394. Id.
395. Thus Hatch's apology to her ". . . if the Senator has misconstrued what I'm saying—and I think you have—I apologize, but that isn't what I'm saying."
396. Richard Grenier, "Profiles in timidity . . . and absurdity," *Washington Times*, July 28, 1993, page G1, commenting on editorial treatment of Moseley-Braun by the *New York Times*, and the *Washington Post*.
397. "Ms. Moseley-Braun's Majestic Moment," *New York Times*, June 24, 1993, Section 1, Page 18, column 1.
398. "Moseley-Braun has a .500 day," *Chicago Tribune*, July 27, 1993, p. 12.
399. Suzanne Fields, "Whitewashing Racism," *Washington Times*, July 29, 1993, p. G1.
400. Press commentary was not uniformly critical of Moseley-Braun for her attempt to silence Hatch. The *San Francisco Chronicle*, for example, in an editorial, appeared to laud Moseley-Braun's behavior in both the Hatch and Confederate flag episodes, and praised "This eloquent daughter of slavery [who] gave the Senate a sensitivity lesson." Indeed the *Chronicle* appeared to condemn Hatch for having the temerity even to cite "the notorious 1857 *Dred Scott* decision." "Moseley-Braun speaks out," *San Francisco Chronicle*, July 26, 1993, p. A12.

401. Stephen Chapman, "Abortion, Slavery Analogy: It's Entirely Too Accurate," *Orlando Sentinel*, July 30, 1993, p. A13.

402. Id. For a recent treatment of the notion, inherent in this part of the text, that our politics demands free expression of political ideas, see Cass R. Sunstein, *Democracy and the Problem of Free Speech* (New York: Free Press, 1993).

403. *Lochner v. New York*, 198 U.S. 45 (1905).

404. *Allgeyer v. Louisiana*, 165 U.S. 578 (1897) (9–0 decision, opinion written by Rufus Peckham, ruling that the due process clause of the Fourteenth Amendment guarantees the right to enter into lawful contracts).

405. United States Constitution, Article I, §10, provides in pertinent part that "No State shall . . . pass any . . . Law impairing the Obligation of Contracts. . . ."

406. United States Constitution, Amendment XIV, provides in pertinent part that "No State shall . . . deprive any person of life, liberty, or property, without due process of law. . . ."

407. United States Constitution, Amendment V, provides in pertinent part that "No person shall be . . . deprived [by the federal government] of life, liberty, or property, without due process of law; nor shall private property be taken for public use, without just compensation."

408. *Holden v. Hardy*, 169 U.S. 366 (1898).

409. There are many biographical volumes on Holmes, who is usually regarded as the greatest of the Supreme Court Justices, save John Marshall. Two recent excellent works by legal scholars on the man often believed to be the only "authentic sage" ever to sit on the Supreme Court are Richard A. Posner, editor, *The Essential Holmes* (Chicago: University of Chicago Press, 1992), and G. Edward White, *Justice Oliver Wendell Holmes and the Inner Self* (New York: Oxford University Press, 1993). Two other recent biographies have also been well received: Liva Baker, *The Justice from Beacon Hill: The Life and Times of Oliver Wendell Holmes* (New York: Harper Collins, 1991), and Sheldon M. Novick, *Honorable Justice: The Life of Oliver Wendell Holmes* (Boston: Little Brown, 1989).

410. *Lochner*, 198 U.S. at 75.

411. Bork, supra note 371, at 49.

412. Cf. United States Constitution, Article I, §10 (the contracts clause), and Amendment V (the "just compensation" clause of the Fifth Amendment). See supra notes 405–406 for the two relevant texts.

413. See Chapter Two, supra, text accompanying Notes 341–360. On the importance of property rights and natural law theory to the framers of the Constitution see also James W. Ely, Jr., *The Guardian of Every Other Right* (New York: Oxford University Press, 1992).

414. Chapter Two, supra, text accompanying Notes 366–368.

415. Eugene W. Hickock and Gary L. McDowell, *Justice vs. Law: Courts and Politics in American Society* (New York: Free Press, 1993.

416. Id., at 106.

417. Id., at 96.

418. Id., at 106–107.

419. *Schechter Poultry Corp. v. United States*, 295 U.S. 495 (1935).

420. Ibid.

421. In particular *United States v. E.C. Knight Co.*, 156 U.S. 1 (1895), which had held that the Sherman Antitrust Act of 1890 could not be used to regulate manufacturing, but that Congress's regulatory power was limited to *interstate commerce*.

422. *Morehead v. New York ex rel. Tipaldo*, 298 U.S. 587, 618 (1936).

423. *Muller v. Oregon* 208 U.S. 412 (1908).

424. *Adkins v. Children's Hospital*, 261 U.S. 525 (1923).

425. See generally William E. Leuchtenburg, "The Origins of Franklin D. Roosevelt's 'Court-Packing' Plan," 1966 *Supreme Court Review* 347, 356–357.

426. Quoted in Gerald Gunther, *Constitutional Law: Cases and Materials* (Mineola: Foundation Press, 1975), 9th edition, pp. 169–170.

427. See generally Leuchtenburg, supra note 425.

428. Drew Pearson and Robert Allen, *The Nine Old Men* (Garden City, New York: Doubleday, Doran & Co., 1936).

429. "No matter whether th' Constitution follows th' flag or not, th' supreme coort follows th' iliction returns." Finley Peter Dunne, "The Supreme Court's Decisions," in *Dissertations by Mr. Dooley* (New York: Harper, 1906), pp. 21, 26 (1911), quoted in Fred R. Shapiro, editor, *The Oxford Dictionary of American Legal Quotations* (Oxford: Oxford University Press, 1993), p. 392.

430. *West Coast Hotel v. Parrish*, 300 U.S. 379 (1937).

431. *NLRB v. Jones & Laughlin Steel Corp.*, 301 U.S. 1 (1937).

432. See generally Karl Klare, "Judicial Deradicalization of the Wagner Act and the Origins of Modern Legal Consciousness, 1937–1941," 62 *Minnesota Law Review* 265 (1978).

433. For the texts of these worries articulated by the Antifederalists, see Bernard Bailyn, editor, *The Debate on the Constitution* (Library of America, Vol. I & II, 1993), and for the connections among the Antifederalist fears of denial of trial by jury, the 1789 Judiciary Act, and the Bill of Rights see, e.g., Maeva Marcus and Natalie Wexler, "The Judiciary Act of 1789: Political Compromise or Constitutional Interpretation?" in Maeva Marcus, editor, *Origins of the Federal Judiciary: Essays on the Judiciary Act of 1789* (Oxford: Oxford University Press, 1992), pp. 13–39.

434. On this movement see generally Stephen B. Presser & Jamil S. Zainaldin, supra note 382, at 763–791 and sources there cited. See also the recently

published set of readings edited by William W. Fisher III, Morton J. Horwitz, and Thomas A. Reid, *American Legal Realism* (New York: Oxford University Press, 1993).

435. Melvin I. Urofsky, "The Depression and the Rise of Legal Liberalism," a subheading of the entry for "History of the Court," *Oxford Companion*, supra note 389, p. 394.

436. David B. Rivkin, Jr., "Health Care Reform vs. The Founders," *Wall Street Journal*, September 29, 1993, Section A, page 19.

437. *West Virginia State Board of Education v. Barnette*, 319 U.S. 624 (1943).

438. *Minersville School District v. Gobitis*, 310 U.S. 586 (1940), Mr. Justice Frankfurter writing for the majority.

439. On this last see, e.g., the comments of Justice Chase to John Fries, supra, Chapter Two, text accompanying notes 336–339.

440. See, e.g., Justice Scalia's dissent to Justice Kennedy's opinion in *Lee v. Weisman*, 112 S.Ct. 2649, 2678–86 (1992).

441. Peter Charles Hoffer, "Felix Frankfurter," in *Oxford Companion*, supra note 389, pp. 314, 316.

442. *West Virginia St. Bd. of Educ. v. Barnette*, 319 U.S. 624, 646 (1943) (Frankfurter, J., dissenting).

443. 319 U.S., at 649, quoting from *Missouri, K. & T. Ry. Co. v. May*, 194 U.S. 267, 270.

444. See generally his seminal article, James Bradley Thayer, "The Origin and Scope of the American Doctrine of Constitutional Law," 7 *Harvard Law Review* 129 (1893). On Thayer's landmark essay see the symposium celebrating its centenary in Volume 88, Number 1 of the *Northwestern University Law Review*, Fall 1993.

445. 319 U.S., at 649, citing "Art. III, New York Constitution of 1777."

446. See the letter from James Madison to Thomas Jefferson, October 24, 1787, in Bailyn, supra note 433, at 192, 198–200, in which Madison elaborates his reasons for wanting to give the United States Supreme Court a power to veto state legislation.

447. *Barnette*, 319 U.S., at 650.

448. Id.

449. *Barnette*, 319 U.S., at 651.

450. Id.

451. Id., at 652.

452. See Chapter One, supra. There appear to be some First Amendment areas in which Frankfurter did favor a balancing test, notably those in which the government sought to regulate harmful speech, but because of Frankfurter's stand in *Barnette* I disagree with the recent assertion by Cass Sunstein that Frankfurter "waged a crusade for balancing and against absolutism under the First Amendment and indeed in every area of constitu-

tional law." Cass R. Sunstein, *Democracy and the Problem of Free Speech* (New York: Free Press, 1994), p. 7.

453. *Barnette,* 319 U.S., at 653.

454. Id.

455. Id., at 654.

456. Gerard V. Bradley, "Beguiled: Free Exercise Exemptions and the Siren Song of Liberalism," 20 *Hofstra Law Review* 245, 308 (1991).

457. See Bradley, supra note 456, at 308–309.

458. *Employment Division v. Smith,* 110 S.Ct. 1595 (1990).

459. Bradley, supra note 456, at 315.

460. 110 S. Ct. 1595, 1597 (1990).

461. As expressed by Frankfurter himself in his majority opinion in *Minersville School District Bd. of Educ. v. Gobitis* 310 U.S. 586, 594–595 (1940), the case that was reversed by *Barnette.* For Scalia's use of Frankfurter see *Smith,* 494 U.S. 872, at 879.

462. 110 S.Ct., at 1600, as quoted in Bradley, supra note 456, at 246.

463. The quoted language is from Bradley, supra note 456, at 247, but it captures the essence of the new act. Clinton signed the bill on November 16, 1993. See, e.g., for the events leading up to the bill's signing, David E. Anderson, "Signing of Religious Freedom Act Culminates Three-Year Push," *Washington Post,* November 20, 1993, page C6.

464. O'Connor herself advocated the application of the same standard in *Smith.* 110 S.Ct., at 1608 (O'Connor, J., concurring).

465. On the meaning of the First Amendment in this regard, see Chapter Four, infra, text accompanying notes 705–742. On the impolity of the substance of the Religious Freedom Restoration Act, and its lack of accordance with the original understanding of the First Amendment, see generally Bradley, supra, note 456.

466. *Barnette,* 319 U.S. at 653.

467. Id.

468. Id., at 653–654.

469. Id., at 654.

470. Id., at 654.

471. Id.

472. Id.

473. Id., at 655.

474. This explains Frankfurter's dissent in *Everson v. Board of Education of Ewing Township* 330 U.S. 1 (1947), in which the majority held that New Jersey could reimburse parents of Catholic school children for the costs of bus transportation to and from the school, so long as the same bus transportation was available to public school students.

475. *Barnette,* 319 U.S., at 655.

476. Id., at 659.

477. Ibid.
478. Id., at 660.
479. Id., at 661.
480. Id., at 665.
481. Id., at 667.
482. Ibid.
483. See generally Chapter Two, supra.
484. See Chapter Four, infra, text accompanying Notes 710–724.
485. *Abington School District v. Schempp,* 374 U.S. 203 (1963).
486. *Engel v. Vitale,* 370 U.S. 421 (1962).
487. See Gordon S. Wood, *The Creation of the American Republic 1776–1787* (Chapel Hill: University of North Carolina Press, 1969), pp. 34, 65–70.
488. Michael Kent Curtis, "Incorporation Doctrine," *The Oxford Companion,* supra note 389, 426. For the case that makes clearest that it is "selective" incorporation that is involved see *Palko v. Connecticut,* 302 U.S. 319 (1937). This has been an area of white-hot controversy among the scholars, many of whom have strived to defend the "selective incorporation" view as a legitimate exercise of the Supreme Court's powers. See generally Richard L. Aynes, "On Misreading John Bingham and the Fourteenth Amendment," 103 *Yale Law Journal* 57 (1993). The classic, and generally accepted, position that the Fourteenth Amendment *did not* incorporate the entire bill of rights (through the Fourteenth Amendment's privileges and immunities clause) was Charles Fairman, "Does the Fourteenth Amendment Incorporate the Bill of Rights?" 2 *Stanford Law Review* 5 (1949). Fairman did take the position, however, that the due process clause of the Fourteenth Amendment could be used to "enforce against the states only those rights 'implicit in the concept of ordered liberty.' " Aynes, supra, at 58. This meant, however, that Fairman could be taken as supporting the idea of "selective incorporation." This view too is dubious. See, for the most widely cited rejection of *both selective and total incorporation,* Raoul Berger, *Government by Judiciary* (Cambridge: Harvard University Press, 1978). Berger's reading of the historical data convinced him that the framers of the Fourteenth Amendment "did not intend that any of the first eight amendments should be made applicable to the states through the Fourteenth Amendment." Aynes, supra, at 60, citing Berger, supra, at 115–119.
489. See generally, Raoul Berger, *Government by Judiciary,* supra note 488. There may have been some indications to the contrary, however. According to one recent commentary: "Several of the amendment's framers suggested that privileges or immunities of citizens of the United States included rights in the Bill of Rights [and thus could have been triggered by the clause in the Fourteenth Amendment prohibiting any states from interfering with the privileges and immunities of citizens of the United

States]. In 1866, no senator or representative explicitly contradicted them on this point and a number suggested the [Fourteenth] Amendment protected the constitutional rights of American citizens. Yet most congressmen did not address the point and others made remarks that some have read as inconsistent with application of the Bill of Rights to the states." Curtis, supra note 488, at 426. For a further development of this point, attempting to hang the validity of selective incorporation on the words of Congressman John Bingham, the principal author of Section One of the Fourteenth Amendment, see Aynes, supra note 488, at note 57. In any event, whatever may have been in the minds of some of the framers of the Fourteenth Amendment, according to the principles of original understanding espoused here, it is impossible to sustain the claim that the Fourteenth Amendment gives carte blanche to the United States Supreme Court for selective incorporation of provisions in the Bill of Rights in a manner that fundamentally alters the relationship between the state and federal governments.

490. For these "Antifederalist" arguments in favor of Bill of Rights see generally Bernard Bailyn, supra note 433.

491. See *Gitlow v. New York*, 268 U.S. 652 (1925), where the doctrine was assumed to be correct, and see *Stromberg v. California*, 283 U.S. 359 (1931), the first case in which the Supreme Court actually forbade a state from proceeding against an individual on the grounds that the Fourteenth Amendment's due process clause incorporated the First Amendment by its use of the term "liberty."

492. *Cantwell v. Connecticut*, 310 U.S. 296 (1940).

493. For an excellent collection of the key Supreme Court cases dealing with religion, and incisive commentary on them see Terry Eastland, editor, *Religious Liberty in the Supreme Court: The Cases that Define the Debate over Church and State* (Washington, D.C.: Ethics and Public Policy Center, 1993).

494. *Everson v. Board of Education of Ewing Township*, 330 U.S. 1 (1947).

495. 370 U.S. 421 (1962).

496. Jefferson, *Writings* (New York: Library of America edition, 1984), p. 510.

497. As summarized in Leo Pfeiffer, "Everson v. Board of Education of Ewing Township," in *Oxford Companion* supra note 389, pp. 261, 262. The cite to Madison's document is James Madison, "Memorial and Remonstrance Against Religious Assessments," 1785, in Robert A. Rutland & William M.E. Rachal editors, *Papers of James Madison* (Charlottesville: University Press of Virginia), Vol. 8, p. 295.

498. Thomas Jefferson to Thomas Richie, December 25, 1820, reprinted in *Writings*, supra note 496, at 1446.

499. *Wallace v. Jaffree*, 472 U.S. 38, 91–114 (1985).

Notes

500. See generally Chapter Four, infra, text accompanying Notes 705-745. For an earlier lonely voice in dissent see Justice Stewart in both *Engel v. Vitale*, 370 U.S. 421, 440–50 (1962), and *Abington School District v. Schempp*, 374 U.S. 203, 308–320 (1963). In two dissents in those cases Justice Stewart argued the case for the Establishment Clause's simply prohibiting a particular sect, and giving no warrant for general judicial attacks on all religion.
501. *Abington School District v. Schempp*, 374 U.S. 203 (1963).
502. *Wallace v. Jaffree*, 472 U.S. 38 (1985).
503. See discussion of *Lee v. Weisman*, in Chapter One, supra.
504. Joseph F. Kobylka, "Abington School District v. Schempp," *Oxford Companion*, supra note 389, p. 1.
505. Cf. William Rehnquist's dissent in *Wallace v. Jaffree*, supra, 472 U.S. 38, 106.
506. On the efforts of the twentieth-century American community to pursue the separation of church and state, and particularly to eliminate prayer in the schools, see Naomi W. Cohen, *Jews in Christian America: The Pursuit of Religious Equality* (New York: Oxford University Press, 1992). A recent review of Cohen's book observed that "A society willing to recognize Judaism's equal worth might have been sufficient and spared them much pain. But something within their own development, perhaps their growing secularization, compelled them to make separationism the heart of a strategy to win religious equality." Henry L. Feingold, "Book Review," 98 *American Historical Review* 1672 (1993).
507. For scholarly treatment of these issues see particularly Suzanne Last Stone, "In Pursuit of the Counter-Text: The Turn to the Jewish Legal Model in Contemporary American Legal Theory," 106 *Harvard Law Review* 813 (1993). While there is a current movement on the part of some American Jewish legal scholars to reenvision the Jewish-American legal tradition as a religiously based, communitarian jurisprudence (the late Robert Cover of Yale was a prominent example), it appears that the predominant theme of American Jewish constitutional scholars well into the middle of the twentieth century was one of assimilation, even glorification, of the individualistic American liberal tradition: "In the classical era of liberal legal scholarship, [Jewish-American legal scholarship] either looked for the Jewish roots of American law or presented Jewish law as an exemplar of then-prevailing Western liberal legal themes." Id., at 815. Professor Stone in particular notes the recent work of Jerold Auerbach, see, e.g., *Rabbis and Lawyers: The Journey from Torah to Constitution* (Bloomington: Indiana University Press, 1990), which argues that "American Jewish acculturation largely involved the transfer of allegiance from a sacred to a secular legal system, from the Torah to the Constitution." Id. Even Louis Brandeis, the great Supreme Court Justice, and

father of the sociologically influenced "Brandeis brief," claimed that the "twentieth-century ideals of America had been the age-old ideals of the Jews." Id., at 816, citing Allon Gal, Brandeis of Boston (1980), p. 126 (quoting Brandeis).

508. Indeed, it appears that in at least one instance the ACLU has made efforts to seek out non-Jewish families as plaintiffs. Joseph Kobylka, "Abington School District v. Schempp," *Oxford Companion*, supra note 389, p. 1.

509. Jacob Neusner, "Who's Afraid of the Religious Right," *National Review*, December 27, 1993, at 37 (quoting Prager).

510. The notion may be beginning to reach even the Yale Law School. See generally Stephen Carter, *The Culture of Disbelief: How American Law and Politics Trivialize Religious Devotion* (New York: Basic Books, 1993), for the realization that the chattering classes wrongly fail to recognize the importance of religious belief. Alas, Carter fails to translate this perception into a sensible program linking morality to religion, and while he wants the courts more liberally to recognize the demands of particular sects he has little to say about how the Court might reverse its jurisprudence condemning religion in the public square.

511. This is the theme of the persuasive Myron Magnet, *The Dream and the Nightmare: The Sixties Legacy to the Underclass* (New York: William Morrow and Co., 1993).

512. A relic perhaps of Jewish jurisprudence's Talmudic or Old Testament faith in the individual's ability to wrestle with the Lord by getting God to implement his own principles of law, to keep his covenant with the Jewish people, so long as they keep theirs. Thus in orthodox Judaism there is a stoic and unquestioning adherence to a plethora of laws of social conduct. This stoic and unquestioning adherence to what is believed as absolute law is reflected in the ACLU's unquestioning application of its doctrines of individual freedoms even in areas where corresponding social duties (not intentionally to inflict mental distress on others) might be present. Thus the ACLU stuck to its principles and defended the purported right of American Nazis to march in Skokie, a suburb of Chicago which contained many survivors of the holocaust, even though it might have been argued that whatever rights to publish or proclaim their views the Nazis possessed ought to have been exercised in a manner that did not flagrantly seek to inflict mental distress on particular members of the Skokie community. On the perils of absolutism in other aspects of First Amendment theory see generally Cass. R. Sunstein, *Democracy and the Problem of Free Speech* (New York: Oxford University Press, 1993).

513. The village of Skokie, Illinois, which contains a strong and vocal Jewish community, successfully secured an injunction against a Nazi march down its main street, arguing that the march improperly fostered hatred of Jews. The ACLU supported the Nazis' right to march, claiming that

the granting of an injunction to stop them violated their First Amendment free-speech rights. The ACLU similarly attacked a Skokie ordinance which required groups to post a $350,000 insurance bond before marching. The United States Supreme Court, in a *per curiam* action, declared the injunction unconstitutional. *Village of Skokie v. Nat'l Socialist Party of America*, 432 U.S. 43 (1977) (per curiam) (reversing the denial of a stay of the injunction against the Nazis, and remanding to the Illinois state courts for further proceedings), *on remand*, 51 Ill. App.3d 279, 366 N.E.2d 347 (1977) (modifying the injunction), *vacated* 29 Ill. 2d 605, 373 N.E.2d 21 (1978). A related line of cases resulted in the declaration that the insurance bond requirement was also unconstitutional. *Collin v. Smith*, 447 F.Supp. 676 (N.D.Ill.) *aff'd* 578 F.2d 1197, 1210 (7th Cir. 1978). See generally, on the Nazis and Skokie, Donald A. Downs, *Nazis in Skokie* (South Bend: University of Notre Dame Press, 1985) (criticizing the use of the First Amendment to allow the Nazis to march). See also the review of Downs's book by Edward L. Rubin, then acting professor of law at the University of California, Berkeley, "Nazis, Skokie, and the First Amendment," 74 *California Law Review* 233 (1986).

514. *Lee v. Weisman*, discussed in Chapter One, supra.

515. Full disclosure probably requires me to confess that I am now much more comfortable with most Christian doctrines, and while in my second marriage I still insisted on stomping on a glass at our wedding, we were married by an Episcopalian minister. My spiritual nourishment is now mostly provided from C.S. Lewis and from Roman Catholicism. Like the figure in the Jewish joke, I am sometimes tempted to address Christians as "fellow *goyim*." I hope, in a spirit of Judeo-Christain charity, I can be spared the wrath traditionally directed against the apostate.

516. Feingold, "Book Review," supra note 506.

517. *Reynolds v. Sims*, 377 U.S. 533 (1964).

518. *Baker v. Carr*, 369 U.S. 186 (1962).

519. Jack W. Peltason, "Baker v. Carr," *Oxford Companion*, supra note 389, pp. 56, 57.

520. Jack W. Peltason "Reapportionment Cases," in Id., at 710.

521. 377 U.S., at 562.

522. See supra, text accompanying note 489.

523. Section 2 of the Fourteenth Amendment provides: "Representatives shall be apportioned among the several States according to their respective numbers, counting the whole number of persons in each State, excluding Indians not taxed. But when the right to vote at any election for the choice of electors for President and Vice President of the United States, Representatives in Congress, the Executive and Judicial officers of a State, *or the members of the Legislature thereof*, is denied to any of the male inhabitants of such State, being twenty-one years of age, and citizens of

Notes

the United States, or in any way abridged, except for participation in rebellion, or other crime, the basis of representation therein shall be reduced in the proportion which the number of such male citizens shall bear to the whole number of male citizens twenty-one years of age in such State." (Emphasis supplied)

524. *Black's Law Dictionary* (St. Paul: West Publishing Co., 6th ed., 1990), p. 581.

525. See, e.g., the exchange of published letters in support or rebuttal of James Wilson's speech in favor of the proposed Constitution delivered at a public meeting in Philadelphia, October 6, 1787 (Bailyn, supra note 433, Vol. I, pp. 63–69). "An Officer of the Late Continental Army" (possibly the Western Pennsylvania politician William Findlay) took a representative Antifederalist stand when he argued that under the proposed Constitution, "The *sovereignty* of the different states is *ipso facto* destroyed in its most essential parts." Id. at 97, 98.

526. A representative debate regarding the need for a Bill of Rights and the threats posed to the states from the proposed federal judiciary took place on the floor of the North Carolina Constitutional Convention, between the Antifederalist Samuel Spencer and the Federalist William R. Davie, on July 29, 1788. Id., at 888–96.

527. Gordon E. Baker, "Reynolds v. Sims," *Oxford Companion*, supra note 389, p. 733.

528. Id.

529. 377 U.S. 533, 624–625, quoted in Baker, supra note 527.

530. On this point see generally Alexander M. Bickel, *The Supreme Court and the Idea of Progress* (New York: Harper & Row, 1970).

531. And if using Samuel Chase as typical offends, then remember that James Wilson is said to be "second only to Madison as an architect of the Constitution." See Raoul Berger, "The Constitution and the Rule of Law," 1 *Western New England Law Review* 261 (1978), reprinted in Raoul Berger, *Selected Writings on the Constitution* (Cumberland, VA: James River Press, (1987), pp. 292, 294.

532. *Colegrove v. Green*, 328 U.S. 549 (1946).

533. 328 U.S., at 556.

534. 369 U.S., at 251.

535. *Miranda v. Arizona*, 384 U.S. 436 (1966). According to one recent commentator, *Miranda* represents "The Warren Court's revolution in American criminal procedure['s]. . . . high point (or, depending on one's perspective, its low point). . . . [It is] the most famous, and most bitterly criticized, confession case in the nation's history." Yale Kamisar, "Miranda v. Arizona," *Oxford Companion*, supra note 389, p. 552.

536. I have tried to capture from memory the words we usually hear from police procedural television programs. The more scholarly way of putting

it, apparently, is that police are required to advise criminal suspects of these particular constitutional rights: (1) the right to remain silent; (2) the reminder that anything said could be used against the suspect; (3) the right to counsel; and (4) the related reminder that counsel would be provided for indigents. Susette M. Talarico, "Miranda Warnings," *Oxford Companion*, supra note 389, p. 554.

537. In *Malloy v. Hogan*, 378 U.S. 1 (1964), decided two years before *Miranda*, the Supreme Court first declared that the Fifth Amendment's strictures against self-incrimination were incorporated into the Fourteenth Amendment's "due process" clause. Justice Harlan, joined by Justice Clark, dissented in *Malloy* because he objected to the "selective incorporation" of the Fifth Amendment against the states. Harlan preferred to continue the jurisprudence announced in *Twining v. New Jersey*, 211 U.S. 78 (1908), where the court had refused to apply the incorporation doctrine, and where instead, "state practices were to be judged in terms of basic principles of justice implicit in the Fourteenth Amendment's Due Process Clause, apart from and independent of the specific— and historically determined—privileges and safeguards laid down in the Bill of Rights." Harlan was, alas, fighting a losing battle. Donald P. Kommers, "Malloy v. Hogan," *Oxford Companion*, supra note 389, p. 519.

538. The key "selective incorporation" of the Sixth Amendment into the Fourteenth Amendment against the states is probably another Warren Court opinion, this time by Justice Black. In *Gideon v. Wainwright*, 372 U.S. 335 (1963), the Supreme Court held that indigents charged with felonies had a constitutional right to be aided by appointed counsel.

539. The quote is from Benjamin Cardozo's opinion in *People v. Defore*, 242 N.Y. 13, 21; 150 N.E. 585, 587; *cert. denied* 270 U.S. 657 (1926) ("the criminal goes free because the constable has blundered").

540. 384 U.S., at 457–458.

541. 384 U.S., at 505 (Harlan, J. dissenting).

542. Id., at 516–517.

543. Said Harlan, "Nothing in the letter or the spirit of the Constitution or in the precedents squares with the heavy-handed and one- sided action that is so precipitously taken by the Court. . . ." Id., at 525–26.

544. "There is now in progress in this country a massive re-examination of criminal law enforcement procedures on a scale never before witnessed," Harlan explained. "There are also signs that legislatures in some of the States may be preparing to re-examine the problem before us." Id., at 523. Harlan expressed his concern that "long-range and lasting reforms be frustrated by this Court's too rapid departure from existing constitutional standards." Id., at 524.

545. Id., at 518–19.

546. *Mapp v. Ohio*, 367 U.S. 643 (1961).
547. See, e.g., Malcolm Richard Wilkey, "The Exclusionary Rule: Why Suppress Evidence?" 62 *Judicature* 215 (1978).
548. *Nix v. Williams*, 467 U.S. 431 (1984). The quoted material is from a discussion of the case in Thomas Y. Davies, "Exclusionary Rule," *Oxford Companion*, supra note 389, pp. 264, 266.
549. *See United States v. Leon*, 468 U.S. 897 (1984), where the Court held that the exclusionary rule will not bar the use of evidence obtained pursuant to a search for which the police have obtained a search warrant, even if the warrant is later ruled to be invalid.
550. 347 U.S. 483 (1954).
551. *Plessy v. Ferguson*, 163 U.S. 537 (1896).
552. See generally, Raoul Berger, *Government by Judiciary*, supra note 488.
553. Michael Kent Curtis, "Equal Protection," *Oxford Companion*, supra note 389, p. 257.
554. *Sweatt v. Painter*, 339 U.S. 629 (1950).
555. *McLaurin v. Oklahoma State Regents for Higher Education*, 339 U.S. 637 (1950).
556. 339 U.S., at 642.
557. On this strategy see e.g., Mark V. Tushnet, "Legal Defense Fund," *Oxford Companion*, supra note 389, p. 497, and for a more extended treatment see Mark V. Tushnet, *The NAACP's Legal Strategy Against Segregated Education 1925–1950* (Chapel Hill: University of North Carolina Press, 1987), and Richard Kluger, *Simple Justice* (New York: Knopf, 1975) (the full story of the *Brown* case).
558. See for this story, e.g., Dennis J. Hutchinson, "Unanimity and Desegregation," 68 *Georgetown Law Journal* 1 (1979).
559. 347 U.S., at 492.
560. Id., at 489–90, 492–93.
561. Id., at 494.
562. In Footnote 11, at 495, Warren cited "K. B. Clark, *Effect of Prejudice and Discrimination on Personality Development* (Midcentury White House Conference on Children and Youth, 1950); Witmer & Kotinsky, *Personality in the Making* (1952), c.VI; Deutscher and Chein, "The Psychological Effects of Enforced Segregation: A Survey of Social Science Opinion," 26 *Journal of Psychology* 259 (1948); Chein, "What Are the Psychological Effects of Segregation Under Conditions of Equal Facilities?" 3 *International Journal of Opinion and Attitude Res.* 229 (1949); Brameld, "Educational Costs," in *Discrimination and National Welfare* (MacIver, editor, 1949) 44–48; Frazier, *The Negro in the United States* (1949), 674–681. And see generally Myrdal, *An American Dilemma* (1944)."
563. *Stell v. Savannah-Chatham County Bd. of Educ.* 220 F. Supp. 667

(S.D.Ga. 1963), reversed 333 F.2d 55 (5th Cir.), cert. denied 379 U.S. 933 (1964).

564. For two of the most famous sustained criticisms of the Warren Court along these lines see Herbert Wechsler, "Toward Neutral Principles of Constitutional Law," 73 *Harvard Law Review* 1 (1959), and Alexander Bickel, *The Supreme Court and the Idea of Progress* (New York: Harper & Row, 1970).

565. *Harper v. Virginia Bd. of Elections*, 383 U.S. 663, 677 n.7 (1966) (Black, J. dissenting). Black was undoubtedly wrong about the amendments completely outlawing all racial discrimination. The amendments are limited to prohibiting such action by state officials. The implication appears to be that private individuals are still free to discriminate.

566. Morton J. Horwitz, "Forward: The Constitution of Change: Legal Fundamentality Without Fundamentalism," 107 *Harvard Law Review* 30, 69 (1993), quoting from Alexander M. Bickel, "The Original Understanding and the Segregation Decision," 69 *Harvard Law Review* 1, 64 (1955).

567. Id., at 69, citing Bickel, supra note 566 at 63, 65.

568. On this point see the comments regarding Justice Scalia's footnote 6 in the *Michael H.* case, Chapter Four infra, text accompanying note 769.

569. 349 U.S. 294 (1955).

570. *Green v. County School Board of New Kent*, 391 U.S. 430 (1968).

571. Dennis J. Hutchinson, "Green v. County School Board of New Kent County," *Oxford Companion*, supra note 389, p. 347.

572. Lino Graglia, "Affirmative Discrimination," *National Review*, July 5, 1993, at 26.

573. Id. at 27–28.

574. Quoted in Jared Taylor, *Paved with Good Intentions: The Failure of Race Relations in Contemporary America* (New York: Carroll & Graf, 1992), p. 126.

575. Title VII, §703(j) of the Civil Rights Act of 1964, quoted in Taylor, supra note 574, at 126.

576. *Griggs v. Duke Power Co.*, 401 U.S. 424 (1971).

577. *Ward's Cove Packing Co. v. Atonio*, 490 U.S. 642 (1989).

578. *Swann v. Charlotte-Mecklenburg Board of Education*, 402 U.S. 1 (1971).

579. Id., at 30.

580. Lino A. Graglia, "When Honesty is 'Simply Impractical' for the Supreme Court: How the Constitution Came to Require Busing for School Racial Balance," 85 *Michigan Law Review* 1153, 1154 (1987) (reviewing Bernard Schwartz, *Swann's Way: The School Busing Case and the Supreme Court* (New York: Oxford Univeristy Press, 1986)).

581. *Smuck v. Hobson*, 408 F.2d 175 (D.C.Cir. 1969).

582. Bork, supra note 371, at 75.

583. See Id., at 75.
584. See, e.g., Dennis J. Hutchinson, "Brown v. Board of Education," *Oxford Companion*, supra note 389, p. 95.
585. According to Raoul Berger, "the framers [of the Fourteenth Amendment] employed 'equal protection of the laws' to express their limited purpose: to secure the [property and contract] rights enumerated in the [1866] Civil Rights Act, and those only, against *discriminatory* State *legislation.*" Berger, supra note 488, at 133. Among the rights *not* enumerated in the Civil Rights Act, of course, were racially integrated public schools and a racial balance in the workplace. Thus, for Berger, and anyone else devoted to the "original intent" of the Fourteenth Amendment, it could not support the construction the modern Supreme Court has put on it. See generally Id., at 117–33.
586. For the manner in which the Court's assimiliationist aims were frustrated by the means chosen in the busing decisions, see Graglia, supra note 580, at 1154. Pat Buchanan observed that "After the Supreme Court decision of 1954, Washington's racial composition began to change with startling speed . . . The white residents of the nation's capital were running away from integration." Patrick J. Buchanan, *Right from the Beginning* (Washington, D.C.: Regnery Gateway, 1990), p. 115. When Buchanan was in Junior High, in 1952–53, the public schools with which his Catholic school competed were 100 percent white, but by the time he graduated from high school, the public high schools in the District "were all desegregated, and on the way to becoming 100 percent black. Within a decade, the *de jure* segregation of '54 was replaced by a *de facto* segregation that endures to this day." Id., at 116.
587. For the sad story on how we now spend huge amounts on American 'schools with little return on our investment see Taylor, supra note 574, at 292–296, 332–333, 336–338 (noting our high expenditures for education, and noting that the problem for many black school children is not inadequate funding for schools, but rather the collapse of stable family life, and the spiral into truancy, sexual license, crime, and drugs which results from that collapse).
588. Almost everything has been tried to reverse this flight from the inner city schools. In terms of resources expended the most massive effort was probably Kansas City's "magnet school" plan, where approximately $500 million in new tax revenues have been expended in attempts to lure whites back from the suburbs. In order to accomplish this plan the federal courts have had to reverse the local taxing authorities' decisions—they balked at the high cost of the plan, but the Federal District court ordered them to proceed, and was upheld, ultimately, by the Supreme Court, *Jenkins v. Missouri*, 495 U.S. 33 (1990). See generally, ArLynn Leiber

Presser, "Broken Dreams," *American Bar Association Journal,* May 1991, p. 60.

589. As a result of the Restrictive Covenant Cases, of which *Shelly v. Kraemer,* 334 U.S. 1 (1948) is the most famous. In these cases the Court held that state court enforcement of racially restrictive covenants violates the equal protection clause of the Fourteenth Amendment, and that the enforcement of racial covenants by the federal courts violates the due process clause of the Fifth Amendment. As is true with *Brown,* it is possible to criticize these racially restrictive covenant cases as instances of the Court expanding the reach of the amendments in a manner that ignored the original understanding and failed to explain why competing constitutional analyses were rejected. See generally Wechsler, supra note 564, at 29–31.

590. Taylor, supra note 574, at 334.

591. Buchanan, supra note 586, at 338.

592. See Mark Tushnet, *The NAACP's Legal Strategy against Segregated Education, 1925–1950* (Chapel Hill: Univeristy of North Carolina Press, 1987). Tushnet points out that the preeminent black leader of the first half of this century, W.E.B. DuBois, broke with the NAACP in the mid–1930s, after strongly disagreeing with that organization's desire to pursue desegregation litigation. DuBois had insisted that the NAACP would make better use of its resources, and blacks would be better served, by focusing on racial empowerment, particularly economic empowerment, rather than an extended course of litigation. He feared (with reason) that such litigation might eliminate legal segregation but still leave blacks no better off in countless other ways. Id., at 8–10. Tushnet concluded that the NAACP's decision to litigate may have seemed right, even inevitable, to the primary figures themselves (such as Thurgood Marshall), but that, in retrospect "it may be worth wondering whether DuBois was right." Id., at 165. See also L. Michael Seidman, *Brown and Miranda,* 80 *California Law Review* 673 (1992), which makes the point that *Brown* and *Miranda* have not delivered what was expected or promised by their advocates.

593. *Roe v. Wade,* 410 U.S. 113 (1973).

594. The quoted language is from *Palko v. Connecticut,* 302 U.S. 319, 325.

595. 410 U.S., at 174–77.

596. *Abortion and Divorce in Western Law* (Cambridge: Harvard University Press, 1987).

597. See, e.g., Philip C. Metzger, "Politics and the High Court," *New York Times,* July 1, 1993, §A, p. 19.

598. Ruth Bader Ginsberg, "Speaking in a Judicial Voice," 67 *New York University Law Review* 1185, 1198, 1205 (1993) (Text of Ginsberg's

speech, given at the twenty-fourth James Madison Lecture on Constitutional Law, at New York University School of Law, on March 9, 1993).

599. On Ginsburg's equal protection argument for allowing abortion rights see generally Terry Eastland, "Mainstream Radical," *American Spectator*, November 1993, p. 66; and Jeffrey Rosen, "The Book of Ruth: Judge Ginsburg's Feminist Challenge," *New Republic*, August 2, 1993, p. 19.

600. See, in particular, the dissenting opinion of Chief Justice Rehnquist, 410 U.S., at 173–174.

601. On this point see Justice Rehnquist's dissent, 410 U.S., at 174 ("While the Court's opinion quotes from the dissent of Mr. Justice Holmes in *Lochner v. New York*, 198 U.S. 45, 74 (1905), the result it reaches is more closely attuned to the majority opinion of Mr. Justice Peckham in the case").

602. Blackmun testified to his longtime connection with the Mayo Clinic, as its chief counsel, at his confirmation hearings. See generally, "Harry A. Blackmun: Hearing before the Senate Judiciary Committee," 91st Cong., 2d Sess. 7 (1970).

603. 410 U.S., at 163.

604. See generally 410 U.S., at 161–164.

605. 410 U.S., at 163–164.

606. See, e.g., the views of Judge Ruth Bader Ginsburg, referred to supra note 599.

607. For the details see Jared Taylor, *Paved with Good Intentions: The Failure of Race Relations in Contemporary America* 21–61 (New York: Carroll & Graf, 1992). The essence of the research findings which Mr. Taylor reports is that where applicants for particular jobs, for housing mortgages, or for educational or professional opportunities have similar qualifications, minorities, particularly blacks, generally do as well or better than do white applicants. Educational or economic level is a much better indicator of who succeeds in American society than is race.

608. See Chapter Three, supra, text accompanying notes 576–577.

609. For the elaboration of Ms. Guinier's views, see her recently-published *The Tyranny of the Majority: Fundamental Fairness in Representative Democracy* (New York: Martin Kessler Books/Free Press, 1994).

610. *Chisom v. Roemer*, 111 S.Ct. 2354 (1991) (state judicial elections are subject to the Voting Rights Act § 2 requirement that minority bloc voters have the opportunity to elect judges of their choosing). The Supreme Court's extension of this "right" has led to a rash of lawsuits. See, e.g., Mark Curriden, "Around the South: Tennessee Lawsuit," *Atlanta Constitution*, November 16, 1993, at A3 (article discusses lawsuits in various states by blacks contesting the election of judges). The Court has recently granted *certiorari* on two court of appeals rulings which seem to

slow the extension of the Voting Rights Act to judges by enforcing a high burden of proof on the plaintiffs. See *Magnolia Bar Association, Inc. v. Hawkins*, 994 F.2d 1143 (1993), (cert. granted Nov. 23, 1993); *League of United Latin American Citizens v. Texas Att'y General*, 999 F.2d 831 (1993), (cert. granted Nov. 30, 1993).

611. See generally Stephen B. Presser and Jamil S. Zainaldin, *Law and Jurisprudence in American History* (St. Paul: West Publishing Co., 2nd edition, 1989), pp. 268–269, for the relevant excerpts from Tocqueville.

612. Id.

613. *Richmond v. J. A. Croson Co.*, 488 U.S. 469 (1989).

614. Chapter One, supra, text accompanying notes 164–171.

615. See Chapter One, supra, text accompanying notes 76–77.

616. James E. Jones, Jr., "Richmond v. J.A. Croson Co.," in Kermit Hall, editor, *The Oxford Companion to the United States Supreme Court* (New York: Oxford University Press, 1992), p. 736.

617. See Chapter One supra, text accompanying notes 149–171.

618. See, e.g., Meg Vaillancourt, "State Vows to Help Minority-owned Businesses," *Boston Globe*, Oct. 30, 1993, at 29 (detailing the running battle in Boston between proponents of set-asides and opponents who point to fraud in the programs); Doris Sue Wong, "Two Contractors Indicted in Alleged Bilking of State," *Boston Globe*, December 4, 1992, at 39 (two set-aside recipients allegedly lied about minority involvement to get contracts).

619. For the Supreme Court case upholding the FCC's "set-aside" practice see *Metro Broadcasting, Inc. v. FCC*, 110 S.Ct. 2997 (1990).

620. 110 S.Ct. 2997 (1990).

621. Id., at 3029, O'Connor, J. dissenting. For critical comment on the majority's presumption that race could be used as a proxy for the presentation of particular views, see Stephen L. Carter, *Reflections of an Affirmative Action Baby* (New York: Basic Books, 1991), pp. 36–37.

622. See the history and rationale behind the peremptory challenge covered by Justice White in *Swain v. Alabama*, 380 U.S. 202, 212–220 (1965), the last major case in which the Supreme Court drew the line at extending equal protection tenets to peremptory challenges. The key Supreme Court cases undermining this purpose on the basis of race were *Batson v. Kentucky*, 476 U.S. 79 (1986) (The exercise of racially discriminatory peremptory challenges offends the Equal Protection Clause when the offending challenges are made by the state); *Powers v. Ohio*, 499 U.S. 1364 (1991) (same), *Edmonson v. Leesville Concrete Co.*, 500 U.S. 2077 (1991) (Equal protection clause is also offended in civil cases, when private litigants exercise similar challenges), and *Georgia v. McCollum*, 112 S.Ct. 2348 (1992) (Equal protection also violated when criminal defendants exercise peremptory challenges on the basis of race).

623. 112 S.Ct., at 2359.

624. In that opinion Thomas also indicated that were it open to challenge he would *not* have accepted the view that a criminal defendant's use of peremptory strikes was state action which could be construed to violate the Fourteenth Amendment. Id. Because the respondents made no such challenge he felt constrained to agree with the majority—that if it was state action to exercise peremptory challenges on the basis of race by private parties in civil actions the same should hold for criminal defendants.

625. Id., at 2360. Thomas also pointedly observed, "In effect, we have exalted the right of citizens to sit on juries over the rights of the criminal defendant, even though it is the defendant, not the jurors, who faces imprisonment or even death. At a minimum, I think that this inversion of priorities should give us pause." Id. Thomas's words about eliminating peremptory strikes were clearly prophetic. The latest step along the road was the Supreme Court's recent dubious decision ruling gender-based peremptories unconstitutional. *J.E.B. v. Alabama*, 62 *U.S. Law Week* 4219 (No. 92–1239, 1994).

626. Stephen Carter, supra note 621, Chapter 4, "Racial Justice on the Cheap."

627. Id., e.g., at 72 ("All the efforts at seeking to justify racial preferences as justice or compensation mask the simple truth that among those training for business and professional careers, the benefits of affirmative action fall to those least in need of them."), and 233 ("[F]or all that it has assisted the black middle class, affirmative action has done nothing at all for the true victims of racism.").

628. Such programs that ought to be undertaken, Carter believes, include the delivery of better health care, better education for parents, or head start-type projects to prepare children to take advantage of educational opportunities.

629. See, e.g., Carter, supra note 621, at 89, where Carter makes plain that he wants no lowering of standards, and where he goes so far as to maintain that to admit minority members to professional schools who possess lower grade-point-average and standardized test scores than those required of whites is wrong.

630. Id., at 67.

631. Id., at 36.

632. Id., at 197.

633. Id., at 210–211.

634. Id., at 210–211.

635. Id., at 228.

636. Steele won the National Book Award in 1991.

637. Shelby Steele, *The Content of Our Character: A New Vision of Race in*

America (New York: St. Martin's Press, 1990), p. 90. Steele notes that this program was basically the agenda of the Republican Ronald Reagan. Steele emphasizes his belief that "*The most dangerous threat to the black identity is not the racism of white society (this actually confirms the black identity), but the black who insists on his or her own individuality,*" Id., at 72 (emphasis in the original). Steele defines the values of individualism as "the work ethic, the importance of education, the value of property ownership, of respectability, of 'getting ahead,' of stable family life, of initiative, of self-reliance," and further indicates that these values are "raceless and even assimilationist," and "urge us toward participation in the American mainstream, toward integration, toward a strong identification with the society, and toward the entire constellation of qualities that are implied in the word individualism. These values are almost rules for how to prosper in a democratic, free enterprise society that admires and rewards individual effort." Id., at 95.

638. Id., at 28, 80.
639. Id., at 113. Steele stresses, "The fact is that after twenty years of racial preferences, the gap between white and black median income is greater than it was in the seventies." Id., at 116. He further notes that "fewer blacks go to college today than ten years ago; more black males of college age are in prison or under the control of the criminal justice system than in college. This despite racial preferences." Id., at 124. He also indicates that "between 1976 and 1989, blacks have endured a drop in college enrollment of between 53 and 36 percent while white enrollment increased 3.6 percent," Id., at 152, and that "Black college students . . have the lowest grade point average and the highest dropout rate of any student group in America . . ." Id., at 162
640. Id., at 39–53, 116–118, 134–138. As Steele explains, Id., at 90, "Since there are laws to protect us against discrimination, preferences only impute a certain helplessness to blacks that diminishes our self-esteem. The self-preoccupied form of white guilt that is behind racial preferences always makes us lower so that we can be lifted up."
641. Id., at 91.
642. Id., at 172.
643. Carter, supra, note 621, at 133. For more on the point that one is condemned if one tries to argue that racism is *not* the continuing cause of black economic problems, see Jared Taylor, *Paved with Good Intentions, The Failure of Race Relations in Contemporary America* (New York: Carroll & Graf, 1992), pp. 9–19.
644. Carter, supra, note 621, at 103.
645. Id., at 118.
646. For the history of the "color-blind Constitution" ideal, a powerful argument that it is consistent with the original understanding of the Four-

teenth Amendment, and a similarly impressive argument that it represents the best hope for the future, see Andrew Kull, *The Color-Blind Constitution* (Cambridge: Harvard University Press, 1992).

647. As Stephen Carter notes, one valid use of affirmative action concepts is "the provision of opportunities for people of color who might not otherwise have the advanced training that will allow them to prove what they can do." Carter, supra note 621, at 26.

648. 163 U.S., at 559.

649. See Chapter Three, supra, text accompanying notes 379–387.

650. 488 U.S. 469, 520–28 (1989). Scalia, though concurring in judgment, disagreed with Justice O'Connor's dictum that "state and local governments may in some circumstances discriminate on the basis of race in order (in a broad sense) 'to ameliorate the effects of past discrimination.' " Id. at 520, quoting from O'Connor's opinion at 476–77.

651. On "balancing," see Chapter One, supra, text accompanying notes 149–171.

652. Lino A. Graglia, "Affirmative Discrimination," *National Review*, July 5, 1993, p. 31.

653. 495 U.S. 33 (1990).

654. See ArLynn Leiber Presser, "Broken Dreams," *American Bar Association Journal*, May 1991, at 60, for an illuminating article about the failure of the Kansas City plan to achieve the goal of voluntary, citywide integration of the public schools.

655. As Shelby Steele explains in *The Content of Our Character*, the logic of reparations:

> overlooks a much harder and less digestible reality, that it is impossible to repay blacks living today for the historic suffering of the race. If all blacks were given a million dollars tomorrow morning it would not amount to a dime on the dollar of three centuries of oppression, nor would it obviate the residues of that oppression that we still carry today. The concept of historic reparation grows out of man's need to impose a degree of justice on the world that simply does not exist. Suffering can be endured and overcome, it cannot be repaid. Blacks cannot be repaid for the injustice done to the race, but we can be corrupted by society's guilty gestures of repayment.

Steele, supra note 637, at 119.

656. See, e.g., Mari J. Matsuda, "Looking to the Bottom: Critical Legal Studies and Reparations," 22 *Harvard Civil Rights-Civil Liberties Law Review* 323 (1987), which suggests that critical legal scholars, and by extension all legal scholars, should take a page from critical race theorists and look to the historically dispossessed for their principles of law and justice. Deriving law "from the bottom," insists Matsuda, would elabo-

rate a legal right to reparation, quite distinct from any moral right. Professor Matsuda's piece begins with an extraordinary suggestion that left-leaning law professors might be tried for their beliefs:

> When you are on trial for conspiracy to overthrow the government for teaching the deconstruction of law, your lawyer will want black people on your jury. Why? Because black jurors are more likely to understand what your lawyer will argue: that people in power sometimes abuse law to achieve their own ends, and that the prosecution's claim to neutral application of the law is false.

Id. (citations omitted). Even a relatively moderately left-leaning legal scholar, such as the highly respected Cass Sunstein of the University of Chicago's law school, appears to regard existing distributions of wealth and power as highly suspect, and has recently written a book offering a theory of the First Amendment designed in part to counteract those existing distributions. See generally Cass R. Sunstein, *Democracy and the Problem of Free Speech* (New York: Free Press, 1993).

657. See generally, L. A. Times Staff, *Understanding the Riots: Los Angeles Before and After the Rodney King Case* (Los Angeles, CA: Los Angeles Times, 1992).

658. See Roger Parloff, "Maybe the Jury Was Right," *American Lawyer*, June 1992, at 7 (describing the entire contents of the King tape, which included crucial sections, edited out of the television version, that showed King disobeying repeated police orders and physically shaking off the officers who initially tried to lay him prone on the ground); see also Elizabeth F. Loftus and Laura A. Rosenwald, "The Rodney King Videotape: Why the Case Was Not Black and White," 66 *Southern California Law Review* 1637 (1993) (discussing the reasons why the videotape must be placed within the context of other evidence in order to be conclusive in a court of law).

659. The constitutional principle of "double jeopardy"—that no one should be tried twice for the same offense—was almost abandoned by its traditional defenders in the King case. After the initial state court verdicts of acquitting the officers who subdued King, the national and California branches of the American Civil Liberties Unions (ACLU) split over the issue of double jeopardy. The national ACLU has long supported a strict approach to double jeopardy—that is, a person cannot be tried twice for the same crime, period. After the state court trial, however, the California chapter of the ACLU began urging the Justice Department to try the L.A. policemen on federal civil rights charges. The national chapter suspended its opposition to double jeopardy so that the organization could debate the issue. In April of 1993, however, the national organization did

reaffirm its traditional stance opposing double jeopardy. See "Nation in Brief: ACLU Says Officers' Retrial is Illegal Double Jeopardy," *Atlanta Constitution*, April 5, 1993, at A4; Ramona Ripston and Paul Hoffman, "King Beating Trial is not a Case of Double Jeopardy," *San Diego Union-Tribune*, April 14, 1993, at B7 (authors were officers in the California ACLU).

660. On Chase's views of the jury see generally Presser and Zainaldin, supra note 616, at 167–177, 231–241 (2nd ed. 1989).

661. See, e.g., *United States v. Dougherty*, 473 F.2d 1113 (D.C.Cir., 1972, opinion by Leventhal, J.)

662. See Ronald J. Allen, "Freedom from Double Jeopardy, Our Lost Liberty," *Wall Street Journal*, March 17, 1993, at A15.

663. This is in the Fifth Amendment: "[N]or shall any person be subject for the same offense to be twice put in jeopardy of life or limb . . ." In *Benton v. Maryland*, 395 U.S. 784 (1969) the Supreme Court held that the clause was incorporated through the Fourteenth Amendment's Due Process clause to forbid any state from subjecting a person to double jeopardy. This reversed a contrary decision in *Palko v. Connecticut*, 302 U.S. 319 (1937).

664. In *Moore v. State*, 55 U.S. (14 How.) 13 (1952), the Court held that the Constitution's principle of "dual sovereignty"—giving some governmental functions to the state and others to the federal government—allowed the two "sovereigns"—the state and the federal government—to prosecute a single defendant for an act which violated the different laws of each. For a history of the role of double jeopardy laws in Anglo-American jurisprudence, see Susan W. Brenner, "S.C.A.R.F.A.C.E.: A Speculation on Double Jeopardy and Compound Criminal Liability," 27 *New England Law Review* 915, 917–29 (1993).

665. See, e.g. *Heath v. Alabama*, 472 U.S. 82 (1985).

666. For example, the following was part of the transcript of the *MacNeil/Lehrer NewsHour*, April 30, 1992 (From Lexis/Nexis):

> MR. LEHRER: Democratic Congresswoman Maxine Waters called a news conference on Capitol Hill this morning to give her reaction. She represents the Los Angeles district where much of the rioting took place. She said she opposed violence, but her constituents did have the right to express their anger.
>
> REP. MAXINE WATERS, (D. CA): I am angry. I am outraged. I think there has been a miscarriage of justice and I suppose I should have known once there was a change of venue and that trial was moved to basically an all white community, but I suppose I was foolish enough to believe that given the very graphic depiction of the beating of Rodney King captured on video that there would be

an undeniable assignment of responsibility to those who had, in fact, beat him. Unfortunately, we saw a verdict that I have no problems in identifying as a racist verdict.

667. *Shaw v. Reno*, 1993 U.S. LEXIS 4406; 125 L.Ed. 2d 511; 61 U.S.L.W. 4818 (1993).

668. §5 of the Voting Rights Act of 1965, 42 U.S.C. §1973c, "which prohibits a jurisdiction subject to its provisions from implementing changes in a 'standard, practice, or procedure with respect to voting' without federal authorization." 1993 U.S. Lexis 4406, at *9.

669. Id., at *11, citations omitted.

670. Id., at *12, citations omitted.

671. Ibid., citing Bernard Grofman, "Would Vince Lombardi Have Been Right If He Had Said: 'When it Comes to Redistricting, Race Isn't Everything, It's the Only Thing'?" 14 *Cardozo Law Review* 1237, 1261, N. 96 (1993).

672. 1993 U.S. Lexis 4406, at *14, *26.

673. Id., at *22.

674. Id., citing "see *Plessy v. Ferguson*, 163 U.S. 537, 559 (1896, Harlan, J. dissenting)."

675. Id., at *22–23.

676. Id., at *24, citation omitted.

677. Id., at *25, citation omitted.

678. Id., at *25, quoting Brennan, J., concurring in part in *United Jewish Organizations of Williamsburgh, Inc. v. Carey*, 430 U.S. 144, 173 (1977).

679. Id., at *25.

680. Id., at *26.

681. See, e.g., Chapter One, supra, text accompanying notes 164- 171 (*Griswold and Poe* opinions of Justice Harlan finding that the state had failed to meet his "strong justification" test).

682. 1993 U.S. Lexis 4406, at *26–27.

683. Id., at *48.

684. Id., at *49 (internal quotations and citations omitted).

685. Id., at *49.

686. Id., at *49–50.

687. Id., at *50, citing 430 U.S., at 167–168.

688. Id., at *50–51.

689. See supra at text accompanying notes 655–656.

690. Other words of Justice O'Connor are well worth quoting in this context. Referring to the special evils attendant to race-based classifications with regard to reapportionment, she wrote:

> A reapportionment plan that includes in one district individuals who belong to the same race, but who are otherwise widely separated by

geographical and political boundaries, and who may have little in common with one another but the color of their skin, bears an uncomfortable resemblance to political apartheid. It reinforces the perception that members of the same racial group—regardless of their age, education, economic status, or the community in which they live—think alike, share the same political interests, and will prefer the same candidates at the polls. We have rejected such perceptions . . . as impermissible racial stereotypes. [citations omitted] . . . If our society is to continue to progress as a multiracial democracy, it must recognize that the automatic invocation of race stereotypes retards that progress and causes continued hurt and injury [citation omitted]. 1993 U.S. Lexis 4406, at *32–33.

691. Id., at *34.

692. See supra, text accompanying notes 618–647.

693. 1993 U.S. Lexis 4406, at *34–35, quoting from Justice Douglas's dissent in *Wright v. Rockefeller*, 376 U.S., at 66–67 (internal citations omitted).

694. The language, of course, comes from Martin Luther King, Jr.'s famous "I Have A Dream" speech delivered to 250,000 people at the "March on Washington for Jobs and Freedom," August 28, 1963. The relevant words were "I have a dream that my four little children will one day live in a nation where they will not be judged by the color of their skin but by the content of their character." Reprinted as "Soaring Words that Focused a Movement," *Chicago Tribune*, August 22, 1993, Section 4, page 1.

695. U. S. Constitution, Amendment I ("Congress shall make no law respecting an establishment of religion, or prohibiting the free exercise thereof. . .").

696. "No State shall make or enforce any law which shall abridge the privileges or immunities of citizens of the United States; nor shall any State deprive any person of life, liberty, or property, without due process of law; nor deny to any person within its jurisdiction the equal protection of the laws." U.S. Constitution, Amendment XIV, §1.

697. *Lemon v. Kurtzman*, 403 U.S. 602 (1971).

698. Ibid.

699. Jeffrey Rosen, "Lemon Law," *New Republic*, March 29, 1993, p. 17.

700. Fortunately the Supreme Court appears to be backing away from this implication. A recent Supreme Court decision, for example, held that it was permissible for the state to provide a student at a parochial school a sign-language interpreter where one would have been provided to a public school student. *Zobrest v. Catalina Foothills Sch. Dist.*, 113 S.Ct. 2462 (1993).

701. Jacob Neusner, "Who's Afraid of the Religious Right?" *National Review*, December 27, 1993, at 38.

702. Rosen, supra note 699, at 18.

703. Id., at 18.
704. Id.
705. R. Kent Newmyer, "Story, Joseph," *Oxford Companion*, supra note 617, p. 841. For the full details on Story's life see Newmyer's magisterial and brilliant biography, R. Kent Newmyer, *Supreme Court Justice Joseph Story: Statesman of the Old Republic* (Chapel Hill: University of North Carolina Press, 1985).
706. Joseph Story, *Commentaries on the Constitution of the United States; with a Preliminary Review of the Constitutional History of the Colonies and States Before the Adoption of the Constitution* (Boston: Hilliard Gray, and Co. and Cambridge: Brown, Shattuck and Co., 1833), p. i.
707. Ronald D. Rotunda and John E. Nowak, "Introduction" to Joseph Story, *Commentaries on the Constitution of the United States* (Durham: Carolina Academic Press, 1987, originally published 1833), p. xiv.
708. Id., at xv.
709. Cass R. Sunstein, *Democracy and the Problem of Free Speech* (New York: Free Press, 1994), p. xii.
710. Rotunda and Nowak, supra note 707, at xiii.
711. Story, supra note 707, at 698–699.
712. See Chapter Two, text accompanying notes 336–339.
713. Story, supra note 707, at 699.
714. Ibid.
715. Ibid.
716. Id., at 700.
717. Ibid.
718. Id., at 701.
719. Gov. Kirk Fordice of Mississippi ignited a national controversy in November 1992, when he said, in an address to a conference of Republican governors, that America was "a Christian nation." Another governor asked him if he meant "Judeo-Christian nation," and Governor Fordice indicated that he did not. Richard L. Berke, "With a Crackle, Religion Enters G.O.P Meeting," *New York Times*, November 18, 1992, at A23. Governor Fordice probably meant no more than to refer to the main source of American values throughout most of our history, but the politically correct police rushed to the scene. Very quickly some Jewish leaders and some liberals jumped to condemn his remarks, as suggesting that some people (non-Christians) were not welcome in America. Myrna Shinbaum, "ADL Response to Gov. Fordice Remarks on 'Christian Nation'," *U.S. Newswire*, Nov. 18, 1992 (on LEXIS). As he had intended no such exclusionary message, Fordice went on *Crossfire* to defend his remarks, CNN Transcripts, November 18, 1993 (LEXIS), but, realizing that his remarks had unintentionally given offense, he soon felt constrained to apologize. "Governor Says He's Sorry

for 'Christian' Comment," *Orlando Sentinel,* November 21, 1992, at A16.

720. Story, supra note 707, at 701.

721. Ibid.

722. Id., at 702.

723. Id., at 702–703.

724. Id., at 703 (emphasis added).

725. *Lee v. Weisman,* 112 S.Ct. 2649, 2668 (1992), citing "1 Annals of Cong. 434 (1789)" (United States Congress, *The Debates and Proceedings in the Congress of the United States* (Washington: Gales and Seaton 1834–1856, 42 v.) (emphasis supplied).

726. Id., citing Annals, supra, note 25, at 729 (emphasis supplied).

727. Id., citing Annals, supra, note 725, at 731 (emphasis supplied).

728. See *Everson v. Board of Education,* 330 U.S. 1, 16 (1947) ("In the words of Thomas Jefferson, the clause against establishment of religion by law was intended to erect 'a wall of separation between church and state.' ")

729. *Weisman,* supra note 725, 112 S.Ct. at 2669, citing Linda Grant DePauw, editor, *Documentary History of the First Federal Congress of the United States of America* (Senate Journal) (Baltimore: John Hopkins University Press, 1972), Vol. 1, p. 136.

730. Id., citing Leonard Levy, *The Establishment Clause: Religion and the First Amendment* (New York: Macmillan, 1986), p. 81.

731. Id.

732. 112 S. Ct., at 2669.

733. Id., citing 1 Documentary History, supra, note 729 at 151 (Senate Journal).

734. Id., citing "ibid."

735. Ibid.

736. Id., citing 1 Documentary History, supra note 729, at 166.

737. Ibid.

738. Ibid.

739. Souter, an intellectually honest scholar, does concede, Id., at n. 2, that "Some commentators have suggested that by targeting laws respecting 'an' establishment of religion, the Framers adopted the very nonpreferentialist position whose much clearer articulation they repeatedly rejected. See, e.g., Robert L. Cord, *Separation of Church and State: Historical Fact and Current Fiction* (New York: Lambeth Press, 1988), pp. 11–12. For Souter, however, "the indefinite article before the word 'establishment' is better seen as evidence that the Clause forbids any kind of establishment, including a nonpreferential one. If the Framers had wished, for some reason, to use the indefinite term to achieve a narrow meaning for the Clause, they could far more aptly have placed it before the word 'religion.' " For this point Souter relies on see Laycock, " 'Nonpreferential'

Aid to Religion: A False Claim about Original Intent," 27 *William & Mary Law Review* 875, 884–885 (1986).
740. *Weisman,* supra note 725, 112 S.Ct., at 2669–70.
741. On this point see Cord, supra note 739.
742. See Michael W. McConnell, "Accommodations of Religion: An Update and a Response to the Critics," 60 *George Washington Law Review* 685 (1992) (nonsectarian accommodation of religion is always permitted by the establishment clause and may, at times, be required by the free exercise clause).
743. Justice Scalia, in particular, is a modern exponent of this ancient view, and has been critical of attempts to find the "intent" of a group of legislators. See, e.g, Michael D. Sherman, "The Use of Legislative History: A Debate between Justice Scalia and Judge Breyer," 16 *American Bar Association Administrative Law News* Summer 1991, pp. 1, 13–14.
744. The seminal article is H. Jefferson Powell, "The Original Understanding of Original Intent," 98 *Harvard Law Review* 885 (1985). See also, H. Jefferson Powell, "Rules for Originalists," 73 *University of Virginia Law Review* 659 (1987) (on the importance of looking beyond both the comments of individual legislators and the text of the document itself to "the cultural context that gave their constitutional views meaning and urgency." (Id. at 674) when interpreting the Constitution).
745. See generally Chapter Two, supra.
746. Pat Buchanan, "Crossfire," CNN transcript, June 7, 1993 (LEXIS) ("We all believe [Weisman] is an absurd ruling, it's not rooted in the Constitution, the Supreme Court's a renegade court.").
747. Id.
748. See, e.g., editorial, "Mississippi Prays," *Wall Street Journal,* December 6, 1993, at A14, noting the trials and tribulations of the principal at Wingfield High School in Jackson, Mississippi. For three days the students began their day by having the president of the student government read the prayer "Almighty God, we ask that you bless our parents, teachers, and country throughout the day. In your name we pray, Amen." The editorial notes that as a result of the reading of the prayer, "Lord, all hell broke loose"—the principal of the school was fired, a rally in support of the reading of the prayer at the state Capitol drew four thousand people, and three hundred students of Wingfield walked out of classes in protest. The *Wall Street Journal* stated, in conformity with the thesis here presented, that

> Not surprisingly, some Mississippians see a link between the decline of the schools [in terms of student achievement and student discipline] and a morally frazzled society, and believe that a little more attention to spiritual matters might help. State Senator Mike Gunn

is sponsoring legislation that would withhold state funding to schools that prohibit voluntary prayer. Id.

749. The *Wall Street Journal* notes that following the Supreme Court's decision regarding the student-initiated prayer at the Houston high school graduation, "In May, a federal judge in Boise, Idaho, issued a similar ruling. In response, Tennessee passed a law permitting public school students to lead nonsectarian prayers during noncompulsory school events." Id.

750. Linda Greenhouse, "Religious Groups Can Use Schools," *New York Times*, June 8, 1993, p. A1.

751. Greenhouse, supra note 750, at A10.

752. *Lamb's Chapel v. Center Moriches Union Free Sch. Dist.*, 113 U.S. 2141, 2149–50 (1992).

753. See Chapter Three, supra, text accompanying notes 461–465.

754. On the strength of support for RFRA see Terry Eastland, "Religion, Politics & the Clintons," *Commentary*, January 1994, p. 40.

755. The argument is often cast in terms of whether or not one believes that the "fetus" is a person, and modern abortion debate appears to use the terms "fetus" and "embryo" interchangeably. I begin the discussion by using the word "embryo" because it signifies development of the fertilized egg from conception, while "fetus" actually refers to a "fully-formed" embryo. See, e.g., *The Concise Oxford Dictionary* (Oxford: Oxford University Press, 3rd Ed., 1944), pp. 370, 440 (entries for "embryo" and "fetus"). Thus the question of whether an "embryo" is a person appears to be a more difficult metaphysical one. See generally the interesting review by Katha Pollit of Roger Rosenblatt's *Life Itself: Abortion in the American Mind* (New York: Random House, 1992), in *The Nation*, May 25, 1992, p. 718, where she indicates that Rosenblatt, who claims to be prochoice, has a "penchant for anti-choice language: It's always the fetus, and sometimes the unborn child, never the embryo (the accurate, rarely used word for what is aborted during the first trimester)."

756. For the ostensible intractability of the issue, coupled with an attempt to arrive at compromises which, not surprisingly, result in the reaffirmation of their authors' basically prochoice positions see Rosenblatt, supra note 755, and Lawrence Tribe, *Abortion: The Clash of Absolutes* (New York: W.W. Norton, 1992).

757. William Blackstone, *Commentaries on the Law of England* (Chicago: University of Chicago Press facsimile, 1979), Vol. I, p. 125.

758. Id., at 125–126.

759. Tribe, supra note 756, at 67.

760. On the history of American decisions and legislation before *Roe v. Wade*, see Rosenblatt, supra note 755, at 82–93, and Tribe, supra note 756, at 34–49.

761. Rosenblatt, supra note 755, at 183.
762. Id., at 184.
763. Id. at 188–189. Of the 83 percent, "14 percent said it should be legal only to save the life of the mother; 35 percent in cases of rape, incest, and to save the life of the mother; 27 percent, for any reason, but not after first three months of pregnancy; 7 percent, legal at any time during pregnancy and for any reason; and 7 percent said abortion should be prohibited in all circumstances." Id., at 188.
764. See, e.g., the Introduction and Chapter One, *passim*.
765. See Chapter One, supra, text accomapnying notes 205–208.
766. See Chapter Two, supra, text accompanying note 343.
767. *Michael H. v. Gerald D.*, 491 U.S. 110 (1989).
768. 491 U.S., at 122, quoting *Snyder v. Massachusetts*, 291 U.S. 97, 105 (1934) (Cardozo, J.).
769. See Scalia's footnote 6, 491 U.S., at 127–128 discussing this problem, and discussing the objections raised by Justices O'Connor and Brennan.
770. Id., at 128.
771. Id., at 137, Brennan J., dissenting.
772. Id., at 110, quoting *Moore v. East Cleveland*, 431 U.S. 494, 549 (1977) (White, J. dissenting).
773. *Eisenstadt v. Baird*, 405 U.S. 438 (1972).
774. *Griswold v. Connecticut*, 381 U.S. 479 (1965).
775. *Ingraham v. Wright*, 430 U.S. 651 (1977).
776. *Vitek v. Jones*, 445 U.S. 480 (1980).
777. *Stanley v. Illinois*, 405 U.S. 645 (1972).
778. *Roe v. Wade*, discussed in Chapter Three, supra, text accompanying notes 593–606.
779. *Planned Parenthood v. Casey*, 112 S.Ct. 2791 (1992).
780. This appears to be the thesis as well of Robert A. Burt's *The Constitution in Conflict* (Cambridge: Harvard University Press, 1992).
781. *Rust v. Sullivan*, 111 S.Ct. 1759 (1991).
782. The Clinton administration has since rescinded the "gag rule."
783. Freedom of Choice Act of 1993, 1993 H.R. 25 (March 24, 1993) (LEXIS). For a scathing criticism of the act, see Stephen Chapman, "Abortion Rights and the Limits of Public Tolerance," *Chicago Tribune*, April 22, 1993, Section 1, p. 25.
784. Chapman, supra.
785. Chapter Three, supra, text accompanying note 436.
786. Ronald Dworkin, *Life's Dominion: An Argument about Abortion, Euthanasia, and Individual Freedom* (New York: Alfred A. Knopf, 1993).
787. See generally the essays collected in Ronald Reagan, *Abortion and the Conscience of the Nation* (Nashville: Thomas Nelson Publishers, 1984).

788. Dworkin, supra note 786, at 11–13, 24–25.
789. See Id. at 87–88.
790. Id., at 95–97 (Dworkin discusses rape, but the same arguments would apply to incest, which he touches on at pages 32–33).
791. See Id., at 32–33, 94.
792. See, e.g., Ronald Reagan, supra note 787, pp. 18, 19, 22, 25, 30, 34, 36, 38.
793. See, e.g., Rosenblatt, supra note 755, Tribe, supra note 756, and Dworkin, supra note 786.
794. Mary Ann Glendon, *Abortion and Divorce in Western Law* (Cambridge: Harvard University Press, 1987).
795. Id., at 18–19.
796. See Chapter One, supra.
797. *City of Akron v. Akron Center for Reproductive Health, Inc.* 462 U.S. 416, 465 (O'Connor, J. dissenting).
798. *Roth v. United States*, 354 U.S. 476, 505 (1957) (Harlan, J. concurring and dissenting, citing Henry Hart, "The Relations between State and Federal Law," 54 *Colorado Law Review* 489, 493).
799. *Kraskin v. Kraskin*, 104 F.2d 218, 221 (D.C.Cir., 1939).
800. Robert A. Burt, *The Constitution in Conflict* (Cambridge: Harvard University Press, 1992).
801. Kathleen M. Sullivan, "The Nonsupreme Court," 91 *Michigan Law Review* 1121, 1126 (1993), citing Burt, supra note 800, at 350–351.
802. Learned Hand, *The Bill of Rights: The Oliver Wendell Holmes Lectures* (Cambridge: Harvard University Press, 1958), p. 73.
803. See Chapter One, supra.
804. For criticism of *Casey* in this regard see, e.g., Michael Stokes Paulsen, "The Many Faces of 'Judicial Restraint,' " 1993 *Public Interest Law Review* 3, 14, 17–19.
805. See Paul Carrington, "Of Law and the River," 34 *Journal of Legal Education* 222, 227 (1984).
806. Inside the academy, of course, as Easterbrook and Fischel have recently noted, an idea gains rather than loses attractiveness for its novelty, which is generally of more importance than its accuracy. Frank Easterbrook and Daniel Fischel, *The Economic Structure of Corporate Law* (Cambridge: Harvard University Press, 1991), p. 31. To be outrageous is often as attractive as to be novel, particularly among younger scholars dizzy with theory.
807. Chapter Four, supra, text accompanying notes 667–694.
808. The belief seems to be found in the later work by Unger, for example, most notably *The Critical Legal Studies Movement* (Cambridge: Harvard University Press, 1986), and see also Peter Gabel & Duncan Kennedy, "Roll Over Beethoven," 36 *Stanford Law Review* 1 (1984). Utopian

aspirations are eschewed by other Critical Legal Studies scholars, most notably in Robert Gordon's rejoinder to Paul Carrington, defending the CLS'ers against the charge that they are "legal nihilists." Robert Gordon, "'Of Law and the River' and of Nihilism and Academic Freedom," 36 *Journal of Legal Education* 1 (1985).

809. See generally Roberto Unger, *Knowledge and Politics* (New York: Free Press, 1975).

810. William J. Bennett, "Commuter Massacre, Our Warning," *Wall Street Journal*, Friday December 10, 1993.

811. Id.

812. Id. See Terry Eastland and William J. Bennett, *Counting by Race: Equality from the Founding Fathers to Bakke* (New York: Basic Books, 1979). The phrase "counting by race" was Eastland's.

813. Id.

814. For another powerful statement of the theme that what is wrong with American society is a failure to teach traditional morality in the wake of the sixties' abandonment of that morality, see Myron Magnet, *The Dream and the Nightmare: The Sixties Legacy to the Underclass* (New York: William Morrow and Co., 1993).

815. Russell Kirk, *The Conservative Mind* (Chicago and Washington, D.C.: Regnery Books, Seventh Revised ed. 1986), pp. 8–9.

816. See generally Russell Kirk, *America's British Culture* (New Brunswick, N.J.: Transaction Publishers, 1993).

817. See the Introduction, text accompanying notes 32–41.

818. David J. Katz, "Note, Grand Jury Charges Delivered By Supreme Court Justices Riding Circuit During the 1790s," 14 *Cardozo Law Review* 1045, 1056 (1993).

819. Samuel Chase, Manuscript Jury Charge Book, Vertical File, Maryland Historical Society, Baltimore, Maryland (charges from 1799, 1802, 1803, 1805, and 1806).

820. See also text accompanying note 815, supra (Russell Kirk's essential postulates of conservatism).

821. See Jefferson's *Notes on the State of Virginia*, in Thomas Jefferson, *Writings* (New York: Library of America, 1984), pp. 123, 272.

822. The starting point is usually thought to be the important Footnote Four in *United States v. Carolene Products Co.*, 304 U.S. 144 (1938), in an opinion in which four Justices concurred, which suggested that the Fourteenth Amendment might require heightened scrutiny for legislative measures directed at particular religions or national or racial minorities or "against discrete and insular minorities."

823. See generally Magnet, supra note 814.

824. There is a hunger even in some parts of the legal academy for such a return to a more organic constitutional theory. On the Left the theory has shown

up as "Republicanism" as outlined by Cass Sunstein and Frank Michel-
man, and on the Right as "Communitarian theory" as outlined by Mary
Ann Glendon and others. See Cass Sunstein, "Beyond the Republican
Revival," 97 *Yale Law Journal* 1539 (1988); and Frank Michaelman,
"Law's Republic," 97 *Yale Law Journal* 1493 (1988); Mary Ann Glen-
don, *Abortion and Divorce in Western Law* (Cambridge: Harvard Univer-
sity Press, 1987), and *Rights Talk: The Impoverishment of Political
Discourse* (New York: Free Press, 1991).

825. Hamilton, according to one of his most brilliant biographers, never advocated government solely by "the rich and well born," but he undoubtedly
believed that he would find the leadership of the future nation among the
officers and other well-educated men with whom he served and in that
class into which he had married. See Forrest McDonald, *Alexander Hamilton: A Biography* (New York: Norton, 1979, 1982 paperback edition),
p. 69.

826. For a nice description of the framers' elitism, reflecting their status as
"gentlemen," see Russell Kirk, *The Conservative Constitution* (Washington: Regnery Gateway, 1990), pp. 35–48.

827. See generally *Federalist 51*, in Bernard Bailyn, editor, *The Debate on the
Constitution* (New York: Library of America, 1993), Vol. II, pp. 163,
164.

828. In a recent piece, Professors Gary Lawson and Steven Calabresi noted
(referring to *Federalist 51*):

> The Framers made no mistake. [They] sought to structure the
> federal government to avoid reliance on the good motives of either
> the citizens or the governors . . . [citation omitted]

Gary Lawson and Steven Calabresi, "Foreword: The Constitution of
Responsibility," 77 *Cornell Law Review* 955, 957 (1992). As Linda K.
Kerber remarked in her excellent study of the Federalists, *Federalists in
Dissent: Imagery and Ideology in Jeffersonian America* (Ithaca: Cornell
University Press, 1970), the Federalists were not able to share the "cheer-
ful Jeffersonian assumption" that men were naturally virtuous: "Their
attitude stemmed partly from the old Puritan awareness of man's natural
depravity, but even more it stemmed from an understanding of the extreme fragility of their experiment in democracy and an awareness of the
substantial demands for self-restraint and individual responsibility that
republican government places on its citizens." Id., at 202.

829. Ellis Sandoz writes at length about the influence that Christianity and
biblical rhetoric had on the Revolution, the framing of the Constitution,
and the writing and adoption of the Bill of Rights, in *A Government of
Laws: Political Theory, Religion, and the American Founding* (Baton
Rouge: Louisiana State University Press, 1990).

830. See Chapter Two supra, text accompanying notes 336–339.
831. Chase Jury Charge Book, supra note 819, at 14.
832. See Chapter Two supra, at pp. 101–106.
833. Chase Jury Charge Book, supra note 819, at 22–23.
834. These appear abridged in Presser & Zainaldin, supra note 611, at 135–141.
835. See generally the pieces by Michelman and Sunstein, supra note 824.
836. See Chapter Four, supra, note 824.
837. Symposium, "Who's Afraid of the Religious Right?" remarks of Kirk Fordice, *National Review*, December 27, 1993, at 39.
838. Id., at 38 (comments of Jacob Neusner).
839. Chapter Four, supra, text accompanying notes 713–714.
840. To be fair to Governor Fordice, he found himself unable completely to agree with Rabbi Neusner that "the 'Christian Right' has a 'crisis of euphemisms' and a failure to 'find the right euphemisms.' " Fordice did, however, note that he was "in substantial agreement" with Neusner, and saw him as a "fellow striver" embracing religion, celebrating moral values that flowed from religion, and "therefore embattled and besieged at a time in our history when high values, morals, and good character are sorely needed," symposium, supra note 837, at 39. Where Fordice said he differed from Neusner, in addition to the point about euphemisms, was that "his God and my God are not the same in that mine comprises Father, Son, and Holy Spirit. I can live with that if he can." Ibid. Presumably the governor sought to emphasize the Christian message of the Gospel and personal redemption through a sacrificial Saviour, which was, of course, missing from Neusner's "message."
841. Id., at 41 (Remarks of Ralph E. Reed, Jr).
842. See, e.g., Richard Epstein, *Takings: Private Property and the Power of Eminent Domain* (Cambridge: Harvard University Press, 1985), Stephen Macedo, *Liberal Virtues: Citizenship, Virtue, and Community in Liberal Constitutionalism* (New York: Oxford University Press, 1990), and Stephen Macedo, "Morality and the Constitution: Toward a Synthesis for 'Earthbound' Interpreters," 61 *University of Cinncinnati Law Review* 29 (1992). See also, for the importance of Lockean property theory to the framers and its further development, James W. Ely, *The Guardian of Every Other Right* (New York: Oxford University Press, 1992).
843. See *Federalist* 78, in Bailyn, *Debate*, supra note 827, Vol. II, at 467, 474.
844. See the observations on the power and prestige that law and lawyers have in America in Alexis de Toqueville, *Democracy in America*, excerpted in Presser and Zainaldin, supra note 611, at 258, 267–70.
845. For the story of how much of the ideology of what was to become American politics sprang from the English eighteenth-century centers of

manufacturing and commerce, see, e.g., Albert Goodwin, *The Friends of Liberty: The English Democratic Movement in the Age of the French Revolution* (Cambridge: Harvard University Press, 1979).

846. The Equal Rights Amendment (ERA) was first introduced to Congress in 1923. In 1972, it passed in Congress and was sent to the states for ratification. In 1982, it failed to pass constitutional muster—three/fourths of the states, or thirty-eight—by three states. The text of that amendment was as follows:

> Section 1. Equality of rights under the law shall not be denied or abridged by the United States or by any State on account of sex.
> Section 2. The Congress shall have the power to enforce, by appropriate legislation, the provisions of this Article.
> Section 3. This Amendment shall take effect two years after the date of ratification.

On the Amendment, and its failure to be ratified, see e.g., Renee Feinberg, *The Equal Rights Amendment: An Annotated Bibliography of the Issues, 1976–1985* (Westport, CO: Greenwood Press, 1986); See also Susan Louise Randall (Dissertation on file, Univ. of Utah 1979), "A Legislative History of the Equal Rights Amendment 1923–1960" (University Press Microfilms facsimile ed., 1982).

847. "Hearings on Measures to Protect the Physical Integrity of the American Flag," Hearings before the Committee on the Judiciary, United States Senate, One Hundred First Congress, First Session, on S.1338, H.R. 2978, and S.J. Res. 180 (August 1, 14, September 13, and 14, 1989), Serial N. J–101–33 (printed for the use of the Committee on the Judiciary, G.P.O., 1989), p. 186.

848. Id., at 189.

849. *Senate Comm. on Judiciary, Voluntary School Prayer Constitutional Amendment, S. Rep. No.* 165, 99th Cong., 1st Sess. (1985).

850. Walter Dellinger, "The Sound of Silence: An Epistle on Prayer and the Constitution," 95 *Yale Law Journal* 1631, 1631 (1986). In his Yale Law Journal article, Professor Dellinger made the case, now rejected by the Supreme Court, that a moment of silence (for prayer or otherwise) is a constitutionally acceptable practice even without a school prayer amendment.

851. See generally *Roe v. Wade,* 410 U.S. 113 (1973), and *Griswold v. Connecticut,* 381 U.S. 479 (1965).

852. See text accompanying notes 847–848, supra.

853. George Washington to John Armstrong, April 25, 1788, Bailyn, *Debate,* supra note 827, Vol. II, pp. 420–21.

854. Professor Tribe advocated a flag protection statute, which was passed, and contrary to Professor Tribe's prediction, was found unconstitutional by the Supreme Court. Professor Tribe lamented that a constitutional amendment was not only unnecessary, but represented dangerous trifling with the Bill of Rights. See generally "Hearings on Measures to Protect the Physical Integrity of the American Flag," Hearings before the Committee on the Judiciary, United States Senate, One Hundred First Congress, First Session, on S.1338, H.R. 2978, and S.J. Res. 180 (August 1, 14, September 13, and 14, 1989), Serial N. J–101–33 (printed for the use of the Committee on the Judiciary, G.P.O., 1989), pp. 141–171 (Testimony of Lawrence Tribe).

855. See *Federalist* 78, in Bailyn, *Debate,* supra note 827, Vol. II, pp. 467, 472.

856. See, e.g., the testimony of Dean Geoffrey R. Stone, supra note 847.

857. See Bruce Ackerman, *We the People: Foundations* (Cambridge: Harvard University Press, 1990), pp. 319–22.

BIBLIOGRAPHY

PRIMARY SOURCES

Cases

Abington School District v. Schempp, 374 U.S. 203 (1963).

Adkins v. Children's Hospital of D.C., 261 U.S. 525 (1923).

Allgeyer v. Louisiana, 165 U.S. 578 (1897).

Baker v. Carr, 369 U.S. 186 (1962).

Batson v. Kentucky, 476 U.S. 79 (1986).

Benton v. Maryland, 395 U.S. 784 (1969).

Bishop v. Wood, 426 U.S. 341 (1976).

Board of Education of the Westside Community Schools v. Mergens, 496 U.S. 226 (1990).

Brown v. Board of Education, 347 U.S. 483 (1954).

Calder v. Bull, 3 U.S. (Dallas) 386 (1798).

Chisom v. Roemer, 111 S.Ct. 2354 (1991).

City of Akron v. Akron Center for Reproductive Health, Inc. 462 U.S. 416 (1983).

Colegrove v. Green, 328 U.S. 549 (1946).

Collin v. Smith, 447 F.Supp. 676 (N.D.Ill.) *aff'd* 578 F.2d 1197, 1210 (7th Cir. 1978).

Commonwealth v. Aves, 35 Mass. (18 Pick.) 193 (1836).

Currie's Administrators v. The Mutual Assurance Society, 4 Hen. & M. (14 Va.) 315 (1809).

Bibliography

Edmonson v. Leesville Concrete Co., 500 U.S. 2077 (1991).

Eisenstadt v. Baird, 405 U.S. 438 (1972).

Employment Division v. Smith, 110 S.Ct. 1595 (1990).

Engel v. Vitale, 370 U.S. 421 (1962).

Everson v. Board of Education of Ewing Township 330 U.S. 1 (1947).

Fletcher v. Peck, 6 U.S. (6 Cranch) 87 (1810).

Garcia v. San Antonio Metro. Transit Authority, 469 U.S. 528 (1985).

Georgia v. McCollum, 112 S.Ct. 2348 (1992).

Gideon v. Wainwright, 372 U.S. 335 (1963).

Gitlow v. New York, 268 U.S. 652 (1925).

Goldman v. Weinberger, 106 S.Ct. 1310 (1985).

Green v. County School Board of New Kent, 391 U.S. 430 (1968).

Griggs v. Duke Power Co., 401 U.S. 424 (1971).

Griswold v. Connecticut, 381 U. S. 479 (1965).

Harper v. Virginia Bd. of Elections, 383 U.S. 663 (1966).

Heath v. Alabama, 472 U.S. 82 (1985).

Holden v. Hardy, 169 U.S. 366 (1898).

Ingraham v. Wright, 430 U.S. 651 (1977).

Jaffree v. Board of School Commissioners, 554 F.Supp. 1104 (S.D.Ala. 1983).

Jenkins v. Missouri, 495 U.S. 33 (1990).

Jones v. Clear Creek Independent School Dist., 930 F.2d 416 (5th Cir. Tex. 1991), *vacated and remanded* 112 S.Ct. 3020 (1992).

Jones v. Clear Creek Independent School Dist., 977 F.2d 963 (1992), *rehearing en banc denied* 983 F.2d 234 (1992), *cert. den.*, 124 L. Ed. 2d 697, 61 U.S.L.W. 3819 (U.S. 1993).

Kraskin v. Kraskin, 104 F.2d 218 (D.C.Cir., 1939).

Lamb's Chapel v. Center Moriches Union Free Sch. Dist., 113 U.S. 2141 (1992).

League of United Latin American Citizens v. Texas Att'y General, 999 F.2d 831 (1993).

Lee v. Weisman, 112 S.Ct. 2649, 120 L. Ed. 2d 467 (1992).

Lemon v. Kurtzman, 403 U.S. 602 (1971).

Lochner v. New York, 198 U.S. 45 (1905).

Malloy v. Hogan, 378 U.S. 1 (1964).

Magnolia Bar Association, Inc. v. Hawkins, 994 F.2d 1143 (1993).

Mapp v. Ohio, 367 U.S. 643 (1961).

Marbury v. Madison, 1 Cranch 137 (1803).

McCulloch v. Maryland, 17 U.S. (4 Wheat) 316 (1817).

McLaurin v. Oklahoma State Regents for Higher Education, 339 U.S. 637 (1950).

Metro Broadcasting, Inc. v. FCC, 110 S.Ct. 2997 (1990).

Michael H. v. Gerald D., 491 U.S. 110 (1989).

Minersville School District v. Gobitis, 310 U.S. 586 (1940).

Miranda v. Arizona, 384 U.S. 436 (1966).

Moore v. State, 55 U.S. (14 How.) 13 (1852).

Morehead v. New York ex rel. Tipaldo, 298 U.S. 587 (1936).

Muller v. Oregon 208 U.S. 412 (1908).

Nix v. Williams, 467 U.S. 431 (1984).

NLRB v. Jones & Laughlin Steel Corp., 301 U.S. 1 (1937).

Palko v. Connecticut, 302 U.S. 319 (1937).

People v. Defore 242 N.Y. 13; 150 N.E. 585; *cert. denied* 270 U.S. 657 (1926).

Planned Parenthood v. Casey, 112 S.Ct. 2791 (1992).

Plessy v. Ferguson, 163 U.S. 537 (1896).

Poe v. Ullman 367 U.S. 492 (1961).

Police Department of Chicago v. Mosely, 408 U.S. 92 (1972).

Powers v. Ohio, 499 U.S. 1364 (1991).

Reynolds v. Sims, 377 U.S. 533 (1964).

Richmond v. J. A. Croson Co., 488 U.S. 469 (1989).

Roe v. Wade, 410 U.S. 113 (1973).

Roth v. United States, 354 U.S. 476 (1957).

Rust v. Sullivan, 111 S.Ct. 1759 (1991).

Schechter Poultry Corp. v. United States, 295 U.S. 495 (1935).

Schneider v. State, 308 U.S. 147 (1939).

Scott v. Sandford, 19 How. (60 U.S.) 393 (1857).

Shaw v. Reno, 1993 U.S. LEXIS 4406; 125 L.Ed. 2d 511; 61 U.S.L.W. 4818 (1993).

Shelly v. Kraemer, 334 U.S. 1 (1948).

Smith v. Board of School Commissioners of Mobile County, 655 F.Supp. 939 (S.D.Ala. 1987).

Bibliography

Smith v. Board of School Commissioners of Mobile County, 827 F.2d 684 (11th Cir. 1987)

Smuck v. Hobson, 408 F.2d 175 (D.C.Cir. 1969).

Snell v. Savannah-Chatham County Bd. of Educ. 220 F. Supp. 667 (S.D.Ga. 1963), *reversed* 333 F.2d 55 (5th Cir.), *cert. denied* 379 U.S. 933 (1964).

Stanley v. Illinois, 405 U.S. 645 (1972).

Stromberg v. California, 283 U.S. 359 (1931).

Swain v. Alabama, 380 U.S. 202 (1965).

Swann v. Charlotte-Mecklenburg Board of Education, 402 U.S. 1 (1971).

Sweatt v. Painter, 339 U.S. 629 (1950).

Twining v. New Jersey, 211 U.S. 78 (1908).

United Jewish Organizations of Williamsburgh, Inc. v. Carey, 430 U.S. 144 (1977).

United States v. Callender, 25 Fed. Cas. 239 (C.C.D. Virginia, 1800).

United States v. Carolene Products Co., 304 U.S. 144 (1938).

United States v. Thomas Cooper, 25 Fed. Cas. 631 (C.C.D.Pa. 1800).

United States v. Dewey, 37 F. Supp. 449 (1941).

United States v. Dougherty, 473 F.2d 1113 (D.C.Cir., 1972).

United States v. Henfield, 11 Fed.Cas. 1099 (C.C.D.Pa., 1793).

United States v. Hudson & Goodwin, 11 U.S. (7 Cranch) 32 (1812).

United States v. Insurgents, 26 F.Cas. 499 (C.C.D.Pa. 1795).

United States v. E.C. Knight Co., 156 U.S. 1 (1895).

United States v. Leon, 468 U.S. 897 (1984).

United States v. Lyon, 15 Fed. Cas. 1183 (C.C.D. Vermont, 1798).

United States v. Nixon, 418 U.S. 683 (1974).

United States v. Trans-Missouri Freight Association 166 U. S. 290 (1897).

United States v. Robert Worrall, 28 Fed. Cas. 774 (C.C.D.Pa. 1798).

Van Horne's Lessee v. Dorrance, 28 F.Cas. 1012, 2 Dal. 304 (C.C.D.Pa., 1795).

Village of Skokie v. Nat'l Socialist Party of America, 432 U.S. 43 (1977).

Vitek v. Jones, 445 U.S. 480 (1980).

Wallace v. Jaffree, 472 U.S. 38 (1985).

Ward's Cove Packing Co. v. Atonio, 490 U.S. 642 (1989).

Ware v. Hylton, 3 U.S. (Dallas) 199 (1796).

West Coast Hotel v. Parrish, 300 U.S. 379 (1937).

West Virginia State Board of Education v. Barnette, 319 U.S. 624 (1943).

366

Bibliography

Wheeldin v. Wheeler, 373 U.S. 647 (1963).

Young v. American Mini Theatres, 427 U.S. 50 (1976).

Zobrest v. Catalina Foothills Sch. Dist., 113 S.Ct. 2462 (1993).

Manuscripts

Samuel Chase, Manuscript Jury Charge Book, Vertical File, Manuscript Division of the Maryland Historical Society, Baltimore (1798–1800, 1802–03, and 1805–06).

Printed Collections

Bernard Bailyn, editor, *The Debate on the Constitution* (New York: Library of America, 2 vols., 1993).

Bernard Bailyn, editor, *Pamphlets of the American Revolution* (Cambridge: Harvard University Press, 1965).

Harry A. Blackmun: *Hearing before the Senate Judiciary Committee*, 91st Cong., 2d Sess. 7 (Government Printing Office, 1970).

Stephen Douglas, "Mr. Douglas' Speech, First Lincoln-Douglas Debate, Ottawa, Illinois," reprinted in *Abraham Lincoln: Speeches and Writings 1832–1858* (New York: Library of America, 1989), p. 495.

Max Farrand, editor, *Records of the Federal Convention of 1787* (New Haven: Yale Univeristy Press, 1911; rev. ed. in 4 vols., 1937; rpr. 1966).

William W. Fisher III, Morton J. Horwitz, and Thomas A. Reid, *American Legal Realism* (New York: Oxford University Press, 1993).

Julius Goebel, Jr., et al, eds., *The Law Practice of Alexander Hamilton: Documents and Commentary* (New York: Columbia University Press, 1964).

Gerald Gunther, *Constitutional Law: Cases and Materials* (Minela, NY: Foundation Press, 9th ed. 1975).

Hearing of the Senate Judiciary Committee, Morning Session, September 16, 1991 (Federal News Service, on LEXIS).

Hearings on Measures to Protect the Physical Integrity of the American Flag, Hearings before the Committee on the Judiciary, United States Senate One Hundred First Congress, First Session, on S.1338, H.R. 2978, and S.J. Res. 180 (August 1, 14, September 13, and 14, 1989), Serial N. J–101–33 (printed for the use of the Committee on the Judiciary (Government Printing Office, 1989)).

Bibliography

Senate Judiciary Committee, *Hearings on Voluntary School Prayer Constitutional Amendment, S. Rep. No. 165,* 99th Cong., 1st Sess. (G.P.O., 1985).

Senate Judiciary Committee, *Hearings on the Confirmation of Ruth Bader Ginsburg as Associate Justice of the United States Supreme Court,* July 22, 1993 (Federal News Service, on LEXIS).

Russell Kirk, editor, *The Portable Conservative Reader* (Harmondsworth: Penguin Books, 1982).

Thomas Jefferson, *Writings* (New York: Library of America, 1984).

MacNeil/Lehrer NewsHour, April 30, 1992 (Transcript, on NEXIS).

James Madison, "Memorial and Remonstrance against Religious Assesments," 1785, in Robert A. Rutland & William M.E. Rachal, editors, *Papers of James Madison* (Charlottesville: University Press of Virginia, 1973), vol. 8, p. 295.

Maeva Marcus, James R. Perry, et al, editors, *The Documentary History of the Supreme Court of the United States, 1789–1800: Appointments and Proceedings,* Vol. 1 (New York: Columbia University Press, 1985); *The Justices on Circuit, 1789–1800,* Vol. 2 (New York: Columbia University Press, 1988).

James Madison, Alexander Hamilton, and John Jay, *The Federalist Papers* (Isaac Kramnick editor, Harmondsworth: Penguin Books, 1987).

Griffith J. McRee, *Life and Correspondence of James Iredell,* (New York: Peter Smith, 1949).

The National Intelligencer, Philadelphia, August 10, and August 12, 1803.

Richard A. Posner, editor, *The Essential Holmes* (Chicago: University of Chicago Press, 1992).

Stephen B. Presser & Jamil S. Zainaldin, *Law and Jurisprudence in American History* (St. Paul: West Publishing Co., 2nd ed. 1989).

Ellis Sandoz, editor, *Political Sermons of the Founding Era 1730–1805* (Indiniapolis: Liberty Press, 1991).

Fred R. Shapiro, editor, *The Oxford Dictionary of American Legal Quotations* (New York: Oxford University Press, 1993).

The George Washington Papers (selected, edited, and interpreted by Frank Donovan) (New York: Dodd, Mead & Co., 1964).

Francis Wharton, editor, *State Trials of the United States During the Administrations of Washington and Adams* (Philadelphia: Carey and Hart, 1849).

James Wilson, *The Works of James Wilson* (Robert G. McCloskey, editor) (Cambridge: Harvard University Press, 1967).

SECONDARY SOURCES

Books

Bruce Ackerman, *We the People: Foundations* (Cambridge: Harvard University Press, 1991).

Nelson W. Aldrich, Jr., *Old Money: The Mythology of America's Upper Class* (New York: Knopf, 1988).

Hadley Arkes, *Beyond the Constitution* (Princeton: Princeton University Press, 1990).

Jerold Auerbach, *Rabbis and Lawyers: The Journey from Torah to Constitution* (Bloomington: Indiana University Press, 1990).

Bernard Bailyn, *The Ordeal of Thomas Hutchinson* (Cambridge: Harvard University Press, 1974).

Luther Baldwin, *Whiskey Rebels: The Story of a Frontier Uprising* (Pittsburgh: University of Pittsburgh Press, rev. ed. 1968).

Liva Baker, *The Justice from Beacon Hill: The Life and Times of Oliver Wendell Holmes* (New York: Harper Collins, 1991).

Carl L. Becker, *The Heavenly City of the Eighteenth Century Philosophers* (New Haven: Yale University Press, 1932).

Robert Bellah, et. al., *Habits of the Heart: Individualism and Commitment in American Life* (Berkeley: University of California Press, 1985).

Raoul Berger, *Government by Judiciary* (Cambridge: Harvard University Press, 1977).

Richard B. Bernstein with Jerome Agel, *Amending America: If We Love the Constitution So Much, Why Do We Keep Trying to Change It?* (New York: Times Books, 1993).

Albert J. Beveridge, *The Life of John Marshall* (Boston: Houghton-Mifflin, 1919).

Alexander Bickel, *The Supreme Court and the Idea of Progress* (New York: Harper and Row, 1970).

Black's Law Dictionary (St. Paul: West Publishing Co., 6th ed., 1990).

William Blackstone, *Commentaries on the Law of England* (originally published 1765, Chicago: University of Chicago reprint, 1979).

Allan Bloom, *The Closing of the American Mind: How Higher Education Has Failed Democracy and Impoverished the Souls of Today's Students* (New York: Simon & Schuster, 1987).

Daniel J. Boorstin, *The Mysterious Science of the Law* (Cambridge: Harvard University Press, 1941).

Bibliography

Robert Bork, *The Tempting of America: The Political Seduction of the Law* (New York: Free Press, 1990).

Stephen R. Boyd, editor, *The Whiskey Rebellion: Past and Present Perspectives* (Westport, CT: Greenwood Press, 1985).

David Brock, *The Real Anita Hill: The Untold Story* (New York: Free Press, 1993).

Richard Brookhiser, *The Way of the Wasp: How it Made America and How It Can Save It . . . So to Speak* (New York: Free Press, 1991).

Patrick J. Buchanan, *Right from the Beginning* (Washington, D.C.: Regnery Gateway, 1990).

Edmund Burke, *Reflections on the Revolution in France* (Harmondsworth: Penguin Books, 1969).

Robert A. Burt, *The Constitution in Conflict* (Cambridge: Harvard University Press, 1992).

Denise Lardner Carmody and John Tully Carmody, *The Republic of Many Mansions: Foundations of American Religious Thought* (New York: Paragon House, 1990).

Stephen Carter, *The Culture of Disbelief: How American Law and Politics Trivialize Religious Devotion* (New York: Basic Books, 1993).

Stephen Carter, *Reflections of an Affirmative Action Baby* (New York: Basic Books, 1991).

Robert Lowry Clinton, *Marbury v. Madison and Judicial Review* (Lawrence: Kansas University Press, 1989).

Naomi W. Cohen, *Jews in Christian America: The Pursuit of Religious Equality* (New York: Oxford University Press, 1992).

Robert L. Cord, *Separation of Church and State: Historical Fact and Current Fiction* (New York: Lambeth Press, 1988).

Robert Cover, *Justice Accused: Antislavery and the Judicial Process* (New Haven: Yale University Press, 1975).

William Winslow Crosskey, *Politics and the Constitution* (Chicago: University of Chicago Press, 1953).

H. T. Dickenson, *Liberty and Property: Political Ideology in Eighteenth-Century Britain* (London: Weidenfeld and Nicolson, 1977).

Donald A. Downs, *Nazis in Skokie* (South Bend: University of Notre Dame Press, 1985).

Ronald Dworkin, *Life's Dominion: An Argument about Abortion, Euthanasia, and Individual Freedom* (New York: Knopf, 1993).

Bibliography

Frank Easterbrook and Daniel Fischel, *The Economic Structure of Corporate Law* (Cambridge: Harvard University Press, 1991).

Terry Eastland and William J. Bennett, *Counting by Race: Equality from the Founding Fathers to Bakke* (New York: Basic Books, 1979).

Terry Eastland, *Energy in the Executive: The Case for the Strong Presidency* (New York: Free Press, 1992).

Terry Eastland, editor, *Religious Liberty in the Supreme Court: The Cases that Define the Debate Over Church and State* (Washington: Ethics and Public Policy Center, 1993).

James W. Ely, Jr., *The Guardian of Every Other Right* (New York: Oxford University Press, 1992).

Thomas Emerson, *The System of Freedom of Expression* (New York: Random House, 1970).

Richard Epstein, *Takings: Private Property and the Power of Eminent Domain* (Cambridge: Harvard University Press, 1985).

Renee Feinberg, *The Equal Rights Amendment: An Annotated Bibliography of the Issues, 1976–1985* (Westport, CT: Greenwood Press, 1986).

Felix Frankfurter & James Landes, *The Business of the Supreme Court* (New York: Macmillan, 1971).

Mary Ann Glendon, *Abortion and Divorce in Western Law* (Cambridge: Harvard University Press, 1987).

Mary Ann Glendon, *Rights Talk: The Impoverishment of Political Discourse* (New York: Free Press, 1991).

Julius Goebel, Jr. I *A History of the Supreme Court of the United States: Antecedents and Beginnings to 1801* (New York: Macmillan, 1971).

Joseph Goldstein, *The Intelligible Constitution: The Supreme Court's Obligation to Maintain the Constitution as Something We the People Can Understand* (New York: Oxford University Press, 1992).

Albert Goodwin, *The Friends of Liberty: The English Democratic Movement in the Age of the French Revolution* (Cambridge: Harvard University Press, 1979).

John Grisham, *The Firm* (New York: Doubleday, 1991).

Lani Guinier, *The Tyranny of the Majority: Fundamental Fairness in Representative Democracy,* (New York: Martin Kessler Books/The Free Press, 1994).

Kermit Hall, editor, *The Oxford Companion to the United States Supreme Court* (New York: Oxford University Press, 1992).

Learned Hand, *The Bill of Rights: The Oliver Wendell Holmes Lectures* (Cambridge: Harvard University Press, 1958).

371

Bibliography

Jeffrey Hart, *Acts of Recovery: Essays on Culture and Politics* (Hanover and London: University Press of New England, 1989).

Eugene W. Hickok, Jr. editor, *The Bill of Rights: Original Meaning and Current Understanding* (Charlottesville: University Press of Virginia, 1991).

Eugene W. Hickok and Gary L. McDowell, *Justice vs. Law: Courts and Politics in American Society* (New York: Free Press, 1993).

Morton J. Horwitz, *The Transformation of American Law 1780–1860* (Cambridge: Harvard University Press, 1977).

Thomas Jefferson, *The Jefferson Bible: The Life and Morals of Jesus of Nazareth* (with an introduction by F. Forrester Church and an afterword by Jaroslav Pelican, Boston: Beacon Press, 1989).

Linda K. Kerber, *Federalists in Dissent: Imagery and Ideology in Jeffersonian America* (Ithaca: Cornell University Press, 1970).

Alfred H. Kelly, Winfred A. Harbison, and Herman Belz, *The American Constitution: Its Origins and Development* (New York: Norton, 7th ed., 1991).

Russell Kirk, *America's British Culture* (New Brunswick: Transaction Publishers, 1993).

Russell Kirk, *The Conservative Constitution* (Washington, DC: Regnery Gateway, 1990).

Russell Kirk, *The Conservative Mind from Burke to Santayana* (Chicago and Washington, D.C.: Regnery Books, 7th rev. ed., 1986).

Richard Kluger, *Simple Justice* (New York: Knopf, 1975).

Anthony T. Kronman, *The Lost Lawyer: Failing Ideals of the Legal Profession* (Cambridge: Harvard University Press, 1993).

Thomas Kuhn, *The Structure of Scientific Revolutions* (Chicago: University of Chicago Press, 2nd ed. 1971).

Andrew Kull, *The Color-Blind Constitution* (Cambridge: Harvard University Press, 1992).

L. A. Times Staff, *Understanding the Riots: Los Angeles before and after the Rodney King Case* (Los Angeles, CA: Los Angeles Times, 1992).

H.H. Walker Lewis, *Without Fear or Favor: A Biography of Chief Justice Roger Brooke Taney* (Boston: Houghton Mifflin, 1965).

Leonard W. Levy, *Original Intent and the Framers' Constitution* (New York: Macmillan, 1988).

C. S. Lewis, *Mere Christianity* (New York: Macmillan Co., 1958).

Stephen Macedo, *Liberal Virtues: Citizenship, Virtue, and Community in Liberal Constitutionalism* (New York: Oxford University Press, 1990).

372

Bibliography

Myron Magnet, *The Dream and the Nightmare: The Sixties Legacy to the Underclass* (New York: William Morrow, 1993).

Maeva Marcus, editor, *Origins of the Federal Judiciary: Essays on the Judiciary Act of 1789* (New York: Oxford University Press, 1992).

James McClellan, *Joseph Story and the American Constitution: A Study in Political and Legal Thought with Selected Writings* (Norman: University of Oklahoma Press, 1971).

Forrest McDonald, *Alexander Hamilton: A Biography* (New York: Norton, 1979).

Forrest McDonald, *Novus Ordo Seclorum: The Intellectual Origins of the Constitution* (Lawrence: University Press of Kansas, 1985).

John Marshall, *The Life of George Washington* (New York: Walton Book Co., 1930).

Richard K. Matthews, *The Radical Politics of Thomas Jefferson: A Revisionist View* (Lawrence: University Press of Kansas, 1984).

J. Miller, *Crisis in Freedom: The Alien and Sedition Acts* (Boston: Little, Brown, 1951).

William E. Nelson & Robert C. Palmer, editors, *Liberty and Community: Constitution and Rights in the Early American Republic* (New York: Oceana Publications, 1987).

R. Kent Newmyer, *Supreme Court Justice Joseph Story: Statesman of the Old Republic* (Chapel Hill: University of North Carolina Press, 1985).

Sheldon M. Novick, *Honorable Justice: The Life of Oliver Wendell Holmes* (Boston: Little Brown, 1989).

Conor Cruise O'Brien, *The Great Melody: A Thematic Biography of Edmund Burke* (Chicago: University of Chicago Press, 1992).

David O'Brien, *Judicial Roulette: Report of the Twentieth Century Fund Task Force on Judicial Selection* (Washington, D.C.: Priority Press, 1988).

Merrill Peterson, *Adams and Jefferson: A Revolutionary Dialogue* (Athens: University of Georgia Press, 1976).

Stephen B. Presser, *The Original Misunderstanding: The English, the Americans, and the Dialectic of Federalist Jurisprudence* (Durham: Carolina Academic Press, 1991).

Susan Louise Randall (Dissertation on file, Univ. of Utah 1979) *A Legislative History of the Equal Rights Amendment 1923–1960* (University Press Microfilms facsimile ed., 1982).

Jack N. Rakove, editor, *Interpreting the Constitution* (Boston: Northeastern University Press, 1990).

373

Bibliography

Ronald Reagan, *Abortion and the Conscience of the Nation* (Nashville: Thomas Nelson Publishers, 1984).

Martin Redish, *Freedom of Expression: A Critical Analysis* (Charlottesville: Michie Co., 1984).

A. G. Roeber, *Faithful Magistrates and Republican Lawyers: Creators of a Virginia Legal Culture 1680–1810* (Chapel Hill: University of North Carolina Press, 1981).

Norman L. Rosenberg, *Protecting the Best Men: An Interpretive History of the Law of Libel* (Chapel Hill: University of North Carolina Press, 1986).

Roger Rosenblatt, *Life Itself: Abortion in the American Mind* (New York: Random House, 1992).

J.J. Rousseau, *The Social Contract* (Harmondsworth: Penguin Books, 1968).

Michael Sandel, *Liberalism and the Limits of Justice* (Cambridge and New York: Cambridge University Press, 1982).

John Sanderson, *Biography of the Signers to the Declaration of Independence* (Philadelphia: R.W. Pomeroy, 1827).

Ellis Sandoz, *A Government of Laws: Political Theory, Religion, and the American Founding* (Baton Rouge: Louisiana State University Press, 1990).

Ellis Sandoz, editor, *The Roots of Liberty: Magna Carta, Ancient Constitution, and the Anglo-American Tradition of Rule of Law* (Baton Rouge: Louisiana State University Press, 1993).

Charles B. Sanford, *The Religious Life of Thomas Jefferson* (Charlottesville: University Press of Virginia, 1984).

Bernard Schwartz, *Swann's Way: The School Busing Case and the Supreme Court* (New York: Oxford University Press, 1986).

Geoffrey Seed, *James Wilson* (Millwood, NY: KTO Press, 1978).

Paul Simon, *Advice and Consent* (Washington, D.C.: National Press Books, 1992).

Thomas P. Slaughter, *The Whiskey Rebellion: Frontier Epilogue to the American Revolution* (Westport, CT: Greenwood Press, 1986).

Charles Page Smith, *James Wilson* (Chapel Hill: University of North Carolina Press, 1956).

James M. Smith, *Freedom's Fetters: The Alien and Sedition Laws and American Civil Liberties* (Ithaca: Cornell University Press, 1956).

Dinesh D'Souza, *Illiberal Education: The Politics of Race and Sex on Campus* (New York: Free Press, 1991).

Shelby Steele, *The Content of Our Character: A New Vision of Race in America* (New York: St. Martins Press, 1990).

374

Bibliography

Donald H. Stewart, *The Opposition Press of the Federalist Period* (Albany: State University of New York Press, 1969).

Shannon C. Stimson, *The American Revolution in the Law: Anglo-American Jurisprudence Before John Marshall* (Princeton: Princeton University Press, 1990).

Joseph Story, *Commentaries on the Constitution of the United States; with a Preliminary Review of the Constitutional History of the Colonies and States Before the Adoption of the Constitution* (Boston: Hilliard Gray, and Co. and Cambridge: Brown, Shattuck and Co., 1833, reprinted Durham: Carolina Academic Press, 1987).

Cass R. Sunstein, *Democracy and the Problem of Free Speech* (New York: Free Press, 1993).

Jared Taylor, *Paved with Good Intentions: The Failure of Race Relations in Contemporary America* (New York: Carroll & Graf, 1992).

Lawrence Tribe, *Abortion: The Clash of Absolutes* (New York: Norton 1990).

Mark V. Tushnet, *The NAACP's Legal Strategy against Segregated Education 1925–1950* (Chapel Hill: University of North Carolina Press, 1987).

Mark Tushnet, *Red, White, and Blue: A Critical Analysis of Constitutional Law* (Cambridge: Harvard University Press, 1988).

Roberto M. Unger, *The Critical Legal Studies Movement* (Cambridge: Harvard University Press, 1986).

Roberto M. Unger, *Knowledge and Politics* (New York: Free Press, 1975).

G. Edward White, *Justice Oliver Wendell Holmes and the Inner Self* (New York: Oxford University Press, 1993).

Christopher Wolfe, *The Rise of Modern Judicial Review: From Constitutional Interpretation to Judge-Made Law* (New York: Basic Books, 1986).

William M. Wiecek, *The Guarantee Clause of the U.S. Constitution* (Ithaca: Cornell University Press, 1972).

Garry Wills, *Inventing America: Jefferson's Declaration of Independence* (New York: Doubleday and Co., Inc., 1978).

Garry Wills, *Lincoln at Gettysburg: The Words that Remade America* (New York: Simon & Schuster, 1992).

Garry Wills, *Under God* (New York: Simon and Schuster, 1990).

Gordon S. Wood, *The Creation of the American Republic 1776–1787* (Chapel Hill: University of North Carolina Press, 1969).

Bibliography

Articles

T. Alexander Aleinikoff, "Constitutional Law in the Age of Balancing," 96 *Yale Law Journal* 943 (1987).

Henry Allen, "Hot Disputes and Cool Sowell," *Washington Post*, October 1, 1981, p. C1.

Ronald J. Allen, "Freedom from Double Jeopardy, Our Lost Liberty," *Wall Street Journal*, March 17, 1993, p. A15.

David E. Anderson, "Signing of Religious Freedom Act Culmin tes Three-Year Push," *Washington Post*, November 20, 1993, p. C6.

Associated Press release, "Federal Appeals Judge Criticizes 2 Jurists, The New York Times," *Orlando Sentinel*, June 14, 1992, p. A23.

Richard L. Aynes, "On Misreading John Bingham and the Fourteenth Amendment," 103 *Yale Law Journal* 57 (1993).

J.M. Balkin, "What Is a Postmodern Constitutionalism?" 90 *Michigan Law Review* 1966 (1992).

C. Edwin Baker, "Scope of the First Amendment Freedom of Speech," 25 *University of California at Los Angeles Law Review* 964 (1978).

Gordon E. Baker, "Reynolds v. Sims," in Kermit Hall, editor, *The Oxford Companion to the United States Supreme Court* (New York: Oxford University Press, 1992), p. 733.

Susan Baxter, "The Last Self-Help Article You'll Ever Need," 26 *Psychology Today* 70 (1993).

William J. Bennett, "Commuter Massacre, Our Warning," *Wall Street Journal*, December 10, 1993.

Raoul Berger, "The Constitution and the Rule of Law," 1 *Western New England Law Review* 261 (1978), reprinted in Raoul Berger, *Selected Writings on the Constitution* (Cumberland, VA: James River Press, 1987), p. 292.

Richard L. Berke, "With a Crackle, Religion Enters G.O.P Meeting," *New York Times*, November 18, 1992, p. A23.

Alexander M. Bickel, "The Original Understanding and the Segregation Decision," 69 *Harvard Law Review* 1 (1955).

Robert H. Bork, "Neutral Principles and Some First Amendment Problems," 47 *Indiana Law Journal* 1 (1971).

Gerard V. Bradley, "Beguiled: Free Exercise Exemptions and the Siren Song of Liberalism," 20 *Hofstra Law Review* 245 (1991).

Susan W. Brenner, "S.C.A.R.F.A.C.E.: A Speculation on Double Jeopardy and Compound Criminal Liability," 27 *New England Law Review* 915 (1993).

Bibliography

Pat Buchanan, "Crossfire," CNN Transcript, June 7, 1993 (LEXIS).

Paul Carrington, "Diversity!" 1992 *Utah Law Review* 1105.

Paul Carrington, "Of Law and the River," 34 *Journal of Legal Education* 222 (1984).

Stephen L. Carter, "Does the First Amendment Protect More Than Free Speech?" 33 *William & Mary Law Review* 871 (1992).

Stephen Chapman, "Abortion Rights and the Limits of Public Tolerance," *Chicago Tribune*, April 22, 1993, Section 1, p. 25.

Stephen Chapman, "Abortion, Slavery Analogy: It's Entirely Too Accurate," *Orlando Sentinel*, July 30, 1993, p. A13.

Mark Curriden, "Around the South: Tennessee Lawsuit," *Atlanta Constitution*, November 16, 1993, p. A3.

Michael Kent Curtis, "Equal Protection," in Kermit Hall, editor, *The Oxford Companion to the United States Supreme Court* (New York: Oxford University Press, 1992), p. 257.

Michael Kent Curtis, "Incorporation Doctrine," in Kermit Hall, editor, *The Oxford Companion to the United States Supreme Court* (New York: Oxford University Press, 1992), p. 426.

Robert Dawidoff, "The Jeffersonian Option," 21 *Political Theory* 437 (1993).

Thomas Y. Davies, "Exclusionary Rule," in Kermit Hall, editor, *The Oxford Companion to the United States Supreme Court* (New York: Oxford University Press, 1992), p. 264.

Walter Dellinger, "The Sound of Silence: An Epistle on Prayer and the Constitution," 95 *Yale Law Journal* 1631 (1986).

Finley Peter Dunne, "The Supreme Court's Decisions," in *Dissertations by Mr. Dooley* (New York: Harper, 1906), p. 21.

Terry Eastland, "Mainstream Radical," *American Spectator*, November 1993, p. 66.

Terry Eastland, "Religion, Politics & the Clintons," *Commentary*, January 1994, p. 40.

Editorial, "Mississippi," *Wall Street Journal*, December 6, 1993, p. A14.

Editorial, "Moseley-Braun has a .500 day," *Chicago Tribune*, July 27, 1993, p. 12.

Editorial, "Moseley-Braun Speaks Out," *San Francisco Chronicle*, July 26, 1993, p. A12.

Editorial, "Ms. Moseley-Braun's Majestic Moment," *New York Times*, June 24, 1993, Section 1, p. 18.

Bibliography

Editorial, "New Court Pick Fits Bill," *Christian Science Monitor*, June 16, 1993, p. 18.

Editorial, "Not a Prayer," *Boston Globe*, June 13, 1993, p. 84.

Walter Ehrlich, "Roger Brooke Taney," in Kermit Hall, editor, *The Oxford Companion to the United States Supreme Court* (New York: Oxford University Press, 1992), p. 857.

James W. Ely, Jr., "Four Horsemen," in Kermit Hall, editor, *The Oxford Companion to the United States Supreme Court* (New York: Oxford University Press, 1992), p. 309.

Thomas Emerson, "Toward a General Theory of the First Amendment," 72 *Yale Law Journal* 877 (1963).

Charles Fairman, "Does the Fourteenth Amendment Incorporate the Bill of Rights?" 2 *Stanford Law Review* 5 (1949).

Henry L. Feingold, "Book Review," 98 *American History Review* 1672 (1993).

Suzanne Fields, "Whitewashing Racism," *Washington Times*, July 29, 1993, p. G1.

Kirk Fordice, "Symposium, Who's Afraid of the Religious Right?" remarks of Kirk Fordice, *National Review*, December 27, 1993, p. 39.

Charles Fried, "Manners Makyth Man: The Prose Style of Justice Scalia," 16 *Harvard Journal of Law and Public Policy* 529 (1993).

Peter Gabel & Duncan Kennedy, "Roll Over Beethoven," 36 *Stanford Law Review* 1 (1984).

Ruth Bader Ginsberg, "Speaking in a Judicial Voice," 67 *New York Univeristy Law Review* 1185 (1992).

Mary Ann Glendon, "What's Wrong with the Elite Law Schools," *Wall Street Journal*, June 8, 1993, p. A14.

John D. Gordan III, "United States v. Joseph Ravara: Presumptuous Evidence," "Too Many Lawyers," and "A Federal Common Law of Crime," in Maeva Marcus, editor, *Origins of the Federal Judiciary: Essays on the Judiciary Act of 1789* (New York: Oxford University Press, 1992).

Robert Gordon, " 'Of Law and the River,' and of Nihilism and Academic Freedom," 35 *Journal of Legal Education* 1 (1985).

"Governor Says He's Sorry for 'Christian' Comment," *Orlando Sentinel*, November 21, 1992, p. A16.

Lino A. Graglia, "Affirmative Discrimination," *National Review*, July 5, 1993, p. 26.

Lino A. Graglia, "When Honesty is 'Simply Impractical' for the Supreme

Bibliography

Court: How the Constitution Came to Require Busing for School Racial Balance," 85 *Michigan Law Review* 1153 (1987).

Blu Greenberg, "Ginsburg Nomination: Good Vibes," *New York Newsday,* June 22, 1993, p. 77.

Linda Greenhouse, "Religious Groups Can Use Schools," *New York Times,* June 8, 1993, p. A1.

Richard Grenier, "Profiles in timidity . . . and absurdity," *Washington Times,* July 28, 1993, p. G1.

Tom Grey, "Do We Have an Unwritten Constitution?" 27 *Stanford Law Review* 703 (1975).

Bernard Grofman, "Would Vince Lombardi Have Been Right If He Had Said: 'When It comes to Redistricting, Race Isn't Everything, It's the Only Thing'?" 14 *Cardozo Law Review* 1237 (1993).

Jane Halsema, "Law Firms Offer Second Path for Non-Partners," *San Diego Business Journal,* January 2, 1989, p. 22.

Henry M. Hart, Jr., "The Relations between State and Federal Law," 54 *Columbia Law Review* 489.

Suzette Hemberger, "Dead Stepfathers," 85 *Northwestern University Law Review* 220 (1990).

Michael deCourcy Hinds, "Robertson Trying to Put Prayer in School," *New York Times,* April 16, 1993, p. A12.

Russell Hittinger, "Liberalism and the American Natural Law Tradition," 25 *Wake Forest Law Review* 429 (1990).

Peter Charles Hoffer, "Felix Frankfurter," in Kermit Hall, editor, *The Oxford Companion to the United States Supreme Court* (New York: Oxford University Press, 1992), p. 314.

Morton J. Horwitz, "Forward: The Constitution of Change: Legal Fundamentality Without Fundamentalism," 107 *Harvard Law Review* 30 (1993).

Morton J. Horwitz, "Republicanism and Liberalism in American Constitutional Thought," 29 *William and Mary Law Review* 57 (1987).

Dennis J. Hutchinson, "Brown v. Board of Education," in Kermit Hall, editor, *The Oxford Companion to the United States Supreme Court* (New York: Oxford University Press, 1992), p. 95.

Dennis J. Hutchinson, "Green v. County School Board of New Kent County," in Kermit Hall, editor, *The Oxford Companion to the United States Supreme Court* (New York: Oxford University Press, 1992), p. 347.

Dennis J. Hutchinson, "Unanimity and Desegregation," 68 *Georgetown Law Journal* 1 (1979).

Bibliography

Illinois Legal Times Roundtable, "Associates Tell All," *Illinois Legal Times*, June 1991, p. 1.

James E. Jones, Jr., "Richmond v. J.A. Croson Co.," in Kermit Hall, editor, *The Oxford Companion to the United States Supreme Court* (New York: Oxford University Press, 1992), p. 736.

Mary Jordan, "More Attorneys Making a Motion for the Pursuit of Happiness," *Washington Post*, September 4, 1993, p. A3.

Yale Kamisar, "Miranda v. Arizona," in Kermit Hall, editor, *The Oxford Companion to the United States Supreme Court* (New York: Oxford University Press, 1992), p. 552.

Thomas E. Kauper, "Penumbras, Peripheries, Emanations, Things Fundamental and Forgotten: The *Griswold* Case," 64 *Michigan Law Review* 235 (1965).

David J. Katz, "Grand Jury Charges Delivered by Supreme Court Justices Riding Circuit During the 1790s," 14 *Cardozo Law Review* 1045 (1993).

Richard S. Kay, "Adherence to the Original Intentions in Constitutional Adjudication: Three Objections and Responses," 82 *Northwestern University Law Review* 226 (1988).

Richard S. Kay, "The Illegality of the Constitution," 4 *Constitutional Commentary* 57 (1987).

Martin Luther King, Jr., "Soaring Words that Focused a Movement [The "I have a dream" speech]," *Chicago Tribune*, August 22, 1993, Section 4, p. 1.

Karl Klare, "Judicial Deradicalization of the Wagner Act and the Origins of Modern Legal Consciousness, 1937–1941," 62 *Minnesota Law Review* 265 (1978).

James T. Kloppenberg, "The Virtues of Liberalism: Christianity, Republicanism, and Ethics in Early American Political Discourse," 74 *Journal of American History* 9 (1987).

Joseph F. Kobylka, "Abington School District v. Schempp," in Kermit Hall, editor, *The Oxford Companion to the United States Supreme Court* (New York: Oxford University Press, 1992), p. 1.

Donald P. Kommers, "Malloy v. Hogan," in Kermit Hall, editor, *The Oxford Companion to the United States Supreme Court* (New York: Oxford University Press, 1992), p. 519.

David Lauter, "Hillary-Bashing Becoming a Part of GOP Campaign," *Los Angeles Times*, August 19, 1992, p. A1.

Gary Lawson and Steven Calabresi, "Foreword: The Constitution of Responsibility," 77 *Cornell Law Review* 955 (1992).

Bibliography

Douglas Laycock, " 'Nonpreferential' Aid to Religion: A False Claim about Original Intent," 27 *William & Mary Law Review* 875 (1986).

Andrew Leigh, "Leaders & Success," *Investor's Business Daily*, October 11, 1991, p. 1.

William E. Leuchtenburg, "The Origins of Franklin D. Roosevelt's 'Court-Packing' Plan," 1966 *Supreme Court Review* 347.

Ralph Lerner, "The Supreme Court as Republican Schoolmaster," 1967 *Supreme Court Review* 127.

Elizabeth F. Loftus and Laura A. Rosenwald, "The Rodney King Videotape: Why the Case Was Not Black and White," 66 *Southern California Law Review* 1637 (1993).

Stephen Macedo, "Morality and the Constitution: Toward a Synthesis for 'Earthbound' Interpreters," 61 *University of Cinncinnati Law Review* 29 (1992).

Earl M. Maltz, "The Failure of Attacks on Constitutional Originalism," 4 *Constitutional Commentary* 43 (1987).

Earl M. Maltz, "Foreward: The Appeal of Originalism," 1987 *Utah Law Review* 773.

Earl M. Maltz, "Some New Thought on an Old Problem — The Role of the Intent of the Framers in Constitutional Theory," 63 *Boston University Law Review* (1983).

"Titus Manlius" [Alexander Hamilton], *The Stand* (April 7, 1798).

Maeva Marcus and Natalie Wexler, "The Judiciary Act of 1789: Political Compromise or Constitutional Interpretation?" in Maeva Marcus, editor, *Origins of the Federal Judiciary: Essays on the Judiciary Act of 1789* (New York: Oxford University Press, 1992), pp. 13–39.

Ruth Marcus, "Gloom at the Top: Why Young Lawyers Bail Out," *Washington Post*, May 31, 1987, p. C1.

Mari J. Matsuda, "Looking to the Bottom: Critical Legal Studies and Reparations," 22 *Harvard Civil Rights-Civil Liberties Law Review* 323 (1987).

Michael W. McConnell, "Accommodations of Religion: An Update and a Response to the Critics," 60 *George Washington Law Review* 685 (1992).

Edwin Meese III, "Interpreting the Constitution," Address before the American Bar Association, Washington, D.C., July 9, 1985.

Philip C. Metzger, "Politics and the High Court," *New York Times*, July 1, 1993.

Frank I. Michaelman, "Foreword: Traces of Self-government," 100 *Harvard Law Review* 4 (1986).

Bibliography

Frank Michaelman, "Law's Republic," 97 *Yale Law Journal* 1493 (1988).

Liza Mundy, "The pro bono hustle; Legal work performed without charge for a worthy cause," *Washington Monthly*, September 1989.

Richard S. Myers, "Book Review," 42 *Journal of Legal Education* 619 (1992).

"Nation in Brief: ACLU Says Officers' Retrial is Illegal Double Jeopardy," *Atlanta Constitution*, April 5, 1993, p. A4.

William E. Nelson, "Changing Conceptions of Judicial Review: The Evolution of Constitutional Theory in the States 1790–1860," 120 *University of Pennsylvania Law Review* 1166 (1972).

Jacob Neusner, "Who's Afraid of the Religious Right?" *National Review*, December 27, 1993, p. 37.

R. Kent Newmyer, "Story, Joseph" in Kermit Hall, editor, *The Oxford Companion to the United States Supreme Court* (New York: Oxford University Press, 1992), p. 841.

Gene R. Nichol, "Constitutional Judgment," 91 *Michigan Law Review* 1107 (1993).

Robert C. Palmer, "Liberties as Constitutional Provisions: 1776–1791," in William E. Nelson & Robert C. Palmer, *Liberty and Community: Constitution and Rights in the Early American Republic* (New York: Oceana Publications, 1987), p. 55.

Roger Parloff, "Maybe the Jury Was Right," *American Lawyer*, June 1992, p. 7.

Michael Stokes Paulsen, "Book Review," 10 *Constitutional Commentary* 221 (1993).

Michael Stokes Paulsen, "The Many Faces of 'Judicial Restraint,' " 1993 *Public Interest Law Review* 3.

Jack W. Peltason, "Baker v. Carr," in Kermit Hall, editor, *The Oxford Companion to the United States Supreme Court* (New York: Oxford University Press, 1962), p. 56.

Jack W. Peltason, "Reapportionment Cases," in Kermit Hall, editor, *The Oxford Companion to the United States Supreme Court* (New York: Oxford University Press, 1962), p. 710.

Adam Pertman, "Legal Changes Explored to Redress Bias," *Boston Globe*, June 21, 1993, p. 1.

Leo Pfeiffer, "Everson v. Board of Education of Ewing Township," in Kermit Hall, editor, *The Oxford Companion to the United States Supreme Court* (New York: Oxford University Press, 1992), p. 261.

Katha Pollit, "Book Review" [of Roger Rosenblatt's *Life Itself: Abortion in the American Mind* (1992)] *The Nation*, May 25, 1992, p. 718.

Bibliography

H. Jefferson Powell, "The Original Understanding of Original Intent," 98 *Harvard Law Review* 885 (1985).

H. Jefferson Powell, "Rules for Originalists," 73 *University of Virginia Law Review* 659 (1987).

ArLynn Leiber Presser, "Broken Dreams," *American Bar Association Journal,* May 1991, p. 60.

Stephen B. Presser, "Et Tu Raoul? Or The Original Misunderstanding *Misunderstood,*" 1991 *Brigham Young University Law Review* 1484.

Stephen B. Presser, "Locking in Liberalism," *Tribune Books, Chicago Tribune,* October 6, 1991, Sec. 14, p. 5.

Kathryn Preyer, "United States v. Callender: Judge and Jury in a Republican Society" in Maeva Marcus, editor, *Origins of the Federal Judiciary: Essays on the Judiciary Act of 1789* (New York: Oxford University Press, 1992), p. 173.

Ralph E. Reed, Jr., "Symposium, Who's Afraid of the Religious Right?" remarks of Ralph E. Reed, Jr., *National Review*, December 27, 1993, p. 41.

Ramona Ripston and Paul Hoffman, "King Beating Trial Is Not a Case of Double Jeopardy," *San Diego Union-Tribune*, April 14, 1993, p. B7.

David B. Rivkin, Jr., "Health Care Reform vs. The Founders," *Wall Street Journal*, September 29, 1993, p. A19.

Paul C. Roberts, "Debt, Lies, and Inflation," *National Review*, August 31, 1992, p. 31.

Jeffrey Rosen, "The Book of Ruth: Judge Ginsburg's Feminist Challenge," *New Republic*, August 2, 1993, p. 19.

Jeffrey Rosen, "Lemon Law," *New Republic*, March 29, 1993, p. 17.

Ronald D. Rotunda and John E. Nowak, "Introduction" to Joseph Story, *Commentaries on the Constitution of the United States* (Durham: Carolina Academic Press, 1987), p. xiv.

William H. Rehnquist, "The Notion of a Living Constitution," 54 *Texas Law Review* 693 (1976).

Gary D. Rowe, "Note, The Sound of Silence: *United States v. Hudson & Goodwin*, The Jeffersonian Ascendency, and the Abolition of Federal Common Law Crimes," 101 *Yale Law Journal* 919 (1992).

Edward L. Rubin, "Nazis, Skokie, and the First Amendment," 74 *California Law Review* 233 (1986).

Herman Schwartz, "Property Rights and the Constitution: Will the Ugly Duckling Become a Swan?" 37 *Amererican University Law Review* 9 (1987).

L. Michael Seidman, "Brown and Miranda," 80 *California Law Review* 673 (1992).

Michael D. Sherman, "The Use of Legislative History: A Debate Between Justice Scalia and Judge Breyer," 16 *American Bar Association Administrative Law News* 1 (Summer 1991).

Suzanna Sherry, "Civic Virtue and the Feminine Voice in Constitutional Adjudication," 72 *Virginia Law Review* 543 (1986).

Suzanna Sherry, "Natural Law in the States," 61 *University of Cinncinnati Law Review* 171 (1992).

Stephen A. Siegel, "Lochner Era Jurisprudence and the American Constitutional Tradition," 70 *North Carolina Law Review* 1 (1991).

Thomas A. Smith, "Note, The Rule of Law and the States: A New Interpretation of the Guarantee Clause," 93 *Yale Law Journal* 561 (1984).

Carrol Smith-Rosenberg, "Discovering the Subject of the 'Great Constitutional Discussion,' 1776–1789," 79 *Journal of American History* 841 (1992).

Thomas Sowell, "Supreme Court Sinks Teeth Into Self-Anointed," *Rocky Mountain News*, March 18, 1992, p. 62.

Suzanne Last Stone, "In Pursuit of the Counter-Text: The Turn to the Jewish Legal Model in Contemporary American Legal Theory," 106 *Harvard Law Review* 813 (1993).

Kathleen M. Sullivan, "The Nonsupreme Court," 91 *Michigan Law Review* 1121 (1993).

Cass Sunstein, "Beyond the Republican Revival," 97 *Yale Law Journal* 1539 (1988).

Cass Sunstein, "Interest Groups in American Public Law," 38 *Stanford Law Review* 29 (1985).

Susette M. Talarico, "Miranda Warnings," in Kermit Hall, editor, *The Oxford Companion to the United States Supreme Court* (New York: Oxford University Press, 1992), p. 554.

James Bradley Thayer, "The Origin and Scope of the American Doctrine of Constitutional Law," 7 *Harvard Law Review* 129 (1893).

Clarence Thomas, "Why Black Americans Should Look to Conservative Policies," The Heritage Lectures No. 119, *Heritage Foundation Reports* (June 18, 1987).

Lawrence Tribe, "Foreword: Toward a Model of Roles in the Due Process of Life and Law," 87 *Harvard Law Review* 1 (1973).

Mark V. Tushnet, "Legal Defense Fund," in Kermit Hall, editor, *The Oxford*

Bibliography

Companion to the United States Supreme Court (New York: Oxford University Press, 1992), p. 497.

Melvin I. Urofsky, "The Depression and the Rise of Legal Liberalism," a subheading of the entry for *History of the Court*, in Kermit Hall, editor, *The Oxford Companion to the United States Supreme Court* (New York: Oxford University Press, 1992), p. 394.

Meg Vaillancourt, "State Vows to Help Minority-owned Businesses," *Boston Globe*, October 30, 1993, p. 29.

William W. Van Alstyne, "Closing the Circle of Constitutional Review from *Griswold v. Connecticut* to *Roe v. Wade*: An Outline of a Decision Merely Overruling *Roe*," 1989 *Duke Law Journal* 1677.

Julian S. Waterman, "Thomas Jefferson and Blackstone's Commentaries," 27 *Illinois Law Review* 629 (1933).

Herbert Wechsler, "Toward Neutral Principles of Constitutional Law," 73 *Harvard Law Review* 1 (1959).

Barbara Dafoe Whitehead, "Dan Quayle Was Right," *The Atlantic*, April 1993, p. 47.

Malcolm Richard Wilkey, "The Exclusionary Rule: Why Suppress Evidence?" 62 *Judicature* 215 (1978).

Christopher Wolfe, "The Original Meaning of the Due Process Clause," in Eugene V. Hickok, Jr., editor, *The Bill of Rights: Original Meaning and Current Understanding* (Charlottesville: University of Virginia Press, 1991), p. 213.

Doris Sue Wong, "Two Contractors Indicted in Alleged Bilking of State," *Boston Globe*, December 4, 1992, p. 39.

J. Skelly Wright, "Professor Bickel, the Scholarly Tradition, and the Supreme Court," 84 *Harvard Law Review* 769 (1971).

INDEX

Index

388

Index

Hand, Learned, 259
Harlan, John M.
  "color-blind" Constitution, 210–
  211
  Griswold opinion, 54
  Miranda dissent, 176–178,
  198
  Poe v. Ullman opinion, 54–55
  Reynolds v. Sims dissent, 171–173,
  198
  states' rights, 254
Hart, Jeffrey
  equality, 38–39
  recapturing spirit of the Constitu-
  tion, 11
Hatch, Sen. Orrin, 136–137
*The Heavenly City of the Eighteenth
  Century Philosophers*, 261
Henfield, Gideon, 98–99
Heritage Foundation lecture, 35
Hickock, Eugene, 142–143
Hill, Anita, 31
Holden v. Hardy, 140
Holmes, Oliver Wendell, Jr.
  civil theology and, 61
  Lochner v. New York dissent, 141,
  148, 149, 200
Hopkins, Richard J.
  government of laws, not men con-
  cept, 34
  rule of law embodying principles of
  reason and justice, 46
Hot Water War, 106, 109–115
Humphrey, Sen. Hubert, 186

I

Interstate commerce
  FDR and, 144–146, 149
Iredell, James
  criticism of *Calder* decision, 118–
  119

Fries trial, 110–111
Supreme Court power, 79

J

Jay, John, 87–88
Jefferson, Thomas
  Callender pardon, 104
  common law crimes jurisdiction,
  99
  concept of democracy, 6–8, 23
  election of, 17
  obligation of wealthy, 267
  religious freedom, 7, 45
  republic definition, 37
  rights to education, 8
  separation of church and state,
  163–165
  spiritual instruction of youth, 165–
  166
Jehovah's Witnesses
  flag salute case, 153
Judicial review, 77–82, 130, 198–
  199, 258
Judiciary Act of 1789, 63, 67–68,
  97–98, 100, 147
Judiciary Act of 1802, 95–96
Juries
  challenges to, 206–207
  "jury nullification," 217
  powers of, 216–217
  right to trial by, 147–148, 149
Justices
  choosing, 257–259
  reduction in number of, 259–260

K

Kansas
  *Brown v. Board of Education of
  Topeka*, 65, 179–192, 201

392

Index

Swann v. Charlotte-Mecklenburg
Board of Education, 187–188

Sweatt v. Painter, 181

T

Taney, Roger, 130–139, 195, 200

Taxes. See also Northampton insurrection; Whiskey Rebellion
federal tax calculation, 109
progressive taxation, 63–65, 73–74
school desegregation and, 212–213

Taylor, Col. John, 7

Taylor, Jared, 191

Thayer, James B., 152

Thirteenth Amendment, 68, 211

Thomas, Clarence
affirmative action views, 210
Anita Hill case, 31
background, 25–26
Heritage Foundation lecture, 35
jury challenges, 207
natural law, 35–36
nomination, 25, 32–33, 73, 198
views, 26–27, 28

Tradition concept, 244–246

Treason
in England, 108
two means of committing, 108
Whiskey Rebellion, 106, 107–109

Tribe, Lawrence
flag desecration amendment, 285
"Greenhouse Effect," 56
right to privacy, 58

Twentieth Century Fund, 32

U

Undue burden standard, 52–53

Unger, Roberto, 261–262, 263–264

United Daughters of the Confederacy, 137–138

United States District Court for the Northern District of Alabama, 14–15

United States v. Callender, 102–104, 258

United States v. Trans-Missouri Freight Association, 17

Universal suffrage, 94–96

V

Van Alstyne, William W., 53

Van Devanter, Willis, 18

Van Horne's Lessee v. Dorrance, 125–126, 142

Virginia
slavery, 132–133

Voting Rights Act of 1965, 188, 204

W

Wagner Act, 147

Wall Street Journal
Rivkin's column on health care reform, 149

Ward's Cove Packing Co. v. Atonio, 187

Warren, Earl
Eisenhower's view of, 27
"great trilogy" of cases, 170–192

Washington, DC
tracking in schools, 188

Washington, George
amending the Constitution, 285
"Farewell Address," 12–13

Washington Times
Confederate flag insignia, 138

Waters, Maxine, 218

The Way of the Wasp, 278

397